Becoming British Columbia

John Douglas Belshaw

Becoming British Columbia
A Population History

UBCPress · Vancouver · Toronto

17 16 15 14 13 12 11 10 09   5 4 3 2 1

Printed in Canada on ancient-forest-free paper (100 percent post-consumer recycled) that is processed chlorine- and acid-free, with vegetable-based inks.

Library and Archives Canada Cataloguing in Publication

Belshaw, John Douglas
    Becoming British Columbia : a population history / John Douglas Belshaw.

Includes bibliographical references and index.
ISBN 978-0-7748-1545-1 (bound); ISBN 978-0-7748-1546-8 (pbk.);
ISBN 978-0-7748-1547-5 (e-book)

    1. British Columbia – Population – History. 2. British Columbia – History. I. Title.

HB3530.B7B45 2009   304.609711   C2008-906206-X

Canadä

UBC Press gratefully acknowledges the financial support for our publishing program of the Government of Canada through the Book Publishing Industry Development Program (BPIDP), and of the Canada Council for the Arts, and the British Columbia Arts Council. ·

This book has been published with the help of a grant from the Canadian Federation for the Humanities and Social Sciences, through the Aid to Scholarly Publications Programme, using funds provided by the Social Sciences and Humanities Research Council of Canada.

Printed and bound in Canada by Friesens
Set in Stone by Artegraphica Design Co. Ltd.
Copy editor: Deborah Kerr
Proofreader: Dianne Tiefensee
Indexer: David Luljak
Cartographer: Dr. Ross Nelson, Thompson Rivers University

UBC Press
The University of British Columbia
2029 West Mall
Vancouver, BC V6T 1Z2
604-822-5959 / Fax: 604-822-6083
www.ubcpress.ca

To Diane

Contents

Illustrations

Acknowledgments

One ought to be wary of personal motivations in any scholarly project, so I lay my cards on the table. Adopted as an infant, I have invested way too much time mulling over the sorts of things that concern demographers: nuptiality, fertility, household size, birth-spacing, and the life-course. Having lost a parent at a young age, I was introduced to morbidity and mortality, single-parenthood, and the spatial disconnect between household and house. The time I've spent obsessing about these features of my own life and of those near and dear to me might account in some measure for my assertion that British Columbian history is fundamentally a demographic history.

As I indicate in Chapter 1, demographic history occupies a peculiar place in the intellectual firmament. Demography – one half of the equation – is starkly empiricist and deeply rooted in the social sciences. Years ago, as a callow youth, I sat in on Tim Dyson's demography seminars at the London School of Economics. (At the time, demography was not one of my interests, and I attended mostly out of a sense of intellectual duty. I took copious notes but struggled to stay focused and even awake through the mid-afternoon doldrums. The fact that I still have the notes from that class is testament to Professor Dyson's clarity and ability as an educator.) The focus was very much on methodological issues, which Dyson could describe with remarkable, casual ease. Although demography has a predictive disposition – tea leaves for academics, journalists, marketers, and politicians alike – it is also evidence, footprints in the snow of an earlier society. *Historical* demography marries the methodological with the analytical and a wide-angle view of historical processes. What that means is that a book such as this is neither fish nor fowl, as my publisher's readers have pointed out. And, frankly, I'm fine with that. So, I want to thank those anonymous scholars who commented on earlier drafts and suggested I pull it this way or push it that way: I didn't ignore your suggestions; I decided to remain true to a particular vision. Cheers just the same.

The material contained in this book grew out of a series of individual studies and papers to which a substantial number of friends and colleagues contributed. Portions (mostly now modified) appeared as articles in the *Journal of the Canadian Historical Association*, the *London Journal of Canadian Studies*, and the *Western Historical Quarterly*, and as a chapter in *Beyond the City Limits*. Editors and peer readers improved the materials I submitted, and their contribution deserves to be recognized. Integral research support came from individuals engaged through the Work Study Program at what was then the University College of the Cariboo, including Marcy D'Aquino, Gillian Cheney, Lindsay Hank, Sarah Houston, Mary Koehn, Amanda MacKay, Jeffrey Preiss, Sheri Thom, and Jeremy Willis. Papers were presented at departmental colloquia at Thompson Rivers University, the University of Victoria, and the University of Wolverhampton, at Canadian Historical Association conferences at Calgary in 1994, Laval in 2001, and Dalhousie in 2003, the Western Historical Association Conference in Denver in 1995, and the conference of the British Association for Canadian Studies in April 2000. I am grateful for constructive comments, suggestions, and assistance from Allan Bogue, Gérard Bouchard, Lisa Dillon, Lynette Gallant, Peter Gossage, Lorne Hammond, Cole Harris, Kris Inwood, Genevieve Later, Julie Macdonald, Richard Mackie, Robert McCaa, Patricia McCormack, Jeff McLaughlin, Tim Rooth, Eric Sager, and Martin Whittles, colleagues at Wolverhampton University, the students in my Population History and BC History courses over the years, and for a period of Thompson Rivers University-funded research leave in 1998. Marvin McInnis was kind enough to reply to my queries regarding his approach to marital fertility statistics. Anonymous readers for the journals *BC Studies* and *Ethnohistory* also made a contribution. In the early 1990s, there emerged in British Columbia a consortium of historians interested in demographic issues. Their ranks included Patrick Dunae, John Lutz, Robert McDonald, Ruth Sandwell, and Duane Thomson, to all of whom I owe a debt of gratitude. Elizabeth Duckworth and Susan Cross at the Kamloops Museum and Archives and Joan Newman at the Anglican Diocese of Cariboo Archives in Kamloops (now part of the Anglican Provincial Synod of BC and Yukon Archives) were characteristically generous with their assistance. The V-Ps Academic at Thompson Rivers University and North Island College, Drs. Mark Evered and Martin Petter respectively, gave me the space and encouragement to see this book to fruition. Rose Delap very generously granted me a peek into the world of Charles Lee and Jessie Hing, for which I continue to feel privileged. James Manuel kindly took me on a walk back two centuries through a Secwepemc village site on the North Thompson and shared his knowledge of indigenous land use. With these people I am happy to share any credit that comes our way; as to blame for errors, I shall take that all for myself.

. This book has been published with the help of a grant from the Canadian Federation for the Humanities and Social Sciences, through the Aid to Scholarly Publications Programme, using funds provided by the Social Sciences and Humanities Research Council of Canada (SSHRC). The splendid go-to-guys for SSHRC money at UCC/TRU were, at the time, Trevor Davis and Tom Dickinson. The SSHRC also provided funding for a census database that demonstrated its value on many occasions. Professor Duane Thomson (formerly of Okanagan University College) took the initiative to post the data on the internet; assistance in doing so came from the Royal British Columbia Museum. Additional financial support for this study came principally from Thompson Rivers University's Scholarly Activity Committee, chaired by my colleague and then vice-president academic, Dr. Neil Russell.

Finally, I have to acknowledge the contribution of Jean Wilson at UBC Press, who took on this project as her retirement approached. Her staff and colleagues, especially Megan Brand and Darcy Cullen, were critical in taking the manuscript through the production phase and were good natured throughout.

To put the course of this project into demographer's language, it has carried me through one mortality, a divorce, two household formations, a nuptiality, no fertility, and repeated local migrations. As well, it has seen me through a decade of diminishing life expectancy and two bum knees. When it started, I was inspired and supported by my two sons and my daughter; as it concludes, I am indebted to two stepsons and a stepdaughter for their encouragement. Above all, as always, and without fail, I am indebted to my friend, partner, colleague, and inspiration, Diane Purvey, to whom this unworthy book is dedicated.

Acronyms

ASFR	Age-specific fertility rate
CBR	Crude birth rate
CDR	Crude death rate
CMR	Crude marriage rate
C/WR	Child/woman ratio
GFR	General fertility rate
GMFR	General marital fertility rate
GLFR	General legitimate fertility rate
GIFR	General illegitimate fertility rate
I_f	Overall fertility index
I_g	Marital fertility index
I_h	Illegitimate fertility index
I_m	Index of marriage
SDR	Standardized death rate
TFR	Total fertility rate

Becoming British Columbia

1
Cradle to Grave: An Introduction

In the 1880s, when the Canadian Pacific Railway was being surveyed and laid alongside the Thompson Rivers in British Columbia's southern Interior, European Canadians began building substantial houses at the townsite of Kamloops. By the early 1890s, some of the structures had aspirations. A few included chimneys assembled from rounded river rocks, verandas that announced an imperial link to India, Victorian features such as turrets, leaded windows, gingerbread trim, and substantial brickwork as well. Sadly, many early builders used sand from the riverbanks when they were mixing their mortars. A century later the foundations of the oldest houses in the city are, in many cases, dissolving. The sand pours out between the bricks or river rock; the concrete foundations bulge and slough away. What once, long ago, seemed like a robust base on which to build a monument to British Canadian domestic-cultural values runs away like time.

Of all the varieties of history, population, or demographic, history has arguably the lightest grip on the academic and public imagination. As the historiographer Ged Martin laments, "Somehow [population history] seems to be almanac stuff, beneath the dignity of the creative and analytical scholar."[1] And though it is true that the local Chapters is as unlikely to have a section dedicated to economic history as it is to have one on population history, books on the Wall Street Crash of '29 do manage to find a home on its shelves (albeit surrounded by studies on the rise and fall of Adolf Hitler). Is this because *demographics* is for predicting the future, not dissecting the past? Or is it because it is assumed that writers of economic, political, social, or cultural histories have done their demographic spadework at the outset? After all, one wouldn't build an analysis of the Industrial Revolution or Confederation or the post-war boom or the Age of Television without having a sense of the numbers of people involved, would one? Given the substantial quantities of time and effort invested in gathering materials, developing a design, and marshalling expertise and skills before putting one's hand to the task, wouldn't one spend the few extra bucks for a sack of Portland Cement?

Like the oldest houses in Kamloops, histories are often constructed with inadequate concern for the foundation. And the foundation of every human history is its people. The history of British Columbia, in particular, has been written in the absence of a systematic understanding of the engines of demographic change in the past and how they exist in a reciprocal relationship with human agency, or choices. The reasons for this lack of attention to the basic building blocks, I argue here, are complex. The consequences are much the same as those facing the Victorian piles: regardless of the elaborate and pretty trim, the whole structure of our historical knowledge is in some jeopardy.

Why write a history of British Columbia's population? It is, in some ways, an old-fashioned and parochial approach. Earlier histories of the province all focused on population growth. We have, in a sense, been there and done that. Arguably, it is too narrow a subject: British Columbia is but one of ten provinces in Canada and, even now, its population is only slightly greater than 4 million. There are more people in Metro Toronto than in the whole of Beautiful BC. If British Columbia had more national or regional or global influence, one might say this sort of study is in order. But it doesn't pack that kind of punch, not on the Pacific Rim, nor even in Canada. What's more, the subject is not very theoretically alluring in that it does not suggest a post-colonial fascination with discourse. So why bother? There are many answers; I offer but one.

British Columbia is a splendid laboratory in which one may test to destruction any number of historical orthodoxies. This is especially true of population history. The region has always been home to a rich constellation of cultures, arguably more so before European contact than thereafter. But, facing the Pacific and with its back to Canada and the rest of the continent, it remains a crossroad of North America, Europe, and Asia. The imperial experiments of the eighteenth and nineteenth centuries accelerated traffic through this intersection, some of which stayed. Industrial capitalism was in the ascendant in Britain when the colonial era began on the coast, shaping the kind of settlement society that would emerge and – hard on the heels of the appearance of genuinely racist ways of thinking of the world – the character of relations between peoples. British Columbia was established, too, at the very moment when households in Britain and other industrializing economies were experiencing one of the landmark demographic changes in recent history: the fertility transition from large families to progressively smaller ones. It coincided, too, with the spread of that bureaucratic instrument of measurement known as *the census*. The regional resource-extraction-based economy made BC a "Man's Province," an extraordinary twentieth-century baby boom made it a young person's province, and the mildest climate in Canada made it an elders' province too.

In short, British Columbia's history combines an Aboriginal story with an imperial tale, a highly contained industrial revolution with an accompanying cultural transformation that picks up speed through the era of modernization, a rhetorical slate on which differing and conflicting demographic stories could be – and were – inscribed. The big picture of running totals could well be far more dramatic than anything Europe or the rest of North America has to offer. The finer details of sex ratios, marital behaviour, fertility transitions, and race-based demographically different experiences are not less startling.

A British Columbian population history is not only desirable but *necessary*. It tests orthodoxies about population history generally, and it challenges historians of the region to think again. What is argued between the covers of this book is that we face huge challenges in accounting for nineteenth-century imperial and Aboriginal experiences; we have badly misunderstood one of the underpinnings of early twentieth-century social history; the sex ratio imbalance worked differently than common sense suggests it should; immigration was a massively important factor in growth, but it was paced by natural increase and driven more by a high mortality rate than by a weak fertility rate; population has been the very business of successive British Columbian regimes, and they have not behaved especially well; and, finally, British Columbia's demographic past is every bit as extraordinary as that of Quebec, which means many shibboleths about Canadian population history need to be reconsidered.

The task of the present work is to show how fundamental an understanding of the demography of the past is to the business of history. Indeed, it demonstrates how population is at the centre of History with a capital H. As a resource, this book provides academics, students, policy makers, and the public at large with the principal themes of the demographic history of the westernmost Canadian province. Also, it seeks to suggest future directions for the examination of this population. Striking a balance has been a challenge: one reader might like a more technically sophisticated and narrowly focused book; another might call for something more accessible to a larger audience. To the former, I would say that the polish here is less in the demography and more in the history; to the latter, I would say, I hope the technical sidebars are helpful. Obviously, this study cannot hope to be exhaustive; nor does it lay hubristic claims to being definitive (it is *A*, not *The, Population History* of BC); nevertheless, a lot of important ground is covered with an eye to encouraging more.

This chapter provides, first, an introduction to the mission of demographic history. That is followed by an assessment of the ways historians have treated the chief population issues in BC's past. It is argued that, far from being an approach that is unfashionably numerate in a post-modern era of inquiry, demographic history in the Far West is laden with critical rhetorical/linguistic issues and preconceptions that have successfully colonized historical writing. Revisiting British Columbian population history is thus a necessary first step toward a timely reconsideration of the larger historical problem of Pacific Canada.

Getting at the Demography of the Past
Modern interest in demography as a special field of historical study begins with the Reverend Thomas Malthus' late eighteenth-century *Essay on the Principle of Population,* in which he linked variations in marriage and birth rates to economic change. More than one hundred years later, the field developed as a bridge between economic and social history, continuing to highlight the various ways in which changes in nuptiality, fertility, and mortality rates affect community formation and economic performance. For many historians, including Britain's Peter Laslett and Tony Wrigley, America's John Demos and Tamara Hareven, and Quebec's Louise Dechêne and Gérard Bouchard, demographic history offered a method by which the lives, loves, and deaths of the plain people of the past could be disclosed. By scrupulously examining church and state registers, and by applying continuously refined quantitative techniques, we could recover, in Laslett's famous phrase, the world we have lost.[2]

In English-speaking Canada, the demographic past of the common people has not faced the same kind of scrutiny. There is not, as yet, a national demographic history of Canada, although some efforts in that direction have been made by sociologists.[3] There are many studies (described in this volume's Suggested Reading), but little to tie them together. This reflects in part the breadth of the field of demographic history, both regionally, and more importantly, along specialist lines, including examinations of fertility, nuptiality, and family formation. Whatever has been accomplished with respect to Central Canada, there is currently little on the shelves on the Canadian West as a whole and British Columbia specifically. This is unfortunate for, as Wrigley put it, "When it became demonstrable that the demographic constitution of a society had an important bearing on many of its other characteristics and it was impossible to regard its demographic constitution as secondary to some other aspect of its economic or social makeup, it also became essential to change its logical status."[4] Despite the best efforts of a handful of historians, neither the recognition of the importance of demographic history nor the change in its status have occurred in Western Canada, particularly not west of the cordillera.

With what do historical demographers concern themselves that we ought to welcome their work in Western Canada? Historians of population are principally interested in the critical elements of demography: marriages (or household formation), births (a.k.a. fertility), deaths (mortality), and in- and out-migrations. These are hardly straightforward. The ideas of *household formation* and *marriage,* when measured over time, usually assume an adherence to certain social practices that, however, may be in flux. Marriage is, obviously, one of those social institutions that is not universally accepted as a necessary prerequisite to new household formation. Likewise, divorce carried a very different social meaning at the start of the twentieth century than it does a hundred years later. One might also point to adoption/fostering as an element of household formation that was defined differently over time and measured differently by government and church agencies in the past.[5] Nevertheless, if one wishes to identify changes in the population of any jurisdiction and to determine how those changes came about, the place to start is with the basics.

The principal challenge to establishing a demographic history of any jurisdiction is the quality of information available.[6] The fact that the general trends of British Columbia's population history can be described through a wide-angle lens is, in itself, a fact that is worthy of note. The nineteenth century, in which two colonies and a province were established, was the first in which statistical investigations became mainstream. For a variety of reasons, which include the growth of the modern state, census taking became a common practice in industrializing nations. Britain, having assumed the lead in this respect, spread its bureaucratic methods across its empire.[7] Achieving agreement on what was to be measured in the pre-Confederation Canadian censuses was not easily accomplished, and the burden of that sometimes acrimonious dispute was one inheritance of the larger new Dominion in general and British Columbia in particular.

Before 1880, attempts to amass information on the region's population were sporadic, inconsistent, and sketchy.[8] What censuses might have been collected before the arrival of Europeans are lost to us. Head counts were, very unscientifically, performed by a variety of visitors to the region thereafter.[9] A more systematic Hudson's Bay Company (HBC) census of Aboriginal communities was collected in the 1830s, with an eye to understanding the peoples with whom the company traded. Parish and congregational records were, as well, maintained from the earliest days of Fort Victoria. These documents would be complemented by Customs House records, civic/municipal tax lists and population surveys, and, increasingly from the mid-nineteenth century, assessments of the school-age population. From the 1850s, the Colonial Office made repeated but unheeded requests that the local administration maintain a register of births, deaths, and marriages. In 1866, a Colonial Office proposal to register marriages in the united colony, for example, was rejected by the local administration because it was felt that settlers knew one another's affairs so well it would be redundant.[10] Two years later,

Governor Frederick Seymour sourly described what he viewed as the impediments to a vital statistics registry: "The population is greatly scattered. The majority are Indians whom we could hardly expect to register one of the three great events of their life. Many of the white men are living in a state of concubinage with Indian women far in the Interior. They would hardly come forward to register the birth of some half breed bastard."[11] On the eve of British Columbia's entry into Confederation, Governor Anthony Musgrave was no less pessimistic and only slightly less caustic. He wrote to the Colonial Office about the difficulties bound to face a proposed vaccination campaign on the Pacific coast, given "the impossibility of establishing any efficient system for the registration of Births in a wild Country like this."[12] Rising secularism and the failure of a state religion to take root, however, ensured that data collecting and analyzing functions associated with vital statistics and the census became the responsibility of the provincial and federal governments, not the church. The extension to British Columbia of the Dominion of Canada's census machinery did not occur until 1881, because the province entered Confederation too late in 1871 to be included in that decennial effort. In its stead a local and questionable mini-census was conducted, a necessary step – and useful foil – in claiming moneys from Ottawa.[13]

The first registration of something like the whole population in British Columbia, therefore, is the Dominion census of 1881. Although it offers our earliest glimpse into the lives of workaday British Columbians who left behind few other records, the 1881 census is far from unimpeachable. Eric Sager, a key figure in the 1901 census sample project, has put it very well: "It is no longer possible, if it ever was so, to treat routinely generated information in historical sources as a transparent window into the social reality of the past." The census and similar records are created in a fluid social context that categorizes and recategorizes with passing generations. Place of birth might be less important at one time than ethnicity or religious affiliation; place of residence might be a coin toss from one decade to the next between de jure and de facto – the difference between one's legal home address and where one hangs one's hat. From 1891 through the mid-twentieth century, the official census definition of *family* was so flexible as to be downright slippery: it might include any group of individuals living under the same roof who dined together, or it might exclude every kind of household except for those in which a husband and wife cohabit. Locating children in the census is even more problematic: they are counted where they are found and not always with their parents. Children thus show up in institutions or in the households of other biological families, and thereby disappear from the census's metaphorical photograph of *the family*. Even if we set aside contested definitions of what is enumerated and how, severe limitations hampered those who collected the data in the first place. As Alan Brookes said of the 1861 New Brunswick census takers, most did the best they could, but "by twentieth-century standards that was not very good."[14] The nineteenth-century enumerators in British Columbia were mostly unprepared, and in the course of their duties they encountered difficulties that may have produced statistical inaccuracies.[15] One recruit to the 1891 census recalled his efforts around the coal-port of Union Bay: "It took me about a week, doing it all on foot. A horse would have been an encumbrance, as I had to cross fences everywhere and hunt out people in the field."[16] As historian Patrick Dunae writes, "Many of the standard themes of British Columbia's history – notably the tyranny of terrain and the challenge of distance, regionalism and sectional rivalry, alienation from Eastern Canada, anti-Asian sentiment, and ambivalent attitudes towards aboriginal peoples – were hallmarks of the census of 1891."[17] It is safe to say that these constraints proved resistant to change well into the late twentieth century. Indeed, the process of gathering population data is still subject to serious criticism: the 2006 Canadian census quickly attracted accusations of incompetence in its execution and incompleteness in its final product.

Of the barriers erected in the way of census taking, no barbed wire fence was as difficult to negotiate as race. It was one of the most powerful and durable ideas of the era in which the census was conceived. Race defines the sort of questions that were asked, but it also limits the utility of our statistical record.[18] Much of the British Columbian *demographic project* was constructed within a dichotomy between the growth of the European population and its competition with Aboriginal and Asian peoples. *British* British Columbians, the colonial charter group, saw themselves engaged in building what Patricia Roy has called a "White Man's Province"; consequently, priority was given to the white population's demographic categories, with long-term negative impacts inevitably falling upon the First Nations peoples in particular – as was the case also in other areas of British colonial settlement.[19] As Robert Galois and Cole Harris observe, the census – the principal tool for measuring population change – was "an instrument of the growing regulatory power of the modern nation-state and a reflection of the cultural myopia and the racial and gendered assumptions of the white Canadian society that devised and administered it."[20] When non-whites were counted (by whites, of course), errors of fact did not precisely *creep* in: they *stormed* in. For example, by far the most common name recorded in the 1881 census in the southern Interior is "Ah": there were 282 of them. Transcription problems associated with Chinese family names and the accurate differentiation between first/common and last names might be anticipated, but "Ah" appears to have had little basis in fact. It may have been a guttural pause, an "um" or "er" preceding the answer to the enumerator's question. One Chinese Canadian claims that his ancestor, a prominent mine manager and merchant, was known to local authorities, the press, and local historians as "Ah Loy," although his true name – not exactly a secret identity – was Leung Chong.[21]

Less well-known Chinese immigrants could scarcely expect to be treated with greater care. Further complications arose from the Chinese practice of sojourning –spending a few years in the Pacific Northwest before returning to China with sufficient funds in hand to improve the financial lot of their families. Similarly, collecting data on the Aboriginal community has long been a fraught pursuit. Categorization offers the first challenge: the distinction between Status Indian and Non-status Indian is a colonial legal artifact that invades the statistical machinery of the state before the First World War. Even the census itself, which provides one kind of information, was criticized a century ago by Aboriginal leaders who (very reasonably) feared it was an instrument for further reducing reserve lands.[22] Department of Indian Affairs numbers have been considered more trustworthy by historians, but for demographic purposes, one must inevitably turn to the reports of the Vital Statistics Department of BC, created in 1871.[23] Even that source is of limited utility in comprehending the life events of non-whites. Given the diversity and challenge of the province's landscapes and peoples, imperfect official surveys were inevitable; those imperfections occurred within a specific historical context.

The difficulties associated with the enumeration of Asian and Aboriginal populations by white census takers was but one stumbling block to reliable census results. The resource-extraction economy necessitated and produced high levels of labour transience. In addition to the seasonality of work in the fisheries and canneries, the forests and the sawmills, there was the short life expectancy of mining communities with which to contend. The whole of a large Kootenay silver town might exist for fewer than ten years and thus fall completely between the cracks of decennial censuses. The mobility of a wage-labour population that went to wherever the jobs appeared was a further obstacle, one that was less important in more rural, sedentary, and agrarian parts of Canada. Working-class British Columbians, "especially casual or itinerant labour and the unemployed, are certain to be under-represented," according to one study of the 1891 census.[24] Also, there was geography to take into account. Many communities – whether deep in the coastal fjords or perched atop a mountain or scattered across the Peace River Valley – were so remote from the centres of bureaucratic power that they escaped enumeration.[25] Some Euro-Canadian communities, such as those of the Doukhobors, actively resisted the intrusion of vital statistics gathering and thus remained off the census record radar for many years. In terms of *reliability*, then, British Columbian population data from the nineteenth century to the present raise some questions.

With respect to *validity* ("the extent to which [the data] are meaningful indicators of the underlying concepts which we wish to explore"), the information at our disposal contains much that ought to interest the social and demographic historian, and a great deal that is genuinely useful. As

Michael Anderson has argued, "In historical demography there are clearly problems with the reliability of the data – but these are, at least in theory, susceptible to arithmetical adjustment. In contrast, there are fewer problems of validity, since we share with contemporaries the idea that burials normally imply a dead body, and baptisms a birth, and it is births and deaths that we wish to measure."[26] To paraphrase Wrigley, "the paucity or incompleteness of the source materials" may threaten to "leave the subject impoverished and peripheral," but this ought to stimulate methodological questions in such an important area, and not deter inquiry.[27] The outcomes of careful demographic history are, quite simply, potentially too rich to be overlooked.[28]

It is, indeed, possible to say a great deal about the population of British Columbia over the past two hundred years. Never more so than at the present time. Access to century-old enumerators' notebooks, the development of machine-readable data bases, the microcoding of all the nineteenth-century Dominion censuses, and the availability of an enormous quantity of data (and analysis) on the internet have revolutionized the possibilities and practices. This study makes use of a variety of such sources, although the focus here is more on small but essentially comprehensive local surveys, rather than huge aggregates or inch-deep-but-four-thousand-mile-wide national samples. The most significant of these larger collections – the Public Use Microdata Samples (PUMS) – has been explored, but I decided early on that focusing on these sources would entail a significantly different kind of project and would distract from the broad goals of this study. (I acknowledge that other demographers and historians will disagree.) The method chosen for this book, a combination of aggregate census and vital statistics numbers with details tweaked out from the microcosmic level, allows for a good beginning to be made.

Historians, Colonization, and the Linguistic Turn

Despite the recurrence of themes that are critically demographic in their premises – development, gendered roles, widespread popular and institutionalized racism, the rise of a numerous and militant working class, democratic parliamentary politics, and success measured in population numbers – the underlying assumptions about the province's population history have not been subjected to systematic scrutiny.[29] What exists is fragmented and mostly cursory. Why is it that so little is known of BC's population history beyond the most basic "running total" aspects? The case I make briefly here is that the region's demographic history has been neglected because of the very centrality of population to the project of imperial province building.[30] How and why this is the case is worth considering. As importantly, the consequences of thinking we know whatever it is we think we know need highlighting.

The main works devoted specifically to BC's population history can be briefly enumerated and described. There are no monographs on the subject other than this, although several articles published in scholarly journals make a promising start. The earliest contribution was that of F.W. Howay, who, in 1930, outlined the "settlement and progress" of the province from Confederation to the Great War.[31] In this pioneering effort, as in so many that followed, demography largely serves a political history narrative; as well, numbers are assumed to be clinically objective. *Growth,* in Howay's day, was unquestionably good and synonymous with *progress.* Peter Ward's 1983 introduction to the population history of Western Canada displays more demographic integrity, but it deals principally with the population history of the Prairie West, drawing on the published census reports.[32] A 1990 article by Jean Barman – expanded upon in her book *The West beyond the West: A History of British Columbia* – also synthesizes Canada census material in a useful and necessary fashion.[33] Both Barman and Ward provide historians working on British Columbia with a reminder that population patterns established in the early years of settlement were distinctive in Canada but also of long-term significance to the emerging society west of Alberta.

Of the other works concerned specifically with population issues, a consequential few might be summarized. Early in her career, Barman produced an overlooked study of voter behaviour in Vancouver based on a close reading of the interwar census returns. Galois and Harris' "Recalibrating Society: The Population Geography of British Columbia" deals specifically with the enumerators' census of 1881, challenging in many respects the accepted wisdom on nineteenth-century demographics in the province without, however, extending the implications of their conclusion into later years. The links between empirical demography of the Ward and Barman variety and the ideology of settlement are more clearly spelt out in an article by Allen Seager and Adele Perry. They "mine the connections" between population and divisions in the workforce predicated on race and gender. Perry subsequently broadened the discussion of the implications of a lopsided sex ratio in the nineteenth century. Jeremy Mouat, too, in a keen-eyed study of the Kootenay mining town of Rossland, explores gendered roles and their links with population recruitment and community identity. My own earlier research exploits population studies to devise an understanding of social relations in the province more than one hundred years ago. A distinctive approach has been made by Ruth Sandwell, who applies insights derived from the new cultural history to the question of rural communities in a very urban province, focusing her attentions on demographic clues to the economic and survival strategies of settlers on Saltspring Island. There is also the work of James Gibson, Robert Galois, and Robert Boyd on smallpox epidemics among the indigenous population, and the assortment of studies on troubled race relations in British Columbia, including Ward's *White Canada Forever* and Roy's three volumes *A White Man's Province, The Oriental Question,* and *The Triumph of Citizenship.* An unusual source provides noteworthy insight into twentieth-century developments: in 1984 BC Tel, the province's telephone monopoly at the time, published a study of British Columbia's population with an eye to projecting growth in the regional market. This slim tome begins with a concise but well-crafted demographic history of the province from 1961 to 1981, based entirely on published materials. The author, Robert Malatest, raises many questions that ought to be considered by students of population history, including cohort survival rates and the statistical trade-offs between an aging population and a generation that has enjoyed a greater provision of medical care than any before it. Another unusual study examines the spatial demography of mortality but only for the last five years of the 1980s. Wider in its breadth and purpose is Julie Macdonald's overview of population for the British Columbia Department of Vital Statistics that covers the hundred years between 1891 and 1990. Macdonald's work does not employ a historical methodology, but it is painstakingly assembled and happily relied upon here. Similarly, Herbert Northcott and Jane Milliken's *Aging in British Columbia* tackles the social policy questions associated with a burgeoning seniors population, grounding their study in solid demographic methods.[34]

If there is a common thread to be found in most of these studies, it is a sense that British Columbia's population history – characterized by substantial and sustained growth – is implicitly (and for good or ill) a tale of victory, of the triumph of a particular imperial and/or national goal. European and Asian occupation of British Columbia and its subsequent economic transformation were carried on within an ideological context in which demography and power continually overlap. Dorothy Chunn puts it extremely well: "During the late nineteenth and early twentieth centuries, strategies aimed at recruiting white Anglo immigrants were implemented. Concomitantly, repressive strategies for *othering* non-Anglo racial and ethnic groups were put in place, including denial of entry to British Columbia, expulsion from the province, and segregation/containment within the province." Chunn's focus is on citizenship and, in this instance, the rise of eugenics, but her observations apply with equal force to demography. Similarly, in a study of colonial gender relations, Perry has shown how "imperial discourse that accorded white women a special role as harbingers of empire rendered this demographic problem a political one." Tina Loo demonstrates elegantly how the abstract notions associated with British justice and colonialism came to have concrete manifestations that impacted populations in BC. In a similar vein, Kay Anderson's *Vancouver's Chinatown* reveals the ways in which racial segregation was linguistically conceived, actualized, and reinforced. The extent to which this was also true of the larger demographic project is evident in Barman's earlier studies of the better-off British immigrants in BC. The imperial ethos is clearly announced in Bishop Hills' boast of Victorian-era Victoria that "the great heart of the people beats with that of England." It echoes, as well, in historic documents that reassure potential upper-class immigrants that "a similarity of race and character, of manners and customs, of sympathies in aim, in those among whom the newly-arrived emigrant from England is cast, [will] all combine to make him feel at home." And it can be seen inscribed in Latin above the front doors of pretentious Britons in British Columbia: "Those who cross the seas change their clime, not their mind." That this discourse had a demographic agenda as well as a cultural one is beyond dispute.[35]

Just as "the whites ... largely constructed the social categories and ... dominated the province" by 1881, so too has their vocabulary dominated historical thinking.[36] In very few – quite possibly none – of the nineteenth-century Colonial Office papers dealing with proposals to insinuate Britons into British Columbia is the desired population described as *workers. Settlers,* instead, is the term used almost exclusively.[37] The *frontier* describes the then boundary of European occupation. *City,* especially in the parlance of boosters, could refer to any settlement that was, or might shortly become, incorporated, regardless of population size or economic sophistication. Throughout the twentieth century, *development* and its close relations indicate a stage in, or a state of, linear progression from labour-intensive, technologically simple economic activities to more complex activities in which economies of scale are affirmed and recognizable, whether in mining, logging, fish packing, distribution, energy production, or farming. The *populating of British Columbia,* a phrase that appears in a variety of guises over 150 years, ignores the depopulating of Aboriginal communities, emphasizes the rise of (especially) Euro-North American numbers, and identifies growing immigration from Asia as a *false* population, one that needs to be subsumed. (One can burrow deeper: according to a 1907 edition of the *Saturday Sunset,* white Vancouverites "lived in homes"; Chinese Vancouverites "infested warrens.")[38] Indeed, the term *whites* was itself employed in curious ways: insofar as it stands in for anyone who is not Asian or Aboriginal, its catchment sometimes extended to include blacks and ethnic Hawaiians. All of these terms remind us that British Columbia was historically and consistently a demographic project.

This framework of discourse is as evident in the historiography as it is in the archival record. According to Allan Smith, the generation of provincial historians whose dominance faded after the Great War produced work that could be characterized as "special pleading on behalf of development, empire and self-made men."[39] His conclusion, that subsequent generations of historians shook off that prejudice, is premature when reckoned in terms of *demographic* development, which had tenacious imperial roots. And although the ethos of resource exploitation might receive a more jaundiced or at least critical eye from historians, population did not. Just as nineteenth- and twentieth-century promoters gauged British Columbia's progress on the basis of white settlement, a similar measure was graphically rendered on maps in the 1958 magnum opus of Margaret Ormsby.[40] The imperial agenda could be seen as well when Norbert MacDonald framed poor Asian-white relations on the coast in such a way as to exclude the former from their own city: "over the years Vancouverites and Seattlites showed little difference in their opinion and treatment of migrants from the Orient."[41] "Vancouverites" in this context are whites concerned to control the racial composition of *their* growing city; Asian residents, however long they might have been based in the west coast cities, are depicted as non-citizens, or (as Anderson sharply observes) as a "counter-idea."[42] Although Roy took as her objective the task of explaining "why white British Columbians wanted to make theirs a 'white man's province,'" she configured her analysis in a manner that isolates economic and cultural imperatives from purely demographic ones. References are repeatedly made to the Euro-Canadians' fear of being "overrun," a sure sign that the numbers game was at the forefront of attempts to secure white capitalist hegemony.[43] Studies like Roy's, which emphasize economics, and Ward's (which posit a more cultural explanation for institutional racism in BC) miss the linguistic point: *development,* a euphemism for capitalism, is both an economic program and a cultural artifact.[44] And it barely conceals a demographic objective as well, one that Arthur Lower critiqued as long ago as 1962, when he wrote, "Our attitude towards population has simply been that of 'The Boosters' Club;' 'bigger and better,' has been virtually the only criterion."[45]

There are other examples from the historiography on which to draw. In Robert McDonald's study of community formation in proto-Vancouver, the definition of "frontier" refers "loosely to the period when settlement was beginning and the social order was relatively unfixed." "Frontier" thus presumes a successful outcome of the settlement process (a "beginning" suggests an end or, better still, *ends*) without questioning its implicit ideological ambition. To quote Norbert MacDonald once more, the flow of immigrants from the British Isles, especially from the Edwardian era on, "has had a profound effect on all aspects of Vancouver's life. Indeed the influence is so pervasive, long standing, and taken for granted that there has been very little scholarly investigation of it."[46] He could not be more right. The problematic of *Britishness* and the objective of *settlement* itself have been invisible because of their ideological precedence: everything that was not of the charter/baseline British community or that did not favour settlement of a particular kind was highlighted by contemporaries as a *social* or *economic* problem and seized upon by historians as a *scholarly* problem. The history of anti- or counter- or phony settlement has therefore been closely studied; the phenomenon of *population* has not.

The social and symbolic construction of British Columbia's demography raises questions that run to the heart of social and political history. As demographer Roderic Beaujot states, "organized human societies determine how population problems are defined, and these definitions delimit legitimate solutions." Similar concerns were raised in the 1960s by Michel Foucault, who alerted scholars to the "biopolitical" agenda of the nineteenth-century state that incorporated whole panoplies of metrics. In British Columbia the definitional process occurred in the context of British imperialism, and, in that framework, *race* was early defined as a problem. To quote Karen Anderson again, "In the ambition to build a dominant 'Anglo' identity and community, the state sought to secure popular legitimacy by defining people of Chinese origin in opposition to all that could be made to stand for 'white' Canada." This urge toward exclusionism was summed up neatly in an either/or fashion by a Lower Mainland newspaper in 1900: "are we to be a British Province or an annex of Oriental Kingdoms?" The answer was tied, of course, to numbers. The symbolic use or value of population created a political and social tension between the need for more free labour and the fear of the wrong sort of immigrant (i.e., Asian). Restrictions were imposed that would, on the one hand, limit Chinese immigration and, on the other, discourage wage-labour immigrants from becoming independent farmers. The infamous British Columbian head taxes thus might be usefully considered alongside the provincial legislature's decision to keep land prices higher than on the Canadian prairies or in Washington State. These factors very clearly conditioned the character of the population and affected its ability to increase naturally, to live long lives, to become residentially stable, or to endure long-term transience. Without an understanding of the demographic element of British Columbia's story, the policy and societal outcomes do not make sense; the former is the canvas on which the latter was painted.[47]

This book revisits the history of Canada's Pacific province through a demographic lens. To that end, the overall patterns and causes of population change are described and assessed. What this book is *not*, is a highly technical exercise in statistics. The data used and presented here are meant to be accessible while inviting further refinement and debate. The organization of the chapters that follow is meant to serve readers whose demographic interests are not comprehensive. Chapter 2 provides a historical demographic narrative of the region since the eighteenth century. I believe this is an important exercise in demonstrating how the story – familiar to historians and to many British Columbians – might be recast by paying closer attention to demographic themes and concerns. Subsequent chapters deal with thorny aspects and/or scholarly problems in demographic history as they apply to the situation in the Far West. The first of these, Chapter 3, examines the decline of Aboriginal populations down to the twentieth century, raising questions about both the reliability of what data we have and the methodologies available to historians of pre-census populations. Chapter 4 describes the contours and implications of a long-term male surplus in the population as a whole. Trends in fertility, including the vexed question of British Columbia's fertility transition, are examined in Chapter 5. The growth of the population by means of immigration is a critical part of the British Columbian story, aspects of which are examined in Chapter 6. The penultimate chapter explores mortality rates and is followed by a chapter of conclusions in which the cynical treatment of populations by the state in this province is laid out for dissection. Throughout this study, two mid-sized British Columbian communities – Kamloops and Nanaimo – are used to illustrate the diversity of demographic experiences across the province in the pre-First World War period, although this evidence is augmented by materials on Vancouver, Rossland, Victoria, Kincolith, and other centres.[48] An effort has been made here to render the statistical information in such a way as to be accessible to a general readership while providing academics with grist for various mills.

The spelling of Aboriginal place names merits a brief note. Wherever possible, I have favoured the forms most widely used at the present time. Thus, *Nlaka'pamux* rather than *Nlha7kápmx* or *Thompson Indians*. In other instances, versions that are more faithful to and respectful of Aboriginal self-descriptions – such as Tsilhqot'in rather than *Chilcotin* – are privileged, regardless of popularity. There is no single hard and fast rule in these matters, a reflection of the point to which post-colonialism has brought us. As well, I have elected to give the island named for Vancouver a possessive apostrophe when referring to it as a separate colonial entity prior to union with the mainland colony in 1866.

I will close this introduction with yet one more caveat. Whatever advantages population histories provide to an understanding of the past, they contain a dangerous tendency toward reductionism. This is part of a tradition that goes back to Malthus, if not to the Old Testament. The library shelves groan under the weight of alarmist accounts (*The Population Bomb* by Paul Ehrlich), oversimplified links between demography and economy (*The Pig and the Python: How to Prosper from the Aging Baby Boom* by Cork and Lightstone), and more scholarly studies that, despite significant strengths, treat some aspect of demography as though it were the grail, pitching a particular population-driven thesis of human history that ignores/minimizes/glosses over a host of other historical agencies. In this lattermost camp, I would include the otherwise delightful *Boom, Bust and Echo* by David Foot and Daniel Stoffman and *The Household and the Making of History* by Mary S. Hartman.[49] The present study does not offer up One Big Theory of population, but it does maintain that population forces played – and continue to play – a key role in the history of British Columbia. Again, the message *here* is that population forces are important underlying structures – the foundations – of what is built on top. And, as is commonly the case with faulty foundations, their defects are transmitted throughout the whole of the structure. The choices that are made thereafter – including decisions to limit immigration, to impose racist sanctions, to embrace pro-natalist policies – are the points where conscious human agency intersects with demography, where choice takes the helm again.

2
Weddings, Funerals, Anything: The British Columbian Demographic Narrative

British Columbia's demography is set within competing storylines. Areas with more monolithic racial/ethnic compositions that have not faced repeated invasions or sustained occupation by newcomers (at least not since Malthus was a young vicar) have far less problematic demographic histories. Indeed, all of the older provinces and much of the rest of Western Canada have less complicated immigration and succession histories. British Columbia's demography in the period since European contact (in the Far West this means from the 1770s) is a multifaceted tale of population crises that cuts along lines of collapse, invasion, and displacement. These are themes that would be familiar to any student of Aboriginal history, pretty much anywhere in Canada. For the European element west of the Rockies, the chief essence of the saga has been arrival, ascendancy, dominance. Part of that chronicle fine-tunes the newcomer category to delegitimize American claims and to measure British Columbia's performance against that of the rest of the Dominion while positioning the largely Anglo-Saxon intruders at the centre and non-Europeans at the periphery. From an Asian perspective, this looks rather different again: a strong flavour of repeatedly frustrated efforts to establish a continuing and self-sustaining trans-Pacific presence is coupled with a unique experience of demographic oppression (in the biological sense), segregation, exile, and dispossession, all of which is crowned – for some at least – with legitimation, integration, and proliferation, though late in the day. There is also a starkly gendered story to be told, for this is a province in which the balance between men and women differed profoundly from Canadian norms. For each group that participates in the populating and population of British Columbia, the account might be described as a struggle for demographic hegemony. Approached chronologically, the first chapter in this contest is the most terrifying, for, if one word can sum up the demographic epic in the hundred years between European-Aboriginal contact to Confederation, it is *Death*.

First Nations Populations before Contact

Before the arrival of Europeans, the First Nations of what is now British Columbia were many in numbers, tongues, and cultures. If we take pre-Columbian Canada and the United States as a whole, possibly no region contained so great a number of people living in such high densities as the Pacific Northwest. A rich food and material base enabled economic and commercial success up and down the coast, from the mouth of the Columbia River to Alaska. The British Columbian coast was a cultural hothouse in which elaborate visual and performance arts (including architecture, engineering, dance, wood and stone carving, and metalwork) could thrive with the support of a vital economic order. Throughout the vast Interior of the territory, more than a dozen distinct nations (most of which depended on river and lake fishery economies tied to the annual salmon runs and augmented by a range of hunting and gathering activities and extensive trade networks) carved out very different niches. Demographically, these were thriving peoples. In some respects and from time to time, they prospered too much: population pressures and demands produced frictions that culminated in raids and wars. Under such conditions, there was instability as some villages and whole nations expanded, divided, advanced, and retreated. Maps 2.1 and 2.2 show the approximate distribution of the principal First Nations in the late eighteenth century, along with villages named in the text.

By the time British Columbia entered Confederation, much of this social and population order was in severe decline. So dramatic was the collapse of some Aboriginal communities that it was widely believed that the First Nations as a whole were on the brink of extinction. Although true in some cases – the Pentlatch, to take but one example, were reduced to a handful and then absorbed into the Komoux – the imagined disappearance of the First Nations in the nineteenth century was a misapprehension that had material consequences.[1] For one thing, the imperial and Canadian presence increasingly believed that the urgency to sign treaties with indigenous communities had passed. As a result of the disinterest shown by London, Victoria, New Westminster, and Ottawa in formalizing a new arrangement with Native peoples, Aboriginal societies experienced further hardships into the twentieth century. Various forces contributed to what can only be described as an Aboriginal population crisis, a chapter in what William Denevan called, thirty years ago, "possibly the greatest demographic disaster in the history of the world."[2] It was this upheaval that laid the foundation for the kind of newcomer society that would emerge in the second half of the nineteenth century.

Archaeological evidence points decisively to human occupation in the British Columbia region as early as ten thousand years ago. The most ancient human sites discovered to date are in the Interior, where population densities are widely accepted to have long been lower than on the resource-rich coast.[3]

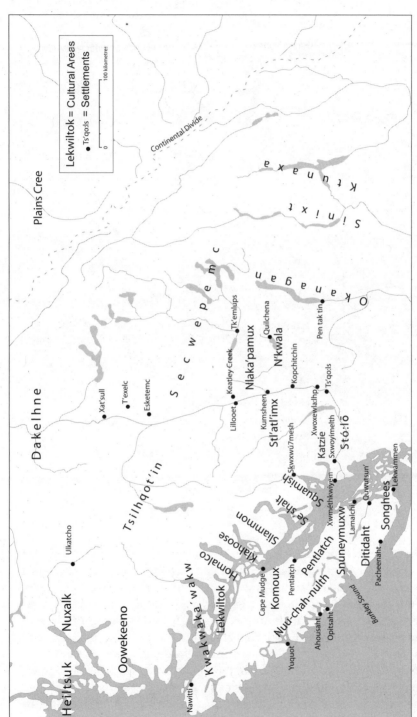

Map 2.1 Distribution of First Nations, c. 1775: South

Map 2.2   Distribution of First Nations, c. 1775: North

The cultures resident throughout the whole region at the time of European contact in the late eighteenth century had deep roots but were the product of fluid territorial expansion and contraction. Two examples from the Interior should suffice. The ethnographer James Teit tapped sources who reported that, as late as 1750, the Secwepemc held the northern Okanagan Valley from Salmon Arm to the upper end of Okanagan Lake and as far east as the Arrow Lakes; they were, of course, subsequently pushed out of those districts.[4] The case of the Nicola/N'Kwala provides another dramatic example: probably a southern offshoot of the Athabaskan-speaking Tsilhqot'in, they were eventually hemmed in by their neighbours on all sides and, by the late nineteenth century, overrun by and absorbed into the Thompson/

Nlaka'pamux, the Okanagan, and the Secwepemc Nations.[5] Pre-Columbian British Columbia was, in short, a dynamic human ecology in which mobility of whole communities occurred.[6]

If pre-contact movement and political struggle are difficult to chart, the fundamentals of Aboriginal demography prior to contact are even more so. Fertility and mortality rates are simply not known. Even if we could ascertain the fertility of one Aboriginal community in the past, it would be an act of purest ignorance to extend it generally. Cultural practices pertaining to age at first marriage and infant rearing could be highly localized and widely disparate: even if life expectancies were uniformly low, other cultural and external factors could significantly impact the number of surviving children that a woman might produce at, say, Gitwangak, Ahousaht, Lax Kw'alaams, Tk'emlups, or Esketemc. In part, this is because substantial social and economic differences existed between Interior and coastal population communities.

Societies on the Northwest Coast were exceptionally well endowed by nature. An abundant food base dominated by salmon, herring, oolichan, shellfish, and sea mammals produced communities of relatively high densities and complexity. Historians of human population would highlight these features: it is unusual for non-agrarian societies to reach the kind of population levels that maritime peoples of the Northwest Coast achieved. Typically, these were tightly packed foreshore villages of longhouses built from handmade cedar timbers. Wealth was, of course, unequally available, and some villages were much larger than others. In the Interior, where resources were not so abundant and where the climate inclines to greater extremes, the early nineteenth-century explorers employed by the HBC and the North West Company (NWC) encountered somewhat smaller populations dependent on seasonal salmon runs, hunting, and gathering. These were, on the whole, semi-nomadic societies whose primary villages nevertheless could run to more than a thousand individuals. The NWC fur trader and explorer Simon Fraser can be cited: in 1808 he encountered a community at or near Kumsheen/Lytton with a population of about twelve hundred.[7]

Household or family structures differed between the coastal and Interior communities but also within either zone. The *kekuli* (pithouse) of the Interior Salish was a response to environmental parsimony in the drylands: there were no building materials to compare with the Douglas fir stands on the coast, so accommodations evolved accordingly. Kekulis lacked the capacity to hold individuals and property comparable to what was typical of the bighouses belonging to the Kwakwaka'wakw; *household* units were thus necessarily smaller in the Interior. Nevertheless, the riverine societies reached significant levels of density. At Keatley Creek in the Lillooet area, for example, pithouses dating from a millennium ago and earlier have been measured to a maximum of twenty-five metres in diameter amid clusters of kekulis that might have sustained a total population between five hundred and a thousand individuals "or even more."[8] Kekulis from the late pre-contact period were more commonly six to seven metres in diameter, and their size appears to have diminished further in the eighteenth century.[9] Accounts from the post-contact period estimate that kekulis (which mark winter settlements primarily) included thirty to forty related individuals – although the Victorian ethnographer Charles Hill-Tout reckoned twice as many – and that there were usually three or four kekulis to a cluster.[10] Villages therefore contained between 90 and 320 individuals.[11] It is unclear, however, whether this pattern was reduced in the prehistoric period or after contact. And, to be sure, some villages were much larger: in 2005, a controlled burn on the North Thompson waterfront of Kamloops Indian Reserve No. 1 revealed a landscape sculpted by dozens of kekuli pits of uncertain age. Elsewhere in the Interior, the Athabaskan-speaking nations, the Sinixt, and the Ktunaxa tended toward smaller and more mobile hunting groups of a hundred per unit or fewer. Their housing can be characterized as tipis or conical lodges that could be easily assembled or disassembled for the sake of mobility.[12]

On the coast, settlement and household patterns were distinctly different from anything else in Canada. Huge longhouse complexes dominated most villages, or at least the winter villages. Simon Fraser described two longhouses – one in the Chilliwack area and the second at the mouth of the Fraser at Musqueam/Xwméthkwiyem – as more than 180 metres long, and 457 metres by 27 metres respectively.[13] Ponder those numbers: the Chilliwack longhouse is nearly as long as two football fields end-to-end; the Musqueam/Xwméthkwiyem structure, though narrow, had a floorspace of more than twelve thousand square metres. The scale of these buildings suggests large populations organized around substantial and ordered social structures: design, construction, and decoration would require both high numbers and task specialization. Moreover, the coastal villages could contain considerable numbers of longhouses. One account of the destruction of the Clayoquot Sound village of Opitsaht in 1792 reports "upwards of 200 houses, generally well built" by local standards, and an estimated population of approximately twenty-five hundred.[14]

The absence of a pre-Columbian census of the region means that we are left with estimates based on archaeological evidence, oral tradition, and European-generated observations from the early period of contact. According to a 1990s survey by Robert Muckle, "Estimates of the First Nations population in the mid-eighteenth century range from 80,000 to 500,000 or more, although most anthropologists accept estimates between 200,000 and 300,000."[15] In the context of Aboriginal Canada as a whole, these are large numbers, even at the low end. Regardless of which figure we favour, it is clear that Aboriginal populations fell dramatically by the 1870s. When British Columbia entered Confederation, there were about 26,000 "Indians" left alive in the territory, the barest fragment of what must have been a vibrant crucible of cultures.[16] There are several explanations for this collapse, although virgin soil epidemics certainly had the greatest impact.

Invasive Species: Bacteria and Firearms

In all likelihood, it was smallpox that laid waste to considerable numbers. An imported exotic disease against which Aboriginal North and South Americans had no natural immunities (hence the term "virgin soil" epidemic), smallpox was devastating wherever it occurred.[17] Aboriginal unfamiliarity with the disease compounded the problem as people turned, naturally, to tried and tested healing practices, some of which were inappropriate for highly communicable diseases. Very seldom does smallpox appear to have carried off fewer than 30 percent of an infected population, and there are accounts that suggest upward of 75 percent perished in some communities. Even in Europe and Africa, where smallpox was an unwelcome companion of humanity for centuries, epidemics produced huge death tolls. There is no reason to imagine that the arrival of smallpox in British Columbia produced anything less than a demographic catastrophe.

Historians and anthropologists have assembled a chronology of major epidemics that has expanded quantitatively and qualitatively over the last two decades. Sarah Campbell argues for a smallpox pandemic that reached the Columbia Plateau (at least as far north as the forty-ninth parallel) and possibly the Northwest Coast as early as c. 1525. Her evidence comes from the archaeological record and is largely based on village site abandonment and shrinkage, as well as food refuse accumulation.[18] Wilson Duff, Robert Boyd, and Cole Harris present evidence for a smallpox epidemic that hit the British Columbia coast (and possibly the Interior as well) in the 1770s or '80s. This outbreak may have originated on the Great Plains, in the Columbia River basin, with the 1775 Spanish expedition to the Northwest Coast led by Juan Francisco Bodega y Quadra, in Russian trade posts in Alaska, or in a combination of all four.[19] Elizabeth Fenn makes the case for an extension across the cordillera of the 1781-82 plague on the plains, but carefully dismisses the evidence for earlier outbreaks and alternative sources of smallpox in the eighteenth century.[20] Boyd also argues for a second outbreak, in the early nineteenth century, which was followed by a third smallpox epidemic in 1836-38. The latter epidemic first appeared in Alaska and spread south through the Tlingit to the Tsimshian on the mid-coast and the Haida on the Queen Charlotte Islands, stopping short of the northern Kwakwaka'wakw and sparing the Nuxalk as well.[21] HBC traders reported mortality rates of about one-third on the north coast, a figure supported by other contemporaries.[22] Demographic impacts carried economic implications: the smallpox epidemics of the 1830s among the Tlingit are thought to have eliminated, disproportionately, the older members of the community "who were more traditional, more conservative, more superstitious and more hostile to the Russians." Smallpox thus had an important impact on the Alaskan fur trade and on cultural transformation among the Tlingit.[23]

Apart from a relatively isolated outbreak among the Nuu-chah-nulth communities of the west coast of Vancouver Island in 1875, the last and best documented smallpox epidemic in the historical period occurred in 1862-63, affecting the majority of British Columbian Aboriginal groups in some measure. Arriving on a ship from San Francisco, smallpox dispersed quickly through the trading community of Salish, Haida, Tsimshian, and Kwakwaka'wakw gathered at Victoria. Within a matter of weeks, the epidemic was raging. Rather than quarantine the affected community, the colonial government responded by forbidding further Aboriginal arrivals into the port and, disastrously, sending non-local Aboriginals to their respective home territories. The effect was to disseminate smallpox rapidly along the coastline, up the Fraser Canyon, and overland from Bella Coola into the Cariboo through the spring and summer of 1862.[24]

In the face of this disaster, some Europeans scrambled to establish a firebreak of inoculation.[25] On the Lower Mainland, in the Fraser Canyon, and along the Thompson River, missionaries (whom Boyd describes as "the true heroes of the 1862 smallpox epidemic"), fur traders, and government officials treated the local population on the eve of the epidemic, saving many lives.[26] On the whole, however, the progress of smallpox was unimpeded, and it spread speedily (even through areas where inoculations took place), burning itself out in the winter of 1863.

James Teit reported from the southern Interior nearly forty years later, "If the evidence of the old people can be relied on, [smallpox] must have carried off from one-fourth to one-third of the [Nlaka'pamux]"; he adds, "thousands of Indians throughout the interior of British Columbia succumbed to it." Boyd claims that in some places the mortality ran to 50 percent, and in others perhaps as much as 80 percent. According to Jack Irvine, an eyewitness to the epidemic's progress in Victoria, the undertakers faced a grim task: "the Indians died by the score, quit[e] a few whites also. There was a place to put the whites but the Indians were carted off on the outskirts, & a hole dug & in [the corpse] went & [the undertaker went] back for more. The man that had this job was paid seventy five [cents] a head & his helper the same [sic]." Among the Nuxalk one Royal Navy officer observed that "in a week [of the outbreak], nearly all the healthy had scattered from the lodges and gone to encamp by families in the woods, only it is feared, to carry away the seeds of infection and death in the blankets and other articles they took with them." His tragic account continues: "Numbers are dying each day; sick men and women were taken out into the woods and left with a blanket and two or three salmon to die by themselves and rot unburied; sick children were tied to trees." This was the last major smallpox epidemic in British

Columbian history, and we know its effects to have been disastrous across the territory. Duff considered it the "most terrible single calamity to befall the Indians of British Columbia," and Andrew Yarmie states that approximately twenty thousand Aboriginal lives were lost in a few short months.[27] Though it is scarcely imaginable, it is possible that this horror was several degrees milder than earlier, less well-documented epidemics.

Other microbial fellow travellers of the European intrusion made their presence known from the last half of the eighteenth century. Syphilis and gonorrhea appear to have arrived with the first exploratory missions in the 1770s.[28] It is clear from the journals of James Cook's expedition that sexual intercourse occurred between the British sailors and the women of the Nuu-chah-nulth villages, and that syphilis or some other venereal affliction passed in at least one direction.[29] Certainly, by 1792, the Spanish at Nootka Sound observed "the terrible ravages of syphilis" among their hosts.[30] Venereal infections, according to explorers' and fur traders' accounts, circulated swiftly, no doubt assisted by the existence of a sex trade.[31] The spread of syphilis in particular may have negatively impacted female fertility. Further complicating the picture is the arrival within a generation or two of other exotic diseases. Whooping cough was introduced to the northern Columbia Plateau in 1807 and 1808, but it is not clear that it was fatal.[32] Tuberculosis is another disease that may or may not have indigenous roots or may have followed European contact in the early period.[33] Elevated mortality rates from disease in the mid-1820s may have been associated with smallpox or measles among the Hul'qumi'num. Malaria, too, visited the Northwest Coast in the 1830s and was variously described as fever, ague, cholera, typhus, and influenza. Its impact was probably contained to what is now Washington State, although it is important to note its presence.[34] Measles appeared in 1847-48 along avenues that are in dispute. Boyd argues for a southern source spreading north in the wake of the HBC steamer *Beaver;* Galois counters that the *Beaver* unintentionally delivered measles directly to the Tsimshian territory at and around Fort Simpson, from whence it spread along Aboriginal trade lines on the coast and deep into the Interior, affecting the Tahltan at and near Fort Stikine, the Natliwoten around Fort Fraser, and, in all likelihood, the Sekani at Fort McLeod. There is also evidence that measles scoured the Okanagan in late 1847, reaching Fort Kamloops, Fort Alexandria, and possibly the Spences Bridge and Lytton area. In this manner, the two waves very nearly collided on the Cariboo Plateau.[35] Measles was a killer in the Interior, claiming thirty-five people "in the vicinity" of Fort Kamloops, though it was evidently less fatal in the Cariboo, perhaps due to fur trader John Tod's attempts at inoculation.[36] According to one account, the Sekani near Fort McLeod suffered from measles and starvation in 1850, but it is far from clear whether a causal link existed between the two; nor is it certain that the reported loss of one-third of their number that year is accurate. Other, less catastrophic, exotic, and sometimes fatal diseases include influenza, dysentery, and scarlet fever.[37]

Once Aboriginal numbers were in decline, they were not necessarily pitched into free fall. Nonetheless, a number of factors may have worsened the mortality crisis among Aboriginal populations. First, older and perhaps indigenous diseases (among which scholars now believe we should include hepatitis and various respiratory and gastrointestinal afflictions) held the whip hand over a population weakened by exotic diseases. Just prior to the gold rush of 1858, famine haunted British Columbia – as it did almost every other quarter of the planet at the time – and reportedly claimed many lives across the Interior.[38] Average life expectancy at birth was probably not much greater than thirty years among pre-contact North Americans: as everywhere else in the pre-modern world, life was – if not nasty and brutish – very probably short.[39] Certainly, there is nothing to suggest that Hobbes' famous iron law softened for the better in the contact era. Also, nineteenth-century observers were sometimes aware of demoralization among First Nations borne of heightened mortality rates and loss of land and freedom of movement. Europeans on the scene described this phenomenon as taking the form of otherwise inexplicable illnesses. As well, the suicide rate was observed to increase among some Aboriginal groups.[40] It is reasonable to think, also, that the Potlatch Laws, which sought to destroy one of the most fundamental glues in regional Aboriginal societies, may have had unintended demographic consequences. Potlatching was an important element in determining and legitimizing the social relations on which marriages (and thus reproductive activity) were based. The potlatch announced clan relations, and in doing so it greased the wheels of nuptiality. And, rather obviously, potlatches were opportunities to select marriage partners (either directly or on behalf of one's children and other dependants). Aboriginal people's nineteenth- and twentieth-century battles against the Potlatch Laws were, in this respect, a struggle for demographic opportunity. Though not directly related to exotic diseases, these depopulation factors need at least to be mentioned.

The pendulum swings of history being what they are, the impact of exotic bacteria has taken centre stage, whereas the conscious efforts of European intruders to destroy Aboriginal British Columbians have skulked out of the spotlight. It may be the case that, comparatively speaking, interracial warfare was less consequential in British Columbia than elsewhere in the history of European-Aboriginal relations in the Americas. This was the position taken by Wilson Duff as he dismissed imperial violence as a significant factor in depopulation. I cannot absolutely concur. Murderous conflict between the contact parties *did* have demographic impacts, although they may be difficult to track.

Armed struggle took a variety of forms, many direct and some oblique, but nonetheless dependably lethal. For example, in 1785, Captain James

Hanna evidently killed twenty or more residents of Nootka Sound in retaliation for the theft of a single iron chisel; the destruction of Opitsaht, mentioned above, surely resulted in a significant death toll; and sixty Haida were killed by the captain and crew of the American trade ship the *Columbia* in 1791. Probably the most spectacular act of homicide in the sea-based fur trade era is associated with the American ship, the Tonquin, on the west coast of Vancouver Island in 1811. Set to self-destruct by the last of its crew – their own number all but exterminated by the Clayoquot – the explosion is said to have claimed more than a hundred aboriginal lives.[41] The unquantifiable but brutal massacre of First Nations peoples by prospectors from California rushing through the Columbia-Okanagan in 1858 is given its due in a study by Daniel Marshall that describes, as well, the Fraser River War in the same year. The Nlaka'pamux were the leading victims, although the number of mortalities on either side remains unknown to historians. It is entirely likely that more than one hundred lives were lost in the canyon and around the forks of the Thompson and Fraser Rivers that summer, most of them Aboriginal. Less direct were the actions of the HBC. Where the British Canadian traders felt that they no longer enjoyed the full cooperation of Aboriginal traders and neighbours, or where the company's financial interests were no longer served, or in cases where retribution for the murder of white and allied traders was viewed as necessary, forts were often closed down. By the early nineteenth century, white traders had created such a level of dependency on the part of Aboriginal partners that withholding European manufactures from a local economy could have mortal effects. At Fort St. John in 1823, the murder of a clerk and four voyageurs by the Beaver/Dunne-za was avenged by closing the post (threats to do so having been the original cause of tensions). The effect was to deprive the Dunne-za of guns and ammunition they now needed to hunt both trade furs and food animals. Four years later, one observer reported that many of the Dunne-za had starved to death as a consequence of the fur traders' retreat.[42]

In terms of direct conflict, the pre-eminent agency to inflict losses on the Aboriginal population was the Royal Navy. By way of examples, in 1861, a party of Haida in Victoria was accused of theft and was pursued and engaged by a British gunboat at Cape Mudge; four Haida (and one British crewman) perished in the ensuing battle. The 1862 killing of Frederick and Caroline Marks by a group of Quw'utsun' people on Saturna Island was avenged with the murder of five of the Lamalchi and the destruction of their village on Kuper Island by the crews of the *Forward* and the *Grappler*. The death of William Brady at the hands of another group of Quw'utsun' in 1863 resulted in the execution of seven more individuals. In the 1860s, a small sloop connected with the illicit whiskey trade was sacked by the Ahousaht and its crew of three murdered; the Royal Navy base at Esquimalt dispatched HMS *Sutlej* and the aptly named *Devastation,* ostensibly to restore order and to arrest the guilty parties. In the process of doing so, the navy burnt to the ground nine villages (common practice since the *Columbia*) and killed at least thirteen Aboriginals before bringing any suspects to trial. Lethal gunboat diplomacy culminated in the 1860s, at about the same time that imperial laws were being freshly imposed across mainland British Columbia. (As Jean Barman notes, of the twenty-seven individuals sentenced to hang by Judge Matthew Baillie Begbie, twenty-two were Aboriginal people.) The *Sutlej* played a part, too, in the dispatch of a warparty against the Tsilhqot'in in 1864, which ended with the hanging of five men including their leader, Klatsassin. Robin Fisher indicates that the "Chilcotin War," in which a total of twenty-three individuals are known to have been intentionally killed, may have been followed by a famine among the Tsilhqot'in, leading to further deaths.[43] The numbers of fatalities involved in this litany are small, but they probably understate the number of indirect casualties incurred due to resource and/or village destruction by the navy and/or British colonial troops, not to mention the hardships involved in fleeing further attacks. This is not an exhaustive list of colonial-era murders, but it gives one a sense of both the regularity of conflict and how its indirect demographic impacts extend to wholesale destruction of communities, the creation of refugee populations, the loss of food stocks, and the likelihood of immediate hardship, famine, and vulnerability. Although these are grim considerations worth keeping in mind, at the end of the day they would pale next to the toll taken by exotic diseases (see Chapter 3).

Populations bottomed out (or reached their *nadir*) at different times across British Columbia. Overall, the aggregate curve had finally troughed in 1929. Assigning definitive numbers to the respective nadirs is difficult because of nineteenth-century census-taking practices that relied on estimates, as well as the Indian Act's practice of redefining certain Aboriginals as "non-Indians."[44] Aboriginal women, for example, lost their Indian status if they married non-Aboriginal men; their offspring were subsequently defined as non-Aboriginals as well. The same was not true of the increasing number of Aboriginal children born of Aboriginal fathers and non-Aboriginal women living on reserves. On the whole, the ways in which the state *made Indians* were capricious, and the demographic study of Aboriginal British Columbia thus becomes bogged down in bureaucratic constructions of racial categories.[45] When we look at nadirs, then, we need be mindful that they do not include every British Columbian of First Nations ancestry; nor are many who are included entirely Aboriginal. It is, in short, messy.

Aboriginal population recovery rates, an integral part of this topic, are another opaque element. Oral histories suggest that recoveries followed directly on the heels of epidemics. Boyd quotes from one account of a Lower Mainland people: "Little by little the remnant left by the disease grew into a nation once more, and when the first white men sailed up the Squamish in their big boats, the tribe was strong and numerous again."[46] The significance of this coastal Aboriginal testimony lies in its insistence that eighteenth-century exposure to exotic disease was something from which Aboriginal communities could bounce back, and rather quickly too. Without knowing more about the natural fertility and mortality rates of First Nations communities before sustained contact began, one cannot project how long it would take for the population to rebound fully. In the case of the Great Plague of London in 1665, one account estimates that recovery took about 150 years.[47] Given that Aboriginal control over land and resources was progressively eroded in the century that followed contact, it is possible – though in no way certain – that recovery was held back by exogenous factors. And some authors have argued that there was a steep biological price to sexual contact with Europeans in the eighteenth and nineteenth centuries. The "appalling consequences" of venereal diseases included infertility and infant mortality, although the evidence to support such assertions is not crystal clear.[48] Unfortunately, the question of fur-trade-era population recovery has not been rigorously explored by scholars: I can only endorse Boyd's observation that, "Even though there is no solid evidence for numerical rebound of any Northwest Coast population [in the nineteenth century], the topic of locally elevated contact-era birth rates is potentially significant and should be investigated further."[49] What can be said for certain is that First Nations numbers mounted a dynamically rising recovery curve in the twentieth century. By the 1960s, the Aboriginal fertility rate was about twice that of the non-Aboriginal community.[50]

Invasive Species: The Newcomer Era
Europeans and Asians first appeared on the Northwest Coast in the last quarter of the eighteenth century, but their colonies took root only in the second quarter of the nineteenth century. The composition of the earliest invasive communities was very mixed, and the demographic behaviour of the region's fur-trade-era population reflected its peculiar economic context. That interlude was completely eclipsed by the arrival of thousands of opportunists in the gold rush of 1858-63. Thereafter, much of the newcomer population bled away until the 1880s when the construction of the Canadian Pacific Railway reinvigorated settler interest in the region. The population from that time until the Great War expanded hopefully. Or, rather, explosively. From an approximated base of about thirty-six thousand in 1871 – the majority of which was Aboriginal – British Columbia grew more than tenfold by 1911 (see Table 2.1). Spread over a huge territory, this might escape observation, but, in the main, the late Victorian and Edwardian-era population increase was concentrated in a few centres and valleys. The effect was to leave older demographic orders to carry on in more rural and less Europeanized reaches of the province while obliterating the *ancien population régime*

Table 2.1

Population of Canada and BC, 1851-1911

	Canada		British Columbia		
Year	Number	Change (%)	Number	Change (%)	% of Canada
1851	2,436,297	–	55,000	–	–
1861	3,229,633	32	51,524	-6.32	1.60
1871	3,689,257	14	36,247	-29.70	0.98
1881	4,324,810	17	49,459	36.50	1.14
1891	4,833,239	12	98,173	98.50	2.03
1901	5,371,315	11	178,657	142.10	3.33
1911	7,206,643	34	392,480	119.70	5.45

Source: F.H. Leacy, ed., *Historical Statistics of Canada*, 2nd ed. (Ottawa: Statistics Canada, 1983), A2, A12.

in others. This resettlement phase was, more accurately, a period of colonization, in the sense that biological opportunity now complemented economic opportunity. Immigration would remain an important – indeed, the *most* important – influence before 1914, but newcomers rapidly established a demographic regime of their own, one that lay across the fault lines of gender, race, and class. It appeared first in the context of fur trade society.

Russian, Spanish, American, and British interests dominate the European side of the fur trade story on the coast, although the Spanish slipped from the scene at the time of the French Revolution. Notwithstanding the impact of European viruses upon the region's indigenous peoples, the newcomers established few demographic benchmarks before the 1820s. The first British post – established by John Meares at Yuquot (Friendly Cove) in the late 1780s – was mostly populated by Chinese labourers, some 130 of whom Meares had recruited from Canton.[51] Any newcomer toehold on the Northwest Coast in the eighteenth century was, however, temporary. That did not preclude a demographic impact. Miscegenation doubtless occurred and the Native oral tradition records voluntary interracial sexual activity as well as a sorry record of sexual brutality visited by European mariners upon Aboriginal women.[52] These were very limited demographic changes, certainly in the days of the sea-based fur trade. Land-based fur trading, however, necessitated the establishment of posts and forts, permitting a more long-term demographic story to begin, albeit very slowly. Montreal's NWC entered the north and north-central part of the mainland territory via the Saskatchewan and Peace River systems in the 1790s while the American-owned Pacific Fur Company worked its way into the Interior along the Columbia River-Okanagan Valleys system as far north as Kamloops by 1811. That post and others in New Caledonia (as the region was known on British maps) were taken over by the Nor'westers during the War of 1812. In 1821, the NWC merged with the HBC of London, and the posts and forts throughout the Interior came under the administration of the latter firm. Also in the 1820s, the HBC's governor, George Simpson, initiated an aggressive policy of fort construction along the coast, which produced Forts Langley, McLoughlin, Simpson, Stikine, Durham, Victoria, and Rupert by the end of the 1840s. This strategy was aimed in part at breaking the back of Russian and American trade in the region, and in that respect it was successful.

The demographic impact of the land-based fur trade era was neither extensive nor dynamic. As the Hudson's Bay Company's records reveal, the number of traders and staff in the forts and posts was meagre. At the smaller operations there might be no more than a half-dozen men. At Thompson's River Post (Fort Kamloops), the number was reduced in the late 1820s from nearly two dozen to fourteen, but even this small number abandoned the post seasonally every summer. The full-blown forts (such as Langley, Simpson, and, later, Victoria) might contain as many as fifty French Canadians, Metis, Orkneymen, Iroquois, and Hawaiians. These newcomer numbers were augmented by wives obtained from the local Native communities. As ethnohistorian Jo-Anne Fiske notes of life within the walls of Fort Simpson, "the female presence was restricted to [Tsimshian] noblewomen living as partners with the high-ranking traders and to [Aboriginal] common women employed for mundane domestic labour." In many cases, the influential Aboriginal wives also brought domestic slaves into fur trade society. Just before the gold rush and after thirty years of operation, it is estimated that the largest of the fur trade communities, Fort Langley, contained a polyglot population of this kind numbering fewer than two hundred.[53]

The fur trade era's demographic dynamic was weak precisely because of its economic structure and goals. Chief Factor James Douglas, like many of his contemporaries in the HBC, believed that settlement and the fur trade were antithetical.[54] An exception to the general rule of piecemeal recruitment during the fur trade arose in the company's experiment with Wakefieldian colonization measures. The gist of this principle – a brief global fad among English imperialists – was to screen immigration by manipulating land prices. High prices kept out "squatters, paupers, and land speculators"; other means would be found to attract a labouring class.[55] The goal was to establish a population with ready-made (and approved) social relations, such as those between master and servant, between industrialist and worker, between patriarch and household. This can be illustrated in the company's attempts to exploit the Vancouver Island coal seams. The foundation of a mining operation was laid at Fort Rupert in 1839 at the north end of the island; Scottish colliers and their families were subsequently recruited from Ayrshire and Lanarkshire in 1848. This was the first *industrial* resource-extraction community on the Northwest Coast, but it was doomed to failure: within a year of their arrival, a large number of the disenchanted miners had abandoned the operation, most having fled to Victoria, Sooke, and even San Francisco; all but a handful (including some returnees) eventually wound up at the new community of Fort Nanaimo. They were joined in 1854 by a second cohort of miners and their families, recruited this time from England's Black Country. These two groups of immigrants – unusual because they were recruited on contracts, unusual because they came as intact families, unusual because they were industrial wage-labourers – were the very foundation of white British Columbia's demography. More so than any of the elite families of the Hudson's Bay Company's "squirearchy" in Victoria, the men, women, and children of Fort Rupert and Nanaimo were the first genuine and lasting building blocks in the whole newcomer population edifice.[56]

Elsewhere in the territory, the norms of fur trade society prevailed. Inter-marriage – formal or not – between Hudson's Bay Company traders and Aboriginal women was commonplace at all the trading posts in the pre-Confederation period. As Jay Nelson writes, "intermarriage ... simply constituted an extension of prevailing [Aboriginal] practices, an effective means of entangling strangers in a series of kinship obligations." Effective *and* widespread. One Orkneyman in the employ of the company may have been exaggerating only slightly in 1861 when he wrote that "the custom of living with Indian women was universal." Some HBC traders had successive Native partners: John Tod's career as a serial monogamist is reckoned to have started in Rupert's Land and continued at Thompson's River Post, where he took Sophia Lolo as his fourth and final bride thirty-five years later (and with whom he produced seven children). Historian of the fur trade era Richard Mackie estimates that "several thousand Native women had some form of contact with British fur traders west of the Rockies before 1843, and not all of them were reciprocal or permanent relationships." There were, for all intents and purposes, no European females among the fur trade company personnel, so this was not a settlement or colonizing project in the truest sense, although it produced many descendants. Some, as Mackie suggests, were the product of unwanted sexual relations in which the fur traders were the offenders. Although the literature on this subject tends to focus on the social and economic impacts of intermarriage, from a demographic point of view it has at least two consequences that matter: first, intermarriage and/or concubinage (and, sadly, cases of rape) inevitably led to the rise of a hybrid demographic; second, Aboriginal women who were more or less permanently connected with European men were effectively lost to the wholly Aboriginal demographic pool. These connections fostered the growth of a "fur trade society," they helped grow hybrid communities around the fur trade posts, and they may have contributed to the survival of parts of the Aboriginal gene pool, but at the end of the day they contributed to Europeanization of the population.[57]

It is important to recall that not all of the traders were Euro–North Americans. A sizable Hawaiian population augmented that of the whites. The Pacific Fur Company began recruiting and importing Hawaiian labour in 1811; the NWC and the HBC followed suit. The Hawaiians (or Kanakas) probably numbered between one and three hundred at the peak of their migrations to the Northwest Coast in the 1840s, but their community was almost entirely male, and, as Tom Koppel notes, a good number "migrated to the Native community," partly in order to find brides. Of course, the Kanakas had more frequent opportunities to return to their homeland than did the British or Canadians in the region. Nevertheless, families did appear and settlements were established near the Hudson's Bay Company forts but also on the Gulf and San Juan Islands where the Kanakas represented a bulwark against American intrusion.[58]

The first half of the nineteenth century, then, witnessed general and localized changes in population character, distribution, and behaviour, some of which was distinctive, if not unique. To summarize, Aboriginal depopulation was well under way, and European/Euro-Canadian settlement, albeit slight, had begun; the Kanakas were only one part of a multinational labour force that included local Natives, Aboriginal slaves, Iroquois, Orkneymen, and Lowland Scottish and English Black Country coalmining families; Aboriginal women entered into a variety of domestic and sexual relations with Europeans and Pacific Islanders, producing small mestizo populations across the socio-economic spectrum of fur trade society; and immigration (and, importantly, emigration) was sustained by the sea-going character of British and American commerce in the region. So, whereas the Aboriginal population was in severe decline, the newcomer population was too meagre to grow significantly from its own resources, even assuming extensive intermarriage with First Nations women. That single fact bode ill in the face of mid-century American expansionism, and it would not satisfy British imperial ambitions.

In the 1840s, the Hudson's Bay Company came under pressure from Westminster to settle the region with loyal British subjects. The border dispute with the US was resolved in 1846 – the Oregon Territory was cut in half at the forty-ninth parallel – and British sovereignty, on paper at least, was fireproofed against American "manifest destiny" all the way north to Russian Alaska. With a little breathing space at its disposal, the Colonial Office in 1849 gave the HBC a decade in which to demonstrate its commitment to building a settler community. The response was distinctly lacklustre.[59] On the eve of the mainland gold rush, the total non-Aboriginal population on the colony of Vancouver's Island amounted to less than 1,000, of whom fewer than one-third might be regarded as farmers or industrial labourers rather than fur traders, plain and simple. This population was divided principally

between 232 in Victoria, 154 in the village's environs, and 150 or so at Nanaimo.[60] Among the newcomers, the sex ratio was reckoned to be roughly
three males to every female, and this probably entails a flexibility of racial
definitions as regards the females. There were fewer than 300 newcomers
on the mainland. This was an inauspicious beginning.[61] The stampede of
miners and various hangers-on to Fort Victoria, the Fraser River, and the
Cariboo Plateau changed all that.

The Gold Rush Years and Colonial Years, 1858-66

The demographic impact of the gold rush was immediate, but its extent remains unclear. Because ships' captains kept poor records – presumably so as
to defy legal constraints on the numbers of passengers they carried – it is
impossible to know with absolute certainty how many people came to the
region in 1858. From San Francisco no fewer than 15,398 individuals were
recorded as bound for the Fraser River in that year, but the total is no doubt
closer to 20,000.[62] Most of these newcomers entered the British territory
through the island colony's capital, Victoria, heading to the new mainland
colony of *British Columbia*. Others took advantage of a short-lived shortcut
from Bellingham Bay to the Abbotsford area and so remain even more fugi-
tive to the historian of immigration. The third and equally obscure human
migration was the bloody trail up the Columbia-Okanagan system, through
which hundreds if not thousands of forty-niners migrated.

There were, despite the boasts of imperialists and their twentieth-century
heirs, few truly new settlements created in this movement of humanity:
colonies of newcomers mostly planted themselves alongside or over top of
Aboriginal villages wherever the landscape and the mineral potential looked
most accommodating. This was the case most notably at New Westminster
(Sxwoyimelth), Hope (Ts'qo:ls), Yale (Xwoxewla:lhp), and Boston Bar (Kop-
chitchin) – from the mouth of the Fraser River to the height of navigation –
and along the Cariboo Wagon Road at Ashcroft, Lytton (Kumsheen), Lillooet,
Fort Alexandria, and Quesnel.[63] Still other, smaller communities were erected
to serve the needs of the "gold crusaders," such as Port Douglas, Spences
Bridge, Savona, and Soda Creek – each of which have very long histories as
human settlements. There was, also, a cluster of logging villages on Burrard
Inlet that was later swallowed up into the metropolis of Vancouver. Effectively all of these loci, too, mirrored Aboriginal settlement histories. Only a
few centres – and some of them, such as Richfield and of course Barkerville,
were quite large – occurred at least somewhat off the map of First Nations
population geography. The point to note here is that there is hardly a settlement in the province in which human occupancy has not been continuous
since long before the newcomer era began. This pattern of reoccupation was
repeated in secondary gold rushes that followed in the Boundary District in

1860, on the Stikine River in 1862, and on the northernmost reaches of Shuswap Lake, in the Big Bend area of the Columbia River, and around Omineca in 1871. There were, as well, abortive efforts on the Queen Charlotte Islands/Haida G'waii from the early 1850s through the remainder of the century. The cumulative demographic effect of these lesser stampedes was marginal when compared to the "Fraser excitement."

The first wave of gold rush population intrusion was marked by a diversity of nationalities. The short-lived boomtown of Port Douglas, tucked onto the north shore of Harrison Lake, provides an exemplary inventory: in 1861 it was said to contain ninety-seven Chinese, forty Americans, twenty Mexicans, seventeen Europeans, and six "coloured" people, along with an estimated seven hundred First Nations people.[64] The mix, from place to place, could vary dramatically, but Americans were numerous throughout the colony, as were British, continental Europeans, Australians, and Canadians. From June 1858 on, hundreds of Chinese men arrived from San Francisco; they were joined by as many as two thousand more who tramped from Portland, Oregon, to New Westminster and another four thousand who arrived directly from Hong Kong in 1860.[65] Italians and other Europeans added diversity to the population of whites, and many subsequently settled into the coalmining communities of Nanaimo, Wellington, Extension, Ladysmith, and Cumberland.[66] (According to the eminently quotable Dr. John Helmcken, the immigrants from France and Germany were "not gutter spawn," but nor were the newcomers handpicked on the basis of their upbringing, moral probity, and intelligence.)[67] There were, as well, about one hundred Jews in Victoria from the US, Australia, and Britain.[68] African Americans made up another, larger block, one that – like the Jewish community – displayed an atypically close sex ratio.[69]

National or ethnic or racial diversity, in fact, was countered by a high degree of uniformity when it came to gender. The gold crusaders were overwhelmingly male, especially in the heart of the gold rush in the Cariboo. There, in 1863, the ratio of men to women ran as high as 220:1, although within five years it fell to a more reasonable 3.53:1 due to the exodus of frustrated men and the arrival of a large number of entrepreneurial women. These demographic qualities, along with the impecunious character of so many fifty-eighters, caused governmental alarm and produced largely unsuccessful immigration experiments to stabilize the single male population in order to build up the colonial foundations. There was, for example, a noteworthy infusion of almost one hundred female settlers in Victoria in 1862 and 1863 as part of an Anglican Church initiative. The "bride ships" are British Columbian history's answer to the filles du roi of New France, but their demographic impact was nothing like the same. There were, as well, those newcomers who sought to take advantage of the retailing side of the boom and often arrived with intact family households. Other family households were established by newcomer miners who entered into relationships with Aboriginal women.[70]

Given the colonial administration's concern for preserving regional sovereignty, it is hardly surprising that attempts were repeatedly made to enumerate and comprehend this influx. Adding to the state's amateurish census-taking efforts were the newly established mechanisms of parochial record keeping, as churches sprang up across the territory to serve the whites and to Christianize the Natives and Asians. However dramatic the impact of the gold rush, the Colonial Office's gloomy view of things failed to lift. As late as 1867 one official in London wrote to his superiors,

> I do not know why we should go out of our way to lead settlers to make an erroneous choice. I by no means agree that it is good general policy to try to swell the English population in B[ritish] Columbia. The fewer Englishmen that are committed to the place, the better it may prove to be in no distant times. As to hoping that we can by Emigrants round Cape Horn outnumber the natural flow of Emigrants from California and the United States, one might as well make the old experiment of keeping out the Ocean with a mop.

This pessimism did not carry the day in the end, but financially assisted emigration to the region from Britain was negligible – not the case in other Pacific Rim colonies – and the local regimes contributed very little more. Neither seemed in a hurry to invest money in population surveys.[71]

What were the numbers involved in the gold rush? Some accounts take the total of the newcomer invasion as high as 50,000, but that is roughly double contemporary accounts and almost certainly folds in various agricultural populations and the colliery community at Nanaimo.[72] According to a dispatch from Governor James Douglas, the population of newcomers on Vancouver's Island reached 3,024 in 1861; 2,350 of these individuals resided in Victoria and the surrounding area (perhaps half the number who briefly resided in the village in 1859-60), and the majority of the remainder lived at Nanaimo. By 1863 Victoria had reached the 6,000 mark, and newcomer intrusion progressed further up-island where "an empty landscape favourable to colonial settlement resulted from diseases like smallpox and the [inter-tribal] warfare that characterized the early and mid-nineteenth century."[73] On the mainland, New Westminster's population was around 1,000, whereas Yale peaked in 1860 at about 5,000, Lillooet in 1862 at 431, Fort Alexandria at 250, and Barkerville in 1863 at more than 10,000.[74] Smaller communities of a few dozen inhabitants survived along the main transportation corridors; this list includes Lytton, Fort Alexandria, and Quesnel Forks on the Fraser River system, and Ashcroft and Kamloops along the Thompson

River and Brigade Trail system. Several of these smaller communities were able to outlast the larger gold rush centres because their economic base was largely given over to agriculture (as was the case in the Fraser Valley near the old fur trade post at Fort Langley) and cattle ranching (in the Thompson, Okanagan, and Nicola Valleys).[75] A few gristmills appeared in the Interior in these years as part of an early service economy geared to exploiting the needs of prospectors and miners. Limited economic diversification of this kind probably contributed more to long-term population prospects than did the gold excitement itself.

By the mid-1860s, the flow of migration had reversed. The chief goldfields were exhausted, and the major lodes had fallen into the hands of better-capitalized organizations that squeezed out the independent prospector. From a peak of perhaps as many as ten thousand, the Cariboo population fell to a mere thousand in 1870. The Chinese population across the two (now united) colonies was reckoned to have fallen to fewer than two thousand by 1868.[76] Some of the men who abandoned prospecting and the gold towns did not necessarily leave British Columbia. Some joined the growing community of coalminers on the western shores of Georgia Strait. Reversing the flow in some small measure was a contingent of British army engineers, or "Sappers." They first established a base called Sapperton about a mile upriver from the mainland colony's capital at New Westminster and then penetrated deep into the goldfield regions. Over one hundred of their number – many with wives – subsequently established ranches in the Interior or moved to the Lower Mainland's fertile Fraser Valley to farm. The Sappers were unusual in their ability to form family households. Of the fifty-eighters who remained in the colony into the Confederation era, Jean Barman writes that "few possessed the resources to secure a female partner from elsewhere by inviting out an old sweetheart or visiting back home."[77] Perhaps they did not need to do so. As Table 2.2 reveals, the real number of white women in the colony began to rise in 1867, increasing by more than 250 percent in one year to a total of 1,618 in 1868. Though Euro-North American women were still a tiny minority, their arrival at this time was testimony to improved economic opportunities for females, principally in domestic service in Victoria and New Westminster. It also reflects the family-based economic order on the Vancouver Island coalfield, to which entire families were recruited. Of course, the earliest Euro-North American households were generating girls, a fact that needs to be taken into account. And the rising number of newcomer women generally, announces the plentiful marital opportunities that existed in the colony. Although the male population would experience reverses, the female population would not. It continued to grow, however slowly, in both real and proportional terms, to Confederation. Overall – and despite net losses of white population in 1864, 1866, and 1868 – the European newcomer numbers continued to expand very gradually from immigration.

Table 2.2

Colonial European population, 1855-70

Year	Male	Change (%)	Female	Change (%)
1855	509	–	265	–
1861	1,456	186	192	-28
1862	1,991	37	326	71
1863	6,978	251	360	10
1864	1,419	-80	354	-2
1865	5,708	302	547	55
1866	2,629	-54	443	-19
1867	5,410	106	1,569	254
1868	4,806	-11	1,618	3
1869	5,811	21	2,456	52
1870	5,782	-0.5	2,794	14

Source: United Kingdom, Colonial Office, Blue Books of Statistics, British Columbia, 1857-71, *British Parliamentary Papers.*

In the space of ten years, then, the newcomers had established a productive demography, one in which the critical mass necessary to sustained natural increase was evident and in which the agencies and instruments conducive to encouraging and managing immigration were in place. In terms of the white "frontier," the roller-coaster ride of numbers was impressive but inconclusive; in the white women's demographic story, 1866-67 marked a turning point.

As an Aboriginal story, the gold rush was insult added to injury. The initial incursion of outsiders in 1858-60 brought episodes of interracial violence and murder (notably of Native people by white intruders). The damage inflicted on salmon-spawning streams along the Fraser and Thompson River systems by panning and hydraulic mining was severe and led to famine. The arrival of smallpox at Victoria in 1862 was nothing short of catastrophic (see Chapter 3). The loss of land through the creation and enforcement of reserves also had consequences, as one Aboriginal community after another consolidated around the strongest remaining nodes. All of these elements combined to reduce the Native population at a pivotal moment.[78]

The cumulative effect of newcomer and Native emigration, movement, and mortality in the late 1860s was to depopulate whole newcomer and Native communities. Communities of Euro-North Americans, Asians, and Aboriginals were drawn to increasingly prominent settlement clusters or towns in which family households would quickly come to dominate; other centres were simply abandoned and became ghost towns. New Westminster, for example, fell by half to about five hundred by 1868, probably the majority of which was made up of Kwantlen, many of whom were taking work in the emerging fish-packing industry.[79] Port Douglas had a population of over two hundred newcomers before the end of 1859, but by 1871 it had effect-ively ceased to exist as a non-Aboriginal centre. By 1866 even Victoria had declined. One newspaperman in the capital wrote, "I find the population reduced, a large proportion of buildings of every class unoccupied."[80] By 1870 the city's population had sunk to three thousand or so. As the towns declined, so too did the number of agricultural inhabitants who would service their needs.[81] Victoria (after 1866 the capital of the now unified colony of British Columbia) was left with an enormous bill for infrastructure, and the territory swiftly acquired an unattractive reputation as "a bankrupt colony, off on the edge of things."[82]

As British Columbia prepared to become the sixth province of the Do-minion of Canada, its population was probably little more than thirty-six thousand. First Nations peoples perhaps constituted three-quarters of that number; the remainder was mainly divided between Asians (homogeneously Chinese) and Euro-North Americans (fractured by conflicting identities as Americans, Britons, "Continental Europeans," and Canadians). According to Barman, "most Europeans" in British Columbia lived on Vancouver's Island, but at least three-quarters of the Chinese population was on the mainland. Between the artificial categories of race, too, was a growing mixed-race popu-lation; of 287 school-age children enumerated in mainland towns "beyond Hope" in 1872, 182 were reckoned by the superintendent of schools to be "half-caste."[83]

In the thirteen years between the start of the gold rush and British Col-umbia's annexation to Canada, the population had both expanded and contracted. The non-Aboriginal element had grown dramatically and then declined. The Native population by the mid-1860s was reeling from the loss of resources, land, and very large numbers of people. The effect of the gold crusade was seismic in that it significantly transformed the demographics and social relations of the territory. The gold rushes also contributed to the province's early urbanization. Towns sprang up to serve prospectors in fairly compact areas, but, more importantly, as the boom ended, large numbers of newcomers descended the Fraser to settle in the four paramount southern centres: Victoria, Nanaimo, New Westminster, and, a bit later, Vancouver. Some stayed on in the cities with an eye to getting a jump on the next gold rush, but most probably did so to take advantage of new economic develop-ments. Just as the gold had washed down the Fraser from the Interior high-lands, the goldminers were pushed downriver to the Fraser delta and Vancouver Island by hunger but pulled too by fresh economic opportunities and a growing Euro-North American female population.

Confederation to the Great War

Population numbers of the new province in 1871 are as impossible to seize as a Prince Rupert mist. The question of the number of settlers became politicized even as negotiations between Victoria and Ottawa were under way. As one historian put it, the delegation sent east to negotiate the Terms of Union "pressed the Conservative ministry to adopt the stratagem of crediting the province-to-be with a fictitious population of 60,000."[84] Indeed, the number 120,000 was bandied about with some recklessness, because the formula for addressing the new province's subsidy (and thus the elimination of the colonial debt) was at stake. Making use of local accounts and a colonial census held in 1870, historians have since settled on the improbably specific total of 36,247, of which 8,576 were categorized as "Europeans," 1,548 as "Chinese," and 25,661 as "Native Indians." In short, the number of newcomers had halved from the peak years of the 1860s, and the First Nations were made into "Canadians" at anywhere from one-third to one-twentieth of their pre-contact number.

Confederation in 1871 brought with it the promise of a railway from Canada. The Canadian commitment did not, however, immediately produce a groundswell of migration from the east to the west, although that was a key reason for the erstwhile province's interest in the Dominion. From 1871 to 1886 immigrants to British Columbia continued to arrive from the Pacific, both from San Francisco – the foremost west coast port in North America at the time – and China. But the diversity of the gold rush era was already in decline: generally speaking, the older the population at this time, the more international; the younger, the more samey. After 1871 the population would narrow to three principal streams, one from each of eastern North America, Britain, and Asia. The enormous appetite for cheap labour evinced by both the construction of the Canadian Pacific Railway (CPR) and the expanding coalmines on Vancouver Island cemented migrant connections with Guangdong. In the ten years after 1876, it is reckoned that approximately 17,000 males and 150 females arrived from China, the vast majority destined to work on the CPR. But another economic and social order was being built as well. The top-hatted easterners who staged the driving of the last spike at Craigellachie were also driving a stake into the heart of gold rush demographics. The gilded make-hay-while-the-sun-shines newcomer population regime, already a shadow by 1886, was subsumed thereafter by a coming generation of "settlers." Where the former had sailed, paddled, trekked, and clawed their way from the sea to the plateau or, even more recklessly, overland from Canada, John A. Macdonald's generation of Canadian colonists rolled in relative ease on steel wheels from the endless flatlands beyond the Rockies. British imperialism is much studied, but think how much *Canadian* imperialism and colonialism there is in the forward posts at Golden and Revelstoke. Within a matter of months, the human destiny of British Columbia was genetically modified by the railway – the Dominion's own double helix.[85]

Growth was not restricted to the Canadian Pacific right-of-way. The Inland Empire that held court in Spokane, Washington, opened the mineral-rich southeastern corner of British Columbia in the 1890s. Communities sprang up to exploit the resources of both the region and the miners. In 1897 there were over three thousand residents in Nelson and another six thousand in Rossland; although more than half the people living in Rossland in 1901 were Canadian, a third were American, and a new wave of immigrants from Southern and Eastern Europe was beginning to appear. This latter group included Italians who arrived in such numbers at Trail that the city became essentially bilingual. There were in the southeast, as well, some five thousand Doukhobors recently arrived from the prairies. Growth also took place in the Okanagan Valley, where gold-rush-era ranches had to make room for orchards and orchardists, first in the north around Vernon, then south through Okanagan Landing and Okanagan Centre on the big lake and Oyama and Winfield to the east to the Mission (Kelowna), Summerland, Naramata, and Penticton. By 1911 there were some 4.4 million fruit trees in the province, more than half of them in the dry Interior.[86] The population of the embryonic province grew dramatically to the early 1900s, but it did so much more by immigration than by natural means.

One distinctive feature of British Columbia's history in this respect is the very limited extent to which immigration was assisted. Recruitment was conducted typically, though not exclusively, by employers whose labour force requirements could not be met in British Columbia. Sometimes, by way of example, white industrialists exploited the Chinese Benevolent Associations, which acted as agents for potential employers of Asian labour. Through their combined efforts, miners, cannery packers, dockworkers, loggers, millhands, and railway builders were drawn in their tens of thousands. In addition, and away from the industrial hotspots, regional boosters sought out rural settlers from clearly defined target areas with the promise of an improved quality of life and a rising standard of living.[87] From the Okanagan Valley, for example, real estate speculators made pilgrimages to Manitoba to seduce frontiersmen and -women with images of bountiful, sunny orchards and "pickings" richer than any seen since the end of the Cariboo gold rush. One xenophobic orchardist wrote in 1912, with an eye to painting the Interior in glowing hues, "you would not wish to find yourself surrounded with garlic eating, foreign speaking neighbours, with whom you could have nothing in common socially. The class of people coming [to the region] are not of that type. They are the very best Canadian stuff." This passage reveals much about the attitudes of turn-of-the-century agrarian Anglo-Saxon settlers, but it also suggests the need to approach the question of settlement and ethnic diversification as not an entirely ad hoc process. Was a generation of "boosters," as geographer Paul Koroscil suggests, "successful in creating a homogeneous, compatible population base"? The role of boosters in selling the province (sometimes to excess) as a suitable site for settlement was consistent with Victoria's strategy as regards Canada.

Private-sector promoters were viewed as critical to the colony's future, but they functioned outside the auspices of official agencies. This is significant insofar as recruitment agents in places such as Australia and South Africa were bankrolled to pay the settlers' way.[88] In British Columbia, the settlers bore the financial burden of migration, a factor that no doubt influenced immigrant self-selection.

The Dominion census of 1881 had its shortcomings, but one could hardly expect perfect coverage in a province of pockets and coves. Nevertheless, the urbanizing areas were evidently well surveyed – with the important exception of Chinese and First Nations residents – and the published and manuscript returns reveal much. The total population of the province in 1881 was reckoned to be 49,459, a 36.5 percent increase over the population estimate of 1871.[89] No fewer than 25,661 British Columbians in 1881 were First Nations people, but the Dominion census takers neglected much of the central plateau and the north, where Native numbers were significant.[90] As many as 4,000 British Columbians were Chinese.[91] There was reckoned to be, as well, somewhat fewer than 300 blacks.[92] To put it another way, the whites were clearly in the minority. As for distribution, fully 40,000 people were thought to be living in "rural" areas – a category that was left undefined – whereas 9,070 (perhaps a third of whom were Chinese) occupied the towns of Victoria, New Westminster, and Nanaimo.[93] The majority, just over 32,000, lived on the mainland, whereas the remaining 17,292 resided on Vancouver Island; nearly three-quarters of the white population lived on or near the Strait of Georgia in the southwest corner of the province.[94] The sex ratio for the entire population was approximately 3:2 – slightly more severe than it had been ten years before – but for the non-Aboriginal population, it had worsened and reached 3:1 (see Chapter 4).[95] Numbers were at last on the upswing, but it is worth recalling that, assuming the 1850s estimates and surveys have any basis in fact, the population of British Columbia in 1881 was still smaller than it had been twenty years earlier. (It is perhaps trivial, but in 1881 there were vastly more horses per capita in British Columbia than in Canada as a whole – 408:1 versus 198:1.)[96]

After the completion of the railway, the number of people in British Columbia boomed, and it did so in particular ways in particular areas. Prime Minister Macdonald's National Policy for Canada's economic modernization was a project built upon three legs: railroad construction, a tariff to protect fledgling Canadian industries, and immigration. All three elements were meant to support each other, particularly as regards the conquest of the prairie west. The policy did not speak directly to the demographic (or economic) needs of British Columbia, but the province became a beneficiary regardless. Population spilled over from the prairies, especially around the turn of the century as the Okanagan and Thompson Valleys were opened up to orcharding, ranching, and other kinds of agriculture. More dramatically, waves of Canadians from Ontario, Nova Scotia, and New Brunswick were hastened west via the new railway. There had been fewer than three thousand Canadians in the province in 1881, rising to nearly twenty thousand (slightly less than half the total population) in 1891; the number of Canadians in BC doubled by 1901, and it doubled again in the ten years that followed.[97] Very quickly the tide of newcomers turned more Canadian and less British.

The population of British Columbia doubled from 1881 to 1891, nearly doubled again from 1891 to 1901, and more than doubled from 1901 to 1911. The pace was being set not only in the new city of Vancouver but in mining areas such as the Vancouver Island coalfield, where the population grew from nearly 10,000 souls in 1881, to 18,229 in 1891, and 27,198 by 1901. By 1911 the city and periphery of Nanaimo, along with Ladysmith and Cumberland – links in a long chain of mining communities – contained roughly 17,000. The Kootenay Census District in the southeast, dominated by Fernie, Ymir, Cranbrook, Nelson, and the many towns of the Slocan, totalled more than fifty thousand in the same year. This super-Malthusian increase would be stopped in its tracks by the First World War, so the arrival in BC of nearly half a million people in the space of a generation was to have lasting importance in terms of culture, values, and political influence. Denominationally speaking, this demographic growth was frozen at the end of a decade in which the numbers of Anglicans, Methodists, Catholics, and adherents of "eastern religions" had roughly doubled, Baptists, Congregationalists, Presbyterians, and Jews had nearly trebled, Lutherans and the Salvation Army had approximately quadrupled, and the numbers of Greek Church members had exploded from 101 to 3,574 – three times the size of the deeply rooted Jewish community. There was growing homogeneity, in that four denominations – Anglican, Presbyterian, Methodist, and Catholic – accounted for 65 percent of the population, but the rise of smaller sects foreshadowed later twentieth-century diversity. It was also during these years – coincidentally, the era when modern national identities were being forged – that the triumphalist chorus of white supremacy found its voice, Canadian-style party politics corrected the local "loose fish" aberration in the provincial legislature, individual landlessness and collective spiritual redemption were thrust upon the First Nations, and the class conflict endemic in an industrial order clashed with the cozy agrarian and pastoral ideals of an anachronistic gentry.[98] It was, in short, a period when a multitude of conflicting visions for the future arrived by rail and sea, an age of competitive foundation setting.

This growth took place against a backdrop of significant large-scale mortalities. Public health measures were slow in coming, and the quality of life – measured in long, robust lives – was not exceptionally high before the war. Consider, for example, the 6,500 Chinese labourers who arrived in Victoria in 1882, of whom it is estimated that 1 in 10 succumbed to scurvy. The next year an epidemic of uncertain character, but also very probably scurvy, claimed perhaps more than 200 Chinese men in the railway camp at Port Moody.[99] A minor smallpox epidemic in 1892 took 28 lives, all of them Aboriginal. Epidemics were otherwise more inclusive mortality experiences, insensitive to racial categories. Typhoid carried off 191 British Columbians from 1898 through 1901; in 1907 the disease returned for a four-year plague that claimed 564 more, all but 78 of them outside of Vancouver.[100] Cholera visited the province thrice before the war, claiming 47 in 1893; another 237 died in a two-part epidemic between 1904 and 1910. An outbreak of scarlet fever killed 17 in 1903, and there was a diphtheria epidemic in 1911-13 that ended the lives of 139. This brief tally alone constitutes more than 2,000 deaths over forty-one years. The pre-war years, then, were a time when illnesses routinely gave rise to mortal fear and in which natural increase was accomplished in the teeth of persistent biological threats.

The key to natural growth in the years from 1881 to 1911 was the rise of nuclear family households across the province. This began in some quarters more rapidly than in others. Nanaimo, for example, was settled in the early 1850s by English and Scottish coalminers who were recruited directly from Britain along with their families. Subsequent cohorts arrived with families in tow or sent for wives and children after establishing a beachhead. Levels of dependency – that is, the share of population under fifteen years or over sixty – regularly exceeded 35 percent from the 1860s on.[101] In the more rural communities of Saltspring Island, fully 40 percent of the population in 1881 and 1891 was under the age of fifteen.[102] Similarly, the towns and cities of the Interior, formerly dominated by "homosocial" communities of males, acquired a more stable population increasingly comprised of families.[103] The proportion of Kamloops' population that was dependent was as high as in more mature newcomer settlements. Even in 1881 nearly 22 percent of the population around Kamloops was under sixteen. That cohort's proportion of the total population would rise to approximately 36 percent in 1891 and 40 percent in 1901. Dependants constituted 28.6 percent of the town's non-Aboriginal, non-Asian population in 1881, so the experience of having children and providing for children would probably have been witnessed across this area of new settlement. Provincial figures are roughly similar, although the Vancouver area recorded dependency rates of only 31.7 percent in 1881 and about 26 percent in 1891.[104] Regardless as to whether these dependency rates were due to natural increase or increasing immigration of children, and regardless of precisely how "dependent" these children really were in an economy that combined unrestricted use of child labour on farms and ranches with underenforced legal restrictions on the use of children in coalmines, the point is to take note of the presence of large numbers of under-fifteens in a region defined in the literature – historical or otherwise – by its adult maleness.

Early Urbanization and Diversity

Although, throughout its history, British Columbia has been ostensibly more urban than rural longer than Canada overall, definitions of what constitutes "urban" have been outstandingly elastic. A contemporary in the 1860s described the four-year-old "city" of New Westminster as sadly typical of so many frontier towns: "Half-a-dozen wooden huts, a whiskey shop, and a post-office, constitute a 'city' anywhere in America."[105] The mainland capital improved, but the boosters' practice of overselling their stock in remote quarters of the province by incorporating chimerical towns and cities did not relent. For example, when Henry and Daisy Phillips were enticed out to the upper Columbia just before the Great War, they found that their city existed only on paper. Within days and weeks their address for mailing purposes changed from the splendid-sounding Invermere to the far more prosaic Wilmer and then to Athalmer. After nearly three years in the valley, the Phillipses and their neighbours still found not so much as a post office in their "town."[106] To assume from the census reports and the puffery of boosters that there was any similarity in the experiences of urbanites in Victoria and New Westminster, on the one hand, and those faux urbanites in bucolic Windermere, Naramata, Ruskin, and Trout Lake is to make a serious critical error. Nor, however, should it be thought that the smaller industrial centres – such as Greenwood, Phoenix, Merritt, Union, and a great many more – were spared classic urban squalor characteristics, including high density housing, poor water, inadequate sewage disposal, and near-toxic air pollution.

Arguably the most outstanding aspect of the pre-1914 newcomer demographic phase was urban growth and the emergence of Vancouver. Down to 1886 there were several communities along Burrard Inlet that primarily survived on the lumber trade: Moodyville, Gastown (or Granville), Stamp's (or Hastings) Mill, Hastings, and Port Moody. These nodes contained 690 non-Aboriginal people, of whom only 149 were female. A third of the "working-age" population was from the British Isles, fewer than one in five from Canada (Ontario, Quebec, and the Maritimes), and the remainder drawn mostly from the US, Europe, and China. There were, as well, Native communities along the saltchuck, which included 375 people in the winter of 1877; another 42 Native people lived on False Creek and a further 92 at Musqueam/Xwméthkwiyem at the mouth of the North Arm of the Fraser. Through the 1860s and '70s, marriage between white men and Native women in the logging towns was a frequent if slowly declining phenomenon.[107]

The completion of the railway to the southwestern shore of Burrard Inlet – just to the west of Granville – settled the question of which community would dominate the others. "Vancouver" became the focus of intensive growth, and it soon challenged the other provincial centres as well. In the first thirty years after Confederation, Victoria and New Westminster (with populations of approximately 5,900 and fewer than 2,500 respectively in 1881) experienced comparative stagnation as the "Terminal City" pulled ahead in the urbanization race. From a population of barely 300 in 1881, the communities hugging Burrard Inlet grew to 13,709 in 1891, after which it easily passed Victoria and reached 120,847 in 1911, nearly 100,000 people being added between 1906 and 1911 (see Appendix A).[108] On the eve of the war, another 20,000 people lived in the nearby suburbs of South Vancouver and Point Grey. This was a rate of growth – the increase from 1901 to 1911 amounted to 271 percent – that resembled but in fact surpassed that of American west coast cities.[109] Like the rest of the province, Vancouver had a large male surplus and a significant Chinese community as well. The metropolis would, however, straightaway come to display a greater diversity in social, economic, ethnic, and religious categories. Vancouver also led the way in becoming more Canadian. From 1881 to 1891, the share of Vancouverites born in Canada but outside of British Columbia leapt from 15.6 percent to 42.5 percent, whereas the percentage of British and American residents grew only slightly; the proportion of the population that was Chinese actually declined from 7.8 percent to 6.1 percent. Very quickly the city had become, to use historian Robert McDonald's phrase, "a relatively homogeneous community," although that "relativity" was very British Columbian.[110]

Vancouver was only part of the urbanization story.[111] As Maps 2.3 and 2.4 and Appendix A illustrate, towns boomed and crashed (and sometimes reappeared) throughout the Victorian and Edwardian years. Mostly, this phenomenon was driven by resource developments. Although the growth of the province in the first decade of the twentieth century tends to overshadow every other statistic from this period, a few details need to be winkled out. First, there were dozens of new settlements established in the years from 1881 to 1891, most of which were associated with resource extraction (chiefly hard-rock mining in the southeast and fish canneries on the coast), railway operations (Revelstoke, for example), and some agricultural expansion (as in the Columbia Valley, the lower Fraser Valley, and the north Okanagan). The total number of people living in these wet-paint communities in 1891 was in excess of 50,000 (more than 15,000 of whom lived in the mining towns of the Kootenays); that is, these towns held more than a third of the provincial population and roughly as many people as there were in all of British Columbia in 1881. Second, if we look at this expansion somewhat differently, in 1891 there were thirty towns with populations of 500 or more, and the vast majority of those towns *did not exist* ten years earlier. By contrast, in 1901 there were thirty-five centres with populations of 500 or more; some towns had been invented anew, others surged across the cut-off line, and still others disappeared, but by my count this activity produced a net gain of only two cities of 1,500 or more (Fernie and Atlin) and five small towns of 500-750 people. In short, the 1880s saw the emergence of a very different human geography in the territory, one in which small-to-medium communities appeared for the first time. Some were shooting stars. Sandon was barely a bush camp in 1891; by 1898 it had 2 to 5,000 people; by the census of 1901, it was sliding badly.[112] Third, the number of towns 500-strong or greater rises sharply to fifty-six in the first decade of the new century, indicating that Edwardian-era growth was not contained to Burrard Inlet. This wave took in the early Okanagan communities of Enderby, Armstrong, and Vernon in the north, as well as Kelowna, Summerland, and Penticton to the south. In fact, the number of communities with populations of 1,000 or more also grew, from twelve in 1891 to eighteen in 1901 and to twenty-three in 1911. Even Kamloops, by 1911 its railway construction boom behind it and stability as a ranching centre secured, more than doubled its population from nearly 1,600 in 1901 to 3,772 in 1911.[113] The Edwardian years thus marked substantial growth of towns and cities across the province and probably contributed more to the making of modern British Columbian society than is generally appreciated.

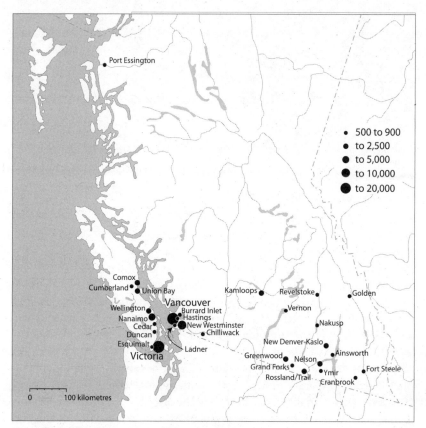

Map 2.3   Urban growth and distribution, 1891

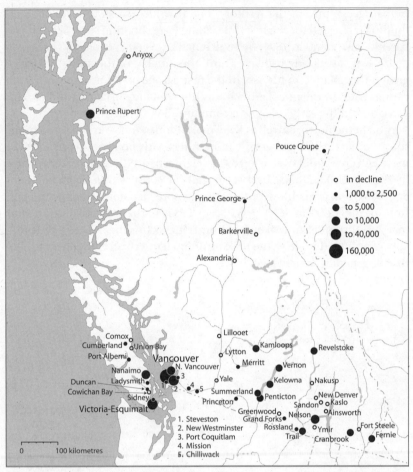

Map 2.4   Urban expansion and depletion, 1921

War and Interwar

Two sports trivia questions – Who won the Stanley Cup in 1915? Who won in 1919?

Answer, the first: the Vancouver Millionaires claimed what has for so many years eluded the Canucks.[114] This fact is of no demographic consequence, but it is so completely forgotten by British Columbians that it cries out for repetition at every opportunity.

The answer to the second question is far more sobering: the finals were cancelled due to Spanish influenza. The initial cases were reported in October 1918 and swept Canada in the month of the armistice. In British Columbia perhaps as much as a third of the population came down with the flu, and it claimed 2,755 lives – nearly half as many British Columbians as died at the front and roughly 1 in every 100 of the population.[115] The death toll in isolated communities was particularly harrowing. In Prince George, for example, one local undertaker handled 21 burials in each of 1917 and 1919, but in 1918 there were 79.[116] At Stoney Creek, a largely Aboriginal community, "people were too ill to make coffins and dig graves, though the church bell rang day and night for the dead." It is reckoned that half the Aboriginal population of the Nemiah Valley was carried off by this epidemic.[117] Even in Vancouver, where public health and medical resources were arguably better than anywhere else in the province, the death toll (at 23.3 per 1,000) was the worst in Canada and perhaps the third worst among major North American centres. According to historian Margaret Andrews, "The streets were darkened with frequent funerals, and fresh flowers and burial plots were in short supply."[118] When one thinks of the Reaper's harvest during the war, it is important to recall that his work did not end when the guns were silenced.

In fact, the demographic breakage of the Great War was so severe that it was hardly tidied away before the next war began. This was true in many Canadian jurisdictions but very much so in BC for several reasons. First, there was the fatal corollary of building a *British* British Columbia in the Edwardian era. The national debate over conscription turned on the comparatively high voluntarism of Anglo-Canadians versus that of Franco-Canadians, but, in point of fact, the Anglo-Canadian numbers were inflated by the response of British immigrants, the majority of whom had arrived during the 1896-1911 immigration boom in the west. British Columbia, trading on its name and ersatz Britishness, had attracted large numbers of British males in these years. (Even in 1921 Britishness remained such a fetish with the locals – fed, no doubt, by nativist xenophobia and imperial zeal left over from the war – that it was claimed, without irony, that one in four "British" Vancouverites had been born in the province.)[119] The effect was that the province's contribution to the rolls of the war dead was particularly high by Canadian standards. Over sixty-two hundred residents – British-born or not – were sacrificed in Europe, the equivalent of more than 4 percent of males between the ages of fifteen and forty. Given the high levels of voluntarism, it was perhaps inevitable that the many returning soldiers at war's end would do such an effective job in spreading the Spanish influenza far and wide.

The loss of young males overseas combined with the post-war epidemic – for a total of about nine thousand – would have been enough to slow growth for the better part of a generation, all other things being equal. But there were hints of things to come before Sarajevo. Between 1902 and 1912, the annual provincial population growth rate fell from a high of 11 percent to a low of 3.6 percent. An economic crash in 1912-13 and the war applied the brakes to a dynamic that was, evidently, already slowing. From 1911 to 1921, the total grew by less than 34 percent, still a respectable rate to be sure, but nothing like the Edwardian period of growth. Had the population carried on doubling through the decade, there would have been 800,000 people in British Columbia in 1921, rather than 524,582. The 800,000 threshold would be not breached until the early 1940s, a further indication of low rates of fertility and the fall in interwar immigration after the brief post-war exodus from Europe of "displaced peoples." It was for these reasons that the interwar era was marked by the solemn promise of soldier settlement schemes and the hoopla of Peace River Block and Okanagan Valley boosters in the 1920s. Over the generation between 1921 and 1941, the provincial population recorded much more modest decennial increases averaging about 25 percent. These slower rates were, nonetheless, consistently much higher than the national average and higher than the Prairie provinces as a group, although Alberta was often a rival in this respect.[120]

It was, perversely, in the midst of this slowdown that the government in Victoria, abetted by allies in Ottawa, decided to introduce the first effective restriction on newcomers. Head taxes before the war had slowed immigration from China (especially that of wives), but there were still some who could afford to pay. Legalistic ploys – such as the 1907 "Gentlemen's Agreement" with Japan that restrained emigration at the source, or the notorious manipulation of the law to forbid immigrants from India to disembark the *Komagata Maru* in 1914 – were effective but short-term solutions. In 1923 the federal government struck boldly and introduced the Chinese Immigration Act, which effectively terminated legal immigration from China and which severely impacted the demographic prospects of both British Columbia as a whole and the regional Chinese in particular. From 1906 to 1942, only 1,074 Chinese women arrived, a fact that clearly inhibited the formation of new Chinese Canadian families. As novelist Sky Lee puts it, in Vancouver's Chinatown from the 1920s on there was "only one thing missing – women!" The act was intended to accomplish three demographic goals: to discourage further aggregation of Chinese numbers, to demonstrate an inhospitality that might lead to Chinese Canadian emigration, and, most importantly, to regulate Chinese fertility. Japanese immigration, also a source of disquiet among the white population, was not affected in a similar way until Pearl Harbor. After V-J Day, however, the tide of repression turned and ten thousand Canadians of Japanese birth or ancestry were pressured to relocate to Japan. Nearly four thousand made the move across the Pacific in 1946.[121] Managing Asian immigration in the interwar years and the post-war era was, in short, much more aggressive than at any time in the past (see Chapter 6).

A factor of signal importance in this era of relative stagnation was the Depression. The international economic crisis is best remembered as an industrial downturn and a disaster in the farming sector. Silenced assembly lines and prairie dustbowls are the emblematic artifacts of the era, certainly in the imaginations of most North Americans. British Columbia did not, of course, share directly in the agricultural disaster, although grain handling along Burrard Inlet certainly suffered. Nor did BC have a sufficiently mature secondary manufacturing sector to fit the blue-collar version of the story. What the province did have, of course, were huge mining and forestry sectors already prone to boom and bust cycles, as was the dependent (and very large) rail transportation sector. When the commodities market collapsed in 1929, jobs in the mines and the woods promptly dwindled.

One needs to state the fact baldly: the Depression cost lives as hunger spread and mortality rose, a fact that contemporaries were often unwilling to acknowledge. Richmond Hobson, for example, described Kamloops as "a sunny healthful town of some five thousand people," despite the fact that the local mortality rate was climbing. In British Columbia's largely capitalist economy, however, labour mobility was a crucial feature on which industries relied, and there were thousands upon thousands of men who searched fruitlessly for work in the mines of the southeast, the forests of the west coast, and, of course, with threshing crews on the prairies. Playing the role of "mecca to the unemployed" since the early twentieth century, Vancouver attracted large numbers of unemployed transient men in the 1930s (not least because of the mild weather). These hoboes and bindlestiffs were a demographic force: overwhelmingly male and crushingly unemployed, most of them very young. The Depression thus assembled different players, but it also worsened the conditions of life for many already on the coast. One measure of a declining quality of life is the incidence and rate of suicide and homicide, both of which increased sharply by about 50 percent from 1929 to 1931; both rates subsequently fell, but as indicators of the emotional, personal, and societal impact of the economic crisis, these are powerful figures. Later in the Depression, in 1937, Vancouver alderman Helena Gutteridge headed a civic housing survey project that discovered four to five hundred Vancouverites (including no fewer than seventy-five children) living in waterfront houseboats or shacks built on piles. Some of these homes, located in the midst of sewer seepage and outfalls along False Creek and along Burrard Inlet as far as Boundary Road, constituted "filthy and distressing" conditions, according to the survey. The *Vancouver Daily Province* reported that "few of the habitations are equipped with sanitary conveniences. Hardly half are equipped with electric light." None were connected to city water supplies.[122] No surprise that mortality rates rose in Vancouver in these years.

For the whole generation of young men and women in the 1930s, the Depression forced a rethinking of older life-course expectations and timings. Marriages were postponed and family sizes were limited in the face of economic uncertainty, as can be seen in Table 2.3 (and Chapters 4 and 5).

Table 2.3

Marriages and births, Vancouver, 1928-39

Year	Marriages	Change (%)	Births	Change (%)
1928	2,347	–	3,812	–
1929	2,585	10.1	3,869	1.5
1930	2,250	-13.0	4,003	3.5
1931	1,767	-21.5	3,730	-6.8
1932	1,633	-7.6	3,450	-7.5
1933	1,776	8.8	3,188	-7.6
1934	2,137	20.3	3,179	-0.3
1935	2,227	4.2	3,248	2.2
1936	2,441	9.6	3,410	5.0
1937	2,783	14.0	3,780	10.9
1938	2,761	-0.7	4,095	5.6
1939	3,496	26.6	4,107	0.3

Source: Canada, Bureau of Statistics, *Vital Statistics, 1929-1939* (Ottawa: King's Printer, 1940).

Nuptiality (the rate of marriage) and fertility rebounded spectacularly after 1938, but only because the business of killing people had once again become industrialized.

The Boom Years

Fewer British Columbians died during the Second World War than in the First – a fact that can be verified at the base of armistice memorials across the province – but there were losses nonetheless. And gains. On the home front, the Second World War revitalized the economy and fired up the demographic jets. The marriage rate shot ahead, peaking in 1942 as jobs and enlistment opportunities opened. Many wartime couples were able, at last, to act on plans laid down and postponed in the 1930s. Having said that, it is noted that the much more important impact of the return to conflict was the so-called baby boom, which can be seen in Table 2.4 as part of a 100 percent increase in the total population from 1941 to 1961 (see also Table 2.5 and Chapter 5). This rise in fertility rates occurred against a backdrop of delayed family/household formation from the 1930s, suddenly improved living standards in the war economy and thereafter, and the arrival, from 1945 on, of large numbers of immigrants in their child-bearing years, many of them "war brides." Today, baby boomers represent a larger per capita share of the Canadian population than is the case in any other G-7 nation, and for much of the late twentieth century, British Columbia was the country's boomer haven without equal. Indeed, in the five years after 1956, natural increase finally (though briefly) outstripped net migration as the leading engine of growth.[123]

Table 2.4

Census year populations, BC and Canada, 1921-2006

Year	Total population (000s)		Decennial increase (%)	
	BC	Canada	BC	Canada
1921	525	8,788	33.66	21.94
1931	694	10,377	32.35	18.08
1941	818	11,507	17.80	10.89
1951	1,165	13,648	42.47	18.61
1961	1,629	18,238	39.81	33.63
1971	2,185	21,568	34.10	18.26
1981	2,824	24,820	29.26	15.08
1991	3,374	28,031	19.46	12.94
2001	4,255	31,021	20.90	10.67
2006	4,320	31,613	1.55	5.40

Note: The Canada census for 2006 gives a total for British Columbia of 4,113,487 and an increase of 5.9 percent over a 2001 population of 3,907,738. The difference arises from incomplete coverage of Indian reserve populations in 2006.
Sources: BC Stats, *BC Annual Population, 1931-2007,* http://www.bcstats.gov.bc.ca/data/pop/pop/BCPop.asp; Statistics Canada, *Population and Growth Components (1851-2001 Censuses),* http://www40.statcan.ca/l01/cst01/demo03.htm; Statistics Canada, *Population and Dwelling Counts, for Canada, Provinces and Territories, 2006 and 2001 Censuses,* http://www12.statcan.ca/english/census06/data/popdwell/Table.cfm?T=101.

Table 2.5

Live birth rate (per 1,000 population), Canada and BC, 1921-90

Year	Canada	BC
1931	23.2	15.0
1941	22.4	18.4
1951	27.2	24.1
1961	26.1	23.7
1971	16.8	16.0
1981	15.3	15.1
1990	15.3	14.6

Note: Patricia E. Roy and John Herd Thompson, *British Columbia: Land of Promises* (Don Mills: Oxford University Press, 2005), 158, draws attention to the difference between BC and Canada in 1951, with birth rates respectively of 24.1 and 27.2. As this table shows, however, the gap between the two was closing at midcentury. What is more important is that they were moving in the same direction after 1941 and would become essentially the same by 1971.
Source: Surinder Wadhera and Jill Strachan, *Selected Birth and Fertility Statistics, Canada, 1921-1990* (Ottawa: Statistics Canada, 1993), 32, table 1b, "Live Birth Rates, Canada and Provinces, 1921-1990."

The sharp and sustained rise in fertility was an international, though not global, phenomenon. True baby booms were witnessed in Canada, the United States, Australia, and New Zealand, although increases in births ("boomlets," according to Angus McLaren) were seen in a number of other countries as well. British Columbia, however, experienced the baby boom differently.[124] The 1930s Depression that preceded it brought large numbers of single unemployed men to Vancouver; women migrated to or stayed in British Columbia during the 1930s in greater numbers than before, and, especially in Vancouver by 1941, there were more women relative to men than at any time since colonization began; the Dominion's entry into the war (well in advance of America's) meant that Vancouver, Prince Rupert, and Esquimalt were buzzing with naval construction a full year before Japanese bombs rained down on Pearl Harbor. These elements combined to produce a precipitous rise in family formation and fertility, much sharper than that seen nationally.[125] And the fertility explosion did not quickly subside. The Korean War sustained the economic and fertility boom into the late 1950s, by which time a pattern of urban and suburban sprawl across the Lower Mainland was plain to see.

The economic and fertility boom was taking place, as well, across rural British Columbia. A growing economy based on traditional and new kinds of resource extraction fed these processes. Hydroelectric power generation, the forest industry, copper mine expansion, a more technologically sophisticated fisheries industry, the rise of the Alcan aluminum smelter operation at Kitimat, an emergent natural gas sector, and a vastly improved road system all supported family formation across the province into the 1960s, despite unemployment rates that were consistently higher than Ontario's.[126] Policies meant to modernize the northern half of the province led to an increase in the region's population from fewer than 50,000 at the start of the Second World War to more than 300,000 by 1971, a proportional improvement from less than 6 percent of the provincial total to 10 percent.

These economic drivers combined with the baby boom to produce a rapid expansion of the public sector. Provincial governments are responsible for education, health, and welfare: those duties became much more pressing with the baby boom, industrial expansion, and widespread labour mobility. Victoria derives significant revenues from resource-extraction royalties: collecting and managing a treasury of taxes on logging and mining in particular demanded the creation of a professionalized bureaucracy. As one historian has put it, the Social Credit regime led by "the demagogic W.A.C. Bennett ... aggressively promoted a virulent form of interventionist state capitalism aimed at wringing the utmost from the province's vast reserves of timber and mineral wealth."[127] Public-sector jobs necessarily increased in number and scope as a consequence and as a reflection of the changing economic-demographic order. This can be seen, for example, in the creation of BC Hydro (the provincial Crown corporation responsible for energy provision and sales) and the wholesale expansion of the health sector.

By the 1960s, the metropolitan socio-economic order was arguably more bourgeois than it had ever been before. Middle-class families and middle-class values depleted energy from the movement toward higher fertility rates. At the same time, the interwar cohort that produced the baby boom was also spent, and working-class families faced unemployment rates approaching double digits for the first time since the 1930s. Timing and cultural change combined to slow and then close the baby boom – sexual revolution or no – just as the sweet life of post-1945 British Columbia started to sour.

As Table 2.6 shows, the 1940s and '50s witnessed significant natural increase in real terms, but newcomers also had a role to play. Stifled in the interwar years, immigration resumed with a vengeance after 1945. By combined means of immigration and natural growth, the population of British Columbia reached 800,000 during the early 1940s; in the thirty years that followed, that many people again would be added through immigration and arrivals from other provinces. Traditional northwestern European sources continued to provide settlers while new veins were briefly mined in Eastern bloc countries – particularly Hungary, from which a whole forestry school was acquired during the troubles of 1956.[128] A noteworthy Portuguese presence appeared in these years as well, principally in the Osoyoos-Oliver area and at the new planned town of Kitimat.[129] Waves of Italians and Greeks also arrived in the 1950s and 1960s, as did smaller numbers of Latin Americans and Caribbean immigrants. White Canadian ethnophobia – as highly evolved in British Columbia as in any other province – softened somewhat after the war crimes trials at Nuremberg, but the road to a policy of multiculturalism was a long one on which British Columbians did not always travel with enthusiasm. Nor did Ottawa. In fact, this situation was largely tailored by federal policy: Europeans enjoyed favourable treatment under Canada's Immigration Act until the 1960s.[130]

In the 1950s, the federal government's frosty official position vis-à-vis Asian immigration started to thaw. As a general rule, protest from the Asian

Table 2.6

Natural increase and net migration, BC, 1931-2001				
	Net migration		Natural increase	
Interval	Number	(%)	Number	(%)
1931 to 1941	82,498	67	41,100	33
1941 to 1951	230,822	66	116,527	34
1951 to 1961	240,081	52	223,791	48
1961 to 1971	392,942	67	192,597	33
1971 to 1981	402,700	69	178,400	31
1981 to 1991	328,300	60	215,286	40
1991 to 2001	479,800	73	178,362	27

Sources: F.H. Leacy, ed., Historical Statistics of Canada, 2nd ed. (Ottawa: Statistics Canada, 1983), Series A349: Changes in the Population through Natural Increase and Migration, 1931 to 1976; BC Stats, "British Columbia Population Forecast – 07/07" http://www.bcstats.gov.bc.ca/DATA/pop/pop/project/bctab2.asp.

community was effective only when the policy door opened a crack; when it was shut tight, it could not be forced ajar. Still, Ottawa had to attend to at least the appearance of even-handedness in the post-war era. Policy initiatives meant to dismantle the anti-Asian framework of laws in Canada were piecemeal and sometimes unconvincing. South Asian and Chinese Canadians received the vote in 1947, and Japanese Canadians did so in 1949. Outwardly more portentous was the repeal of the Chinese Immigration Act in 1947, but this move was effectively nullified by Mao's revolution, which cut off much of the supply of Chinese immigrants after 1949. (Direct travel from China to Canada would not resume until 1974.)[131] Practically speaking, Ottawa's change of heart toward Asians immediately after the war did not extend much farther than allowing into the country the wives and children of Chinese Canadians, and a small quota of about three hundred Indians, Pakistanis, and Sri Lankans beginning in 1951.[132] The curve of tolerance did not move steadily upward: it is true that in 1956 the quota for Indians alone was raised to three hundred, following an aggressive campaign on the part of British Columbian Sikhs, but the 1960s witnessed striking if ominous changes in immigration practices and experiences.[133] At that time Ottawa recognized there was a shortage of workers to meet the country's burgeoning labour needs; simultaneously, a Royal Canadian Mounted Police report claimed that effectively half of the Chinese who had come to the province after the war had done so under false pretences. Many, no doubt, had done so in order to reunite families separated since 1923 or earlier. What is striking in retrospect is the absence from the period of laudatory tales of refugees from the People's Republic of China comparable to those regarding the "boatpeople" of post-revolutionary Cuba and Vietnam or the "defectors" who fled the Warsaw Pact countries. Although they found themselves outside of the law and invisible to broad public sympathy, many Chinese immigrants in these years were engaged in the kind of displacement migration that was a hallmark of the twentieth century. That is not to say that attitudes held by one group of British Columbians toward another were unchanging. The need for new working-class citizens trumped a resurgent white fear of a "yellow peril": soon the restrictions on Asian immigration were softened and eliminated; before the 1970s got under way, Asians were being actively recruited – a policy that had not been embraced since the days of Andrew Onderdonk's exploitation of "coolies" along the CPR mainline.

The increasingly liberal attitude of Ottawa, enshrined in the 1976 Immigration Act, led to further accessions from Asia that pushed the provincial population ever more definitively toward an ethnically diverse composition. In the decade between 1981 and 1991, nearly two-thirds of BC's immigrants came from Asia. Alberta posted a rate of 51.3 percent from Asia, but, as was the case in most other provinces, roughly 25 percent of Alberta's total immigration in the 1980s came from Europe. In British Columbia, European immigration had fallen to below 19 percent. Immigration continued to climb from 13,190 in 1984, peaked at 52,023 in 1996, and fell back to 38,289 in 2001.[134] Arrivals from the Indian subcontinent stabilized, but a fresh wave of Chinese newcomers came ashore at Vancouver. The threat of changes in the status of Hong Kong created a push factor that was quite unlike any experienced by earlier generations of Chinese emigrants. Between 1990 and 1995, roughly half of the 190,000 people who moved to British Columbia came from Hong Kong, the People's Republic of China, and Taiwan.[135]

The character of the immigrants had changed as well as the source of supply. Unlike most earlier immigrant cohorts, the late twentieth-century stampede from Southeast Asia brought high levels of skills, education, ambition, cultural capital, and wealth, provoking a small resurgence of the old racism. By way of an infamous example, the bitter elite of the provincial metropolis coined the phrase "Hongcouver" to illustrate its sense that a new, wealthy cohort from Asia was pounding at its garden gates. (Things certainly could have been much worse: this fresh tide of immigration coincided with the worst unemployment in British Columbia since the 1930s, but a racist backlash based on working-class fears of competition was not revived.) Against the record of cranky intolerance, however, one can place the rise of Asian leaders in the community, exemplified by David Lam (the Hong Kong-born lieutenant governor of BC from 1988 to 1995) and Ujjal Dosanjh (born in India, a Sikh, and premier from 2000 to 2001), among many others.[136]

Another feature that changed dramatically in the mid-twentieth century is age distribution. Before the Great War, the population was dominated by young to middle-aged adult males; children and the elderly were vastly overshadowed, as were women in every age cohort. Statistical levels of dependence (the ratio between individuals between the ages of fifteen and sixty or sixty-five, on the one hand, and those between zero and fifteen years and over sixty or sixty-five, on the other) rose from 25.5 percent in 1911 to 32 percent in 1921, begging the question whether demands for some kind of redistribution of wealth and/or a more interventionist state drew their strength from dissatisfied single unemployed males (a widely touted explanation) or from an adult population with a growing responsibility for younger and elder cohorts. The popularity enjoyed by Anglican missions to Vancouver's Japanese community has been attributed to precisely this kind of demographic pressure. According to one account provided by a Japanese Canadian, "Both father and mother had to work to make ends meet. Dad worked in the mill and mother did housekeeping. That's why they sent us all to kindergarten and later we became involved in Sunday school and all the clubs. It kept us out of trouble and off the streets. Religion didn't really have much to do with it at first."[137] What was understood as "progressive" legislation probably sprang from the same concerns: reform was as much a product of demographics as ideology. That becomes even more clear after the Second World War.

The baby boom delivered an age profile that was more pyramidal than before: the largest cohorts were under fifteen years of age, so much so that they offset the rising numbers of elderly migrants to the province. That baby boom population has continued to dominate the composition of the population as it matures, so that by the 1990s the middle-aged segment (thirty to fifty years old) was sandwiched between two smaller cohorts. Falling fertility, consistently high levels of immigration (from abroad and the rest of Canada), an aging homegrown population, and the addition of retirees from elsewhere contributed to this particular profile. One consequence has been a growing dependency rate that reached 35 percent at the start of the new millennium.

It is, however, the overall pattern of growth in these years that stands central to the story. Not only was the growth of British Columbia's population more rapid than the national average, it increased at a rate that outstripped every other province except Alberta, whose challenge was restricted to the oil patch booms of the 1970s and 1980s.[138] (See Table 2.4, above.) Of course, for every addition, there is, ultimately, a subtraction.

The Great War brought in its train an enhanced appreciation for medical science and important advances in technology. One consequence was a change in the principal causes of death. If we set aside the 10,014 British Columbians who fell in the two world wars and the nearly 2,800 who died in the 1918-19 influenza pandemic, incidental losses of human life were far fewer and of much lower magnitude in the post-1914 period than before. Only the measles outbreak of 1923-24 (in which 114 died) and the fatalities arising from acute poliomyelitis in 1952-53 (74 dead) might be held up as comparable mortality events. More drawn out has been the toll taken by acquired immune deficiency syndrome (AIDS). The province's first recorded case of AIDS appeared in 1981. Over the next five years, nearly one hundred cases were identified, and in 1990 the Department of Vital Statistics attributed a total of 588 deaths to AIDS and HIV infection; in 1993 AIDS/HIV was the third-leading cause of death among British Columbian males between the ages of thirty and thirty-nine, and BC had easily outstripped the other provinces in this area of mortality. In 1994 the trend peaked with 330 deaths. Other relatively new infectious diseases had a far more limited impact. These include Creutzfeldt-Jakob Disease and *Clostridium difficile,* which claimed twenty-five lives apiece between 1990 and 1998. These post-war epidemics share common features: they do not strike with the same force as earlier disease incidents, but they seem rather more reluctant to go away.[139]

As to death from external causes, workplace disasters in the twentieth century were mercifully fewer. Tragic though it was, the death of eighteen men during the construction of Vancouver's new Second Narrows Bridge in

1958 was hardly comparable to that of the hundreds who died in mining explosions in the Victorian era. The provincial economy in the twentieth century nevertheless remained dominated by resource-extraction industries, so a high incidence of workplace deaths – by national and international standards – would continue. Although it was still the case in 1960 that males were at greater risk of injury-related death (430 males to 174 females at a time of near sex parity), the most dangerous environment for accidental deaths was the home. In 1960, 137 males perished from injuries suffered in the home (mostly falls, burns, poisoning, and drowning – in order of frequency), whereas only 83 females suffered similar fates (due to falls, burns, and poisoning). British Columbian males under ten years of age in particular died from drowning accidents, not surprising given the fishing industry and the fact that there is hardly a town in the province that is not built along an inviting river, lake, or inlet. Motor vehicle accidents were another important source of mortality. Road deaths peaked in 1974, falling to 2002 (at which time they spiked briefly), but the rate of death from accidental causes hovered at around 0.7 per 1,000 from the 1950s into the 1990s. In almost every category of death from external causes, First Nations people (males in particular) suffer the dubious distinction of far more severe rates of mortality in the late twentieth century. Whereas the age standardized death rate from motor vehicle traffic accidents per 10,000 population was 1.6 at the provincial level in the early 1990s, it was 5.7 for Status Indians (see Chapter 7).[140]

Embracing Diversity

Between the 1967 centennial and the hundredth anniversary of BC's entry into Confederation, revolutionary changes occurred in the economic, social, and political fabric of the nation and the province. The phenomenon of youth culture (manifest on the west coast in student protests at Simon Fraser University, raucous open-air concerts at Empire Stadium, and the Gastown Riot), the rise of separatist feeling in Quebec, and the growing strength of the Oil Producing and Exporting Countries (OPEC) cartel are elements of this transformation that forced a rethinking of social, political, and economic orthodoxies. After twenty years in office, the Social Credit government of W.A.C. Bennett was retired in 1972 in favour of the New Democratic Party under David Barrett; a generation had grown up under Social Credit, but Social Credit itself had not adjusted for the demographic, social, and economic order it had itself called into existence.

A new era of uncertainties was met by an adjustment in demographic behaviours. Fertility rates continued to fall, as did nuptiality rates (see Chapters 4 and 5). Widespread acceptance of family planning and the use of pharmaceutical contraceptives and induced abortions played a critical role, especially in the 1970s. In that decade, the abortion rate in British Columbia was consistently double the national rate and about 50 percent higher than

that of the next nearest province, Ontario. By the 1980s surgical contraceptive methods – essentially, tubal ligation and vasectomy – gained ground,
much faster than in the United States.[141] It was reckoned in 1995 that 3.3
million Canadians (roughly one in ten) had undergone one procedure or
the other.[142] At the same time, the stigma of "shacking up" was replaced by
the acceptability of common law "cohabitation." Long before Vancouver
acquired the epithet of Hollywood North, Los Angelenos descended on the
city to film *Carnal Knowledge* (1971), a movie that charts a course through
the shoals of sexual relations both within and without the boundaries of
marriage. Twenty years later, British Columbia was chasing only one province
– Quebec – for the highest incidence of common law unions.[143]

A more empirically verifiable indication of changing practices is the divorce
rate. Nationally, the divorce rate was gathering speed even in the early
twentieth century, although there were only three provinces (n.b., British
Columbia was one) with divorce courts. There was a sharp rise in the provincial incidence of divorce in 1945 and 1946 as those who married in haste
at the start of the war began to repent – if not at leisure then certainly in
large numbers. By 1951 the rate per 1,000 population in British Columbia
was about 50 percent greater than it had been a decade earlier, almost double
that of the next most divorce-prone province (Alberta) and more than three
times greater than the national rate. In the 1950s the number of divorces
crept slightly upward in terms of real numbers, but they fell or were stagnant
when measured per 1,000 population – in British Columbia it was a mere
0.9 per 1,000 in 1961. The wholesale overhaul of the federal Divorce Act in
the 1960s ushered in a new era of household formation and transformation,
nowhere more so than in British Columbia.[144] Divorces accelerated in the
1970s, and by the mid-1980s – and the passage of new legislation in 1985 –
one in every three marriages ended in divorce.[145] This was not merely consistent with similar changes at the national level: British Columbians were
setting the pace. West coast mores (including irreligiosity) were often cited
by commentators, as were changes in the roles of women.[146] Whether culture
or economic necessity was the more forceful influence, I cannot say for certain, but it is clear that economic indicators and what were regarded as conventional "family values" were both in decline in these years.

New patterns of nuptiality (and *anti*-nuptiality) disguised another important demographic change. The sex ratio in British Columbia was finally bal-
ancing out; consequently, the status of women in the province was bound
to change. The 1970 report of Ottawa's Royal Commission on the Status of
Women was one milestone of changing gender roles and expectations, as
was the rising number of women in the workforce and improved wages
relative to those received by men. Adult female labour in this environment
had a number of demographic effects, including postponement of marriage

and/or reproduction for younger women and reduction of total fertility among women in their thirties and forties.[147] (This particular explanation for falling nuptiality and fertility rates is sometimes invoked as an explanation, too, for climbing marriage dissolution and, thus, a further fall in marital fertility.)[148] One must add that the 1970s marked the beginning of a period of price inflation that was no longer matched by income improvements in British Columbia, evident most noticeably in skyrocketing house prices. These economic developments placed additional pressure on women to pursue careers outside the confines of homemaker and mother. In sum, changing economic circumstances combined with shifting conceptions of conventional (or, more correctly, a generation's experience and understanding of) gendered roles to impact fertility rates, as did the relationship between divorce and the completion of the family formation phase.

In these years the cohort that West Vancouver author Douglas Coupland labelled *Generation X* became more visible. Successors to the baby boomers, Gen-Xers across North America were to witness a withdrawal of economic opportunities and a renegotiation of the social contract just as they reached adulthood in the late 1970s and early '80s. If the baby boomers grew up in a world that saw economic expansion as the norm, most of Generation X experienced the world as a consistently far less optimistic place. Raised in a culture in which old shibboleths about normative behaviour were already dismantled, Generation X approached family formation not as rebel but as battle-scarred survivor of rapid demographic changes. Coupland recognizes this, prefacing his book with a Pop Art cartoon of a young woman who cheerfully explains to her mother, "Don't worry ... if the marriage doesn't work out, we can always divorce!"[149]

Even as the baby boom was at its peak and a culture of youth was being forged, British Columbian elders were becoming a growing demographic factor. The "grey wave" mostly originated in other parts of Canada. Thanks to the warmer, milder winters that prevail on the southwest coast of Canada, it has become a magnet for retirees. Victoria is, of course, "Canada's leading retirement centre." As well, flatlanders fed up with long and biting winters have moved in their thousands to the dry-belt of the Interior, to communities throughout the Okanagan, the Columbia, the Kootenays, and the Thompson Valleys. In fact, the "grey rush" has only accelerated into the twenty-first century. Quips about Victoria, Comox, and Kelowna serving as "God's waiting room" speak to a simple fact: these centres are not only heavily populated by elders, but their social and physical fabric announces it.[150] Truth be told, there is in British Columbia hardly a city worthy of the name that does not now cater, in some measure, to this lucrative and unstoppable tide. In this respect, as in so many others, the cities of BC have been cockpits of demographic change.

The Century of the City

Urbanization constitutes the larger part of British Columbia's population history in the twentieth century. Appendix A shows the gap between Vancouver and Victoria opening up dramatically from 1911 on. New Westminster, North Vancouver, and other nearby communities rode Vancouver's slipstream of growth as suburbanization began to get traction. As a share of the largest cities' population, Vancouver – and especially Greater Vancouver – was becoming a behemoth. Not only was the emerging conurbation far and away larger than any other city in the province, its *population increase* in the decade after 1941 was greater than the populations of the eight next-largest centres in 1951 combined, Victoria included.

Away from the Terminal City and its immediate neighbours, a more and more stable supporting cast of resource centres and regional market cities brought up the rear. It seems reasonable to think of a fifteen hundred population mark as the cut-off for inclusion in a list of major centres in 1921 and 1931, with the bar moving upward to two thousand in 1941 and three thousand in 1951.[151] This gives us comparable lists of about two dozen apiece. Under those circumstances, there are only five shooting stars: Ladysmith, Pouce Coupe, Ocean Falls, Anyox, and Britannia Beach appear just once and then disappear. By contrast, the top ten lists from 1881 to 1911 look like a revolving door of boom (and bust) towns. Not that flash-in-the-goldpan centres ceased to make an appearance thereafter: Michel, Buckley Bay, Copper Mountain, and Bralorne sprung into life as fully formed communities with eight hundred to a thousand or more, most of which dispersed within a generation. Generally, however, there was growing stability among the cities and towns, but also gaping disparity. A city such as Prince Rupert might post an entirely respectable decennial growth rate of 27 percent at mid-century, but, in reality, it was stuck in a second division of small cities. Twenty-seven centres (all but five of them outside the Lower Mainland) each held between two and twelve thousand people, although eight of these counted fewer than three thousand. This enormous disparity between the metropolis with its suburban satellites and the rest of urban British Columbia merits underlining: after Vancouver (344,800) and Victoria (51,300), the next largest city outside of the Lower Mainland in 1951 was Trail (11,400), followed closely by Penticton (10,500). From 1921 through 1951, this small-city cadre experienced significant growth, but at the end of that period those twenty-seven communities contained fewer than half the number of people living in Vancouver City proper and hardly a third against what was emerging as "Greater Vancouver." Understanding the rough outlines of "urban" in this context is important because the province was arguably the most urban in Canada for much of the twentieth century. The balance between the urban and rural populations is shown in Table 2.7. It reveals an interwar

Table 2.7

Urban and rural shares of population, BC, 1911-2001

Year	Urban (%)	Rural (%)
1911	51.9	48.1
1921	47.2	52.8
1931	43.1	56.9
1941	54.2	45.8
1951	52.8	47.2
1961	72.6	27.4
1971	75.7	24.3
1981	78.0	22.0
1991	80.4	19.6
2001	85.0	15.0

Sources: Veronica Strong-Boag, "Society in the Twentieth Century," in *The Pacific Province: A History of British Columbia,* Hugh J.M. Johnston, ed. (Vancouver: Douglas and McIntyre, 1996), 280; BC Stats, 2001 Census Highlights, http://www.bcstats.gov.bc.ca/data/cen01/c2001hl.asp.

phase of increasing rural growth (notably in the Peace River Block and Okanagan Valley), returning thereafter to an aggressively rising curve of urbanization.[152]

Qualifications must be added. British Columbian cities were *materially* different from one another, but they were also *defined* in different ways over time. Although Burnaby, Surrey, and Coquitlam were among the most rapidly expanding locales in this era, none of the three had a hub that would pass for a central business district. The 33,600 residents of Surrey in 1951 had less in the way of a downtown of their own than, say, the 8,500 of Prince Rupert. Proximity to Vancouver and New Westminster, along with a growing "car culture" and a loosely packed residential land use pattern, sapped what little there was in the way of suburban town centres. The largest cities, in terms of population, thus might be the least city-like. By contrast, the smaller and more self-sufficient towns typically had their own cultural institutions, retailers, government services, newspapers, and so on. Trail – "Home of Champions" – is exemplary in that it sustained theatres, a powerful and distinct sporting tradition, and two vigorous Italian lodges. As the founder and operator of Bennett's Hardware in Kelowna, W.A.C. Bennett was able to capitalize (in business and politics) on both the strong downtown market dynamic of his emerging city and its rapid urban growth.[153] Contemporary promoters of an implicitly rustic "Sunny Okanagan" view of British Columbia were being disingenuous: *civitas okanaganus* more closely describes their world.

Official definitional factors in ranking town and country are also relevant. Down to 1951 the Canada census would include under "urban" any incorporated town, village, or city regardless of population size, as was the case with the Phillipses' Athalmer described earlier. In 1951 the aggregate numbers mattered: the urban population was now "all persons residing in cities, towns, and villages of 1,000 and over, whether incorporated or unincorporated, as well as the population of parts of census metropolitan areas."[154] From the 1961 census through 1971, the definition includes both incorporated and unincorporated spaces with either a population of at least a thousand or a density of a thousand per square mile; the definition also included suburban fringes of incorporated areas.[155] The 1981 census broadened "urban" to include any cluster of settlement with one thousand or more individuals living at a density of no less than four hundred per square kilometre. Two things to note here: first, there is the obvious impact of metrification on geographical and social definitions; second, the idea of "urban" was not uniform, even later in the twentieth century. An urbanite living in a metropolitan centre containing a hundred thousand individuals might be forgiven for thinking that a town of, say, fifteen hundred was in no way, shape, or form an urban space, even in the early twentieth century. By the end of the millennium, the metropolitan share of growth would be so great that Vancouverites could be forgiven for not thinking about rural spaces at all.

Greater Vancouver's share of the provincial population continued to swell in the Cold War era, driven largely by the baby boom and immigration. Much of that expansion took place beyond the city limits of Vancouver proper: across Boundary Road, on the North Shore of Burrard Inlet, and over bridges and through tunnels to the south where farms and forests fell before relentless suburbanization.[156] New highways and freeways and shopping malls were built to facilitate the relocation to the periphery of thousands of city core dwellers who were joined by hundreds of thousands of migrants from other (very often rural) parts of Canada and from other countries. From about 580,000 in 1951, the Greater Vancouver population rose to nearly 1.4 million in 1986, the year of the city's centennial. (Yet, in the middle of this boom, the population of Vancouver City proper experienced at least temporary decline.)[157]

The pace of Vancouver's growth at the end of the century, driven in part by a growing Pacific Rim economic thrust, was outstanding in Canada. As one historian wrote in the 1970s, "the inevitability of future growth surpassing that of Los Angeles and New York remains an article of faith for many Vancouverites."[158] Nonsense, of course, but in the period between 1988 and 1996, the average annual rate of increase was 2.7 percent, easily the leading rate among Canada's largest cities (by contrast, Toronto and Montreal grew by 1.9 percent and 1.0 percent respectively).[159] Regionally,

Vancouver was a leader as well: of the roughly 52,000 international immigrants who arrived in the province in 1996, all but about 4,000 (that is, fewer than 8 percent) went to Vancouver.[160] By the time of the 2001 census, there were 1,987,000 people in the metropolitan region, an increase of over 500,000 since 1986. As was the case in the Cold War years, significant shares of that growth took place on the fringes. Surrey struggled to shake off its bedroom community character as it became the most briskly growing city in the province, albeit a *suburban* city.[161]

As Greater Vancouver's spatial and demographic size increased, so too did its economic dynamism and its political authority in the province. Simultaneously, the demographic complexion of the city effectively parted company with that of the non-metropolitan areas. Vancouver has always been a city of tremendous diversity, and by the 1960s that diversity began perceptibly to challenge and undermine the hegemony of the old, largely white, middle-class elite. Not only did the city and (to a lesser and much slower extent) its immediate environs become more heterogeneous ethnically, economically, culturally, and sexually, but the bible-belt communities of the Fraser Valley offered an increasingly vocal white, conservative Protestant critique of what were seen as decadent urban values and practices. As one provincial Baptist leader put it, "Even a casual look at the geographic configuration of the churches prompts the conclusion that" some conservative Protestant elements "must believe that God is the God of the valleys and the north, but not the God of the cities."[162] Nevertheless, as the centre of economic, political, and media influence in British Columbia, Greater Vancouver defined the late twentieth-century urban experience.

Urbanization, accelerating in other quarters of the province, reflected Vancouver's lead. Regional centres endured relative stagnation in the interwar and the immediate post-war eras. In 1951 Trail held on to the title of fourth-largest centre in the province, and Penticton was close on its heels. Rapid growth in the 1950s and '60s, much of which was determined by infrastructural investment and the move away from a dependence on rail to a reliance on road traffic, promoted new cores and relegated others. Chilliwack, Nanaimo, Prince George, Kelowna, and Kamloops expanded dramatically, taking on many of the classic features of urban centres, including service-based economic activities that challenged and largely surpassed the old resource-extraction or agricultural bases. Nanaimo is a case in point. The last significant coalmines on the east coast of Vancouver Island closed in the 1950s, but Nanaimo recovered on the strength of a forest products industry and a retailing sector that served a growing hinterland along an improved highway system. Similarly, the Edwardian orcharding economy of the central Okanagan gave way to more diversified activity that continued to include, but was not so dominated by, resource-extraction industries. A new ribbon of highways, completed by the 1960s, linked Kelowna – now the largest and most central node – to the rest of the valley, which it quickly came to dominate. Kamloops provides an average growth trajectory for all of these communities during the decade that followed. From a population of about thirty-two thousand in 1966, the community added fifteen thousand over the next five years and ten thousand more by 1976. In the twenty years after 1971, Kamloops grew by about 41 percent, but most of that growth occurred by 1976. The economic downturn of the early 1980s was uncommonly sharp in the Interior, and most major communities – although Kamloops especially – experienced shrinkage. Each of Prince George, Nanaimo, Kelowna, Kamloops, the Fraser Valley conurbation anchored by Abbotsford and Chilliwack, and the sprawling suburbs of the South Fraser delta (Richmond, Langley, Surrey, and Cloverdale) were given provincial universities or university-colleges in the late 1980s and early 1990s; further economic diversification and maturation followed. Nevertheless (and despite an 8 percent growth in Abbotsford in 1996-2001), these secondary cities seem to have plateaued: only Kelowna passed the 100,000 mark by 2001. Their respective sources of growth were different, but only in degree. The dramatic rise of the central Okanagan, for example, was due very largely to the growing Albertan diaspora in that region.[163]

George Woodcock wrote in 1990 that "British Columbia remains a province of small and often still rustic towns," but that view already seems quaintly dated.[164] As Table 2.7 reveals, rural British Columbia held less than one-fifth of the provincial population in 2001. The small towns remain, but most (such as Enderby, Gibsons, and Cache Creek) are profoundly connected to and dominated by regional and provincial hub cities (including, in the case of the East Kootenays centres, the metropolitan gravitational field of Calgary). Other small centres, such as New Denver, Port Alice, and Tahsis – where the population fell 79 percent in the last twenty-five years – have been reduced to the point that rusticity would constitute an improvement. Moreover, BC's small towns are distinct from those found in parts of Canada with stronger agrarian traditions: as centres for industries associated with the forest, the fisheries, or mineral extraction, these villages, towns, and cities operated within the parameters of proletarianization, wage-labour, and time-work discipline. This can be seen in Williams Lake, a cowtown of about five hundred in 1945 that grew over the next thirty-five years into a regional service centre of ten thousand with a large and heavily capitalized forest industry and a service sector that included a growing professional class.[165] Moreover, even the smaller British Columbian cities at midcentury displayed a higher level of density than was found elsewhere in Canada: Kamloops and Kelowna (at 8,090 and 8,517 individuals respectively) had densities in the 4.2 to 5.6 thousand per square mile range, which was considerably higher than that of Calgary or Edmonton, and at least as high as Ottawa's.[166] What "rusticity" one might find in comparable third division communities – including Smithers, Terrace, Vanderhoof, Prince Rupert, Nelson, Castlegar, Trail, Campbell River, Port Hardy, Fort St. John, and Fort St. James – was, by the 1970s at the latest, offset by intensifying integration of the core and periphery economies, easier air travel between regions, and the growing cultural hegemony of televisual urban North America. Indeed, the most rapidly expanding municipality in the period between 1996 and 2001 in terms of percentage growth was Whistler.[167] Until recently a very small and very seasonal town, the ski resort community leads a select, dynamic pack of recreation-oriented centres that are located some distance from the metropolises and, though not truly "urban," are nevertheless urbane. In short, the authentic "rural" experience, if ever it really existed, was retreating in the face of urban middle-class culture, even in the Cariboo, the Kootenays, and the Peace.[168] There are, to be sure, distinctive threads in the provincial urban fabric, but perhaps they were seen most clearly in the capital city.

As a demographic driver, Victoria took a distant – not to say humiliating – second place to Vancouver before the Great War but enjoyed a renaissance more than a century after its founding. The seat of provincial government, it is geographically isolated from the mainland centres of population and economic decision making. Endowed with government offices and services catering to a growing bureaucracy and an exploding retirement population, the city lacked a significant manufacturing and financial role and thus, too, the economic dynamism and demographic potential of Vancouver. Nor did Victoria participate directly in the resource-extraction boom experienced by the rest of the province after 1939. Things began to change in the 1950s. At that time the baby boom created pressure for greater government services, specifically in the areas of education, social policy, and health care. Despite the ostensibly right-wing and anti-bureaucratic character of a succession of Liberal, Coalition, and Social Credit administrations from 1940 to 1972, the size of government necessarily grew. So did Victoria. Employment in government accounted for about 8 percent of all employment in BC in 1961, but in the capital the share was closer to 25 percent. Senior government salaries attracted a variety of services, cultural amenities, and, in 1963, an independent university. Victoria's status as the premier retirement centre in the nation also led to growth in the health care, service, and retail sectors that, as a matter of course, attracted more retirees. Ironically, it was the long years of underachievement through the first half of the century that permitted the survival of many of Victoria's older buildings and rendered unnecessary any midcentury urban renewal programs that would have drastically changed the face of the urban core: as was equally the case in Nelson and Rossland, economic and demographic stagnation in Victoria paid out heritage charm dividends. With a population in 2001 of more than 318,000, Victoria grew tenfold since 1911, almost a third of that in the last twenty-five years.

Conclusion

In the two centuries from contact to the present era, British Columbia's population experienced transformations of a kind and magnitude witnessed nowhere else in North America.[169] Worst case scenario – an Aboriginal population running to nearly half a million people was reduced to fewer than thirty thousand in the space of eighty years. As the shadow of death lingered over the coast and the cordillera, wave after wave of newcomers was lured ashore and inland by coal, by gold, by timber, and by steam and steel. The colonial population regime itself would have lasting impacts, in particular as regards distribution, but it too would be superceded. By the eve of the Great War, and really within the space of a generation, the population profile of the province was turned inside out. What had once been was effectively no more; what was, arrived with a rush; what was yet to come was the subject of ferocious, racist, and mean-minded argument. These transformations were compressed within a remarkable time frame. It was a period over which the concept of "settlement," with all its attendant assumptions of vacant lands and available resources, fell like a suffocating blanket of snow. As historian Adele Perry has written, newcomers "participated in a process of colonization in which Aboriginal dispossession and settler migration were irreparably linked."[170] One population world was buried while the shape of another swiftly emerged.

The Great War marks a watershed in human demography. Death, destruction, and dislocation were clearly implicated, as was the influenza epidemic that followed in its wake. Just as importantly, however, the war ushered in a new era in medical science. Life expectancies began to grow at a pace unseen in the nineteenth century. The infant mortality rate (IMR) began a long-term plunge, and, one by one, the diseases that had tormented humanity for millennia began to lose their purchase. Fertility limitation also became more widespread, accompanying critically important changes in the status of women. With the further advance of formal schooling in the Western world, the whole experience of childhood was also refashioned.[171] This, too, had demographic implications for age at first marriage and early onset fertility. The war, as well, brought with it new killing technologies that would be cleverly upgraded and tested further on British Columbians in the century that followed. In demographic history, as in political and economic history, 1914 was both an end and a beginning.

The "short twentieth century" was marked by growth and demographic maturation. Immigration played a foremost role, but natural increase was now able to achieve at least a significant place. This was singularly true in the baby boom years after the Second World War. Through the century, the rhythms of a boom-bust economy continued to have an impact on households and communities alike. This could be seen in, among other places, Cassiar, Anyox, Ocean Falls, and Tumbler Ridge, towns that exploded and then fizzled out in the course of the twentieth century. Outright decline across the province was avoided, but the 1930s and the 1970s and '80s brought with them a rise in out-migration and a fall in births. Nevertheless, the population grew more than tenfold in the course of the century, from less than 400,000 to more than 4 million (see Appendix B). What is more, British Columbia's rate of increase consistently outpaced that of the nation as a whole, and from 1911 to 1971 the province's share of the national population nearly doubled from 5.45 percent to 10.13 percent.[172] By 1951 British Columbia ranked as the third-largest province and has never been in danger of sliding back into fourth. Between 1951 and 2001, the population of Canada doubled; British Columbia's population explosion was significantly more dramatic. When W.A.C. Bennett began his generation-long career as premier of British Columbia in 1952, there were fewer than 1.2 million people west of the Rockies; when Gordon Campbell's Liberals swept to power in 2001, there were more than 4 million. (Think of the practicalities of governing the province under these circumstances; for Bennett and Campbell, the conditions are worlds apart.) Qualitative changes occurred as well: throughout the modern era, the province pursued a demographic trajectory that in a great many ways sets it apart from the rest of the country.

These are the outlines of the province's demographic history, or at least what we can say of it in light of resources that are partial, incomplete, and sometimes very biased. They are, to be sure, outlines marked repeatedly by extremes. Several of these themes demand closer attention. What follows is an exploration of a few outstanding questions in British Columbia's demographic record.

3
The West We Have Lost: First Nations Depopulation

It is surprising to continue to observe that the enormous implications of First Nations depopulation have been so incompletely recognized by scholars. By this I mean that academics have failed to wrestle fully with the legitimacy of the numbers (low or high); nor have they taken full measure of what (catastrophically or merely horrifically) elevated mortality levels from the eighteenth century through the era of European colonization imply for the history of the region. There are exceptions and they will be cited fully below, but what remains remarkable is the breezy way in which a great many historians and anthropologists treat the legitimacy of and the disparity between proposed Aboriginal depopulation numbers.

To be fair, there are reasons for avoiding the whole question. Simply stated, a high count invites and rightly receives sympathy while dramatically shoring up Native demands for compensation. A low estimate, by contrast, might be wilfully interpreted as proof that Aboriginal peoples in BC could not possibly have intensively utilized the kind of spaces now being pursued in land claims. Even more paralyzing for scholars working in this field is the danger of being accused of "holocaust denial," a possibility that could brake any critical discussion of the data.[1] The answer to this dilemma is not, however, to blindly endorse one set of estimates over another. The question demands to be addressed systematically, although anyone looking for convenient proofs to support one side against the other in this debate will not find what they seek here.

The purpose of this chapter is to demonstrate the strengths and weaknesses of what we think we know about pre-contact Aboriginal populations and their subsequent collapse in the hundred years after Spanish and British vessels first entered the waters off the Northwest Coast. The criticism will be made that this chapter offers nothing new. It's true: I have not one shred of additional evidence to throw into the mix. But the critique made here of the depopulation argument is a distinctive historiographical exercise, one that the field has long needed.

Table 3.1

Contact-era (eighteenth century) population estimates

Author	Estimate	Geographical territory
Low counters		
Mooney (1928)	85,800	British Columbia
Duff (1965)	80,000	British Columbia
Woodcock (1990)	100,000	British Columbia
Barman (1991)	80,000	British Columbia
Cybulski (1994)	80,000	British Columbia coast
Carlson (1996)	75,000	British Columbia
Moderates		
Ubelaker (1976)	119,262	British Columbia
Gibson (1990)	125,000	Northwest Coast
Daugherty (1993)	130,000	Northwest Coast
High counters		
Dobyns (1983)	1,612,622	British Columbia
Ubelaker (1988)	175,330	Northwest Coast
Boyd (1990)	200,000	Northwest Coast
Gibson (1992)	200,000	Northwest Coast
Tennant (1990)	400,000	British Columbia
Harris (1997)	200,000-400,000	British Columbia
Muckle (1998)	200,000-500,000	British Columbia

Sources: Douglas H. Ubelaker, "North American Indian Population Size: Changing Perspectives," in *Disease and Demography in the Americas,* John W. Verano and Douglas H. Ubelaker, eds. (Washington: Smithsonian Institution, 1992), 172-73; Robert T. Boyd, "Demographic History, 1774-1874," *Handbook of North American Indians,* vol. 7: *Northwest Coast* (Washington: Smithsonian Institution, 1990), 135; Wilson Duff, *The Indian History of British Columbia,* vol. 1: *The Impact of the White Man,* new ed. (1965; repr., Victoria: Royal British Columbia Museum, 1997), 55; Jean Barman, *The West beyond the West: A History of British Columbia* (Toronto: University of Toronto Press, 1991), 14; James R. Gibson, "The Maritime Trade of the North Pacific Coast," *Handbook of North American Indians,* vol. 4: *History of Indian-White Relations* (Washington: Smithsonian Institution, 1998), 390; Richard D. Daugherty, "People of the Salmon," in *America in 1492: The World of the Indian Peoples before the Arrival of Columbus,* Alvin M. Josephy Jr., ed. (New York: Vintage, 1993), 52; James R. Gibson, *Otter Skins, Boston Ships, and China Goods: The Maritime Fur Trade of the Northwest Coast, 1785-1841* (Montreal and Kingston: McGill-Queen's University Press, 1992), 4; Henry F. Dobyns, 1983, quoted in David E. Stannard, *American Holocaust: The Conquest of the New World* (New York: Oxford University Press, 1992), 21; Jerome S. Cybulski, "Culture Change, Demographic History, and Health and Disease on the Northwest Coast," in *In the Wake of Contact: Biological Responses to Contact,* Clark Spencer Larsen and George R. Milner, eds. (New York: Wiley-Liss, 1994), 80; and Roy Carlson, "The First British Columbians," in *The Pacific Province: A History of British Columbia,* Hugh J.M. Johnston, ed. (Vancouver: Douglas and McIntyre, 1996), 31; George Woodcock, *British Columbia: A History of the Province* (Vancouver: Douglas and McIntyre, 1990), 56; Paul Tennant, *Aboriginal Peoples and Politics: The Indian Land Question in British Columbia, 1849-1989* (Vancouver: UBC Press, 1990), 11; Cole Harris, *The Resettlement of British Columbia: Essays on Colonialism and Geographical Change* (Vancouver: UBC Press, 1997), 30; Robert Muckle, *The First Nations of British Columbia: An Anthropological Survey* (Vancouver: UBC Press, 1998), 37).

I hasten to add that there is much more to the demographic history of Aboriginal British Columbia than the virgin soil epidemics. There are questions of normal life expectancy, family structure, and fertility, for example, and these cry out for attention too. But this single demographic fact, that tens, if not hundreds, of thousands disappeared in the space of a century hovers over any discussion of Native societies like smoke from a funeral pyre.

An Overview

Estimates of the pre-Columbian population of the Americas vary tremendously, especially north of Meso-America. The Spanish invasion of Mexico and South America was sweeping, and a greater number of nations were contacted and described in a tighter time frame than was the case north of the Rio Grande. There was, in short, a shorter *proto*-contact era in the Aztec, Mayan, and Incan domains, during which population change occurred beyond the view of European witnesses. Also, the Spanish benefited from the bureaucratic legacy of the elaborate societies at Tenochtitlán, Cuzco, and elsewhere. Assembling demographic information in those densely settled nations was, as well, consistent with the Spanish economic order, which relied heavily on Native labour and tribute. Having said that, I must add that there is lively disagreement among scholars as to the size of the pre-contact population in Meso-America, the effects of virgin soil epidemics, and the reliability of Spanish accounts.[2]

The case in North America – especially in Canada – was very different. As the bacteriological frontier of European impact moved westward from the Atlantic and north along the Mississippi and Missouri system, it outran by decades, if not centuries, those European observers who might have provided posterity with a clearer record of human populations in the shadow of exotic epidemics.[3] With few exceptions, Aboriginal populations in Canada were nomadic hunter-gatherers; most First Nations lacked the centralized social structures conducive to census taking. The result is a variety of estimates based on very partial evidence.

The range of numbers proffered by historians and other scholars for indigenous Canada is staggering. James Mooney's 1910 estimate of 302,000 was revised downward by Alfred Kroeber in 1939 to 280,000. Henry Dobyns roared into the debate in 1966 with an estimate of 9,800,000 to 12,250,000 First Nations peoples in pre-Columbian Canada and the US. Three years later Harold Driver was more cautious, proposing 1 million for Canada, Greenland, and Alaska together.[4] The "low counters" did not, however, desert the field: in 1976 Douglas Ubelaker returned to a figure of 2,171,000 for all of North America, and Russell Thornton and Patricia Marsh-Thornton (1981) proposed 1,845,000 for just the coterminous United States. Dobyns replied in 1983 with a new estimate of 18,000,000 for North America as a whole.[5] Olive

Dickason (2002), a historian of Aboriginal Canada who is herself a First Nations person, would not be bound to even "the most widely accepted estimate" of 500,000 for Canada, acknowledging that the range now stretches to "well over 2 million."[6] One important side effect of this debate has been to push in an upward direction the population figures most often cited in less specialized texts. Ronald Wright, in his widely read *Stolen Continents*, notes a contested range between 7 and 18 million for North America but implicitly endorses only the larger figure.[7]

Scholars working in British Columbia have had little more luck in reaching a consensus, and the estimates have become even more disconsonant. There is an overarching chronological pattern of increasing estimates: the lower numbers were proposed in the mid-twentieth century, and the count has been moving upward ever after. The process begins with Wilson Duff's estimate in 1965 that the eighteenth-century population was no less than 80,000, a contention that evidently relied heavily on Mooney's figures.[8] Duff thus provides the baseline for population estimates. Historians Jean Barman and Robin Fisher accept Duff's figure as serviceable, although Barman has lately endorsed a higher, compromise figure.[9] Despite a generally upward trend, in the 1990s anthropologist Roy Carlson reaffirmed his commitment to a more modest total (75,000) for all of British Columbia but allowed that it might be low.[10] In the 1980s and 1990s, Robert Boyd estimated (with audacious precision) that there were 188,344 people on the Northwest Coast in 1770 while suggesting that "there is a good possibility that the actual figure was considerably higher."[11] Boyd also offers figures on the British Columbian section of the Columbia Plateau (the Okanagan and Thompson Valleys, along with the Stl'atl'imx territory) of around 18,000 shortly after contact.[12] The distinguished historical geographer Cole Harris has been slightly more cautious, although he ignores what another author calls "the peril of extrapolating isolated observations of disease-related demographic changes to the population of an entire region."[13] His estimates on the lower Fraser River area led him to conclude that between 200,000 and 400,000 people lived in British Columbia at contact. More recently he seems to suggest that the low end has risen to 300,000.[14] Whatever their weaknesses – and there are many – all of these estimates have the distinction of some scholarly pedigree. Other, higher estimates come from less compelling sources.

Some academics have shown a tendency to top up estimates of British Columbian pre-contact numbers in a manner that has sometimes been reckless. For example, in a 1990 study of white-Native relations over the past two hundred years, political scientist Paul Tennant pushed the limits upward with a figure of 400,000, although he provided no support for what appears to be nothing more than a guess.[15] In a puzzling move, anthropologist Robert Muckle extends the range to 500,000 without providing any reason for doing so. Still more amazing is Dobyns' 1983 estimate of 1,612,622 "pre-Colonial" inhabitants of British Columbia.[16] Dobyns' figure was derived by multiplying an estimated density in the Tsilhqot'in territory (1.7 persons per square kilometre) by the total area of BC (948,601 square kilometres). In the space of two lines, he claims that the resultant figure is both 1,204,723 and 1,204,728 higher than his previous estimate. If we disregard, for the sake of argument, that his multiplier – the total area of British Columbia – is inflated by nearly a thousand square kilometres, the correct number is 1,204,724. This is not splitting hairs: Dobyns provides no justification for his assumption that the Tsilhqot'in density is appropriate as a base figure, and his inability to address details with care does not inspire confidence, especially when a million lives are held in the balance. Perhaps more worrying is the fact that David Stannard uses Dobyns' figure in *American Holocaust*, though oddly enough without citing the source.[17] The effect of Stannard's inclusion of the Dobyns estimate is to suggest that this figure has acquired even the patina of legitimacy, which it has not.

All of these estimates, and others, are reproduced in Table 3.1.

Academics and the Aboriginal Numbers Question

At the time of writing, the tendency is increasingly to favour higher pre-contact numbers than in the past. But what is worrying – and what makes addressing this issue imperative – is the apparent emergence of a consensus on depopulation that is purely conjectural. Muckle's estimate of 500,000 is one example. Not only does he fail to provide sources for his figures, Muckle does not seem to register the terrible implications to the anthropology of the region of a loss of more than 400,000 human lives in the space of a few short years. Given the apparent willingness of academics and the public to seize upon dramatic higher numbers, one can expect to see the half-million figure in print regularly from now on. Similar carelessness in the service of dramatic totals can be found elsewhere, a worrying sign that an unsubstantiated or at least precarious total has prematurely worked its way into the orthodoxy.[18] How did this come to pass? An analysis of the methods used by scholars working in this field reveals problems rooted in sources, interpretation, and method.

Predictably, the earliest demographic catastrophes are the most contestable. Sarah Campbell's findings for the early sixteenth century indicate significant pre-Columbian fluctuations in population, but her evidence for a 1525 smallpox pandemic is weak. There is no way of dating with accuracy her alleged depopulation (she admits the possibility that it could have predated Columbus), or of determining whether it was in fact due to smallpox or some other factor such as warfare.[19] In any event, Aboriginal numbers in the Pacific Northwest would have had more than 250 years to recover before sustained contact began.[20] If there were no further catastrophes, the damage of 1525 could have – should have – been repaired.

Ironclad evidence for smallpox reaching western British Columbia in the late eighteenth century is also lacking. Beginning in 1779, an outbreak of smallpox in Mexico appears to have spread as far south as Chile and north to the Great Plains. On the prairies smallpox attacked the HBC's trading partners and passed westward along the Saskatchewan River corridor.[21] Evidently, the disease made its way to the Lower Columbia by exploiting Native trade and raiding patterns that connected the Snake River region with the foothills beyond the cordillera. In 1782-83, according to Boyd, smallpox reached the British Columbian coast via the Columbia River system from whence it also spread north into the Interior, a thesis that is supported by Elizabeth Fenn in *Pox Americana*.[22] European historical sources are not helpful in confirming this scenario. Accounts from the Lewis and Clark Expedition include evidence of a smallpox epidemic along the lower Columbia River, and there are the solid-looking reports from Russian Alaska and Haida G'waii for the same period.[23] Elsewhere, on the southern and central British Columbian coastline, there is simply nothing that conclusively points to smallpox in the eighteenth century.[24] In fact, Robert Galois' work on the Kwakwaka'wakw highlights the definite absence of any smallpox on the central coast before the nineteenth century, as does Alan McMillan's study of the Makah, Ditidaht, and Nuu-chah-nulth – among whom only the Ditidaht were thought to be affected.[25]

The case for a late eighteenth-century epidemic is presented by Robert Boyd and Cole Harris, and it has quickly achieved wide acceptance. Two bodies of evidence – Native oral traditions and the European historical record – are cited to support the claim that smallpox spread from the Columbia into Georgia Strait. These are, however, ambivalent at best. The oral sources are entirely unclear as regards the date of the epidemics in question. As Harris himself concedes, "ample ground exists for disagreement about the meaning of these fragments," but in his conclusions Harris does not allow for these ambivalences.[26] The critical "smoking pistol" oral account used by Harris comes from "Old Pierre, a Katzie living in the Lower Fraser Valley in the 1930s (when the ethnographer Diamond Jenness recorded a story about Old Pierre's great grandparents' escape from the disease)."[27] Extrapolating from Old Pierre's narrative, Harris asserts a mortality rate of 50-75 percent and concludes that "It is becoming clear that such an estimate is not obviously preposterous."[28] Nor is it conclusive.

Old Pierre's story is problematic. To begin with, one must – with all due respect – question the reliability of a near-octogenarian recalling events that took place another eighty or ninety years before his birth. Clearly, verifiability is a problem that faces the historian in this instance and, it has to be said, oral tradition is not infallible. But there are several alternative readings of Old Pierre's narrative that we might consider.[29] It could be seen as a conflation of several epidemics, culminating in one final, cataclysmic, 75 percent mortality disaster. The gist of his story is one of overpopulation followed by three Malthusian collapses, the last one brought on by smallpox, which Old Pierre identifies with a certitude that eludes every other ethnographic source for the period. We have fairly to absolutely reliable evidence of epidemics in the early 1800s, the 1830s, and the 1860s: does that not suggest the three waves described by Old Pierre? Perhaps the account has been misunderstood: have "eighteenth century" and "1800s" been confused? Toss out those doubts and we are still left with a simple arithmetical question of probability. If Old Pierre's great-grandparents were, as he claimed, young adults present at the time of the alleged 1780s epidemic, we have to make some assumptions about their fertility and that of their descendants. Old Pierre relates that they already had twins; possibly, then, they were in their twenties. That leaves approximately eighty years between the disease event and the birth of Old Pierre, which, for two successful generations, is quite a long time indeed. It is, of course, biologically and physically possible that at least one of those two generations produced a child when they were around forty years of age, but it is an uncomfortable assumption, particularly in a harsh post-epidemic environment. The story probably works better as evidence of a c. 1800 outbreak, but I am inclined to doubt it entirely. Old Pierre combined elements of Christian mythology – including a flood and other purifying acts of "the Lord Above" – with elements of First Nations narrative. There certainly *was* a flood event in the region, associated with the Cascadia quake of January 1700, but the Katzie narrative might be referring to something else entirely. Clearly, the tale comes together from a variety of sources and origins.

To what extent, then, should one trust Old Pierre's unquestioned insistence that the cause of the final calamity was smallpox? If Old Pierre was, as proposed, seventy-five years old in 1936, then he was born in 1861, right on the eve of the 1862-63 smallpox epidemic. Perhaps this was the source of his declaration that smallpox was the guilty party in the 1780s.[30] I think these are legitimate concerns and the sort than any historian should raise about evidence – written, oral, or otherwise. When Harris writes that "the demographic carnage was evident everywhere long before the first province-wide epidemics" of the 1840s and '60s, one can only ask that the evidence be placed in court for cross-examination.[31]

Anthropologist Robert Boyd is undoubtedly the leading figure in this field on the Northwest Coast. He has written a dissertation, several articles, and a book on the subject of exotic diseases on the Northwest Coast and has, as well, made an extensive and authoritative contribution to the Smithsonian's *Handbook of North American Indians*. Boyd's scholarship is detailed and painstaking, and, like Harris, he makes a case for a catastrophic epidemic in the late eighteenth century. There are, however, telling weaknesses in the evidence. James Cook's 1778 expedition made no mention of smallpox on

Vancouver Island's east coast, and Boyd describes George Vancouver's records as "silent on signs of smallpox among Salishan peoples of the Strait of Georgia." The Spanish expedition under Galiano and Valdez may have found indications of smallpox among the Hul'qumi'num near Nanaimo, but they record the presence of survivors, not corpses. There is, therefore, no way of knowing how serious the epidemic was, and it is possible that the pock-marked faces and instances of blindness were after-effects of a venereal disease or some other affliction.[32] This is the position taken by Robin Fisher in 1996, when he observed that "Both syphilis and smallpox result in nasty symptoms and often agonizing deaths, so reactions to even the possibility of their presence among a population were, not unnaturally, more hysterical than scientific. The pock-marked faces seen among Native people in the early contact period are not, in themselves, evidence of pandemics, but rather that some survived even the worst of the introduced diseases."[33] By way of an example, a 1791 report from the Ditidaht of southwest Vancouver Island identifies signs of smallpox in an evidently large community, which indicates many survivors. Moreover, the 1791 account specifically diagnoses smallpox and venereal disease in one local noble, which only raises further the question of which variant of "the pox" the explorers and traders were observing.[34] (Perhaps it was not a pox at all: Robert Galois has shown how European eyewitnesses repeatedly mistook the 1848-50 measles epidemic for smallpox.)[35] The written record is, then, not entirely "silent" on smallpox, but, as Boyd himself concedes, "much of what has [survived] is duplicitous."[36]

Elizabeth Fenn makes an interesting contribution to the discussion, wrestling mightily with the contradictions and gaps in the evidence. She cites accounts from the 1787 Alaska expedition of Captains Nathaniel Portlock and George Dixon. In brief, Portlock sees the scars of smallpox everywhere around Sitka, but Dixon does not. Portlock reckons the date for the epidemic in the 1770s, which Fenn demonstrates as highly unlikely while supporting Portlock against Dixon nonetheless. Fenn quotes Dixon, who claims, "The people are totally free from that long catalog of disease, which luxury and intemperance have introduced amongst more civilized nations." This is a pretty definitive statement that smallpox was not evident, but Fenn rejects it because subsequent accounts record signs of scarring. As Fenn repeatedly, succinctly, and correctly points out, "smallpox comes from where smallpox was." There needs to be a chain of infection stretching back from the Northwest Coast to an area where an epidemic was raging. Is that the case on the western slope? Fenn demonstrates convincingly that sea-borne sources of smallpox before 1782 are unlikely and looks to the Columbia River basin as the probable route of infection. Fenn is correct to point out the extensive commercial links between the many peoples of the region (though she does not really address the role of the Interior populations), but it is indeed a long way from Shoshone territory (where smallpox occurred in 1781-82) to

Haida G'waii, let alone Alaska. Timing would be everything. Transmitting the disease by means of mounted Aboriginal traders and cavalries across the western plains is one thing; getting it across the mountains and over extensive water systems in a timely way is another. And though First Nations were dynamic in trade, they were also often at each others' throats; warfare and no-go zones could have acted as a prophylactic to smallpox.[37]

If the late eighteenth century witnessed a widespread demographic catastrophe in the region, our understanding of its reach is not assisted by this lack of clarity in explorers' accounts. Those snippets of evidence ought to be treated with extreme care.[38] Explorers,' traders,' and ethnographers' records from the eighteenth and nineteenth centuries are not only agonizingly imprecise about population figures, many are ambivalent toward the notion of significant depopulation. One might take, by way of an example, the 1878 reports from Haida G'waii by George M. Dawson – scientist, scholar, and surveyor. Dawson was a man of diminutive physical stature who became a Canadian intellectual giant. He contributed an enormous quantity of first-rate material to the record on the shape and peoples of what was to become Canada. His Victorian sensibilities and prejudices notwithstanding, Dawson was keenly observant and has been happily relied upon by historians, geographers, and anthropologists for the better part of a century. What he had to say about Haida depopulation is, therefore, instructive. Dawson recorded a population around Skidegate and Gold Harbour of about 500, a large portion of which was almost permanently in Victoria on trading missions. Relying on the Reverend W.H. Collinson at Masset, Dawson reported about 700 Haida for the "whole north Coast" of the archipelago. Dawson noted that his local source estimated that as many as 12,000 lived there at some point in time. Moreover, in his published report, *On the Haida Indians of the Queen Charlotte Islands,* Dawson indicated that he was familiar with the HBC censuses of 1836 and 1841 that revealed a Haida population on the islands of 6,593. Dawson acknowledged that the 1860s smallpox epidemic had resulted in severe mortality, and he felt that this went a long way to explain the apparent collapse of the Haida to no more than 2,000. But it is his conclusion on longer mortality history that is of interest here. In his report he wrote, "It is very difficult in all cases to form estimates of the number of aboriginal tribes when first discovered, and it is a common error, from the too literal acceptance of the half fabulous stories of the survivors to greatly overestimate the former population."[39] This dual caution is worth keeping in mind: first, Dawson felt that pre-contact numbers were not very high; second, he felt that his contemporaries had a tendency to high-count. The historian's sources in the debate on Aboriginal depopulation are sparse and set within a context of colonial oppression. It would be condescending, perhaps, to call into question First Nations recollections of better days and whether some parts of the oral tradition might be imbued with a rosy tint, but no more so than the assumption made by British Columbian high counters that silent "voices" on the subject of smallpox constitute vivid and valid testimony.

What European sources there are that do point to a demographic "event," it must be added, can be read in conflicting ways. For example, George Vancouver's expedition in 1792 observed many "deserted" villages, which might suggest depopulation by disease. On the other hand, the British also noted that in these empty sites the longhouses had not been merely left to rot: "the Planks were taken away, but the Rafters stood perfect."[40] Surely this indicates an organized removal rather than either a panicked exodus in the face of an epidemic or the sudden destruction of the villages in question by smallpox. Harris dismisses the possibility that resource-pursuit migrations out of the area might have been a factor: "There is no evidence that Native seasonal rounds took people away in May and June from the coastlines that Vancouver and his officers explored and mapped."[41] But Galois observes that the north coast was a hive of activity associated with the oolichan fishery every spring, extending into May.[42] Daniel Clayton reports that the Clayoquot peoples arrived at Opitsaht annually in December but left the large village for smaller ocean-facing locations, the better from which to hunt.[43] Evidence from other communities on the north coast does not prove an error on the part of Harris (and his informant), but it does indicate regionally specific reasons for movement in the spring and raises the possibility that migration ought not to be too quickly rejected as a factor in the case of the apparently deserted Strait of Georgia. Moreover, where smallpox depopulation is alleged in the journals of explorers David Thompson, Simon Fraser, and other fur traders arriving from the east, the epidemic(s) in question might have occurred a generation later than the alleged 1782 catastrophe.

What we are left with from the eighteenth century is negative evidence of epidemic depopulations: the fact that there were so few people visible in an area that appeared to the Europeans to be capable of sustaining a larger population than that which they found. Obviously, this cannot on its own be taken as irrefutable proof of an encounter with aggressive European microbes. In short, the European record consistently fails to point decisively at an epidemic in British Columbia in the eighteenth century.

The case for early nineteenth-century epidemics is somewhat stronger, but even here scholars disagree with each other. A recurrence of smallpox around 1800 on southern Vancouver Island and in the Fraser Valley and canyon is argued for by Boyd, but Harris notes the absence of consistent evidence of pockmarks in the subsequent ethnographic record.[44] Keith Thor Carlson, in a study of Stó:lō demographics, maintains that "both the oral and documentary evidence better supports a single epidemic in 1782, not two successive ones."[45] If there was a smallpox outbreak around 1800, it was probably a less virulent strain; alternatively, if a 1782 epidemic *did* occur

first, the 1800 episode would have found a population at least partly im-
munized by the earlier exposure.

In any event, one of the conclusions of scholars working the field of dis-
ease-driven mass depopulations is that the stereotypes of epidemics are often
wrong. For example, one must not assume that virgin soil epidemics were
universally catastrophic. Conditions critical to the survival of the disease
vary from location to location and from host to host. As a study of smallpox
on the eastern American seaboard has shown, "smallpox will 'burn itself
out' fairly quickly in dense populations, particularly under 'virgin soil' conditions of virtually 100 percent infection rates."[46] And even under virgin soil
conditions, it is possible that the mortality levels will not exceed 30 percent,
although that is plenty disastrous enough.[47] Evidence for the appearance of
smallpox in British Columbia prior to the 1860s, then, ought not to be
generalized into an all-encompassing epidemic that claimed a majority of
lives. Localized and limited depopulations may be all for which we have
proof.

Once doubt is cast on the accounts of the 1780s and c. 1800 epidemics,
it follows that the 1830s smallpox outbreaks may have been genuine virgin
soil events. Logically, it has to be conceded that the 1836-38 mortality was
either a reappearance of smallpox – in which case virgin soil conditions
would not apply in some areas – or it was a first encounter with smallpox,
in which case it reveals a great deal about the scale of depopulation. Fortuit-
ously for anyone interested in Aboriginal demography, the Hudson's Bay
Company agents on the coast conducted a series of "censuses" in the 1830s
and early 1840s.[48] Their figures provide some indication of the impact of
the 1830s smallpox outbreak, coupled with measles and other afflictions.
According to James Gibson, "the fatality rate among the Tsimshians was
nearly one-third, and among the Haidas it may have been even higher."
Gibson calculates that there were "up to 30,000" Tlingit, Tsimshian, and
Haida when the epidemic struck and that their numbers, overall, were
diminished by "about one-third."[49] This is well below the widely cited figure
of 80-95 percent depopulation under virgin soil conditions, from which one
can conclude one of two things: this was not a virgin soil incident or, and
I think this is more likely, virgin soil epidemics did not necessarily everywhere
claim more than 30 to 50 percent of the population.

Despite the presence of European observers, some questions remain about
the severity of even the 1862-63 smallpox epidemic. Boyd reports on this
outbreak among the Haida. From a population of 8,428 in 1840, the north
coast nation plummeted to about 1,600 when a Dominion census was taken
in 1881. The residual effects continued to be felt into the twentieth century:
the Haida nadir was reached only around 1915 to 1920 when their numbers
bottomed out at 1,049. The post-epidemic fall can be attributed to the loss
of available mates and migration (perhaps seasonal) to the mainland.[50]

Smallpox in the 1860s thus probably claimed as many as 80 percent of the Haida.[51] This scenario is flawed. Boyd argues for virgin soil epidemic conditions in 1862-63 on Haida G'waii while claiming that an encounter with smallpox had occurred some sixty to ninety years earlier. He cannot have it both ways. In studies of other contact areas in North America, it is suggested that virgin soil conditions may be perpetuated by new births and the arrival of (in this case, Aboriginal) migrants.[52] This ought to be treated with caution. Jody Decker argues that, "regardless of how virulent an agent is, it cannot become epidemic in a population unless there are a sufficient number of susceptible new hosts capable of being infected." In short, probably no less than a generation (Decker's model requires thirty to fifty years) would need to pass before a severe epidemic could strike again.[53] Those conditions did not prevail in Haida G'waii, raising these questions: Was it a true virgin soil epidemic (in which case we have to discount earlier alleged smallpox attacks)? Was the 1862-63 epidemic significantly worsened by other factors? Are the numbers just plain wrong? What other factors do we need to consider?

An alternative explanation for village abandonment and apparent or real depopulation is Aboriginal warfare. There is ample evidence in the form of fortified village sites to suggest that armed and lethal conflict was endemic among the British Columbian First Nations, and this is supported by archaeological, ethnographic, and even British eyewitness accounts.[54] Bone trauma found on human skeletal remains suggests increasing warfare or interpersonal conflict in the period from AD 500 to contact, actually declining thereafter. Archaeological and ethnographic evidence from the north coast points to "nearly continuous warfare," although comparable bone traumas are not found in the Strait of Georgia or Haida G'waii.[55] Likewise on the west coast of Vancouver Island, archaeological evidence suggests a chain of conflict around Barkley Sound that began some time before contact, leading to extensive death and dislocation in the Long War of the nineteenth century.[56] Too, in the 1850s, the Pacheenaht of Vancouver Island were, according to a contemporary account, "reduced" to only a handful by "war with the Songish Indians [sic]," a disaster that was subsequently compounded by smallpox or measles.[57] On the central coast and as late as 1862, the Nuxalk were complaining of raids by the Haida, described in one contemporary account as "the bloodhounds of the northwest coast."[58] (Some of the Haidas' reputation for lightning and sometimes devastating attacks may, in fact, belong more rightfully to the Lekwiltok of Johnstone Strait, whose range included southern Vancouver Island and the Fraser Valley.[59]) In the southern Interior, armed conflict was rife in the early nineteenth century. The Salish-speaking peoples of the upper Columbia region of Washington and British Columbia "had long traditions of warfare and raiding."[60] Around 1800 a party of Secwepemc "wiped out" the Athabaskan-speaking N'Kwala band at the north end of Nicola Lake (a.k.a. Guichon's); other groups harried the N'Kwala from the east, west, and south. Although their eastern and western frontiers were subsequently secured by alliances, the N'Kwala continued to suffer attacks from the Secwepemc.[61] Centred at what was once a crossroads of trade and human traffic, the N'Kwala found their territory all too access-ible to ambitious and aggressive neighbours on horseback.[62] By the end of the nineteenth century, the N'Kwala were so squeezed between the Nlaka'pamux, Secwepemc, and Okanagan that they effectively intermarried themselves out of existence.[63] In 1823 the Okanagan chieftain Hwistes-mexe'qEn (a.k.a. Nkwala, Nicola) led a raid on the Stl'atl'imx, for which he reportedly raised a cavalry of roughly five hundred.[64] It is claimed that Hwistesmexe'qEn's campaign to avenge the murder of his father cost his foes in excess of four hundred lives, more if one includes captives taken as slaves.[65] Elsewhere in the province, David Thompson's accounts of the Ktunaxa in the early nineteenth century reported that they had been reduced by warfare and smallpox, but he could not determine which factor was of greater consequence. An 1864 account of a Kwakwaka'wakw raiding party that stopped at Comox reports that their booty included a "large number of captives taken as slaves" from Lummi villages to the south, along with three severed heads: "a man's a woman's and a child's."[66] Despite frankly primitive armaments, it is clear that substantial deaths would result from warfare in the pre- and early contact periods. Archaeologist Alan McMillan's observation with respect to conflict in the Nuu-chah-nulth territory could be applied across much of what is now British Columbia: "Intensification of warfare in the early Historic Period, stimulated by the introduction of firearms and new trade rivalries as well as by a destabilized economy ... resulted in widespread and catastrophic loss of life."[67] Thereafter, firearms technologically worsened the situation, making the death toll in individual conflicts "terribly high," according to Duff: "Murders, massacres to avenge them, and more massacres in retaliation form a constantly recurring pattern."[68]

Raiding for slaves took place throughout the territory and was both cause and consequence of warfare. Oral traditions from up and down the Pacific Northwest indicate that every single Aboriginal group was either engaged in raiding or was being victimized by it and that this was a venerable part of First Nations life.[69] Captives were moved great distances to their eventual owners.[70] Captured coastal people, for example, might find themselves traded via the Stl'atl'imx to other communities still deeper inland. Slavery also oc-curred in the Interior. Ethnologist James Teit's account of the Kumsheen leader Cixpentlem tells of the chieftain's tour of Secwepemc, Nlaka'pamux, and Okanagan territories in 1850, buying up Stl'atl'imx slaves in order to return them to their homeland as a diplomatic gesture.[71] In terms of demo-graphic implications, slavery in pre-European British Columbia constitutes double jeopardy: the slaves' reproductive capacity was lost by the community from which they were taken, but their low status as slaves meant that they usually added little or nothing to the fertility of their host/captor community.[72] As labourers and as commodities, slaves had a value; as dynamic demographic elements, they had little or none at all, even though they might account for as much as a quarter of a First Nation community's population. Whether raiding took place to accumulate slaves or other plunder, or to establish or re-establish territorial boundaries, ethnographic accounts point to the frequency, magnitude, and implications of armed conflict.

There is more unanimity among historians on the ubiquity and vitality of slave raids and warfare than there is regarding epidemics. Fenn reckons that smallpox "is the likelier culprit" behind apparent depopulation in the 1780s but allows for the possibility that war or some other non-disease factor was involved.[73] Gibson maintains that the fur trade increased the incidence of slavery and, with it, raids on Puget Sound and Fraser Valley communities for captives.[74] This phenomenon may have begun as early as the 1760s, following the arrival of Russian traders and European products in Alaska. Warfare and the taking of slaves around the Strait of Georgia in this manner may account for the human bones Vancouver found strewn about at Port Discovery on the Olympic Peninsula and the depopulation (in part, therefore, *relocation*) of the villages assessed by Harris. How widespread and endemic warfare was at any time between contact and the mid-nineteenth century is difficult to judge. European eyewitness reports of "inter-tribal" warfare are sparse, as one would expect in a region in which newcomers were few and geographically isolated before 1858. Nevertheless, HBC records for Fort Langley in 1827-30 indicate that violent clashes occurred on an average of ten incidents per year.[75] Harris, writing in 2002, notes that "the construction of Forts Victoria and Rupert and of a colliery at Nanaimo had reoriented Native trading patterns and the relative economic and geopolitical position of local groups, in so doing almost certainly increasing the frequency and scale of intertribal warfare."[76] Indeed, this may have been the case throughout the region. What we do *not* know is the extent to which raids and warfare constituted *mortal* events. Clearly, it is in the best interests of a slaver to ensure that not everyone in the target community is killed. Moreover, even the "destruction" of a village need not entail the immediate death of every resident: the loss of sufficient numbers of demographically significant members (as slaves or as fatalities) could be enough either to propel the remainder into exile or to bring about a slow depopulation through famine and/or other causes. Either way, indigenous conflict has to be read into the record as a factor contributing to the depopulated landscape that early European observers recorded. European-Aboriginal conflict, to be sure, is not to be ignored as an element in the equation (see Chapters 2 and 7). But, at least until the 1850s, it could not account for the magnitude of depopulation from pre-contact numbers that is the focus of the debate.

The situation, then, is this: the evidence for eighteenth- and early nineteenth-century epidemics is fraught with shortcomings and contradictions. There is strong but fractured evidence for smallpox on the Northwest Coast in the 1780s, the source of which remains, in Fenn's words, "an enigma."[77] But a great many scholars working on the larger demographic question of depopulation have leapt from an incomplete picture of a pandemic to confident estimates of its magnitude. In doing so, a few have produced mega-ballpark numbers over 500,000.

In part, the range can be explained by sampling and what demographer Russell Thornton calls both "depopulation projection" and "retrojection" methods.[78] Mooney relied on ethnographic data, which is to say he was calculating the indigenous population from accounts compiled some time after initial contact between Aboriginal communities and European record makers.[79] If we assume that bacteria ran ahead of the contact frontier via indigenous trade systems, the ethnographic accounts have to be regarded as low in at least some, if not all instances.[80] The question is how low? We cannot know for sure, but a formula has been widely used to leapfrog over virgin soil mortality and run straight to pre-Columbian totals.

Henry Dobyns argues that the nadir of depopulation represents one-twentieth to one twenty-fifth of the initial or pre-Columbian population level. Multiplying the nadir figure by twenty, he argues, would yield a workable pre-contact number.[81] This assumes many things, including the reliability of those nadir numbers. It also assumes that the proportional impact of disease, famine, and warfare was even across the map, a premise that simply cannot be sustained. It is difficult enough to establish reliable estimates for Aboriginal numbers in the post-contact nineteenth century. Even in the twentieth century, problems abound with the census, especially as regards its effectiveness in counting First Nations peoples.[82] Without acknowledging these difficulties, scholars have combined questionable nadir numbers with a shorthand retrojection method in an exercise that is emotive and highly politicized: calculating pre-contact numbers.

Dobyns' methodology has been subjected to repeated critiques, but it remains popular among scholars.[83] The sheer elegance of its simplicity must be regarded as a factor in the survival of the nadir-based approach to retrojection. In British Columbia, Cole Harris has been explicit in his approval of this methodology, though he has not defended the technique. Boyd has applied nadir-based retrojection with more caution, but he clearly accepts it as one of several equally legitimate approaches.[84] Others have merely applied the method without attributing its source, let alone recognizing its shortcomings.[85]

The effects have been dramatic and the origin of the high count is now clear: if, following Dobyns, one multiplies by twenty and twenty-five the available cumulative nadir numbers for thirteen of nineteen British Columbian First Nations groups listed in the *Handbook of North American Indians,* one arrives at retrojected pre-contact numbers of 379,720 and nearly half a million respectively. The results are reproduced in Table 3.2.

Numbers from Brobdingnag
The single greatest demographic question haunting North America is this: how many Aboriginal people were there before contact? From one region to the next, this mystery resists resolution while frustrating a comprehensive understanding of experience and change in the past. One can certainly appreciate the desire of scholars to settle on one figure or another. In the case of British Columbia, we have come to something that approaches a consensus, but we have got there via a method that is highly suspect. What I am emphatically arguing here is *not* that pre-contact populations were necessarily small, but that the evidence for large pre-contact populations is, as yet, simply not there. And it may never be there. Using elementary multiplication tables will not alter that reality. Gulliver's account of Brobdingnag – the land of giants that Swift mischievously placed on BC's southwest coast – is no less fantastical than some of the evidence and argument mustered by historians of the region's depopulation. Harris writes that "the general picture is now fairly clear," and Boyd holds out "hope" that "we have now ... moved beyond the stage of arguing over [the] existence [of epidemics] and whether they indeed had severe and lasting effects on local Native American populations"; even in these respects, I have to disappoint them both.[86] There remains uncertainty as to *when* or even *if* smallpox visited the major settlements of eighteenth-century British Columbia before 1862-63, and until that uncertainty is resolved, we ought not to attempt definitive statements about the disease's impact.[87] To quote demographer Anatole Romaniuc on the subject of national Aboriginal numbers, "None of these estimates has an empirical base solid enough to afford scientific credibility."[88] It would be Pollyannaish to suggest that we agree to disagree, but it is unethical and inappropriate for scholars to ignore that disagreement exists and to neglect its implications for our understanding of the past. Recent historical writing has taken us some distance toward at least part of that goal.

In a pithy assessment of population decline in the southwest corner of the province, Cole Harris argues that the Native "holocaust" issue has been dodged because of its ramifications for the paradigm of *imperial history* on the coast. In the nineteenth century, the dominant Euro-British Columbian narrative included the subjection of the Natives to the "civilizing" influences of European newcomers. Even more recent accounts of the role played by

Table 3.2

Nadir populations and Dobyns-style projections

Group	Earliest census (date)	Nadir (date)	X 20	X 25
Haida	6,693 (1836-41)	588 (1915)	11,760	14,700
Tsimshian peoples[a]	8,500 (1835)	4,015 (1895)	80,300	100,375
Haisla	n/a	392 (1890)	7,840	9,800
Nuxalk	1,940	n/a	–	–
Haihais, Heiltsuk	2,018 (1835)	204 (1890)	4,080	5,100
Oowekeeno/Qweekeno	n/a	n/a	–	–
Kwakwaka'wakw	c. 7,750 (1835)[b]	1,088 (1929)	21,760	27,200
Northern Coast Salish	n/a	n/a	–	–
Nuu-chah-nulth	7,500 (1835)	1,459 (1924)	29,180	36,475
Central Coast Salish[c]	4,160 (1835)	7,000 (c.1900)	140,000	175,000
Stl'atl'imx	1,800	1,100 (1896)	22,000	27,500
Secwepemc	1,600 (1835)	2,000 (1909)[d]	40,000	50,000
Nlaka'pamux	1,100 (1835)	n/a	–	–
Ktunaxa	1,000 (1838)	490 (1887)	9,800	12,250
Okanagan	1,200 (1835)	n/a	–	–
N'kwala	n/a	nil (1900)	nil	nil
Slavey	c. 200 (1881)	c. 100	2,000	2,500
Beaver/Dunne-za	800 (est., 1859)	n/a	–	–
Tsilhqot'in	600 (1837)	550 (1905)	11,000	13,750
Total	46,861	18,986	379,720	474,650
Wilson Duff's total for BC	–	22,605 (1929)	452,100	565,125

a Includes Nisga'a and Gitxsan, along with Tsimshian in British Columbia and those who emigrated to New Metlakatla, Alaska.
b The 1835 figure is provided by Codere as a range between 7,500 and 8,000; I have simply split the difference.
c Includes Halkomelem/Halq'emeylem, Squamish, and North Straits Songhees and Saanich, plus the Nooksack and Clallam from what is now Washington State.
d According to Ignace, influenza in 1918-19 "killed up to one-third of the remaining population on some reserves," but she provides no final figures.
Sources: See the *Handbook of North American Indians*, vol. 7: *Northwest Coast* (Washington: Smithsonian Institution, 1990), for the following: Margaret B. Blackman, "Haida," 357-58; Marjorie M. Halpin and Margaret Seguin, "Tsimshian Peoples: Southern Tsimshian, Coast Tsimshian, Nishga and Gitksan," 282; Charles Hamori-Torok, "Haisla," 311; Suzanne F. Hilton, "Haihais, Bella Bella, Oowekeeno," 320; Helen Codere, "Kwakiutl: Traditional Culture," 367; Eugene Arima and John Dewhurst, "Nootkans of Vancouver Island," 408; and Wayne Suttles, "Central Coast Salish," 473. See the *Handbook of North American Indians*, vol. 12: *Plateau* (Washington: Smithsonian Institution, 1998), for the following: Dorothy I.D. Kennedy and Randall T. Bouchard, "Lillooet," 188; Marianne Boelscher Ignace, "Shuswap," 216; David Wyatt, "Nicola," 221; Bill B. Brunton, "Kutenai," 235-36; and Robert T. Boyd, "Demographic History until 1990," 474, 477. Wilson Duff, *The Indian History of British Columbia*, vol. 1: *The Impact of the White Man*, new ed. (Victoria: Royal British Columbia Museum, 1997), 55.

missionaries and residential schools, for example, are rooted in this kind of discourse, although in a much more critical form.[89] In the earlier version, progress and enlightenment were legitimate goals pursued and often secured; millennium-generation authors deride those goals as phony and Eurocentric but do not necessarily question the demographic context of imperial cultural intrusion. More generally, the history of British Columbia (like that of North America as a whole) is conducted within a narrativized Turnerian myth of European settlement, development, and modernization in which Aboriginal populations play less than a minor role. Elizabeth Furniss has described the literature thus: "North America is presented as an empty, unoccupied wilderness where land is free for the taking and resources are abundant."[90] What is missing? Death. Enormous, unbelievable, incomprehensible, staggering amounts of death, into which the imperial narrative intrudes.

Massive depopulation, to quote Harris once more, "turns the story of the contact process away from the rhetorics of progress and salvation and towards the numbing recognition of catastrophe."[91] The availability of land and opportunity in sites such as British Columbia stems directly from the causal link between virgin soil epidemics and empty or, more accurately, *widowed* lands for settlement. As Richard Mackie has succinctly put it, settlers had "a terrible advantage."[92] Whether blame should be apportioned to Europeans for inadvertently transmitting lethal bacteria is neither here nor there; what is critical to note is that the dominant theme of British Columbian history – Whiggish progress – has remained untarnished by tales of colossal depopulation and that the liberal province-building narrative requires continued inoculation against such horrors.

But Harris takes us beyond recognizing the absence of a piece of critical knowledge to suggesting that historians' failure to look catastrophe in the eye is not an accident, has debilitated historical writing on British Columbia, and is tantamount to holocaust denial.[93] That raises the stakes considerably, and it is something to which all Canadian historians should pay careful attention. The issues are clearly very political and contentious as well. Keith Thor Carlson states the problem with elegant simplicity: "while those who present evidence of higher pre-contact Aboriginal population figures are often seen as taking the moral high ground ... studies producing lower figures are frequently viewed as part of an apologist strategy for reducing European guilt and responsibility for colonialism."[94] It may have once been the case that scholars who favoured high numbers were subject to something like peer sanction. (Harris maintains that Wilson Duff was intellectually hamstrung on the numbers issue in the 1960s, unable to propose a much higher figure because the populations accepted for the rest of Canada and, indeed, for the rest of North America were still so low.)[95] Such constraints no longer apply, and, it has to be said, there is no cost to academics who carelessly endorse high numbers. The range of acceptable arguments in the debate, in short, has tilted the other way.

If we put the politics to one side, the larger point is this: whether one favours a high count or a low count or even an in-between count, that choice will colour the history of British Columbia one endeavours to write. It is therefore essential to consider what lowball and highball figures would do to our orthodoxies (although that is not the purpose of the current study, which allows me to duck that particular responsibility for now). Especially in the absence of absolutely definitive numbers, it is incumbent on Euro- and Aboriginal Canadian historians to consider what their conclusions on First Nations life in the nineteenth century would look like in the light of starkly different demographic possibilities. According to one scholar writing on the British Columbian experience, "Disease was an integral and devastating component in the dialectic of contact."[96] A good point, but what are the consequences of disparate depopulation projections? Gibson states that the 1830s "demographic disaster broke the back of northern Indian resistance to Euro-American encroachment, both territorial and cultural."[97] Surely, varying estimates of the magnitude and timing of depopulation would force a reconsideration of such a definitive statement? What do we make of the missionary period or aboriginal proletarianization in coalmines and fisheries, to take other examples, if there was population stability, severe depopulation, and/or robust repopulation? This is, granted, not neat and tidy. History is a messy business and some ambiguity must always be admitted.

It is possible to close this chapter on a hopeful note. Very lately a new wrinkle has been added to the depopulation debate in the form of a novel methodological approach. It is too early to say for certain whether the "settlement site extrapolation" archaeological model holds the key to determining the pre-Columbian population riddle, but it has the advantage of working with both micro- and macro-level data. As well, its application to the Stó:lō of the lower Fraser Valley has been restrained in its inclusion of a 66 percent mortality rate from smallpox in the 1780s. This method has generated a pre-contact Stó:lō population figure of more than 62,580, a total that points toward higher numbers than those embraced by the low counters but less than half those promoted by the high counters.[98] It is increasingly likely that archaeology will yield whatever answers we are going to get.

4

Girl Meets Boys:
Sex Ratios and Nuptiality

The gold-rush-era newcomer has been characterized as "a somewhat hard-boiled single man aged anywhere from twenty to fifty years and chronically short of cash."[1] One of the most resilient features of the historical demography of British Columbia in the first century of European colonization is, in fact, its maleness. Throughout the Far West of North America, and indeed wherever there was a gold frontier, one finds a similarly skewed sex ratio. In terms of Canadian provinces, this made British Columbia unique, from the Victorian era to the mid-twentieth century.

Imbalanced sex ratios are, in and of themselves, a demographic *phenomenon*, but because sex ratios play into marriage behaviour, or nuptiality, they are components in the ongoing demographic *process*. It is widely (sometimes wrongly) assumed that fewer women mean earlier marriages by a greater share of the women, who thereafter produce more children per woman. Before we examine fertility rates, then, it is essential to interrogate the evidence on sex ratios and nuptiality. This chapter focuses on the period before the Second World War for two reasons: first, because nuptiality becomes less important in family formation after the war, as marital behaviours and norms change, and second, because marriage patterns in the years between Confederation and Dunkirk tie in with the key questions raised in Chapter 5 regarding fertility rates. Questions of exogamy and endogamy in marriage are important in a consideration of nuptiality, and they are addressed in Chapter 6.

Super, Masculine British Columbia

Was British Columbia a "Man's Province"? From the mid-nineteenth century to the Great War, the answer is a resounding yes, especially among the settlement communities.[2] Before 1858, the ratio of white men to white women on colonial Vancouver's Island was nearly 2:1; by 1891 that imbalance would seem a halcyon age of marital opportunity. The gold rush ushered in a decade of dramatically distorted sex ratios across the two colonies, running as high as 19.4:1 in 1863, falling back to 2:1 in 1870.[3] This demography, as one author puts it, "fostered a rough, vibrant homosocial culture created by and for young men."[4] And for *very* young men, too: it was a *boy's* province in which girls were reliably outnumbered – though not always by dramatic proportions. The most severe ratio between men and women was reserved for those over the age of twenty and under the age of fifty. A woman turning twenty in any decade before 1914 left a cohort of near parity and entered one in which men outnumbered women by more than two to one. Place the shoe on the other foot and the British Columbian male who passed into manhood in either 1891 or 1911 saw the number of his male peers double and the likelihood of his finding a wife halved (see Appendix C). One can see instantly what these transitions would mean in the case of what is sometimes called the "marriage market"; teenage women were common within their own cohort, but once they entered their twenties their scarcity was undeniable.[5] These were rhythms of the life-course that characterized the newcomer experience in the region down to 1900.

By the start of the twenty-first century, however, the sex imbalance was no longer ubiquitous. The achievement of relative parity between males and females might be disregarded as simply part of the demographic maturation process, but the truth is that the male surplus in many respects defined human society and life itself in the province in 1911; despite lingering through most of the twentieth century, it no longer did so in 2001. In this fundamental way, the province changed, and it began to do so at the very start of the modern period.

The chronic shortage of women (or oversupply of men) attracted comment from the outset. In the Comox Valley in the 1860s, for example, "two English-women were surrounded by forty-odd 'bachelors' washed up from the gold regions of the world. Most were almost middle-aged, and if they [the men] were thinking of marriage they had come to the wrong place."[6] In 1868 Governor Musgrave described the implications of a 2.77:1 sex ratio among the white settlers across BC as an "evil ... which does more to retard the advance of the Colony than any other."[7] A generation later, by which time the ratio had fallen to 2.3:1, the editor of the *British Columbia Directory* declared the shortage of "help mates for the lonely bachelors" to be "the greatest deficiency of life on the [Cariboo] plateau."[8] By the 1890s, the rise of the coastal logging industry only made the region relatively less attractive to women, and a badly skewed sex ratio survived into the Edwardian years, particularly in the newer areas of settlement. Eva MacLean recalled travelling up the Skeena River on a sternwheeler in 1911: "I was the only woman aboard ... I was going to be alone with *M-E-N* for nearly a week." A contemporary in the Peace River Block, Lucill K. Adems, found that she was "the only white girl in the country for three hundred miles" and that she was outnumbered by white men six to one.[9] The census does not support Adems' account – the ratio was seldom greater than two to one, although it was roughly four to one in the silvery Slocan and the Kootenays in 1911 – but there is no doubt that there remained a surfeit of men.[10] On the eve of the Great War, John Bensley Thornhill, an English travelogue writer in British Columbia, claimed that "much of the madness in Canada is due to the fact that men, after working hard all day, have none of the comforts of home life, and have to be content with their own thoughts and their own inferior cooking." (It was hardly better for the few women in the colony who, according to historian Kathryn Bridge, "did not have the luxury of choosing friendships, but only the necessity of cultivating friendships," although this may not have contributed to the wave of lunacy Thornhill evidently observed.)[11] The surfeit of males was perceived by British Columbian officials as a source of much dissatisfaction in the new settlements. There were fears, sometimes well founded, that an unmarried male population would not sink permanent roots west of the Rockies. Worse, perhaps, it would become a godless proletarian mass leading the province into moral ruin.[12] Attempts to remedy the sex ratio at the macro level met with unrelenting obstacles. As early as the 1860s, efforts were made to directly recruit unmarried British women; the few who elected to emigrate to British Columbia arrived on what came to be known as the "bride ships."[13] Their impact was predictably limited (not least because, under colonial law, a goodly number were too young to marry).

There were abundant reasons for the sex imbalance and its resilience, not the least of which was the economic order of the two colonies and thereafter the new province. Dependent principally on resource-extraction industries rather than agricultural growth, British Columbia was not likely to attract a great many women on their own; nor was it as likely as later farming-oriented settlement areas elsewhere to attract whole families that would include one or more women. As Jeremy Mouat observed in the case of turn-of-the-century Rossland, "the gender imbalance ... indicates not simply the way the world was but the way the world was made." European and Canadian women repeatedly demonstrated the good sense to stay away from places where their economic futures were largely beyond their control.[14] But there was also negative press to consider: the media and political construction of British Columbia as a man's province must have contributed to the continuing shortage of women. For example, one gold-rush-era book on British Columbia and Vancouver's Island argued vociferously against female emigration assistance: "Altogether it is most heartless to send poor girls out, to starve and become outcasts, in a country where there is neither shelter nor defence" against the "crafty bloodthirsty and implacable savage."[15] How influential such lurid works were in conditioning views of BC is beyond determining. Certainly, only a few newcomer women were assisted by organizations such as the United Englishwomen's Emigration Association and the

United British Women's Emigration Association before the first years of the twentieth century. The effect for men was simple: a long career as a husband and a prolific father was unlikely.

Qualifying the Sex Ratios

So entrenched was this phenomenon of extensive and massive maleness that it came to be regarded, then and recently, as a definitive characteristic of British Columbia. Peter Ward embraced this impression when he described pre-Depression BC as a society dominated by "primarily young, single men." Outwardly, many of the newcomer settlement areas deserved the caricature. The goldmining town of Rossland had a 2:1 ratio in 1901, but matters could, and did, get worse: the ratios ran as high as 4:1 in 1881 in the central Interior. This is what a glance at the published census would establish, but a closer look presents a different British Columbia.[16]

The Asian population – drawn first from peasant communities in southern China, later from Japan, and then from India's Punjab – was effectively all male. In either Nanaimo or Kamloops, the number of Chinese women found in any of the census years before the Great War can nearly be counted on the fingers of two hands. Brides such as fifteen-year-old Quie Young of Guangdong or Cherry Jip Ti He of Victoria travelled to the Interior to marry prosperous local merchants, but they were exceptional.[17] Just as exceptional was the experience of Leung Chong, who served as a field manager in the Tranquille Canyon goldmines during the 1860s. This position afforded him the wealth and opportunity to return to China and, at the age of fifty, to marry. He and his new wife then returned to Kamloops where she was part of a very exclusive demographic of Chinese women.[18] Even in the growing Chinese enclave in Vancouver in 1901, there were "fewer than sixty women and children" out of a total population of about two thousand.[19] In 1911 Chinese British Columbians totalled over 19,000, but only 769 of these were women; still more dramatically, the Indian community of 2,292 people (mostly Sikhs) contained only 3 women.[20] The Asian numbers, in short, tilted the aggregate sex ratio.

For the Chinese, one root of the problem was legislative. Beginning in 1885, immigration laws that included the notoriously discriminatory head taxes discouraged Chinese newcomers generally but worked primarily to discourage female arrivals. Exemptions were introduced in 1900 that allowed merchants and their wives to enter the province without paying the $100 per person tax. This is one reason that Guangdonese merchants were more likely to live in a family household than were, say, Chinese railway workers along the CPR mainline. A second reason was relative wealth: a merchant might afford privileges that a labourer could not. Third, far more so than the merchant class, the Chinese labouring population was made up of so-journers, individuals who had no long-term plan or desire to stay in British

Columbia. Some of these men had wives and families in China and so did not intend to establish a North American demographic beachhead. An overwhelmingly male population will, however, attract women, though not exclusively wives: for two decades beginning in the 1880s, one to two hundred women and girls arrived from China as prostitutes and/or concubines.[21] Still, these infusions could not begin to rectify the imbalance that was observable in every Chinese community in the province.

Insofar as "race" formed an effective (albeit socially constructed) barrier between Asians and Europeans in BC, at least so far as marriage was concerned, it would be more appropriate to assess the non-Asian sex ratio separately. What the non-Asian figures indicate is a frontier population that was principally male but not always overwhelmingly so. In Victoria in 1870, there was a male preponderance among the white population of only 1.37:1, although at New Westminster the figure was 2.22:1.[22] Farming communities often displayed a closer balance: to cite two examples, in 1881 the ratio of non-Asian males to females on the Saanich Peninsula and in the Cowichan Valley was nearly even. Some industrial communities, too, recorded sex ratios that were not dramatically distorted.[23] At Nanaimo in 1881, for instance, the ratio was as low as 1.2:1, although by 1891 the gap had widened to 1.98:1, and in 1901 it was wider still at 2.07:1. Among the adult population, the sex ratio was, however, considerably more skewed. In what proved to be the coalfield's worst year, 1881, we find 589 men and 279 women between fifteen and forty-five years of age: a ratio of 2.11:1. The figures for the central Interior were substantially closer, and there was a pattern of decreasing maleness. In 1881 the Yale and Hope Subdistrict was 80 percent male; this dropped to 63 percent in 1891 and 57 percent in 1901. The non-Asian figures for Vancouver are even closer: a general ratio of 1.5:1 (60 percent) is reduced to 1.39:1 (56 percent) once the Asian components are subtracted. Moreover, the Canadian and American communities in Vancouver both stood at about parity, although the British population was more than 62 percent male.[24] Adult women, in sum, represented a more considerable proportion of the province's non-Asian population than has been recognized in the literature.[25]

At a time when population was doubling decennially, it is conceivable that these sex ratios might have smoothed out. In 1891, for example, there were 11,071 men and women in the twenty to twenty-four age group; ten years later they were joined by 19,634 newcomers as they became the thirty- to thirty-four-year-old cohort. But the sex ratio remained almost exactly the same: in fact, the number of men nearly doubled precisely, as did the number of women in the cohort! (See Figures C.2 and C.3 in Appendix C.) The same could be said for the progress of most of the adult-aged cohorts before the war. It was as though British Columbia employed a gender-based quota system. Why this occurred has, to my knowledge, never been explored.

There was no escaping the tyranny of these numbers. For women the ratio meant an abundance of potential spouses – if marriage were the goal – but it also meant inescapable minority status and "the reaffirmation of roles limited to wife and mother or sexual commodity." For as many as one-in-three, sometimes one-in-two men, the sex ratio was a life sentence of bachelorhood and membership in a masculine culture in an economy that privileged muscularity.[26] The lived experience of this demography could be poignant, and it was recalled as such by a former resident of Savona who remembered the neighbourly affection with which the local Sikh men, "lonesome for the children they had left behind," treated the younger English residents.[27] This Indo-Canadian experience reminds us that the sex ratio was tilted more heavily among Asian newcomers than it was for European arrivals.[28] The consequences, too, of choosing a "man's province" was also disproportionately borne by the Asian male community.

Toward a Woman's Province

As the Great War began, the sex ratio in British Columbia was still deeply unbalanced. Perhaps this explains in part why so many British Columbian men enlisted as hostilities erupted: the opportunity to travel and see more of the world (or just to return to Britain for a spell) was not hindered by family obligations. And the appeal of wartime "adventure" included the lure of sexual opportunities as well.[29] How *could* one keep them down in the Kootenays after they'd seen Paris?

The First World War, however, began a revolution in the sex ratio by making the first of a series of cuts into the adult male population. In 1911 there were 1.79 men to every woman in the province and a ratio of 2.44:1 in the twenty to twenty-nine age bracket. By 1921 the provincial ratio had fallen to 1.26:1, most of the change being felt in the thirty to thirty-nine age bracket, from which 10,000 males had been subtracted (more than half sacrificed as cannon fodder in Europe), reducing the cohort ratio to 1.46:1. (The situation improved dramatically in the Chinese community in Vancouver, where the ratio fell to 10:1 in 1921.)[30] The Second World War had a similar impact. In 1941 the ratio of men to women in the cohorts between ages fifteen and twenty-nine falls below parity: mobilization and the removal of male troops to Britain meant that for the first time there was *a surplus of females*. Parity had been approaching rapidly through the 1920s and 1930s, but wartime recruitment plays the decisive role. After 1945 there would be some restoration of the status quo ante bellum, but by 1951 the surplus maleness of the general population was reduced to 1.05:1 – parity, or as near as dammit. There was in that year a female surplus in the five cohorts ranging between ages fifteen and thirty-nine.[31] By 1961 males once again outnumbered females in almost every cohort (the exceptions being the thirty-five to forty-four-year-old cohorts as well as those for sixty-five to sixty-nine and seventy-five and up).[32] One cohort in particular – the fifteen- to nineteen-year-olds of 1941 – passed through successive census years with a slight female surplus intact, no doubt part of the price paid by the "greatest generation" in the bloodbath of 1939-45.

What happened in the 1970s reflected in demographic terms the changing economic complexion of the province and the evolving roles of women. The ten- to fourteen-year-old "Generation X" cohort in 1971 contained 113,235 males and 109,065 females; over the next ten years, as this group became the twenty to twenty-four cohort in 1981, it added only 11,620 males but fully 17,405 females. Over the same decade, twenty-one thousand newcomers bolstered the ranks of males in the fifteen to nineteen cohort of 1971, but their female counterparts were joined by twenty-seven thousand. This age cohort, as it passes through its twenties, is where one would expect to find new immigrants. Clearly, British Columbia was attracting more females than had ever been the case in the past; or, to put it another way, the province was no longer as attractive to males as it had once been. There was, as well, a rising female surplus in the older age brackets, reflecting the greater life expectancy of women who survived their spouses in British Columbia or did so elsewhere before moving west of the Rockies to retire.[33]

In 1981 a long history of aggregate male surpluses was seemingly overturned. In that year, for the first time, females outnumbered males, especially between the ages of twenty and twenty-nine, and over fifty-five years. Female surpluses were also reported in the 1990s, indicating that the demographic tide had evidently turned. In 1991, for example, there were more females than males between twenty-five and forty-five, and over sixty-five.[34] It is interesting to note, however, that male surpluses continued to be reported in the under twenty-five cohorts. These figures suggest that the province was in fact attracting more females or, more significantly perhaps, failing to retain young males into adulthood. The era of female surpluses, however, is signally different from what was witnessed at the start of the century: at that time males *grossly outnumbered* females in almost every age cohort; the reverse has yet to occur.

A Boy's Province
What is most puzzling about the historical sex ratio patterns is the consistent surplus of boys. Gendered hiring practices in British Columbia's resource-extraction economy favoured boys in the early twentieth century, setting an obstacle for a "natural" balance even in the childhood years. But the young male surpluses continued long after boys were effectively legislated and policed out of the workforce. With less economic advantage, there should have been a quick march to parity.

Three hypotheses explain this continued boy surplus, which begins in the cradle. Vital statistics reports covering the whole twentieth century indicate a very clear pattern of more male births than female births. In the zero- (or birth-) to four-year-old bracket – the infant cohort – the sex ratio always slightly favours males. In 1901 and 1981 alike, there was a ratio of 1.05:1 among infants. This differential might be explained in one or more of three ways.

First, it is possible that British Columbian parents were bearing a higher number of males than females. (A late nineteenth-century observer in the Interior wrote that "Nearly every young married woman around has had a baby during the last fortnight, nearly all boys at that.")[35] Some research suggests that, on the whole, male births outnumber female births.[36] But research also suggests that male infant mortality in some circumstances is sufficiently high to eliminate the difference.[37] This appears to have been the case west of the Rockies. Neonatal and infant (birth- to four-year-old) deaths were consistently higher among males than among females. In 1921, for example, there were 71.4 male neonatal deaths per 1,000 but only 56.8 female neonatal deaths; in 1948 it was estimated that the ratio of male to female neonatal deaths in Vancouver was roughly 7 to 5.[38] Even in 1960 there was a marked distinction: 26.7 male versus 20.6 female neonatal deaths. Higher male neonatal mortality throughout this period means that the surplus of males to females therefore points to a higher rate of male births throughout this period.[39]

Second, research on colonial societies suggests that resources are applied differentially to boys and girls from birth, favouring the survival of boys.[40] This rather chilling prospect might then permit the ratio to be represented in a new way: it does not measure the surplus of males from birth but the decay in the number of females by the age of five. This may have been the case in British Columbia, but demonstrating it conclusively is impossible.

Third, it is possible that immigrants who had small girls were marginally less likely to prefer BC as a destination than were settlers who had small boys. Of the three hypotheses, this one is most clearly supported by the data. From the start of the century through every decade, the zero to four cohorts for boys and girls in any census year increase by very similar amounts over the decade that follows. In 1921, for instance, there were 4,471 more females in the ten to fourteen bracket than there had been in the zero to four bracket ten years earlier; for males the difference was 4,789; in 1990 the ten to fourteen category contained 5,647 more girls and 5,820 more boys than the zero to four category in 1981. Respectively, the differences in the 1911-21 and 1981-91 male and female cohorts are 7.11 percent and 3.1 percent; the rate and character of growth in the under-fifteens during the decades between 1901 and 1991 fall roughly in between these poles. In short, males were born in larger numbers or at least survived infancy in greater numbers than females, and the immigration of boys and girls to British Columbia – though almost even – consistently introduced a greater number of boys than girls. This experience of a female deficit in the under-fifteens continues into the current century.

Elders

Demographic surveys tend to focus on sex ratios among the young and young adults, but shifting our attention to the older cohorts in BC alerts us to a long-term feature of this population. In 1901 the ratio between men and women in the thirty to thirty-nine cohort was 2.36:1. If we follow that cohort through to 1941, we are struck by the persistence of the differential. In 1911 the ratio among the cohort born between 1861 and 1871 was 2.25:1; in 1921 it was 1.69:1; in 1931 the ratio between what were now sixty- to sixty-nine-year-olds was 1.58:1; finally, in 1941, the ratio for these septuagenarians stood at 1.34:1. What shrinkage occurred in the ratio could have been due to the loss of males (mostly through premature natural or workplace death or emigration, as this group would have been too old to serve in large numbers in 1914-18) and/or the addition of more females. In fact, the evidence (particularly the stability of the female population) suggests both factors were in play. While the male cohort declined from 1911 to 1941 at rates of 16.4 percent, 12 percent, and 31 percent decennially, the female cohort grew from 1911 to 1921 by 10.9 percent, then fell in the two decades that followed by 5.8 percent and 19.1 percent respectively.[41] What does this mean? A resilient male surplus in this cohort would ensure an ample supply of life-long bachelors and few unwed women; toward the end of the life-course, it would have presented more elderly males in the province's hospitals and retirement homes and proportionately fewer widows than elsewhere in Canada.[42] For some British Columbians, these differentials were writ even larger.

Chinese Canadians in BC were, of course, trapped in a perpetually heavily male society. The 1923 Immigration Act guaranteed the Chinese community a long-term experience of male surpluses by closing the door to most female immigration. This male community aged and did not, could not, shore itself up with heirs. In 1951 nearly 37 percent of the Chinese in Vancouver were males over the age of fifty-five.[43] As one author expressively puts it, for the males and particularly for the older males in the Chinese community down to the 1960s, "life during this period was one of insecurity and, above all, loneliness."[44] Changes in immigration regulations were insufficient in 1947 and in the 1950s to rectify the sex ratio imbalance, although the situation improved somewhat. Separated families were incrementally reunited, weddings – once few and far between in the Chinese community – became commonplace, and in the decade after 1951, the Chinese community in Vancouver doubled in size to just over fifteen thousand.[45] Things were looking up for the post-war generation, but the life-course of the older generation of Chinese Canadians remained frozen in amber. The Chinese community was not large enough in the mid-twentieth century to skew the sex ratio for the whole population as it had in the late nineteenth century, but its experience does alert us to diverse and relevant elements.

Overall, then, male surpluses – though diminished through the twentieth century – remained a defining feature of the province's demography. Two world wars clearly had an impact on that characteristic, but parity (and certainly female surplus) was slow in coming to any cohort. When it did arrive, it sprang from migration pattern changes, not from natural increase. Whether drawn to the westernmost province by work, marriage, or retirement opportunities, female migrants (specifically female adults) have typically arrived in their twenties, or over the age of fifty-five. And it must be added that the male surplus of old appeared wherever the latest thrust of Euro-Canadian economic development took place. Life in the Peace River District during the 1930s, for example, was characterized by a shortage of females; a popular fashion accessory for men in the region was a hatband bearing the "pathetic appeal, 'Single, Willing to be Married.'"[46] By the end of the century, however, people raised in that male surplus environment found that there were more females about. The effect of these sex ratios on marriage patterns and natural growth is of fundamental importance.

First Marriage, Second Marriage

Much demographic behaviour is driven by cultural rather than biological factors. This is nowhere as evident as in the question of when and with whom one might marry. In a region where distinct cultural practices were colliding, one finds diverse experiences of nuptiality. Insofar as marriage (in its various incarnations) is a necessary first step toward family formation, it is of critical importance in a society suffering from severe decline or in one that launches a biological colonization campaign.

Traditional marriage practices among First Nations peoples have survived the work of Christian missionaries, although, in many quarters, they were dramatically altered if not destroyed. Through the nineteenth century, however, it is safe to say that non-European behaviours associated with nuptiality patterns dominated among Native peoples. These indigenous practices impacted, and were impacted by, the depopulation crisis that occurred during the fur trade and colonization periods.

Aboriginal marriage possibilities were constrained throughout most of the region by customs associated with clan systems as well as, in some coastal areas, a class or caste system and slavery. In parts of British Columbia, young boys were adopted out to their mother's brother's household, usually in a different village. There they were raised as part of the uncle's social and political lineage, inheriting title and position when the surrogate father died. Girls, by contrast, were typically raised by their birth parents until they were married to a male from another village who was no less genetically removed than a first cousin. In this manner nuptiality customs perpetuated a pattern of endogamous relations that tied together a network of villages and clans, what Wayne Suttles described as "the intervillage community." This was true of coastal groups and, at the very least, the Interior Salish as well. Further, skeletal and genetic evidence suggests that "the whole of the Northwest Coast did not comprise a single breeding population either historically or pre-historically," which may be taken as evidence for mating practices between proximate groups.[47]

It must be underlined that not every feature of First Nations nuptial customs was tightly regulated. Among the North Coast Salish, marriage could take place "anytime after puberty," whereas the Nuu-chah-nulth married at "about" age sixteen in the late nineteenth century.[48] Father Brabant observed of the Hesquiat that "it is an unusual case when a young woman is not married before she is sixteen. Many of them are joined in wedlock at thirteen and fourteen." Males on the west coast of Vancouver Island married around the age of sixteen or seventeen, although Brabant believed that in this respect standards changed in the last quarter of the nineteenth century: "in the past it was the custom to postpone looking for a wife for a young man who was below twenty or twenty-two."[49] Charles Hill-Tout was vague about what constituted "marriageable age" among the Nlaka'pamux, but he reported that "a man is free to marry whom he might outside his own family."[50] There were, however, other marriage practices that could have had consequences for fertility. Polygyny (the practice of males having more than one active mating female partner and, in some instances, more than one wife) occurred among several of the First Nations. It was "common" among the Stl'atl'imx, where "co-wives resided in the same household, but in different compartments."[51] This practice was, however, an expensive one restricted by the institution of "bride prices." There is evidence to suggest that polygyny increased with the introduction of new wealth during the fur trade period on the coast.[52] The same hypothesis may permit insight into the nuptial record of the famed highland leader Hwistesmexe'qEn, who is reported to have had no fewer than fifteen wives concurrently in the mid-nineteenth century (by whom he is said to have fathered some fifty children).[53] Theoretically, polygyny could have the effect of raising fertility levels, but there is insufficient evidence one way or the other. By way of a counterbalance, divorce also occurred with some frequency and was, apparently, an informal practice achieved "by simple separation."[54] Remarriage was, predictably, also a regular occurrence and one that was regulated. For example, males among the Nuu-chah-nulth peoples practised sororate and levirate remarriage (respectively, marrying a sister of one's deceased wife and the widow of one's brother), although some of their neighbours did not.[55]

Figure 4.1

Marriages and births, BC, 1914-50

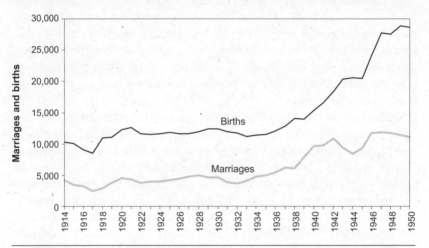

Source: Julie M. Macdonald, "Vital Statistics in British Columbia: An Historical Overview of 100 Years, 1891 to 1990," *Vital Statistics Quarterly Digest* 4, 1 (June 1994): 25-26.

The depopulations of the eighteenth and nineteenth centuries would have played havoc with these nuptial practices. Villages were, of necessity, consolidated, reducing the range of inter-village adoptions; at the same time, the number of prospective spouses belonging to the appropriate clans would have been randomly reduced by disease. To some extent or at least in some quarters, falling population numbers would have applied the brakes to multi-spousal relationships. Widows and widowers would have been more common in the remarriage market than divorcees. The extent to which nuptiality practices therefore inhibited Aboriginal population recovery is unknown, but it logically suggests a problem.

Prescribed nuptial practices were also highly influential among newcomer populations. At the aggregate level (and as may be seen in Figure 4.1), the provincial marriage rate down to the 1940s was a fairly reliable predictor of the birth rate. Social conventions that created an intersection between nuptiality and fertility evidently exercised a powerful influence.

For the European community, the greatest nuptial concern was the distorted sex ratio. How did it affect settler nuptiality to the First World War? The conventional view is that a scarcity of women ensures that almost all adult females are married and that first marriages occur at a young age. Widespread early first marriages and a high level of female nuptiality in British Columbia overall were two consequences of a high male to female ratio down to the 1930s. Take, by way of an example, the experience of female schoolteachers who arrived in the Interior at ages ranging from twenty to twenty-eight. The Anglican bishop at New Westminster recruited instruct-ors for Kamloops, but the English or Eastern Canadian women were "so soon married that the Bishop was always sending for a new one."[56] At the turn of the century, according to anecdotal evidence, the "young school teachers were very much in demand [at dances] and never lacked for partners. Most of them ended up as ranchers' wives."[57] Within four months of taking up a teaching post at Lower Nicola and Quilchena in 1887, Annie McQueen be-came the object of at least two suitors' attentions. Marking her first New Year's Eve in British Columbia, she wrote home to her mother in Nova Scotia about her prospects: "what would you say if I told you that by-and-by I was going to marry a BC businessman, one who is nice, steady, clever and wealthy into the bargain? Mind, I don't say that this is the case, but what would you say if it were?"[58] Within a year she was wed.

One author has claimed that "Marriage and white womanhood became virtually synonymous" in early BC.[59] Likewise, the distinguished Canadian historian Arthur Lower wrote in 1962, with respect to high nuptiality and fertility rates in new areas of European settlement, "The limiting factor is usually the scarcity of women, and what women there are are seldom without either husbands or numerous children."[60] One must be careful not to exag-gerate. Even though the extent of nuptiality in the late nineteenth century in Vancouver and across the rest of the province was easily the highest in Canada, the share of the population that was *never-married* was also signifi-cant.[61] Sometimes the sex ratio is an unreliable predictor of nuptiality.

At the micro level, more complex realities can be detected. The trend to-ward high and early nuptiality is especially visible in Nanaimo, where the sex ratio also set the stage for high rates of remarriage among women.[62] Early marriages were the norm in Kamloops as well, but a larger proportion of the female population between the ages of fifteen and forty-five was unmarried in 1881 and 1891. Nearly three-quarters of the entire adult non-Asian popu-lation in Kamloops was single in 1881. But of the 165 who *were* married, 45 had no co-resident spouse. Ten years later, over 35 percent of the Kamloop-sian cohort was married, but fewer than half of the married individuals lived with co-resident spouses. In other words, large numbers of married men without their wives remained a feature of this frontier community, something that was distinct from Nanaimo's record. This evidence suggests that the practice of sojourning was not monopolized by members of the Chinese community. Similarly, the 1901 sex ratio in Rossland was 2:1, but nearly one in five of the non-Asian married male newcomers had arrived in the mountaintop mining town without their wives (all ninety-four of the mar-ried male Chinese settlers were in Rossland without their wives). There were, as well, about 289 single women over sixteen years of age and sixty widows in Rossland, a fact that confounds the stereotype of early and universal marriage for women on the frontier.

Truth be told, the sex ratio in British Columbia's mining towns was simply not as bad as it was in other cordilleran and west coast locales. Even when the sex ratio was running at around 2:1 in Rossland, Nanaimo, and Ladysmith, it was still statistically possible for as many as one in two of the mining-town males to have co-resident wives. And the reality was not far removed from the probability: in Rossland perhaps one in three men were married, but at Nanaimo nearly half the colliers had wives. By 1911, 57 percent of the male population at Ladysmith was married, and a further 21 percent of the total lived in family households, either as sons or siblings of farmers, widows, or other miners.[63] These figures deserve sober reflection, given the emphasis in the literature on a male-dominated and potentially explosive workforce in British Columbian mining communities.[64] The presence of a substantial married population, one that produced dependent children in large numbers, does not square with facile demographic-determinist theories of frontier social dynamics.

In and around Kamloops, once again a different pattern emerges. In the 1880s and '90s we find that, quite unlike Nanaimo's adult women, who reached nuptiality levels of as much as 93 percent in 1891, the female population of Kamloops between the ages of fifteen and forty was well divided between single and married women.[65] Only 62 percent were married in 1881, and this figure actually fell in 1891 to 58 percent. Even in the cohort most likely to be married – the twenty-five- to thirty-four-year-olds – just 56 percent were married in 1881, rising to a more respectable 79 percent in 1891. The pressures an agricultural economy placed on couples to postpone marriage until some degree of security had been achieved were evident in Kamloops, which lacked the superior and regular wages available to young men in Nanaimo.[66] These were qualities that would reduce the viability of early and widespread marriages. Economic necessity, moreover, encouraged Kamloopsian women to seek careers of their own; economic opportunity permitted them a degree of success.

The 1891 census found fifty-two women working in specified occupations (see Table 4.1), including nine sex trade workers euphemistically described as "dressmakers."[67] Although a 1992 retrospective of the work of the early Victoria photographer Hannah Maynard described her as "an anomaly as a professional woman photographer," she had *two* female contemporaries in Kamloops in the 1890s.[68] Options for women outside of marriage appear to have been more readily available in the Interior than on the island, a factor that probably affected both nuptiality and fertility.[69] There were, to be sure, some common features between island and mainland towns: in both Nanaimo and Kamloops, for example, all but a tiny number of the women lived in family households and not as independent settlers or in groups of unrelated women.

Table 4.1

Occupations of Kamloops women, 1891

Description	Number so occupied
Baker	1
Farmer	1
Hotel keeper	1
Merchant	1
Music teacher	1
General store clerk	2
Milliner	2
Waitress	2
Cook	3
Nun/nun supervisor	3
Nurse	3
Tailor	3
Teacher/school matron	3
Packer	3
Dressmaker (prostitute)	9
Servant	14
Total	52

Source: Canada, Census Enumerators' Manuscript, 1891.

Despite the fortunes of frontier schoolmarms, it does not appear that single women turned their demographic deficit to good use in the British Columbian west. Historian Adele Perry argues that "such tales of colonial marriage" involving upward social and/or economic mobility for females "were more a staple in immigration propaganda than a reflection of female experience."[70] Perry cites anecdotal evidence, but marriage records from Kamloops and the Vancouver Island coalfield also argue her case. Among those who took their nuptials at Nanaimo, miners' daughters favoured miners' sons and so benefited little if at all socially from being "exceedingly scarce."[71] Twenty-six miners' daughters were married in the Presbyterian church at Ladysmith from 1904 to 1915, all but four to miners.[72] At Kamloops, the records of the Anglican Church suggest that, down to 1902, farmers' daughters and farmers' sons were likely couplings, but there were even more daughters of ranchers and farmers who married merchants, clerks, or artisans.[73] This small sample can scarcely be used to determine whether or not upward social mobility was the goal and achievement of Kamloopsian women, but it should be noted that many of the local farmers/ranchers enjoyed socio-economic status superior to that of the local bourgeoisie. The impression is strong, then, that the scarcity model of female nuptiality did not guarantee improved status for young women. One regional historian has put the consequences for women in this environment very nicely: "Some of these frontier women took advantage of this state and so did not adhere rigidly to convention. Others only saw the barriers necessitated by their lack of numbers."[74]

Older women may, however, have fared better. Widow's weeds were almost as likely to be found in the wardrobe of a British Columbian woman as a wedding gown, and a great many of the province's widows dusted off their bridal finery as they plunged into serial marriages. Incidences of widowhood can be gleaned from the census returns. These are perhaps less reliable than some measures because some widows and widowers might credibly describe themselves as single or as still married. Nevertheless, what we learn from the 1881 census is that there were 1,127 widows and 714 widowers self-identified in British Columbia out of a total adult non-Aboriginal population of 18,044. Table 4.2 shows the age distribution of widows and widowers in 1881, revealing a concentration of middle-aged widows but also quite a few in their thirties. This pattern continued in 1891 when there were, for example, 12.2 widows aged twenty to twenty-four per 1,000 women in that age group, as compared to a national figure of 4.2; indeed, in every age category up to seventy-five to eighty-four years, British Columbian women experience a far greater incidence of widowhood than women in any other province. For this share of the adult population – and especially of the adult non-Aboriginal female population – these are significant numbers. They suggest two things. First, the province attracted widows who might have considered it either a good place to find a new husband or a good place to be a widow. This supposition is sustained by the size of the continuing excess of widows over widowers to the eve of the Great War (the range was between 1.1:1 and 1.5:1) and by the concentration of widows in the two main urban centres (where the incidence of widowhood was 46.2 to 57.4 per 1,000 females, as opposed to the provincial average of 43.9 per 1,000). Second, the incidence of widowhood hints at the kinds of workplace dangers faced by British Columbian men, as can be seen clearly in census data from the Vancouver Island coalfield. Finding a new spouse was an option customarily pursued by colliers' widows: seventy-two marriages were registered in a Ladysmith Presbyterian church in the decade before the war, 14 percent of which saw women marrying for the second or third time. Given the number of widows on the coalfield – in 1911 there were 44.4 widows per 1,000 population in the district, and 1 in 5 of British Columbia's widows lived in the colliery towns of Vancouver Island – the practice of remarriage must have quickly become a cultural custom.[75] Few coalfield widows, moreover, lived in households headed by others; they either took charge of their households, remarried, or left the mining district.

Despite the absence of comparable workplace dangers in the central Interior, widowhood in Kamloops was the estate of a far greater number of

Table 4.2

Age distribution of widowhood, BC, 1881

Age cohort	Widows	Widowers
16 to 20	12	5
21 to 30	64	49
31 to 40	155	100
41 to 60	471	320
61 to 70	142	114
71 to 80	41	33
81 to 90	4	4
91+	1	0

Source: Census of Canada, 1881, vol. 1 (Ottawa, 1882), 182-84, table 10.

women and men in 1881 than was the case at Nanaimo. Remarriage was, evidently, less vigorously pursued, possibly because of other economic options for women. One indicator of this degree of opportunity (or necessity, as the case may be) is the fact that over 14 percent of the adult women in the Kamloops area in 1891 were heads of households; to put it another way, 10 percent of all non-Aboriginal, non-Asian households were headed by women. As well, roughly 15 percent of non-Aboriginal, non-Asian women at the confluence of the Thompson Rivers were boarders in Kamloops-area households. To state it differently, about one in every five boarders was a woman. Unlike their sisters in Nanaimo, Kamloops women showed a tendency to live in non-family settings. Relatively low nuptiality rates may offer an explanation: a lower proportion of the female population married on the Interior Plateau, so fewer would have had large numbers of children, and that meant fewer women would have been propelled into a second or third union by the needs of their dependants. Some, of course, took to their heels with widowhood: Charles Lee (alias Leung Kwong Fat) records that his mother, widowed in 1914, left Kamloops and returned to China, taking with her Charles' three sisters.[76]

Historian Peter Ward has written that "Victorian Canada was the promised land for those who wished to wed." Although that might be true for Ontario, men nursing nuptial aspirations in Victorian British Columbia would have found life there more akin to wandering the desert. The sex ratio numbers forbade the emergence of a frontier of equal opportunities, certainly as far as family formation was concerned. Of the 4,962 men between the age of twenty-one and thirty-one appearing in the 1881 census, 3,439 fall into the "never married" category. Marriage was as out of reach for most British Columbian males as a mortgage on Joan Dunsmuir's Craigdarroch Castle, if not more so. And the most potent force determining who, among the males, would or would not marry was the same as that deciding who could afford a coach-and-four: class. Middle-class males were far more likely to be married than were working-class males, especially in Victoria, Vancouver, and New Westminster. This was particularly true in the colonial period, when the establishment reinforced its elite status through selective and strategic marriages. Although local newspaper accounts of weddings are common fodder, what is striking is how many describe opulent services and gifts, even in the late nineteenth century. For example, when George Hoffman (a Canadian Pacific Railway district manager) married Lillian Graham (a Shuswap Lake area farmwoman) the *Kamloops Inland Sentinel* marked the occasion with three column inches detailing the silverware, silk, and chinaware provided for the couple by members of the local economic and social elite.[77] Marriage was not a poor man's game; nor did poorer women necessarily derive much benefit from their scarcity.

Although the focus here has been on nineteenth-century patterns, it is important to note that they survived into the twentieth and occurred, too, in very urban areas. Jean Barman's work on interwar Vancouver reveals a surprisingly similar phenomenon of considerable widowhood during a period of male surpluses. In 1931, more than 10 percent of the adult female population in the city was widowed, and another 22.1 percent was single. This at a time when 54.7 percent of the total adult population was male, of whom 30 percent were single and another 3.6 percent widowed. In the West End and in what Barman calls the "Business District" (Central School, Ward 2, or, less precisely, Yaletown), more than 14 percent of adult women were widows. In those two neighbourhoods, respectively, 47.4 and 77.5 percent of the adult population was male (37.5 percent and 48.5 percent single). Ten years later, despite the explosion in marriages in 1939 and 1940, the city-wide share of adult female widowhood was nearly 13 percent and had risen to 16.8 and 15.7 percent in the two downtown wards.[78] The war had increased the female proportion of the population, but there were still more men, especially in the downtown peninsula, and a third to nearly half were single. Clearly, the connections between sex ratios and nuptiality, even remarriage, resist being reduced to simple odds.

Age at First Marriage

Another aspect of nuptiality is age at first marriage. It is widely assumed that, in communities where a high male to female ratio prevails, the average age at first marriage will be low among the female population.[79] In fact, British Columbian young women – always scarce in the period before the Second World War – married younger *but not that much younger* than women in Ontario, where near parity or female surplus was more typical.[80] In the period from Confederation to the 1930s, the age at first marriage for British Columbian women rose slightly from 22.3 years to 24.8 years, whereas for women in Ontario it climbed in the last half of the nineteenth century and then fell from an average of 26.6 years to 24.9 (and continued to fall until the 1970s).[81] According to the Canada census, women in British Columbia on average married slightly later than their counterparts on the Prairies (23.8 and 22.4 years respectively in 1921), but they married earlier than women in Nova Scotia, Quebec, and Ontario until 1941. As the sex ratio in BC closed, the age of men at first marriage dropped, from 32.7 years in 1891 to 28.5 in 1921.

Peter Ward describes the rise in women's age at first marriage in English Canada (Ontario) before 1900 as "something of an enigma"; British Columbian women's behaviour certainly defies easy explanation.[82] Partly, it may have been a function of the arrival over many years of thousands upon thousands of females in their twenties who were unmarried on arrival but not for long thereafter. The fall in men's age at first marriage most probably occurred because of the arrival of younger male immigrants and the appearance of a BC-born-and-raised male cohort both of which found earlier marrying opportunities.[83] Other marriage timing considerations (and there are many) fall outside the ambit of the present study. What is important to note is that, despite a severely limited female population among the settler community, British Columbia from the 1860s to the 1910s shared the Western world's larger experience of delaying marriages. At least, that was the case in aggregate. A few examples from three locales give a sense of the differences and commonalities.

At Kincolith (also called Gingolx), a small Northwest Coast cannery town near the Alaska border, fifty-four marriages were performed at the mission between 1871 and 1890. Of these, the parish register reveals that forty-two were first marriages for the women, and thirty-six were first marriages for the men. The average age for females marrying for the first time was 19.15 years; for males it was 26 years. The youngest females (five of them) married at the age of 15, but it is possible that they were even younger and that 15 was the earliest acceptable age of marriage.[84] Typically, the men who were *re*marrying were over 35 years of age, but there were a few who were younger and one who was only 24 when he remarried. The range for females was much the same, but, significantly, there is no sign of the age at first marriage rising over the period of a generation. And though it was more likely than not to be the case that the age of each partner was close – twenty-eight of the fifty-four marriages were between partners separated in age by no more than five years – there were startling discrepancies as well. Eleven of the couples were separated by fifteen years or more, the largest gap being that between a 60-year-old groom and a 20-year-old bride. Contrary Kincolith defies almost every aggregate pattern while inviting us to consider how serial marriages for men were even a possibility in the female-scarce Far West.

In Kamloops the pattern, remarkably, is not hugely different from that of Kincolith. Census manuscripts and Catholic Church data show that Aboriginal women (whether married to Native or non-Aboriginal men) appear on average to have had their first-born at the age of 18.[85] Non-Aboriginal women, however, were 22.21 years old on average at first birth. These figures suggest an age at first marriage around 21.5 for non-Aboriginal women and around 17.33 for Native women, assuming that none of these women was pregnant on her wedding day.[86] Church registers corroborate this evidence. The median age at first marriage of Methodist women who wedded in Kamloops between 1891 and 1904 was 19; for men it was 27. In the decade that followed, Methodist women and men married at more advanced ages, 23.66 and 29.78 years respectively. Among the Anglican women married for the first time in Kamloops from 1885 to 1888 and 1892 to 1901, the average age was about 22 years.[87] From 1904 to 1912, age at first marriage for Anglican women climbed to an average of 25.62. The average age for Anglican men at marriage was 34.16 (1885-88), 26.96 among those married between 1892 and 1901, and 30.14 from 1904 to 1912. These samples are small, so caution must be exercised in reaching conclusions, but the trend toward later marriages among every denomination after 1900 appears to have been very strong, and these figures are broadly consistent with their province-wide equivalents. It was, as well, the case that Kamloopsian men married late by national and international standards.[88]

The figures from Nanaimo are different. There, women married earlier on the whole, and they continued to do so into the twentieth century. This probably reflects a disposition toward early marriages among mining populations in Britain, a practice that was transferred to Vancouver Island by immigrants, and one that was evidently deepened in the colony.[89] The average age at *first marriage* among colliers' wives in Britain in the 1880s was 22.46 years; on Vancouver Island, the average age of miners' wives at *first birth* was 20.7 years. Even in the Black Country of South Staffordshire, whence many of the Nanaimo miners originated, 1851 census data reveals an average age of miners' wives at the birth of their oldest co-resident child was 25.84 years.[90] The average age of non-mining males in Nanaimo at the birth of their eldest child was 29.9; for miners, the average age was 27.5. Again, church registers allow us to get closer to the individual and community experience. At St. Paul's Anglican Church from 1862 to 1879 – for many years the only Protestant church in the Nanaimo area – coalfield women were marrying very young. Only slightly more than half of the seventeen weddings for which the bride's age is given involved women who were eighteen or older. The youngest cases were fifteen, but, if we ignore one outlier, the oldest bride in the record was twenty-two.[91] Marriage registers from Ladysmith's Presbyterian Church reveal a similar pattern.[92] For the coalfield's female cohorts, then, early marriages were the general rule and no doubt the primary cause of high fertility levels (see Chapter 5). Men in the coalmining district, however, were more likely to marry slightly later than their British counterparts; for these men, fatherhood began around the age of thirty. It is probably the case that male immigrants to the coalmining communities of nineteenth-century Vancouver Island included large numbers of older bridegrooms, men who perhaps had postponed marriage and parenthood so as to accumulate the funds necessary to leave the British Isles or eastern North America.

One feature of frontier nuptiality that has been observed in other areas of recent European colonization is the tendency of locally born women to marry earlier than immigrant women.[93] If we set aside marriages involving Aboriginal women, the Euro-Canadian women of the Nanaimo area who were born in British Columbia married considerably earlier than their immigrant neighbours. Likewise, Presbyterian women born in Victoria who were wedded there in 1874 were on average 18.6 years old, whereas their non-local peers married at 21.5 years. One sample of more than seventy Presbyterian marriages at Ladysmith in the first fifteen years of the twentieth century shows ten women who were born in the coal district, all of whom married before their twentieth birthday, two of them at age sixteen. Only one Vancouver Island-born woman in this record married in her twenties.[94] The same pattern of early marriages held for British Columbian-born white women in the Thompson Valleys. In the 1890s, for example, there was one case of a British Columbian woman in Kamloops marrying at fourteen (her sister married shortly thereafter, at sixteen). Although none married younger than sixteen years in the 1904-13 cohort, the British Columbians continued to anchor the range of figures. This was especially noticeable among "half-breed" women in 1901, who tended to have their first child a full year earlier than their wholly European neighbours. The youngest brides in church records in the Interior, however, were consistently BC-born, regardless of ancestry.

In short, then, newcomer-era towns were united in a pattern of early marriages, but they parted company on the frequency of nuptiality among women. Marriage came early and to virtually all of the women in Nanaimo, whereas Kamloopsian women stayed unwed for somewhat longer, perhaps permanently. Cultural as well as demographic pressures to marry were evidently less intense in the Thompson Valleys; alternatively, the community may have attracted a slightly older population of unmarried women whose presence at the census affects the statistics. Economic factors cannot be ignored: whatever the sex ratio, the means by which to establish a household would have to be considered. For those settlers who acquired good bottom-land and for those whose wages were secure and substantial, Kamloops and Nanaimo stimulated positive demographic processes. As Donald Eversley observed forty years ago, "Ample food could scarcely fail to have beneficial effects on marriage, fertility, and mortality." In any event, a qualification needs to be added here as regards the significance of early nuptiality: early first marriages might be a factor in increasing fertility, but it may be the case that, as one demographer has put it, women who marry young "tend to have more familial orientations and hence higher family size demands."[95] The jury remains out as to whether circumstantial early first marriages produce high fertility or a cultural/personal inclination toward large families encourages intentional early marriage and early (and large) family formation.

Conclusion

This chapter has principally evaluated the case for a connection between a high sex ratio and nuptiality rates from the beginning of the colonial period through the Second World War. The evidence is sometimes elusive and contradictory, but what can be found reveals important patterns. First, the sex ratio was not as uniformly lopsided in the period before the Great War as some believe, and the province has been in this respect feminizing since the mid-twentieth century. Second, the (somewhat more conditional) sex ratio did not force a pattern of early female nuptiality. Third, widowhood was the lot of many women but so, too, was remarriage, more so in the urban enclaves on the south coast than in the Interior. Fourth, compelling evidence shows an early first marriage regime, especially as regards British Columbia-born women. Fifth, men tended to marry later in life by North American and Western European standards. Finally, marriage rates and reproduction rates were closely related – the significance of which fact is the subject of the next chapter.

5
Ahead by a Century: Fertility

There is a certainty in anecdotal accounts of settler society that thwarts the demographic historian. Women are scarce and therefore quickly and universally married off; children seemingly arrive by the bushel; everybody is healthy and happy, apart from those who die in infancy or in the workplace. Here is an example from the papers of a nineteenth-century newcomer: "there was no such thing known as birth control & there was as a rule big familys from six or seven up to seventeen. [T]his family of seventeen. I myself have known 13 & to the best of my knowledge there were four that died very young [sic]."[1] First, it has to be said that family size across pre-war British Columbia did not approach an average of six or seven children, let alone seventeen. Family sizes were higher in the countryside than in the towns, but not enough to raise the bar as high as that.[2] Second, this sort of account, I believe, is in some measure a reflection of the booster spirit hard-wired into imperially sponsored biological colonies. One could hardly move across the continent or halfway around the world without falling at least partly under the spell of the progressive and optimistic rhetoric that held sway. Third, caveats aside, accounts like this do highlight how demographic reality was filtered through experience. Large families were cause for comment, and cumulatively those comments become contemporary generalization. And there's a reporting pitfall to beware of: for every person who comes from a family of, say, ten siblings, there are nine other siblings who can report the same, a fact that may lead to the misperception that there are, for argument's sake, ten distinct families containing ten children.

Having led with cautions, I note the important truth hidden in the account cited above: before 1914, high rates of female nuptiality and the occurrence of early first marriages produced a rising birth rate in British Columbia. And *that* is extraordinary news.

This upward trend in fertility is highly significant because fertility rates around the Western industrializing world were falling in these very years.

The broadest brushstrokes of the story look like this: In the eighteenth century, mortality rates fell in parts of Western Europe while fertility levels remained at near "natural" levels, leading to sustained and significant population increases. Some time around the middle of the nineteenth century, fertility rates began a long-term decline, a phenomenon known to demographers as a "fertility transition."[3] By the early twentieth century, population growth had slowed significantly along the north Atlantic Rim (in Canada as a whole, total fertility fell from about 7 births per woman to about 4.9).[4] How and why this came about under differing economic, cultural, and political regimes has preoccupied demographic historians for years; why it refused to occur along these lines in France, Hungary, and the United States – where fertility fell before mortality could do the same – has also been a source of interest.[5]

Was there a fertility transition west of the Rockies? The question is salient for a number of reasons. Although fertility rates fell substantially in Canada in the mid- to late nineteenth century, such was not the case in Western Canada – that is, from Lake of the Woods west to the Rockies. The Prairie West saw a postponement of the fertility transition in large part because of the pre-eminence of agriculture and family units of production, a context in which children were regarded more as economic assets and less as dependants. The prairies also attracted settlers from east of "Hajnal's Line," the demographers' boundary that separates Western Europe (late marriage and low fertility) from Eastern Europe (early marriage and high fertility).[6] In British Columbia, however, things were different: First, the agricultural frontier in the farthest west was comparatively small and was overshadowed by an industrial regime built on resource extraction. Second, though ethnicities were diverse, low-fertility British groups dominated the European cohorts, and high-fertility colony builders such as the Mennonites and Hutterites were rare (although a Doukhobor community emerged in the southeast just before the Great War). Third, secularism and a shortage of demonstrative religiosity were noteworthy phenomena in BC, factors that may have reduced the power of prescriptions in favour of families and proscriptions against contraception. Fourth, urbanization proceeded very rapidly on this side of the continental divide, as did the spread of urban ideals. This matters because European and North American city-dwellers were among the first in the modern era to move to smaller families. And fifth, the sex ratio was more heavily weighted toward men than in any other part of the country.[7] The scene was set, therefore, for a reduction in fertility rates that might have rivalled any in the Western world. Historians of population, however, have demonstrated widely – not to say wildly – divergent understandings of the fertility situation in British Columbia: the province is described as either leading the way in the fertility transition or dawdling far behind.

Fertility

There is a difference between the rate of fertility and the absolute physiological capacity to conceive. The latter, sometimes referred to as *fecundability,* is what fertility would look like if no external limits were placed upon it. Since all societies experience cultural and/or environmental constraints on the ability to produce a succession of infants, our attention turns quickly to measuring the rates at which they do so. Fertility obviously depends, first and foremost, on the number of women of child-bearing age, which demographers regard as between fifteen and either forty-five or forty-nine years. Because environments and laws are subject to change, outwardly similar groups of women in the fertile cohort may, over time or across frontiers, generate children at hugely different rates. How these are measured varies in terms of complexity and comparability. The principal systems of measurement are illustrated in sidebars throughout this chapter. They are drawn heavily from Colin Newell, *Methods and Models in Demography* (New York: Wiley, 1998), which has been reprinted many times and remains both definitive and delightfully accessible.

This chapter explores the fertility transition in BC, seeking patterns and explanations for what, in its departure from Western norms, seems to be an unusual historical experience. Briefly, there *was* a fertility transition, but it appears to have been reversed in the last quarter of the nineteenth century by a return to higher rates. In other words, when we shouldn't expect to see low fertility, it shows up; right when we expect to find it falling, it changes direction. But fertility rates were relatively low throughout the period, and, what is more, they remained resistant to national upward trends in the interwar years. The economic and social order of the province played a role and that order was, in turn, reinforced by the peculiarities of the regional fertility transition. What happens to fertility in the years after the Great War is also examined, particularly with respect to the return to the high rates of fertility associated with the mid-twentieth century "baby boom."

British Columbia's Fertility Transition

Disagreements between historians on the course of fertility in this early period are so great that drawing a sketch of this tale is the premier challenge. Jacques Henripin's *Trends and Factors of Fertility in Canada* was published in 1972 under the imprimatur of Statistics Canada (a.k.a. the Dominion Bureau

GFR

The general fertility rate (GFR) measures births against the number of women in their reproductive years. Demographic histories have variously used forty-four or forty-nine as the top limit for women of reproductive age because many women continue to bear children after they reach forty-five and because the published census assembles age categories in five-year cohorts beginning with zero to four (due to this, cohorts end at age forty-four or forty-nine, not forty-five or fifty). It is important to note that a community's GFR based on age fifteen to forty-four will differ from its rate based on fifteen to forty-nine. One must be diligent to compare like with like.

$$GFR = \frac{\text{Births during year}}{\text{Women 15-44 or 15-49 at mid-year}} \times 1{,}000$$

Here's the drawback of the GFR: female populations are not evenly distributed along the age curve. In one decade, they might be clustered in the middle; in the next, the majority might be at either end. In most societies, the reproductive activity of women slows as they approach forty-five, so knowing whether the cohort is younger or older is going to matter.

of Statistics). Henripin argued that the British Columbian general fertility rate (GFR) was nearly 30 percent higher than the national average until 1911.[8] This is a difference of considerable magnitude with startling implications: though revenge-of-the-cradle-era Québécois fertility has become the stuff of legend in Canadian history, by Henripin's reckoning, it was eclipsed by British Columbia's during the last quarter of the nineteenth century. But, and this is of equal importance, according to Henripin, the British Columbian GFR fell sharply from 1891 to the eve of the First World War. This account of the fertility transition in British Columbia was given additional shelf life by Jean Barman in her respected survey of the province's history *The West beyond the West*.[9] For most British Columbians who care to know, then, the orthodoxy for forty years has been league-leading fertility rates that collapsed dramatically before 1914.

Less well known are two other versions of the British Columbian fertility transition, both of which stand Henripin on his head. Marvin McInnis, an economics professor at Queen's University, contributed the Canadian chapters to *A Population History of North America*, published in 2000.[10] McInnis'

Figure 5.1

General fertility rates, BC, 1881-1981

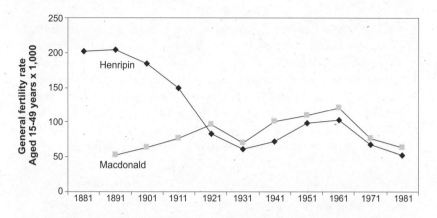

Source: Jacques Henripin, *Trends and Factors of Fertility in Canada* (Ottawa: Statistics Canada, 1972), 18, 21, 357-66, 373-76; Julie M. Macdonald, "Vital Statistics in British Columbia: An Historical Overview of 100 Years, 1891 to 1990," *Vital Statistics Quarterly Digest* 4, 1 (June 1994): 19-45.

evidence for 1891 suggests that BC's I_f (overall fertility index) was 0.344 and was thus lower than the indices for Quebec, Prince Edward Island, New Brunswick, Manitoba, and the Northwest Territories.[11] Figures produced for 1891 by Julie Macdonald are consistent with McInnis' in that they point to a lower fertility rate than Henripin reports.[12] There are, however, important inconsistencies here as well. Macdonald's work with the British Columbian Division of Vital Statistics includes a run of historical data covering the provincial GFR. The rates she produces are a fraction the size of Henripin's for 1891 (see Figure 5.1). The source of disagreement seems to be this: Henripin's 1891-1911 figures are based on *estimates* of both (a) women in the fifteen to forty-nine cohort and (b) births. Macdonald, by contrast, employed data gleaned directly from the Vital Statistics records (that is, *not* estimates) and she measured fertility against the fifteen- to forty-*five*-year-old female cohort. For 1891, Henripin's calculations yield a GFR of 204, quadruple the rate derived from British Columbia's own run of Vital Statistics.[13] Henripin admitted that he lacked solid numbers of births and female age cohorts, and so, devising fairly elaborate formulae that he described in his text, he made an educated but off-target stab. The extent to which these widely republished estimates distort the GFR of other provinces or of Canada as a whole is beyond the scope of this study, but it is very clear that they are significantly out of line with what was recorded in the nineteenth and early twentieth centuries by British Columbian record keepers.[14]

I_f, I_g, I_h, and I_m

Three indices of fertility were developed in the mid-twentieth century to measure real-world fertility against fecundability – that is, the highest fertility that might be something like humanly possible. Ansley Coale devised this system, having observed that Hutterite women in central North America were able to achieve outstanding levels of reproductivity as a result of early marriages and a creed that encouraged almost continual childbearing. I_f represents Coale's overall fertility index; it shows the percentage of children born to a specified female population when measured against Hutterite potential:

$$I_f = \frac{\text{Total number of births in year for female population aged } x}{\text{Female population aged } x \times \text{ Hutterite standard of birth for that cohort}}$$

Typically, the results of all the female cohorts multiplied by the Hutterite standard are added together to produce a fifteen to forty-five (or fifteen to forty-nine) figure.

I_g does much the same, but it uses only married women and *legitimate* births instead of *total* births. This yields the marital fertility index. Similarly, the I_h is the illegitimate fertility index. These two indices rely on the same kind of formula as the overall fertility index.

However, the I_m does not. The index of marriage is described elegantly by Newell as "the ratio of the expected births that would occur to married and to all women if they experienced the standard Hutterite fertility rates."[15]

$$I_m = \frac{\text{Expected births to married women}}{\text{Expected births to all women}}$$

Although Macdonald and McInnis both point to lower fertility rates, they too part company on its dimensions. McInnis reports an overall fertility index lower in BC than in most other provinces, but he also provides a GFR that is higher than Macdonald's. McInnis claims that the GFR for ex-urban BC in 1891 was 132; Henripin claims it was 202; Macdonald puts the GFR for the province as a whole at 53.3.[16] Like Henripin, McInnis reworked the British Columbian statistics along lines that were derived from a study of

Central Canadian demographics.[17] Macdonald, by contrast, worked with birth figures that are in agreement with statistics Ottawa published in the 1890s. The Dominion's figures show BC as having the lowest crude birth rate (CBR) of any province – 23.16 – as compared to 24.98 for the Northwest Territories, 24.5 for Prince Edward Island and Ontario, 25.41 for Nova Scotia, 27.7 for New Brunswick, and 36.86 for Quebec. Faced with three versions of BC's fertility record, one might feel spoilt for choice. By working at the microhistorical level, I have concluded that Macdonald's figures are the most reliable of the three.[18] Census manuscripts for the communities of Kamloops and Nanaimo in 1881 and 1891 support the Macdonald view of things and are consonant with McInnis' findings as regards hinterland I_f as well.[19]

According to Macdonald, British Columbia's fertility curve rose steadily between 1891 and 1921, a development that clearly has critical implications for the demographic and social history of the province. Her scenario differs sharply from BC's standard social historical narrative, which, following Henripin, has for decades been built on the premise that the fertility rate reached its nineteenth-century peak in 1891 and fell thereafter. Although Macdonald and Henripin agree that the population rebounded after 1930 and carried on upward through the baby boom, the point here is that *there was no fertility transition in BC between the 1880s and the First World War:* the low fertility of the early provincial historical era was left behind as British Columbia marched to a different demographic drummer. Why was that the case?

CBR

The crude birth rate (CBR) is the most straightforward of all measures. It is also the least sophisticated. It measures births against *total* population (as opposed to *female* population). The formula looks like this:

$$CBR = \frac{\text{Births in year}}{\text{Population at mid-year}} \times 1,000$$

As Colin Newell points out, because the CBR does not "relate the births to the number of women at risk of having those births," it isn't really a fertility rate: it is, in truth, a population ratio.[20]

Economics, Culture, and Fertility

The classic explanation for the fertility transition combines the economic and social revolutions associated with industrialization and urbanization in Western Europe (specifically Britain) and in eastern North America. Following on a somewhat earlier (but no less profound) shift from high to low levels of *mortality*, life expectancies improved and population grew until – some time around the mid-nineteenth century – *fertility* rates began to fall. This is essentially a supply-and-demand scenario in which the supply of new humans increases until falling mortality softens the demand. Few current demographers would attribute the fertility transition to this equation alone.

The socio-economic changes that evolved through the nineteenth century, often bundled together by social scientists as *modernization,* provide a more rigorous (though still problematic) explanation for falling birth rates. Industrial wage-labour and the decline of the independent family unit of production, better and more widespread formal schooling, public hygiene initiatives, and improvements in medical knowledge are said to have had the combined effect of reducing infant mortality rates.[21] More *surviving children* reduces the need for additional offspring to cover the losses while, at the same time, increasing pressures on family and community resources. Attitudes toward childhood and parenting also change under these circumstances, and, during a period in which household incomes are generally improving and the source of income increasingly shifts to wages secured outside of the family home by adult male breadwinners, the place of children in the household economy is also reconsidered by parents, further strengthening the case for lower fertility.[22] As Quebec historian Peter Gossage writes, however, "more recent theories reflect the inability of these extremely broad concepts to convey the diversity and complexity of historical fertility situations." Demographers do not, generally speaking, make the case that industrialization and urbanization *immediately* produce a fertility decline, and the belief is common that the fertility transition occurs in different cultures and settings historically along various points in the journey from pre-modern through modern.[23]

The coincidence of substantial material improvement overall and fertility decline in the same society offers up a chicken-and-egg scenario: does fertility fall because of economic change or does change in the economic order depend on reproductive factors? British historical demographer Simon Szreter makes a strong case for this distinction while favouring the latter answer: "the attainment of low fertility has apparently been a precondition for sustained economic development over the long term, but economic growth and its entailments are not a necessary part of a general explanation for widespread falling fertility in a society."[24] In other words, industrialization does not cause fertility to fall; rather, falling fertility makes full-scale industrialization possible.

Cultural features, to be sure, are thought to significantly influence the occurrence and character of a fertility transition and ought not to be ignored.[25] One need only mention attitudes (perhaps enshrined in proscriptive legislation) toward contraceptive knowledge and/or technology, and the extension to girls of compulsory schooling legislation. Canadian historical sociologist Angus McLaren, who subscribes very strongly to cultural explanations for fertility change, offers the suggestion that changes in contraceptive knowledge and falling fertility itself influenced the ways women considered reproduction: "once women knew they did not have to become pregnant, they viewed childbirth in a radical new way," one in which "stoicism" was usurped by "fears and concerns."[26]

Whichever factor or factors one concludes played a leading role, to cite Gossage once more, "fertility levels must be treated as the result of choices made, and sometimes not made, by women and men in response to aspects of their environment, and especially to the particular sets of economic opportunities and constraints that they experienced and perceived."[27] Szreter echoes these sentiments, but pushes us closer to the household level at which the key decisions were being made: "Simply to invoke large-scale, impersonal economic forces or cultural change is to remain at an unconvincing distance from the phenomenon and to fail to take into account the significant historical and intra-national variation that is everywhere evident ... The direct agency of change was each set of potential parents and the locus of change was each family household in its local context."[28] True enough, but there are places the historian cannot go: the bedroom door is locked. As the authors of one recent UK study of the nineteenth century put it, "the extreme paucity of surviving, direct evidence on [reproductive] intentions and [contraceptive] techniques is the result of two compounding silences in the historical record. First, until the very end of the nineteenth century there was little public acknowledgement of the widespread nature of the fertility changes occurring. Second, British society had evolved a general code of euphemism and evasion in virtually all sexual matters ... [A]s it was indelicate and vulgar to pursue such matters in explicit public discussion, even the most fearless pioneering sexologists have left remarkably little explicit and direct information on the changes which were occurring."[29] That legacy of discretion – shared by British immigrants (and many other cultures) in British Columbia – forces us back onto aggregate figures showing fertility changes that, naturally, invite macro theories.

The general socio-economic and cultural contexts, to echo Szreter, are not the only explanations, but they *do* matter. For example, one could hardly argue, in the case of Saskatchewan, that industrialization was held back by high rates of fertility. Core-periphery economic and political relations guaranteed an agrarian economy for the Prairies, regardless of what homesteading parents elected to do or not do about family planning. The compromise must be to see how economic forces became *personal* rather than "impersonal." To that end, we must return to those Vancouver Island coalminers who imported traditions of early first marriages and large families.

Colonial-Era Fertility

Nineteenth-century Nanaimo registered a level of community fertility higher than that for British Columbia as a whole. This record-setting was due mainly to the presence of large numbers of coalminers on the east coast of Vancouver Island and, specifically, large number of miners from Britain. In the nineteenth century, colliers in Britain enjoyed relatively good wages at an early age and a consequent ability to marry young and to father families that were, on average, larger than those recorded for other occupational groups. British coalfield women, predictably, were also able to marry early, and – what with a reasonably good quality of life in terms of food and housing in many coalfields – they exhibited high rates of fertility.[30] On the Vancouver Island coalfield, this cultural baggage was combined with a high male to female ratio that contributed further to a widespread phenomenon of early first marriage. Given the number of young wives at Nanaimo, one would naturally anticipate a fertility rate on Vancouver Island higher than even in the Old Country's coalfields. Indeed, in the early 1870s, the *Victoria Colonist* commented approvingly on the robust fertility of Nanaimoites: "[The] ladies of Nanaimo are determined to hold the foremost rank in reproductiveness and are furnishing more liege subjects for Her Majesty than any other locality in the Colony of equal population. By rapid home production we may

C/WR

Another measure sometimes used by historical demographers is the ratio of children under five years of age per 1,000 women between fifteen and forty-four years of age. That measure is called the child/woman ratio (C/WR), and *ratios* are not, technically speaking, *rates*. Nevertheless, the C/WR does, from time to time, present as a fertility index. It looks like this:

$$C/WR = \frac{\text{Children aged 0-4}}{\text{Women aged 15-44}}$$

The C/WR has the estimable advantage of not requiring data on the number of births in a period.

be at last independent of immigration."[31] And, for the next twenty years or so, there were signs of solid rates of fertility. In 1881, for example, the child/woman ratio (C/WR) for the non-Aboriginal, non-Asian population was 0.725:1, compared to Victoria's ratio of 0.676:1 and Washington State's 0.591:1.[32] The general marital fertility rate (GMFR) in Nanaimo was higher than the provincial rate: in 1881 there were 1,038 under-fives for every 1,000 married women and 677 in 1891; the figure for the province was 616 in 1881, but by 1891 BC's GMFR had fallen to about 569.[33] By all indications, then, Nanaimo had an unusually high record of fertility, but it was falling quickly – much faster than in the province as a whole. Why was this the case?

GMFR/GLFR/GIFR

In communities in which marriage reliably precedes reproduction, the general marital fertility rate (GMFR) can be used:

$$GMFR = \frac{All\ births}{Married\ women\ 15\text{-}44\ (or\ 15\text{-}49)} \times 1,000$$

Of course, there's hardly a society on the planet in which marriage precedes *all* births. The GMFR can produce interesting results regardless, but we might try, instead, the general legitimate fertility rate (GLFR):

$$GLFR = \frac{Legitimate\ births}{Married\ women\ 15\text{-}44\ (or\ 15\text{-}49)} \times 1,000$$

We can turn it on its head and measure the general illegitimate fertility rate (GIFR):

$$GIFR = \frac{Illegitimate\ births}{Single,\ widowed,\ divorced\ women\ 15\text{-}44\ (or\ 15\text{-}49)} \times 1,000$$

"Legitimacy" and "illegitimacy" used to have a huge cultural resonance, but birth out of wedlock no longer carries the sort of opprobrium that it once did. For historians, this hardly matters; marital fertility rates can be used to reveal social behaviours over time.

Initially, the economic context of coalfield life was supportive of high fertility. Coalmines were places in which boys could earn relatively good money, thereby offsetting the costs of childhood dependency. These opportunities – crucial in attracting coalmining families from Britain through much of the century – did not last.

The job opportunities for coalmining boys were beginning to shrink as early as the 1860s. Adult male immigrants from China arrived on the scene, and they competed directly for the jobs formerly monopolized by British Canadian boys. Another nail in the coffin of the household wage came in the form of child labour laws, introduced in 1877 (although, to be fair, these regulations were largely toothless). How did this impact fertility levels? By the end of the 1880s, mining families on Vancouver Island were averaging about 2.75 children each; in Britain, the rate among coalmining families was coming down, but it was still higher than four children per family as late as 1911.[34] Nanaimo-area mining families might have demonstrated high rates of fertility by provincial and regional standards, but within the global imperial community of British miners, they had already set off on the road to fertility transition.

There is one last twist to this tale. In the 1880s, local conditions changed again in a way that impacted fertility. Massive fatalities in industrial accidents for which Chinese workers were blamed resulted in the exclusion of Chinese labourers from underground work, thereby restoring the incentive for Euro-Canadian households to raise boys.[35] Through the Edwardian era, then, the curve moves upward from a relatively low point. Having suppressed its fertility to levels well below those of miners in the Old Country, the British mining community of Vancouver Island began to play catch-up.

Several points can be drawn from this state of affairs. First, economic circumstances had an observable impact on fertility. Second, this is especially evident in a single-industry town in which the majority of the community have the same employer, comparable housing conditions and food supplies, similar costs of living, and broadly shared cultural values. The environment for fertility is, in a word, homogenous. Third, a region-dominating high fertility rate quickly gave way to an empire-leading low rate that was not enormously greater than replacement (i.e., 2.1 children per couple). Boys in particular became more dependent and thus more costly. Fourth, this situation did not last. For highly localized reasons, the link made elsewhere between industrialization and the transformation of childhood to a period of dependency (resulting in lower rates of fertility) was stalled and even reversed (resulting in higher rates of fertility).

This evidence suggests that there was, in fact, a fertility transition in BC, but it occurred earlier than one might expect. Additional support for a mid-century movement away from high fertility comes from the rate of marriage.

In the fourth quarter of the nineteenth century, the province as a whole witnessed a higher female nuptiality rate than was seen in most of the rest of Canada, and it was rising. But, as shown in Chapter 4, a high male to female ratio in the 1880s and early 1890s had not produced dramatically extraordinary rates of nuptiality. As the century closed, in other words, different choices were being made. McInnis speculates that the mid-Victorian strategy of limiting births by delaying marriage was being abandoned in late nineteenth- and early twentieth-century Canada; British Columbia may, in fact, have led *the return to patterns of high and early nuptiality*. Once the practice of having fewer children in marriage had become widely accepted, the marriage rate could bob back up to a "normal" level.[36] The dramatically high male to female ratio may have permitted rising levels of nuptiality, but that phenomenon appears to have been delayed, and it did not, in any event, necessarily and automatically lead to *high marital fertility*.

Further, fertility behaviour after the Great War might also suggest the possibility of an earlier transition. From Confederation to 1911, the GFR in British Columbia climbed steadily and at times even sharply by national standards, but it nevertheless remained below the national level. After the war, its upward progress slowed. Standing at 97.3 births per 1,000 women aged fifteen to forty-five in 1921 (versus 108 nationally), the rate remained below that of all other provinces until the 1980s.[37] Wayne McVey and Warren Kalbach capture some of this in their textbook *Canadian Population*.[38] Their graph of CBR trends for Canada and selected provinces from 1921 to 1991 shows BC well behind the other regions and below Canada from 1921 to 1942 and 1945 to 1966. (Oddly, British Columbia is the one province not mentioned in the narrative with respect to this graph!) In other words, fertility was ascending, but on a curve that consistently ran behind the national trends.[39] This twentieth-century movement upward can be seen in a generally sluggish but largely steady climb in the CBR with roots that reach back into the nineteenth century. From 1891 to 1907, the CBR was barely into double digits in British Columbia, hitting a high of 13.23 per 1,000 population in 1898. From 1908 to 1911, it rose from 11.16 to 14.86. In 1912, however, there was a sudden breakthrough to higher numbers: for the next eleven years, the CBR would puncture the 20 births per 1,000 population ceiling on three occasions, and it would never fall lower than 16.39 (in 1916). Insofar as one can rely on the CBR, it shows rising fertility *within the context of a low fertility regime*.

Having established a case for rising fertility against a national and international background of falling fertility, how can we explain it? Several factors can be identified that contributed to this upward trend to 1914. What seems to matter most is sex ratios, age at first marriage, urban growth, and falling infant mortality rates.

Adult sex ratios in British Columbia were tilted heavily in favour of males until the 1950s. But what was the impact of high sex ratios on fertility? Barman cites the sex ratio to explain why the fertility rate "plummeted" (according to her figures), even though the general fertility rate was in fact rising while the sex ratio was falling slowly toward parity. The evidence now points to comparatively low levels of fertility, so clearly the sex ratio did not automatically produce a high fertility rate. One reason it did not do so is because of the presence of large numbers of Chinese males, many of whom were sojourners, many of whom had wives and families in Guangdong or Taishan, and effectively all of whom were out of the competition for the small number of white females in British Columbia. Once socially constructed notions of race and racial boundaries are factored in, the model of female scarcity is tempered – so much so that the assumption that high sex ratios lead to high and early nuptiality followed by high fertility must also be qualified.

Over the longer haul, however, there seems to be an inverse relationship between sex ratios and fertility rates. In 1911, there were 1.79 men to every woman in the province and 2.44:1 in the twenty to twenty-nine age cohort; by 1921 the second ratio had fallen to 1.26:1. What was now the thirty- to thirty-nine-year-old cohort had lost roughly ten thousand males (much of it in European trench warfare), reducing the overall ratio to 1.46:1. Despite this falling sex ratio, fertility continued to jerk upward until the 1920s. So, though a high sex ratio did, from time to time and from place to place, facilitate widespread nuptiality among women in Victorian and Edwardian British Columbia, that did not translate into universally high rates of fertility; nor should the importance of the high sex ratio be overstated.

The upward movement of fertility rates from the 1870s on defined and distinguished life in British Columbia during the Western world's fertility transition. It has been lost sight of because, in part, national aggregate figures

Table 5.1

Birthplaces of non-Aboriginal British Columbians, 1881-1921

							Birthplace					
	BC		Canada		Britain & empire		Asia		Other Europe		US	
	(000s)	(%)	(000s)	(%)	(000s)	(%)	(000s)	(%)	(000s)	(%)	(000s)	(%)
1881	6.5	27	3.5	15	6.0	25	4.3	18	0.8	4	2.3	10
1891	9.4	13	20.7	29	20.7	29	8.9	13	3.1	4	6.6	9
1901	30.6	20	41.0	27	32.0	21	27.0	13	9.4	6	17.2	11
1911	64.3	17	86.4	23	116.5	31	27.0	7	40.1	11	37.6	10
1921	134.7	27	108.9	22	158.9	32	32.7	7	31.7	6	35.0	7

Note: Due to rounding, percentages do not total 100.
Source: Canada, *Sixth Census of Canada, 1921* (Ottawa: King's Printer, 1924).

pull us so strongly in another direction. More critically, the population history of BC, as a tale of wave after wave of newcomers, has deflected attention from those who were born and raised in the West beyond the West. Between 1881 and 1891, the number of residents born in British Columbia increased by half to more than 9,000; ten years later there were 30,640 residents born in the province; that figure doubled again by 1911 (see Table 5.1). And here I will offer a hypothesis.

Ahead by Two Centuries

Victorian British Columbia attracted mainly two categories of people: the very well-to-do and the far less well-to-do. The latter included many hewers of wood, a few drawers of water, and huge numbers of railway workers, miners, and fishermen. Whether European, African, or Asian, the British Columbian newcomer working-class male laboured in difficult, dangerous, and not entirely lucrative resource-extraction and construction industries, all of which were vulnerable to sudden and dramatic boom and bust economic swings. And a great many of these settlers could not afford large families. Some, such as the white coalminers of Vancouver Island, might have fathered large numbers of children, but, even within their culture and industry of high fecundity, they appear to have resisted the urge to do so. On the coalfield, one sees evidence of the declining economic viability of boys; this alone would have dampened the fertility of mining households. But that hardly matters: between 1871 and 1886, railway construction gripped the provincial economy, drawing more and more single (or at least wifeless) men to the west coast. After 1886 and until the mid-1890s, the economy faltered, and it was not until the opening of mining frontiers in the silvery Slocan and the Klondike (as well as new agricultural settlement in the Okanagan and Thompson Valleys) that migration and family building resumed with force.

Meanwhile, on the better side of town, middle-class and upper-middle-class British Columbians were practising the sort of fertility limitation that was fashionable in northwestern Europe. In this context, the legal parameters of fertility control can be mentioned. Briefly, birth control – whether it came in the form of information or contraceptive materials – was illegal in the province from 1892. Having said that, we can be confident that birth control was practised before and after 1892, and that it was probably widespread. Recent research in England's industrial north in the early and mid-twentieth century turned up evidence of extensive reliance on the withdrawal method, which, though hardly foolproof, could be used effectively to limit fertility. Venerable folk recipes for small families were being joined by more "scientific" solutions to the challenge of pregnancy avoidance. From the mid-nineteenth century, urban networks of early family planners linked the periphery to the centre, British Columbia to Montreal, New York, and

London. This was perhaps especially true on Canada's west coast where immigration rates were so great and the base population levels so low that white Anglo-Saxon Protestant newcomers could have a continuing impact on culture and attitudes. As has been observed in the case of Victorian Ontario, "the fertility experience in a population subject to high in-migration must inevitably reflect a continually changing mix of immigrant and developing local values." In Chapter 4 it was shown that significant numbers of young women arrived in the twenty years between 1891 and 1911. They arrived at a time when birth control literature was increasingly available and when they themselves were of an age that the question of fertility was most likely to matter to them at a personal level. If these young women originated in London or Toronto or New York or any of a dozen other major urban centres on the Atlantic Rim, the birth control pamphlets of the day would have been accessible to them in some measure.[40]

Whatever impact birth control advocates may have had in the pre-war era (in BC or elsewhere in the Western world), they were swimming with the tide. Family size began dropping in many parts of mainland Britain in the mid-nineteenth century (first and especially among the middle classes); by the war a substantial shrinkage had occurred in family size for which pamphleteering could not take all the credit. Urbanization, gradually but significantly improved household wages, the stiffening of child labour laws, and a host of other influences led people in this generation to rethink the ideal family size.[41] Throughout the Western world, they reached the same conclusion at roughly the same time: a smaller family was preferable. Bourgeois British Columbians may have accepted this paradigm shift earlier than some, but the likelihood is that their low fertility range was sustained by the international "family planning" and contraceptive movements, and by infusions of middle-class immigrants from precisely those Victorian and Edwardian enclaves of cutting-edge family size planners.[42]

In other words, cultural practices associated with socio-economic class combined with economic conditions to produce a generation that exhibited low fertility behaviour in a variety of British Columbian settings. The effect of these elements would be to reduce fertility generally: those who could least afford children found them economically undesirable; those who could most afford children embraced fertility limitation ideals; and the significant numbers of women who sought careers as teachers, photographers, hotel owners, saloon-keepers, and the like voluntarily removed themselves from the active fertility game.

Having established a fertility regime lower than anywhere else in the country, British Columbians did not need to engage in the fertility transition seen nationwide.[43] Instead, their reproductive activity intensified but always at rates that fell below national levels until the mid-twentieth century. Not only were British Columbians ahead of their contemporaries by a century in terms of fertility limitation, they achieved a fertility rate that remained a benchmark for the province itself for one hundred years. Most importantly, in 1891, their general fertility rate was no less than one hundred points (a different kind of "century") lower than has been widely reported. This finding alone is of considerable importance to the history of the province.

I will close this section by underlining the continuing existence in this period of a discrete Aboriginal demographic order. The Dominion census and Ottawa's Indian agents were not especially scrupulous and thorough when it came to enumerating vital events among the First Nations, but by the mid-1890s coverage seems to have become more comprehensive. Despite neglect, especially of northern bands, the overall evidence on fertility is compelling: Aboriginal peoples had a crude birth rate that was roughly comparable to that of the non-Aboriginal community as a whole. Nevertheless, it was estimated in 1900 that nearly a third of all births in the province were to First Nations women. Hugh Johnston argues that this fact points to a shortage of white women and not to relatively high fertility among First Nations women.[44] It could, in truth, do both.

What is more, these Aboriginal rates were slow to diminish. According to a study of three generations in a pair of Nuu-chah-nulth and Tsilhqot'in communities, colonial-era fertility rates (and presumably contraceptive practices as well) lasted into the twentieth century. As sedentarism became more widespread under the emergent Euro-Canadian industrial and agricultural economy, opportunities to alter First Nations fertility practices increased. The cultural influence of missionary orders is important in this respect, but so too are the health care initiatives that increasingly attended to the high infant mortality rates besetting Native communities. Conversely, it may be the case that tuberculosis was a significant involuntary factor in tempering First Nations fertility; likewise, the retreat of TB may have contributed to rising fertility. What can be known with relative certainty is that age-specific fertility rates (ASFRs) indicate larger numbers of younger women having larger numbers of children in the mid-twentieth century and older cohorts reducing their lifetime fertility.[45] Motherhood came earlier and to more Native women than was the case in the past. This development certainly contributed to a First Nations population rebound.

The mid-1920s mark the nadir of most Native populations in BC. At that point there were a mere 513 births, so nearly matched by 512 deaths. In the fifty years that followed, the Aboriginal death rate per 1,000 was higher than the non-Aboriginal death rate, as was the Aboriginal birth rate. The critical difference is this: though the death rate gap between Natives and newcomers did eventually close, the birth rate gap did not follow suit. So, in the period 1926-1930 the non-Aboriginal birth rate stood at 15.9 per 1,000, rising to 25.3 in 1957 at the end of the baby boom; the Aboriginal birth rate, which began this period at 22.7 per 1,000, rose rapidly to more

ASFR

The shortcomings of the GFR – that is, its inability to take account of clustering along the age range – are addressed by the age-specific fertility rate (ASFR). This requires more data than are often available in censuses. The female child-bearing period of fifteen to forty-four (or to forty-nine) years is divided into five-year cohorts, and each of these is matched to the number of births recorded for that cohort:

$$ASFR = \frac{\text{Births in year to women aged } x}{\text{Women aged } x \text{ at mid-year}}$$

So, x could be fifteen to nineteen or forty-five to forty-nine or one of the five cohorts in between. This means that a community doesn't have one ASFR, it has seven, which is cumbersome and not particularly useful to a broad conversation about fertility. What is more, in the context of British Columbia, the births are recorded by the province's Vital Statistics Department, but the female age cohort information comes from the federal census office. In other words, there's a question mark hanging over whether the numbers are consistent and reliable.

than 50 per 1,000 per annum by the 1950s and peaked in 1960 at 56.9 per 1,000.[46] Wilson Duff pointed to the relative youthfulness of the Native population (which belied a comparatively lower life expectancy) as the cause of this discrepancy and predicted that the fertility levels would balance out in a generation or so.[47] This has not been the case entirely. In the late 1990s, the total fertility rate (TFR) among the "registered Indian population" of British Columbia stood at 2.24, whereas the provincial TFR was much lower at 1.38.[48] It is true that First Nations "entered demographic transition from a traditional high to a modern low almost a century after Canadians of European stock," but Aboriginal people continue to have relatively large numbers of children because Aboriginal communities continue to consist very heavily of young people of child-bearing age.[49] Whatever the underlying causes, there were clearly two very different birth regimes in BC – one linked to an ancient Aboriginal past in the region, the other tied to the values and practices of the modern era.[50]

TFR

One way of making the ASFR more useful is through the total fertility rate (TFR). Since each ASFR relates to a five-year cohort, they are added together and then multiplied by 5. The outcome is divided by 1,000 to give us a rate per 1,000 women:

$$TFR = \frac{\text{Sum of ASFRs} \times 5}{1,000}$$

Like the ASFR, the TFR depends on lots of reliable data, and often those simply aren't available.

BC's Second Fertility Transition

Following on the Victorian-era fertility transition, Western world reproductivity continued to fall, hammered first by the Great War and then by the 1930s Depression. A recovery in fertility levels would not occur until the early 1940s, when the baby boom began. The socio-economic energy that carried the boom into the 1950s was dying down before the sexual revolution of the 1960s. Thereafter, improved access to effective means of birth control and a changed attitude to women's place in the social and economic order led to a precipitous fall in fertility – a *baby bust* – which completed what the Industrial Revolution had begun.[51] By the dawn of the twenty-first century, natural population increase in Canada as a whole was well below replacement levels (and only Newfoundland and Nova Scotia had lower total fertility rates than BC, at 1.38).[52] So, in short, Western world fertility fell in the Victorian and Edwardian eras, kept on falling until the Second World War, reversed itself dramatically for almost twenty years, and then resumed its downward trend. How and why this came about in differing economic, cultural, and political regimes is a question that has engrossed demographic historians for years. What did the twentieth century hold for British Columbia in this respect? How deep were the troughs of low fertility in the interwar years and how high the peaks of the baby boom? Was very secular BC highly receptive to the revitalized birth control movement of the 1960s, or did newer waves of immigrants offset that trend with levels of fertility higher than what was found elsewhere in Canada?[53]

The short answer seems to be that British Columbians initially exhibited the most aggressive resistance to high fertility witnessed in any region in the country. Marvin McInnis' recent turn-of-the-century national survey disaggregates figures for metropolitan and "residual" areas of each province. What his findings disclose is that between 1891 and 1931, the GFR in residual BC fell from 132 to 70 births per 1,000 women aged fifteen to forty-five, whereas the rate in the metropolis dropped from 129 to 50. London, Ontario, may have been "the most avant-garde city in Canada" as regards a low GFR in 1891, but Vancouver led the nation in this respect in both 1921 and 1931.[54] Similarly, although the percentage married in Vancouver was well above the median for the nation's larger centres, *general marital fertility* (GMFR) was down to double digits in 1921, whereas it survived in triple digits in every other medium-to-large city. What is more, Vancouver's performance, while advancing further and faster down the road of fertility limitation in the 1920s, was paralleled by that of BC's residual areas. No non-metropolitan area in any other province could match residual BC, and, with a GFR of 70 births per 1,000 in 1931, hinterland/heartland British Columbia was more "avant-garde" than Montreal, Hamilton, Edmonton, Halifax, Saint John, Kingston, Trois-Rivières, and Quebec City. To be sure, the cities did not have a monopoly on these trends. McInnis notes that, in Canada, small towns and rural areas shared in falling birth rates to a greater extent than did their equivalents in other nations. This was evidently very much the case in British Columbia, perhaps more so than elsewhere in Canada. McInnis finds high fertility in Vancouver (the most urbanized part of an urbanized province, and the part of BC to which immigrants arrived in greatest numbers) but quite spectacularly low fertility in the rest of the province (which includes a great many industrial urban nodes) when measured against the standard of other "residual" areas in Canada.

Although the crude birth rate rose fairly steadily in the province during the first half of the twentieth century, it did suffer some reverses. Through the 1920s, the CBR hovered in the 16 to 18 range, but it declined in 1933, the worst year of the Great Depression, to its lowest level (13.37) since 1909.[55] The 1930s nadir was lower in BC than in any other province, although the fall from 1922 to 1933 was not necessarily as precipitous as it was in Manitoba, Saskatchewan, or Quebec. More to the point, before the Great War, during a time of relative prosperity and relative agricultural expansion in the province, the CBR was as low as it would be in the depths of the Depression.

The focus in the literature on the significance of immigration has had the effect of hiding the fact that the province was becoming vastly more home-grown between the wars.[56] Just the same, it went about doing so at rates below the national average. That, too, would change.

The Baby Boom

If there is one demographic phenomenon with which the general public has some nodding acquaintance, it is the baby boom, the sudden increase in births that began during the Second World War. Its roots, however, run somewhat deeper in British Columbia.

Despite the dampening effect of the 1930s Depression on nuptiality and fertility alike, recovery is visible by the middle of the decade. Running alongside rising marriage rates, the CBR grows from 13.6 to 16.1 by 1938. Faltering briefly in 1939, the upward curve reappears with a vengeance thereafter. In terms of real numbers, total annual births pass the 10,500 mark in 1936 and the 12,000 mark in 1938. Before what is usually understood as the baby boom was under way, a larger cohort was already on the rise.

Of course, what followed made the Depression-era recovery pale by contrast. The years 1940-45 saw the CBR climb rapidly. By the middle of the war, the rate leaps to 20.9.[57] This represents a near doubling of the real number of children born annually. And the rate continues to rise through 1957. It is worthwhile to consider the cumulative effects of this birth rate. From 1914 to 1935 (a period of twenty-two years inclusive), there was an average of 10,125 births per annum for a total of 222,753; from 1936 to 1957 (the next twenty-two years), there was an average of 23,186 births per year for a total of 510,113. From 1925 to 1955, the rate of natural increase (i.e., births less the number of deaths) rises from 9.8 per 1,000 population to 15.9.[58] British Columbia grew from 442,000 in 1914 to 1,487,000 in 1957, and during that period, 732,866 people were born in the province.[59]

As in so many other respects, Vancouver's experience of fertility had a greater statistical impact on the province than did that of any other community. As shown in Figure 5.2, what the number of births and deaths in the city from 1941 to 1990 demonstrates is that, first, the greatest net increase took place in 1957; second, in that year, the baby boom peaked and began to recede; third, the end of the baby boom, despite a population that was both maturing and increasing by immigration, signalled a decline in the *real* number of births right down to the 1990s; and fourth, the falling number and rate of births was countered by a largely stable annual number of deaths, which produced, in the five years after 1971, either nil growth or an actual decrease.[60]

What distinguishes the Canadian baby boom from earlier levels of relatively high fertility is not rising average family size but more widespread incidences of marital fertility. To put it simply, more women were marrying and more of those married women were having children than was the case in the 1920s and 1930s. In British Columbia, however, an important feature was growing family size: in 1951, fourth-born children constituted only 9 percent of all births, and fifths, sixths, etc., combined for 9.5 percent. As the

Figure 5.2

Births and deaths, Vancouver, 1941-90

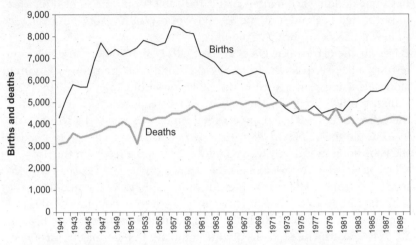

Source: City of Vancouver Planning Department, "The Vancouver Monitoring Program Information Update: Births and Deaths, 1941-1990" (December 1991), 4-6, City of Vancouver Archives, Vancouver, BC.

1950s wore on, fourth-borns rose to 12 percent, and fifth-borns et al. rose throughout the decade, peaking in 1962 at about 16.5 percent.[61] Even so, this "boom" needs to be placed in perspective: in terms of the crude birth rate, the Edwardian era's commanding heights were recaptured only in 1947. The upward trend thereafter continued to 1956-57, when the CBR topped out at 26.1, by which time the number of births per year had reached 36,241.[62] Although 1976 was a particularly low CBR year, the first time the rate fell to a level comparable to that of the 1930s was 1987. That's a long way to travel to catch up to the modern era's fertility transition.

The social ramifications of this demographic tide deserve consideration. On the eve of the Great War, British Columbians below the age of fifteen or over sixty constituted 34 percent of the population. The impact of trench warfare and an aging "pioneer" generation was immense: by 1921, the dependent share of the population had grown to 47 percent. Given the decline in the male population associated with the Great War, an increasing share of the burden of social dependency – both that of the young and the elderly – was borne by women, many of them war widows. Through the interwar years, the level of dependency would hardly change, due in part to an aging population. By 1941, however, nearly 42 percent of the population was not in the "productive" age cohort between fifteen and sixty years of age.[63] For Canada as a whole, the figure was 38 percent – noticeably lower.[64] (See Table 5.2 and Figure C.8 in Appendix C.) In the era following the Second World

Table 5.2

Dependent and producing populations, 1891-1990

Year	Adults (#)	Children (#)	Over 60 years (#)	Dependent (%)
1891	70,783	25,080	2,310	39
1901	129,703	25,080	4,458	38
1911	292,523	91,256	8,701	34
1921	356,727	149,460	18,395	47
1931	484,982	171,178	38,103	43
1941	574,656	175,133	68,072	42
1951	734,686	304,387	126,137	59
1961	954,323	509,143	165,616	71
1971	1,369,625	609,975	205,020	60
1981	1,857,995	588,315	298,200	48
1990	2,089,839	631,593	409,016	50

Source: British Columbia, *The Nineteen Eighties: A Statistical Resource for a Decade of Vital Events in British Columbia* (Victoria: Ministry of Health and Ministry Responsible for Seniors, 1994), 10.

War, pressure from a younger dependent population increased and was augmented by an aging population born before the century began; in practical terms it was further buttressed by the large number of women who were not engaged in paid labour and were, therefore, also dependent. The sex ratio had nearly balanced out by 1951, but the economy still remained skewed heavily toward "masculine" resource-extraction industries. We can see, then, two generations – the interwar and the Cold War generations – separated by demographic characteristics, experiences, and concerns. The interwar generation that rose to adulthood in the 1940s and '50s had grown up at a time when childhood dependency constituted much less than a third of the population and in which responsibility for dependants was borne very widely by war widows; the Cold War generation found its feet when dependency – by age and gender – was much more likely to be the norm and not the exception. In these contexts, the rising pressure on the state, beginning in the 1920s, to shoulder some of the burden of dependency can be seen outside the language of intellectual change and social reform. These were, first and foremost, demographic concerns.

It is only after 1957 that one can begin to see a community-wide movement away from a high fertility regime. British Columbia's experience of fertility transition in the twentieth century looks unusual by European standards. Indeed, most of North America, with its exceptional baby boom pattern, steps outside of the experience of older societies marked more clearly by the demographic consequences of the Industrial Revolution. But European demographers have identified a common denominator that can be applied here: the slowing of the birth rate coincides with the decline of the infant death rate, producing a net balance in births and deaths. As British population historian Robert Woods put it, "high levels of fertility are necessary to match high levels of mortality, and thus ... when infant or childhood mortality begins to decline, marital fertility will also be reduced without adversely affecting the effective level of fertility, that is the supply of new adults capable of reproducing."[65] This occurs at both the household level (where families aim with mixed degrees of precision to achieve an ideal complete size) and across communities, where larger economic and social pressures become more visible.[66] The evidence suggests this was the case in British Columbia.

The Vital Statistics information (tabulated in Appendix D) shows an infant mortality rate in BC that was, from the 1920s, consistently below the national average.[67] However, the province performed markedly better than any other western province in this respect. In 1923, for example, whereas the infant mortality rate in BC was 66.8 per 1,000 live births, it was 85.7, 91.9, and 94.2 in Manitoba, Saskatchewan, and Alberta respectively. Moreover, on 20 January 1939 the *Vancouver Daily Province* could boast that "Vancouver, with an infant mortality rate of thirty per 1000 of population, has the best record on the continent. Twenty-five years ago, the rate was about 180 per 1000." By 1948 the rate had dropped further still to 24.3 per 1,000 births. (The improvement in BC was attributed to the work of the Medical Health Board, initiatives in health education, and better professional medical care; what proved most resistant to their combined efforts was premature birth, reckoned to be the leading cause of infant death to the mid-century.) British Columbia continued to lead Western Canada until 1956, when Alberta posted a slightly better record; by the 1960s, Western Canada as a whole was comparable, although, more often than not, British Columbia retained a slight lead in the region. In Central Canada, Ontario drew ahead in the 1940s, and Quebec did so too but only in the 1970s. On the whole, then, infant mortality rates – which had been very high in some British Columbian communities in the nineteenth century – fell faster earlier and continued to fall (albeit more slowly) through the mid- and late twentieth century. By 1951 the national and provincial levels of infant mortality were almost the same as those for fertility; by 1961 the two rates were virtually identical, and thereafter they continued to gently slide down together, fertility rates rising above infant mortality for the first time in the century in the 1970s and remaining there to the millennium. In the early twenty-first century, British Columbia continues to have the lowest infant mortality rates west of New Brunswick.[68]

Factors contributing to a rise in fertility in the baby boom years would naturally include a falling age at first marriage. High sex ratios are generally thought to lead to earlier ages at first marriage, but, in British Columbia, the trends continued to point in the opposite direction.[69] Age at first marriage appears to have been, on average, in the low twenties for women in the late nineteenth century. Thereafter, it crept up slightly – to around twenty-four from 1921 through 1941 – and then, according to provincial Vital Statistics and Canada census evidence, actually fell steadily throughout the baby boom years.[70] Table 5.3 lays low the long-standing image of early marriages and pregnancies followed by a long career of births: from 1921 to 1961, teen fertility rates were growing, whereas, throughout the century, the rate for older women fell steadily. To put it another way, yes, teen mothers *were* an increasingly active part of the natural increase equation, but young mother-hood did not necessarily lead to sustained fertility. There is something odd about the fact that the evidence points to a falling age at first marriage through the baby boom years. This defies common sense understandings of what happens in a community where the sex ratio is closing: the age at first marriage should rise.[71] The age at first marriage for men was 28.5 years in 1921 and 23.5 in 1971; among women the change was not as severe, but is there in a decline from 23.8 years to 21.0 years from 1921 to 1971.[72] Of course, marriage does not necessarily signal the immediate onset of child-bearing, but in 1960 the age of mothers at first birth was still surprisingly young. Seventy percent of all first births occurred among women between twenty-one and twenty-five years of age and another 27 percent among women below twenty years.[73] Moreover, the number of births to women in the fifteen- to nineteen-year-old cohort increased from 31.6 per 1,000 in 1945 to 73.8 in 1961. Women were marrying young, and more than one in four were having their first child before they were themselves out of their teens. This was not a trend that would last.

Table 5.3

Age-specific fertility rates, 1921-2001, selected mothers' age cohorts

Year	Age cohorts						
	15-19	20-24	25-29	30-34	35-39	40-44	45-49
1921	26.5	140.6	151.7	125.5	79.0	30.8	3.8
1931	23.8	110.7	126.2	94.9	55.8	20.3	2.5
1941	31.4	135.1	135.0	95.0	46.9	16.0	1.6
1951	59.2	192.7	183.1	120.6	62.7	19.7	2.2
1961	73.8	253.7	214.5	128.7	64.7	20.0	1.5
1971	48.9	141.2	136.6	67.5	26.2	6.2	0.4
1981	29.0	99.5	121.9	68.9	19.1	2.8	0.1
1991	24.9	76.8	112.3	83.4	30.5	4.4	0.1
2001	13.4	47.5	85.6	83.6	38.2	7.2	0.3

Sources: BC Stats, "Age Specific and Total Fertility Rates by Local Health Area, 1987 to 2006," http://www.bcstats.gov.bc.ca/data/pop/vital/lha_asfr.asp; Surinder Wadhera and Jill Strachan, "Age-Specific, Total and General Fertility Rates, Canada and Provinces, 1921-1990," *Selected Birth and Fertility Statistics, Canada, 1921-1990* (Ottawa: Statistics Canada, 1993), 64, table 10.

Changes in women's economic and social roles, along with developments associated with the sexual revolution in the 1960s, upset many of these demographic behaviours. The CBR and the real number of births (accompanied by the GFR and the TFR) began to slide in 1958, but there had been slight reversals in the post-war upward trend of the CBR in 1948 and 1950. Anyone watching might have been surprised by the shrinkage of 1958 and 1959, but by 1961 they would have known that the rate was definitely falling. In that year, the CBR dropped to 23.7, the lowest level since 1946. It continued to fall in every year but one until 1979. Through the 1980s, the general trend remained downward: by 1994, the CBR stood at less than 13 births per 1,000 population, a figure that was well below even that of 1933.[74]

These developments can be explained in part by economic conditions and by changing female roles. Rates of engagement with the economy tell part of the tale. The crest of the baby boom came in 1957; the very next year saw the unemployment rate spike to 8.6 percent. In two of the three years that followed, the unemployment rate stayed well above the 8 percent mark. Fertility shrank almost instantly as British Columbians reckoned with the possibility that twenty years had passed since the end of the Depression and another downturn might be just about due. In 1951, roughly one in every four British Columbian women participated in paid labour; by 1961, that had increased to nearly 30 percent; by 1991, the proportion had doubled to 60 percent.[75] Graph the rate of female participation in the paid workforce against the fertility rate in these years and the two lines form a near-perfect X.[76] By the 1980s and 1990s, more and more women were pursuing educational, career, and personal goals that resulted in later marriages, later first births, and fewer career births.[77] As Figure 5.3 illustrates, by 1990, Vancouver women were typically having their first child in their late twenties. The same was true across the province. What is more, a greater proportion of women had their first birth after they turned thirty-five; from 1981 to 1995, the number of infants born to women in the thirty-five to thirty-nine age group rose from 1,768 to 5,645. For the first time in the century, women in the thirty to thirty-four age group were having more births than women aged fifteen to twenty-four.[78] The delay in marriage and first birth could be seen among men as well: British Columbian men on average spent more years single (36.8 years) than their counterparts in any other province except Quebec.[79] These reversals in what was nearly a century-long pattern of earlier-and-more nuptiality were, it has to be said, nothing short of revolutionary in that they were widespread and occurred in a relatively short period of time.

Puzzling questions emerge from some of these data. British Columbians as a whole witnessed a higher nuptiality rate than did most Canadians – and both the provincial and national rates were climbing.[80] Nevertheless, the

Figure 5.3

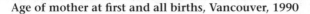

Age of mother at first and all births, Vancouver, 1990

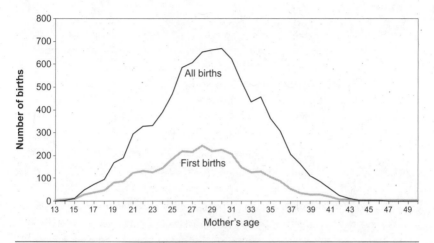

Source: City of Vancouver Planning Department, "The Vancouver Monitoring Program Information Update: Births and Deaths, 1941-1990" (December 1991), 4-6, City of Vancouver Archives, Vancouver, BC.

GFR rose only very slowly in the period to 1945. It must be the case that British Columbians were practising fertility limitation very aggressively indeed. As mentioned above, McInnis speculates that the mid-Victorian strategy of limiting births by delaying marriage was being abandoned in late nineteenth- and early twentieth-century Canada; his own evidence suggests that British Columbia led the way in this respect. A closer examination of nuptiality in British Columbia reveals more complexity.

Figure 4.1 shows the point at which the relationship between nuptiality and births ceased to be automatic. In the interwar years and right through the 1940s, the correlation was clear: as the incidence of marriage fell, so too did the CBR. What is even more striking is the close relationship between these two parallel trends and two other considerations: world events and British Columbia's economic performance.

Declining Marital Fertility in a Global Context

The two world wars had immediate yet outwardly contradictory effects on the crude marriage rate (CMR), shown in Table 5.4. From 1914 to 1918, the CMR was nearly cut in half, from just less than 10 per 1,000 population to 5.2. This fact no doubt reflects the impact of the war, but it is worth noting that British Columbia did not attract large numbers of high nuptiality, high fertility Eastern European immigrants as did the Prairies, so the potential for a falling nuptiality rate was already present. (Having said that, I add that

CMR

The crude marriage rate (CMR), like other "crude" measures, is simplicity itself. It measures marriages against total population per 1,000. Unlike the crude birth rate or the crude death rate, however, the CMR measures social behaviour. In other words, everyone who gets a birth gets a death, regardless of how they feel about it; not everyone chooses to marry, and there are a variety of alternatives to signing a marriage register.

$$CMR = \frac{\text{Marriages in year}}{\text{Population at mid-year}} \times 1,000$$

Age-specific data are more useful, as a great many people in the total population will be too young to be "at risk" of nuptiality. And, conceivably, if everyone were married, the rate would drop to nil the next year. For more precision, then, we have the general marriage rate, or GMR. This measures marital activity (typically by gender) against the population over fifteen years of age, like so:

$$GMR \text{ (Female)} = \frac{\text{Marriages}}{\text{Unmarried females aged 15+}} \times 1,000$$

BC continued to have leading-edge nuptiality rates even without the Eastern European factor commonly used to explain a rising rate nationally.)[81] The CMR recovered somewhat through the 1920s and '30s, but it returned to double digits only in 1940.[82] From 1940 to 1943, it averaged 11.2 per 1,000 population, falling to 9.0 and 9.8 in the last two years of the war. The socio-demographic context of the Great War – a large immediate enlistment (and thus removal) of adult males – was certainly significant in reducing the nuptiality rate in 1914-18, as were widespread female employment opportunities. Why did similar developments in 1939-40 produce not a reduction but an increase in the CMR?

The answer lies in the economic context. Down to 1912, the economy of British Columbia had been growing: the province's Edwardian "Indian summer" was marked by new settlement opportunities in farming districts and boom-times in the Vancouver housing market.[83] That kind of prosperity would not be seen again until well after the Second World War. But it did

Table 5.4

Crude marriage rates, BC and Canada, 1914-50

Year	Crude marriage rates BC	Canada	Year	Crude marriage rates BC	Canada	Year	Crude marriage rates BC	Canada
1914	9.5	–	1927	7.8	7.2	1939	9.9	9.2
1915	7.5	–	1928	7.7	7.5	1940	12.0	10.8
1916	6.9	–	1929	7.1	7.7	1941	9.8	10.6
1917	5.3	–	1930	6.9	7.0	1942	12.4	10.9
1918	5.2	–	1931	5.6	6.4	1943	10.4	9.4
1919	9.0	–	1932	5.1	5.9	1944	9.0	8.5
1920	9.0	–	1933	5.6	6.0	1945	9.8	9.0
1921	8.2	7.9	1934	6.6	6.8	1946	11.7	10.9
1922	6.9	7.2	1935	6.8	7.1	1947	11.4	10.1
1923	7.1	7.3	1936	7.3	7.4	1948	10.9	9.6
1924	7.0	7.1	1937	8.2	7.9	1949	10.2	9.2
1925	7.2	6.9	1938	7.9	7.9	1950	9.8	9.1
1926	7.3	7.0						

Sources: J.M. Macdonald, "Vital Statistics in British Columbia: An Historical Overview of 100 Years, 1891to 1990," *Vital Statistics Quarterly Digest* 4, 4 (June 1994): 25-26; F.H. Leacy, ed., *Historical Statistics of Canada,* 2nd ed. (Ottawa: Statistics Canada, 1983), B75-B81.

not last. There was a severe downturn, beginning with the crash of 1913 and continuing through the war, during which time "people began leaving Vancouver – if they could afford to." From 1912 to 1916, the population of the metropolis was reckoned to have fallen by as much as 20 percent to ninety-six thousand.[84] Despite some economic recovery in the 1920s, the Dirty Thirties more than cancelled out what gains were made so that, by 1932, low confidence in the economy was indicated by a CMR of 5.1 per 1,000, the lowest point in a generation-long trough.[85] Economic recovery thereafter was slow and faltering, finally taking off with the declaration of war and the creation of war-industry jobs. As employment rates recovered, a generation of men and women who had postponed marriage for economic reasons pushed their way to the head of the nuptial queue in the early '40s. The fact that most Canadian troops would not find themselves in combat until 1942 – three years into the war – is relevant too. The CMR peaked at 12.44 marriages just as the war in the Pacific was getting under way. Excepting 1912, when the rate reached 12.9 per 1,000, this was the high-water mark for the century. There was some slippage in 1943-45, but the rate returned to 11.73 in 1946 with demobilization. The CMR would bottom out at 6.71 per 1,000 in 1961, well before the sexual revolution got under way. By that time, however, the relevance of marriage – in a demographic sense – was no longer clear.

Around the time of the Korean War, marriage ceased to be the principal determining factor in the rate of births.[86] Down to the 1951 census, it is safe to say that a rise in the CMR was matched by a rise in the CBR. Suddenly, the old rule of thumb was obsolete: the change is so abrupt that it is difficult to resist calling it unprecedented. The rate of marriage was lower in 1951 than it had been in 1941, but the birth rate grew significantly over the same period, particularly in suburban areas of Vancouver.[87] Over the next ten years, a further steady fall in the rate of marriages occurred against a backdrop of an effectively unchanged rate of births. From 1961 to 1971, however, the marriage rate increased, from 6.71 to 9.33, and – remarkably – the CBR fell by about one-third. A great deal has been made of Quebec's fall in fertility, from an average of 6.37 children per ever-married woman in the female co-hort born before 1896 to 2.23 children per ever-married woman in the cohort born 1941-46 (which is below the Anglo-Canadian level of 2.35), but the BC figures are also outstanding. While the crude rate of marriage hovered between a high of 9.0 and a low of 7.6 per 1,000 population in the 1980s, the CBR continued to sink slowly. In the 1990s, the crude marriage rate slid again, finally dragging the CBR down further with it.[88]

In some measure, the continuing rise in the CBR against a slowing (if not stagnating) CMR reflects the fact that more couples were having more children. Another fact was illegitimacy. In British Columbia, the rate of illegitimacy increased dramatically in the mid-twentieth century, stabilizing to some extent in the post-war period. In Vancouver, the rate per 1,000 births leapt from 52 in 1943 to 96 in 1962. British Columbia as a whole led the country in illegitimacy rates from 1949 through to 1969.[89] It may have been the case that illegitimacy was under-reported in earlier years, but, insofar as the official statistics can be trusted, what stands out is the sharp increase in the rate from 1942 to 1945, when it rose from about 40 per 1,000 live births to nearly 60.[90] Official records also indicate that illegitimate births were more common among Aboriginal mothers than among their non-Aboriginal counterparts. If we set aside the incidences of Aboriginal illegitimacies, the rate among non-Aboriginals was about 45 per 1,000 in 1945. Even among this group, there was a significant rise in illegitimacy, and by all appearances this was a province-wide phenomenon.[91] But, according to conventional wisdom, it should not have been happening at this time. Although the sex ratio was closing, women were still substantially outnumbered by men in these years, so by all rights opportunities for marriage (and thus "legitimate" births) were greater in BC than in Eastern Canada. These data clearly complicate any simplistic description of gender and sexual relations during the ascendant years of middle-class pro-nuclear-family imagery in which *myth* became *Mrs.*[92] The close relationship between nuptiality and fertility was thus undermined in the mid-twentieth century. There is no reason to believe that that fissure has closed: the current rate of "out-of-wedlock" births is about one in five.[93]

Conclusion

In the context of comparable socio-economic orders, British Columbia should have shared in the nineteenth-century fertility transition. Given the high degrees of urbanization prior to the war, the limited opportunities for the family farm economy across most of British Columbia, the ubiquity of industrial wage-labour, and the relative prosperity of many of its middle- and upper-middle-class settlers from Britain and Canada, the province contained all the features conducive to lower fertility and few of the factors that led to higher fertility.[94]

The principal reason that the Henripin/Barman account of sharp fertility decline went unquestioned for so long is precisely because it makes sense. Intuitively, one feels that a fertility transition should have happened in late-nineteenth- and early twentieth-century British Columbia, and one is fearful of throwing out the babies with the bathwater. And, in point of fact, there *is* evidence of a fertility transition – one that was perhaps already completed by the time of Confederation. After that point, however, fertility moves upward into the new century. To be clear, this doesn't bring about a *high* fertility regime *per se*, but it *is* higher (and getting higher) than it was at Confederation and as we move closer to the Great War.

In the "short twentieth century" from 1914 to 1989, fertility in the Far West experiences incredible elasticity. The ramifications of interwar stagnation at a depressed level might be briefly considered. From 1914 to 1935, there was no need to add even one more hospital bed for maternity purposes. In the same period, were it not for interwar immigration, not one additional schoolroom could be justified. Insofar as consumption is driven by the birth rate, purchases of homes, high chairs, bunk beds, and hockey skates would be flat. At the end of the period (just as at the start), there was a cohort of no more than 10,500 BC-born British Columbians who would, in lockstep, fill places in the life-course vacated the year before. This is a generation about whom historians of BC know little, in part because of the second direction fertility took in the mid-century: sharply upward from 1940 to 1956.

The factors that might be invoked to explain these fluctuations do not necessarily behave as we might expect them to. Nuptiality sags and then skyrockets, but it is not as relevant to fertility as it once was. Sex ratios even out, but fertility increases regardless. The pressures to marry young are far less great in the 1940s and 1950s than they were in the nineteenth century, but teen pregnancies increase phenomenally in the post-war years, fuelling a baby boom that rumbles along for nearly two decades.

Nothing, however, is as astounding about the baby boom phase as the speed with which it recedes. The downturn that begins in 1957 is, to date, irreversible, and it signifies a revolutionary change in human fertility behaviour, one that serves to reinforce British Columbia's dependence on immigrants and the consequent opportunity or need to reinvent the culture of the community on a generational basis. Although we should not lose sight of the place of fertility in the province's history, it is to the "Accession of Strangers" that we must now turn our attention.

6
Strangers in Paradise: Immigration and the Experience of Diversity

As the settler-era population grew and became more urban, it simultaneously became more diverse. A contemporary observed, on the eve of the First World War, "One of the noticeable features of the Pacific province is the cosmopolitan character of its inhabitants. Chinese, Japanese, Hindoos [sic], native Siwashes [sic], English immigrants and Canadian-bred citizens, constitute the chief elements in this confusion of races."[1] This revolution in the complexion of the province's population – not a century earlier, it had been almost entirely populated by indigenous peoples – was made possible by the steam technology that provides a backdrop to the colonization of the region. Coal-fired, steam-powered sea travel to the region was one thing, but the new railway – along with increased and improved shipping to Burrard Inlet and Victoria after 1886 – enabled the arrival of immigrants from new sources in southern Europe and the Scandinavian countries as well as Japan and India. Italians appeared in the Kootenays, Danes at Cape Scott, Austro-Hungarians around Kamloops, and Greeks in Vancouver; Sikhs moved from the Punjab to the mill-towns of the Lower Mainland and the Interior; Norwegians took to the fjords on the central coast; and Finns worked the coalmines of Ladysmith and then established a utopian fishing community on Malcolm Island. Although there were clusters, evidence reveals mixing: the strike committee at the Wellington coalmines in 1891 consisted of "one German, one Italian, one Belgian ... and one Russian Finn."[2] In an age of nation-states, nationalities, and a growing concern for racial categories, accounts of ethnic diversity were in fact comments on the absence of homogeneity. British Columbia was distinctive in the British Empire and North America in that its mix of peoples was unique.

The twentieth century witnessed a lull in immigration followed by an enthusiastic resurgence in the period after the Second World War. Initially, this occurred when fertility rates were both substantial and on the ascent. Even under those circumstances, British Columbia's need for additional labour in its factories, offices, and mines was greater than its local supply.

In an age of rising consumerism, moreover, immigration now also represented additional *demand*. There was, in this period, some resumption of British immigration, and additional arrivals came from Western Europe as a whole, but the larger story in the twentieth century is one of reorientation away from the Atlantic world to the Pacific Rim.

That immigration played a primary role in the demography of colonial and provincial British Columbia is without dispute. Benjamin Franklin's explanation for colonial growth two hundred years ago could be pressed into service once more: "This quick Increase is owing not so much to natural Generation, as to the Accession of Strangers."[3] Nevertheless, the character and impact of immigration invite numerous questions and tests. Are immigrants more or less fertile than locals?[4] What is their life expectancy and how does it impact provincial averages? Do newcomers consistently belong mostly to the age cohorts of, say, twenty- to twenty-nine-year-olds? Questions such as these demand separate study. What is introduced in this chapter is a consideration of immigrant sources, some questions regarding what might be called the *Asianizing* of British Columbia's demography, and the manifestation of a community of "Strangers" in rates of exogamy in the years before the Great War.

Immigration by Numbers

An examination of countries of origin as indicated to the census enumerators is an exercise in difficulties. First, the census does not reveal the age at which foreigners emigrated from their homeland, a great frustration to any analysis of immigrant fertility rates. Second, national boundaries and identities change, the foremost example of which is the disintegration of Hapsburg Austro-Hungary after the Great War, raising an obstacle to longitudinal studies of emigrant origins. As well, people lie, especially to officials during periods of international tension. Enumerators themselves may have a limited grasp of world geography, and if they were typical of their contemporaries through much of British Columbian colonial and provincial history, they may have seen the human world through the lens of racism, nativism, and bigotry. What we find in reports on immigration is, therefore, never ironclad.

Cautions on board, the leading patterns and changes over the fifty years before 1921 include a declining proportion of Chinese and other Asian peoples from roughly a fifth of the total provincial population when the Canadian Pacific Railway was being built to barely one in twenty by the Great War.[5] We also see a rising proportion that was *Canadian*, though the Aboriginal share of that number was simultaneously falling. As the Canadian – and especially the British Columbian – segment grew from about 42 percent in 1881 to more than 56 percent in 1911, the British share at the start of the

Edwardian era fell to just over 20 percent. Americans and continental Europeans in 1911 comprised roughly 8 percent apiece, although they both fell to around 5 percent following the war. By 1921 the community was more British than it had been in the early days of the twentieth century: nearly 30 percent hailed from the British Isles. It was also proportionately less Canadian, and only 27 percent of the population was British Columbia-born.[6] So, though the pre-war years are often understood as a period of strong British imperial connections, they in fact witnessed a generation of Canadianization that was followed by a return to British influence. To be sure, no matter how Canadian BC was becoming, the province stood apart from all others in terms of non-European diversity; moreover, it increasingly stood apart from the rest of Western Canada, which was much more European than British.

Table 6.1 shows how the immigrant complexion of the province has changed since the Depression. In each successive decade, the share from Britain, its colonies, and its former colonies has declined as a proportion. So too has the share from the United States, which peaked as a proportion of the provincial population in the 1920s, despite renewed movement across the forty-ninth parallel in the 1960s. Continental European immigration increased in the late twentieth century, a fact that has been overshadowed by the more widely acknowledged Asian immigration.

British Columbia has become only more attractive for immigrants since 1945. Ten percent of all immigrants to Canada made their way to BC in the

Table 6.1

Birthplaces of non-Aboriginal British Columbians, 1931-2001

	Birthplace								
	Canada		Britain & empire		Asia		Other Europe		US	
	(000s)	(%)	(000s)	(%)	(000s)	(%)	(000s)	(%)	(000s)	(%)
1931	352	52.6	188	28.0	38	5.3	59	8.8	34	5.2
1941	490	61.8	181	22.8	24	3.0	62	7.8	36	4.5
1951	798	70.0	193	17.0	15	1.3	89	7.8	42	3.7
1961	1,167	73.4	198	12.4	18	1.2	162	10.2	43	2.7
1971	1,635	76.7	187	8.8	42	2.0	183	8.6	58	2.7
1981	2,208	79.0	188	6.7	134	4.8	201	7.2	63	2.3
1991	2,365	75.6	178	5.8	256	8.4	195	6.4	54	1.8
2001	2,652	74.4	141	4.0	507	14.2	211	6.0	54	1.5

Note: Due to rounding, percentages do not total 100.
Sources: Statistics Canada, *Profile of Citizenship, Birthplace, for Designated Places, 2001 Census,* Catalogue no. 95F0489XCB2001008, 2001; Jean Barman, "A British Columbian View of Regions," *Acadiensis* 35, 2 (Spring/Printemps 2006): 144-56.

1950s, rising to 16 percent in the 1970s, and holding steady at around 14 percent through the remainder of the century. In 1991, the province's share of immigrants who had arrived between 1946 and 1960 was slightly greater than that of all three Prairie provinces (though less than a quarter that of Ontario). In the same year, it was estimated that roughly 1 in every 7.5 immigrants who arrived in Canada between 1981 and 1991 resided in BC.[7] These rates intensify in Vancouver, where 30 percent of the city's population in 1991 was comprised of immigrants (a third of whom had arrived in the period 1981-91 alone), a proportion that comes second only to Toronto (at 38 percent) and well ahead of third-place Hamilton (at 23.5 percent). Of all the major centres in Canada, Vancouver alone included an ethnic group that was neither English nor French – the Chinese – whose share of population passed into double digits.[8] This is manifest in a variety of ways but perhaps most publicly in terms of language: in 1996, 75 percent of British Columbians claimed English as their mother tongue (compared to 80 percent in Alberta), and 1.4 percent claimed French (nearly 2 percent in Alberta), but 22 percent of British Columbians spoke a "non-official" language at home (compared to 16 percent in Alberta).[9] Nearly 7 percent of British Columbians spoke "Chinese" (mostly Cantonese) at home, compared to 3 percent in Ontario; more than 2.6 percent spoke Punjabi, compared to less than 1 percent in Ontario. But that Asianizing process is largely contained to Vancouver and its suburbs: the province-wide figures for 2001 shown in Table 6.1 smooth over diverse patterns of distribution while highlighting the extent to which the province is a far less *British* British Columbia than it once was. Continental Europeans also make up a shrinking share, although the size of the German-speaking population is easily underestimated: British Columbia has the second-largest German-speaking community in the country, representing 2.4 percent of the population in 1996 as compared with Ontario's figure of 1.5 percent.[10]

British Columbia is often held out in Canada as an attractive place to which to move, not least because of the mild climate on the coast. In fact, some British Columbians are prepared to leave what the Provincial Government calls "the best place on earth."[11] In the 1990s, for example, twelve of twenty-eight regional districts across the province experienced either negligible growth from migration or a net loss to other parts of Canada. The districts most hard hit by net losses lay outside of the southwest corner of the province and the Okanagan.[12] This behaviour has not abated: the incidence of emigration has increased steadily if not spectacularly since the late 1970s.[13] The phenomenon of out-migration was particularly strong among people under the age of twenty-four. The province became a net beneficiary of migration in 2002, not because of an end to youthful movement to Alberta, or wherever else the jobs may be, but because of an aggressively continuing rise in arrivals among the forty-five- to sixty-four-year-old cohort and those over sixty-five.[14] Out-migration from the province is largely limited to residents who were not born in the West beyond the West: they are nearly five times as likely to move away than British Columbians who were born in the province. Having said that, I add that British Columbia's in-migrants demonstrate less mobility than in-migrants in any other province (which is to say that Canadians who relocate to BC stay in BC, whereas Canadians who move to Ontario very often have second thoughts). A booster would, at this point, happily intone "The Last Best West." Not entirely true, however. Locally born British Columbians demonstrate a propensity to leave their home province that is even with the national average; the rate is, however, half that of abandonment-prone Albertans and about a third the probability of desertion of their home provinces by Manitobans and Saskatchewanians.[15] Given the concentration of media in Vancouver, it is not surprising that the public's impression is one of generalized expansion, but the fact is that British Columbia's growth is tempered by out-migration.

A photograph of British Columbia's population at any time would thus reveal unique qualities associated with immigration and migration. But it is in the demographic processes stimulated by immigration that the most interesting experiences are to be found. One is considered here: the phenomenon of demography in the choice of marriage partners.

Endogamy and Exogamy

Take Richard McBride. Premier from 1903 to 1915, "The People's Dick" was born in New Westminster and was thus the first native British Columbian to achieve the province's highest elected office. McBride was the son of an Orange father and a Catholic mother. Both parents were, evidently, committed to their respective beliefs, though not strongly to the observance of prejudicial strictures. Could either afford to be choosy? Was that BC's gift to Richard McBride – a homeland in which tolerance and unconventional unions were by-products of making the best of a bad demographic situation? Perhaps. But McBride was not alone, and that is what raises his story above the trivial. Exogamy spread across the territory from early and promising beginnings around fur trade posts through to the war, by which time its parameters had shifted while its practice had grown.

Marital *endogamy* and *exogamy* refer to the practice of choosing marriage partners, respectively, within or without one's own national, ethnic, racial, or religious group. Arguably, it was in the nineteenth century that these options first became an issue for much of humanity. Exogamy was a phenomenon associated with the Age of Imperialism and the Age of Steam, both of which encouraged, facilitated, and indeed depended upon the movement of diverse peoples around the globe. By the second half of the nineteenth century, goldfields and wheat fields alike in the North American west were drawing in a far more cosmopolitan population. The *possibility*, if not the *probability,* of a rise in the number and the variety of exogamous unions thereby increased.

If geography no longer formed the barrier to exogamy that it once did, culture was endogamy's Continental Divide. One quantifiable aspect of beliefs and values is religious identity as reported in censuses and marriage records. The provincial Registrar-General found inter-denominational marriage so noteworthy that, for a time, he tabulated its occurrence in his annual reports. In 1878, for example, he found that nearly one-third of all marriages in BC in that year took place between men and women of different creeds. Now, admittedly the gulf between Presbyterian and Methodist is hardly a chasm, even in the Victorian era, but it still attracted comment.[16] Moreover, of thirty-eight inter-denominational marriages recorded in 1878, eleven involved Roman Catholic brides taking Protestant grooms, and six more saw Catholic men wed Protestant women in the same year. In an age of strident Orangeism elsewhere in Canada – not to mention in Britain – these figures are, as the Registrar coolly put it, "not uninteresting." And the practice did not soon let up. In 1882 more than 40 percent of all registered marriages were inter-denominational; of those, 3 percent involved Catholic men marrying Protestant women and 12 percent, Catholic women marrying Protestant men. That is to say, one-third of all inter-denominational marriages in 1882 took place between a Catholic and a non-Catholic.[17]

This is worth dwelling on. The social constipation one detects in turn-of-the-century newspapers on topics such as race, drink, sports, gender, and ideology belies the diversity of experience and choices in late Victorian and Edwardian British Columbia. The contemporary discourse may well have hinged on fear of the "Other," but practice demonstrates something well beyond grudging tolerance. In the pre-war era, English, American, and British Columbian-born women, for example, tended to be more exogamous than their male counterparts. In addition, it has been estimated that, in 1881 and 1891, the proportion of the male non-Aboriginal rural population that was married to Native women was one in ten and one in twenty respectively.[18] One study of national incidences of exogamy based on ethno-religious origins reveals that fewer than 10 percent of male Canadians in 1871 married outside of their identity group.[19] More so than anywhere else in Canada, if not in the whole British Empire, in British Columbia, the possibilities of dizzying alternative paradigms rose to the surface like bubbles in a Kootenay hot spring.

Interracial marriages are a part of this story, especially between European males and First Nations women. Relationships of these kinds decreased in number through the nineteenth century as settler society physically, economically, and politically marginalized the Natives. Interracial marriage shows up in late nineteenth-century mission and census records – there were some fifteen hundred mixed-race households in the 1880s and '90s – and it is usually set within the context of the gold rush (or subsequent remote resource-extraction industries) and rural life, of which I offer two regional examples.[20] In the Yale Census District in 1881, there were twenty-two Native women married to non-Aboriginal men, a large number of whom were clustered in and around the Cariboo Wagon Road community of Cache Creek. If we extrapolate from the age of the eldest co-resident child, marriage or at least cohabitation began for these women at an average age of about seventeen. An illustration might be made of Cache Creek rancher Charles Augustus Semlin, who became premier of the province in 1898. Apparently, his Native wife was thirty-two at the time of the 1881 census, and her oldest co-resident child was sixteen, suggesting an age at marriage of fifteen or sixteen years.[21] The census data on this community also reveals that half of these interracial marriages began in the gold rush era (the Semlins would have begun living together around 1865) and the other half in the late 1870s to 1880. A north coast fishing village reveals a trend separate from the gold rushes. At Kincolith, one in five marriages performed at the Indian Mission between 1871 and 1890 involved European males and Aboriginal women. One more involved a "mixed-race" male and an Aboriginal woman; another took place between an Aboriginal man and a "half-breed" woman. One must be careful with these data, as representation of racial heritage was and is a vexed problem. Nevertheless, on the face of it, it would seem that the missions and the new industrial economic order on the north coast facilitated interracial marriages in these years.

Although Native and newcomer intermarriage was widespread, these unions had limited demographic impact, especially as they became increasingly stigmatized in an age marked by the misapplication of Darwinian theory. As Jean Barman explains, "Racial boundaries hardened as numbers of newcomers grew, particularly in urban areas. Class considerations compounded the force of race. As everyday behaviour became more public, and social status more dependent upon externalized expectations of behaviour into which an Aboriginal wife simply did not fit, so a number of men with political or social pretensions abandoned their Aboriginal wives and sometimes also their children."[22] Intermarriage continued, but the demographic possibilities represented by a Native community with a slight female surplus and a newcomer population with an excess of males were closed off by new cultural prejudices.[23] In the 1890s, missionaries complained that "there are numbers of White men and Indian women who are living in unlawful concubinage, throughout the Province."[24] Control over the process of marriage and thus the contractual aspects of property ownership and inheritance were at stake, at least so far as organized religion and the state were concerned.[25] Marriages that were not "solemnized in Christian form" were regarded as invalid by the provincial courts, a verdict that weighed heavily against the offspring of Native-newcomer cohabitations who might find themselves

declared, as a corollary, illegitimate.[26] It also weighed against widows especially, one-half of whose property the Crown claimed when their legally
defined "bastards" died.[27] Insofar as marriage constitutes a survival strategy
for individuals and their offspring, marriage *à la façon du pays* between Aboriginals and non-Aboriginals was increasingly turned into a high-risk
business.[28]

Intermarriage between whites and Asians was a non-starter. Scant few
Asian women immigrated to Canada in the nineteenth century, and the
small number who did were likely to arrive as wives or concubines of established Asian settlers, so the likelihood of an Asian woman marrying a non-
Asian man was very slim. Given the under-representation of Euro-Canadian
women in the population as a whole and the inferior economic and social
position of most Asian males in the province, marriages between white
women and Chinese men were just as improbable. Under these circumstances, the barrier of racial antipathy becomes redundant. Marriage did,
however, take place between at least a handful of Chinese men and Aboriginal women. Chow Bing Yit, a forty-niner who made his way to the Fraser
River gold rush and a commercial career in Yale, married a daughter of
Tsah'kwah'lait'sa, a leading figure among the Chilliwack. This integration
of Asian and Amerindian households continued through two subsequent
generations in the Fraser Canyon and elsewhere.[29] The 1881 census found
a community of Chinese men in or near Osoyoos, three of whom were married to (or at least co-habiting with) Native women. To judge from the ages
of their children, the eldest of whom was four, these connections had been
forged in the 1870s.[30] Notwithstanding the fecundity of Ah Lem and Lucy
of Osoyoos, who had six children in less than eleven years, or that of Chow
Bing Yit, his wife, and their heirs, Asian-Aboriginal marriages of this kind
did not have much demographic significance overall.

Within the white community before the Great War, however, the degree
of *international* exogamy is remarkable. And this is no small thing. The concept of the "Other" was not monopolized by sinophobes: these were the
years of hardening national stereotypes in Europe. As Peter Ward points out,
two out of three men and women in contemporary Ontario went to the altar
with "someone from their own community," by which he means their own
town.[31] Nonetheless, data from BC's 1911 *Who's Who* and from church marriage records around the province almost all point in the same direction: in
the period between Confederation and 1914, men and women in British
Columbia took spouses from national backgrounds other than their own.[32]
From 1870 to 1880, the clergy at St. Andrew's Presbyterian Church in Victoria
recorded the country of birth for both partners in 119 marriages: only 43
were between co-nationals (see Tables 6.2 and 6.3). If we add into that
number the English-Scottish and Welsh-English unions, then the total rises
only to 55, roughly half. To put it the other way, 53 percent of the weddings

Table 6.2

Endogamous and exogamous marriages, Victoria Presbyterian, 1870-80

Year	Endogamous marriages		Exogamous marriages	
	Number	(%)	Number	(%)
1870	1	25	3	75
1871	6	56	5	44
1872	8	57	6	43
1873	2	15	11	85
1874	6	35	11	65
1875	1	14	6	86
1876	3	21	11	79
1877	4	50	4	50
1878	3	43	4	57
1879	5	42	7	58
1880	4	33	8	67

Source: Birth, Marriage and Baptismal Records, St. Andrew's Presbyterian Church (Victoria) fonds, Add Mss 1507, BC Archives, Victoria, BC.

Table 6.3

Marriages by birthplace and sex, Victoria Presbyterian, 1870-80

	Scotland		England		Ireland		USA		Germany		BC		Canada	
	M	F	M	F	M	F	M	F	M	F	M	F	M	F
Endogamous	6	6	10	10	3	3	11	11	3	3	1	1	9	9
Exogamous	21	3	10	15	5	3	12	15	8	2	2	18	9	9

Source: Birth, Marriage and Baptismal Records, St. Andrew's Presbyterian Church (Victoria) fonds, Add Mss 1507, BC Archives, Victoria, BC.

involved a man and a woman from different countries. These included a Dane who married an Australian, a Hawaiian who wedded a German, and a Swede who took the hand of an Ontarian. In this sense, Victoria's presbytery was a heterosexual meeting place of nations and cultures that defied an era of amplified nationalism.

Exogamy crept upward in Kamloops, too, as the century ended and opportunities increased. Endogamy survived in some quarters: in the censuses of 1881 and 1891, Ontarians living on or near the banks of the Thompson Rivers were married to Ontarians, English to English, and so on. The exception to this nineteenth-century rule were women born in British Columbia, a large proportion of whom were either Native or had some Native ancestry.[33] By 1901 there was widespread disregard for national boundaries in marriage, and all of Kamloops' BC-born married women had husbands born elsewhere. Groups that exhibited the highest degree of endogamy on the plateau during the Edwardian period include the English (eleven couples), Ontarians (eighteen couples), and Nova Scotians (nine couples). But Ontarians also took to twentieth-century exogamy: of thirty-nine married Ontarian women in Kamloops in 1901, twenty-one had married non-Ontarians. Although the sample is small, it is worth noting that, of nine married American women, seven married exogamously.

International exogamy, like religious exogamy, was a feature of life in western North America but perhaps more so in the regions bounding the Pacific, from California to Alaska. The significance of these exogamous bonds must not be missed: the cosmopolitan pluralistic qualities of the population as a whole were experienced at the household level and not simply from neighbourhood to neighbourhood. Historical geographer Cole Harris observes that exogamy was part of the abandonment of something old – marital parochialness, if you will – and the adoption of something new, a frontier mentality in which categories shifted and modified, producing something like a British Columbian identity. It was, of course, within the context of these loosened cultural boundaries that concerns about racial identity sank deep roots. If anti-Protestant feeling among Catholics (and vice versa) was melting away, how strong would the ramparts of race prove to be? Was the project of a white man's province at risk? Euro-British Columbian alarmists thought so and built the barricades of new prejudices on the ruins of the old.

Canadianizing and Asianizing BC
The role immigration plays in British Columbia's growth during the twentieth century is undeniably important. But it is often overstated, certainly in the sense that immigration automatically denotes the arrival of foreigners. It may well be that, compared to the Prairie provinces, British Columbia was consistently more "cosmopolitan," but some of that heterogeneity was purely Canadian.[34]

Hundreds of thousands arrived in British Columbia from other countries throughout the twentieth century, but after the Second World War more people arrived from other parts of Canada. In 1941 the number of British Columbians born elsewhere in Canada passed the number who were born in Britain and the rest of the empire; ten years later, there were more transmontagne Canadians in the province than all other newcomer groups combined. The Canadians held on to this lead, although their share never surpassed the 1951 peak of nearly 32 percent of the total BC population. In real terms, however, the Canadians climbed from fewer than 200,000 in 1941 to nearly 1 million by the end of the century.[35] Of their number, as can be seen in Table 6.4, the greatest influx before 1931 came from Ontario; thereafter, the number of Prairie migrants dwarfed all migration from Ontario, Quebec, or the Atlantic provinces. What is less striking but perhaps

Table 6.4

Canadian migrants to BC, 1881-1996

	Birthplace							
	Atlantic		Quebec		Ontario		Prairies	
Year	(#)	(%)	(#)	(%)	(#)	(%)	(#)	(%)
1881	784	28	396	14	1,572	56	38	1
1891	5,395	25	2,567	12	11,658	57	957	5
1901	9,575	24	4,329	11	23,642	58	3,194	8
1911	18,569	22	7,496	9	45,518	54	13,097	15
1921	19,235	18	8,240	8	50,361	47	30,117	28
1931	20,853	15	9,226	6	54,486	38	57,970	41
1941	19,639	10	9,627	4	54,160	27	115,627	58
1951	24,906	7	14,968	4	69,818	19	249,608	69
1961	28,366	6	17,704	4	76,016	17	323,025	73
1971	41,275	7	31,465	5	107,295	17	451,760	72
1981	58,160	7	52,640	6	173,345	21	542,940	66
1996	78,250	8	71,715	7	245,095	25	596,480	60

Note: Due to rounding, percentages do not total 100.
Sources: Statistics Canada, "Historical Statistics, Residence and Birth Places of Native-Born Internal Migrants, Natural Increase and Net Migration, Every 10 Years (Persons)," CANSIM table 075-0023; Statistics Canada, *The 1999 Canada Year Book* (Ottawa: Ministry of Industry, 1998), 90.

just as significant is the persistent proportional relationship between migration from regions east of Manitoba. Down to the 1970s, migration from the Maritimes to BC was roughly half the size of the wave from Ontario and roughly double the traffic from Quebec. Only in the 1960s and 1970s did Quebec and Ontario – with vastly larger populations than the four Atlantic provinces combined – begin to send greater shares. To put it another way, Maritimers have been disproportionately represented on the west coast compared to Ontarians and immensely so compared to the Québécois. In the 1980s, the greatest share of British Columbians born in other provinces came from Alberta. The magnitude of this migration is worth underlining: roughly speaking, one in ten Albertans is to be found in BC.[36] First Nations peoples (most of whom are, of course, from British Columbia) improved their share too, but the greatest increase came among the Canadians born outside of BC. Despite what Eastern Canadians might think, BC is the most Canadian of all provinces, in that it contains the greatest representation from the other parts of the country. The traffic is largely one-way: precious few British Columbians deign to move to Central Canada, let alone the Maritimes.[37]

Albertans and other Canadians settled across the province; the distribution of Asian immigrants over the last hundred years or so was more clustered. Japanese fishermen became a mainstay of Steveston's salmon-packing industry early in the twentieth century, and other Japanese sought work in the mines at Cumberland. In 1907 alone – the year of the Anti-Asian Riots in Vancouver – there were more than 5,000 Japanese immigrants, rising to 15,006 in 1921. By 1941 there were reckoned to be nearly 22,000 Canadians of Japanese ancestry, a number that surpassed the Chinese population. The internment of Japanese Canadians during the Second World War (which included removal of nearly 2,000 to camps on the prairies) disturbed the emerging pattern of Japanese settlement. The coastal presence of the Japanese was sharply diminished, but after the war, a good number of internees chose to hang on in the Slocan and Kootenays, for example, places to which they had been forcibly moved but where they found some degree of welcome. By 1951 the majority of Japanese British Columbians lived in rural areas, a dramatic change that took place in a very short time.[38]

The Chinese, of course, have long been the largest and most visible minority in the province. In 1884 they constituted nearly a quarter of the population and were nearly as numerous as the whites, their numbers enormously swollen by the need for cheap railway construction labour. For a time, much of this population was spread throughout the Interior, along the CPR right-of-way. This phenomenon produced several "Chinatowns" and left a trail of Chinese cemeteries from Revelstoke west through the Fraser Canyon but most notably in Kamloops and Ashcroft. The massive contribution made to the local economy by cheap Chinese labour was not enough to insulate the newcomers from Euro-Canadian hostility. The period from 1885 on would see repeated efforts on the part of Victoria and Ottawa to reduce if not stop Chinese immigration. The politically dominant Euro-Canadian community regarded the potential of an Asianized demography with fear and active hostility. This sprang from social Darwinist and outright racist belief systems and was part and parcel of a British imperialist outlook on the world in the Victorian and Edwardian years. The Chinese, however, resisted sanctions and increased their numbers by immigration until the 1920s.[39] A renewal of immigration from China would not begin in earnest until the 1980s. As the new millennium gets under way, the Chinese are a numerically substantial (and growing) share of the provincial population.

The process of Asianizing the population, then, has taken place very unevenly. The initial wave of Asian immigration (that is, c. 1858 to 1923) was more substantial and of greater duration than what has occurred since the middle of the twentieth century. Nevertheless, these first waves were limited by government policies and the force of racism.[40] Port cities such as New Westminster, Victoria, and Nanaimo-Wellington received large infusions, but it was in the Interior gold rush communities that the largest numbers of Chinese were to be found in the years before the building of the CPR. Nodes of Chinese settlement survived in the Interior after the 1860s gold rush, in

Hope and Yale, in Lytton, Lillooet, and Clinton, and in the heart of Gim Shan – "Gold Mountain."[41] One author has claimed that "by 1877 the Cariboo was virtually a Chinese province, with over 50 percent more Chinese than white miners (1510 versus 949)."[42] The locus of this community was Quesnel Forks, where the Chinese population was – in real numbers – smaller than that of Nanaimo or Victoria; along with the much reduced Barkerville and Quesnelmouth, Quesnel Forks could describe itself as mainly Chinese until the 1890s. In point of fact, Buddhism was, at 34.5 percent, the most popular declared religion in the southern Interior in 1881.[43] From the gold rush on, there was a migration out of the Interior and into the cities of the southwest where, joined by new arrivals from across the Pacific, the urban Chinese found themselves housed in enclaves by a combination of city ordinances and an instinct for community survival. This meant that the impact of the Chinese community was felt mostly in a few centres and not evenly across the province. In 1880 there were more than 1,500 residents in Victoria's Chinatown, rising to nearly 3,000 in 1901 and 3,458 in 1911.[44] In 1901 the Chinatowns in Nanaimo and Kamloops contained 503 and 189 Chinese residents respectively; these small real numbers were proportionately very large, as in Kamloops one in ten of the population was Chinese, not much less than in Victoria.[45] By 1941 Nanaimo and Kamloops were joined by only a handful of small cities – Vernon, Nelson, Port Alberni, and Duncan – on the list of communities with significant Chinese populations.[46] At the metropolitan end of the scale, Victoria's Chinese ghetto held a slight edge through the Edwardian era, but Vancouver's overtook it in 1911 with a population of just over thirty-five hundred.[47] Due to grotesque sex ratios, these urban Chinese populations grew almost exclusively through immigration until the 1920s, at which time immigration was stopped and growth was necessarily thrust back on natural processes and the occasional illegal arrival.[48] Although the Vancouver and Victoria Chinatowns survive – as David Chuen-yan Lai points out, largely on the strength of "Chi-eppies" (Chinese elderly poor people) and "Chi-lippies" (Chinese low-income people) – not one of the other "first wave" nodes has done so.[49] Rooted Chinese populations are to be found in virtually every community of modest size, but they long ago entered into the larger mix beyond the gates of the enclave. This is exemplified by the political career of Kamloopsian Peter Wing, who served as mayor of the city from 1966 to 1971 despite the absence of a geographically coherent Chinese voting base.

Immigration from India and Japan follows a similar pattern. The sudden boom in labour demand at the end of the nineteenth century was driven by Euro-Canadian capitalists who could not find a sufficiently large and reliably pliant and cheap workforce in their own communities. Asian workers met the crying need for an industrial proletariat in the province's coalmines, lumbermills, and fisheries. Indian and Japanese immigrants were unlike Chinese settlers in that they tended toward specialization in distinct industrial sectors, though not always in close proximity to one another. Initially, all three national groups displayed dreadful sex ratios (by 1903 only 0.3 percent of the Indian population was made up of adult women), although the Japanese were able to wear down the discrepancy and to build more long-term households as a result.[50] Confronted with barriers to further immigration (such as the "continuous journey" provision that disingenuously permitted arrivals from anywhere on the globe, providing no stops were made along the way), South Asian immigration in particular stagnated from 1914 to the 1950s.

In the years after the Second World War to the 1970s, it looked as though the Asian population – Chinese, Japanese, and Sikh – was very much in decline. The various restrictions on immigration and the Japanese expulsion from the coast (which also entailed "repatriation" to Japan of some four thousand Canadians of Japanese ancestry) combined to halve the real numbers between 1931 and 1951. Recovery began slowly in 1951 (when the census shows the share of Chinese immigrants, for example, who were not children or wives of established Chinese Canadians leaping from 14 percent to 43 percent) and continued down to 1971.[51] But, as the numbers trebled during this second wave of immigration, the share of the Asian population continued to shrink. Although the provincial population was 7.3 percent Asian in 1931, it was a mere 3.5 percent in 1971.[52] Soon thereafter, Toronto's Chinatown surpassed that of Vancouver in size.[53] (Is it cynical to suggest that part of the appeal of multiculturalism in the 1970s and early '80s lay in the fact that there was less proportional ethnic diversity than at just about any time over the previous hundred years?)

It is important to note that during the years between the Second World War and Expo 86, much of the growth in the Asian communities slipped from the Chinese to the Sikhs. Immigration from the subcontinent renewed in the 1950s under the auspices of Ottawa's "sponsorship" immigration policy, achieved some newfound vigour in the early 1960s, but gained real momentum in the 1970s and stabilized thereafter.[54] Although Indian and Pakistani arrivals continue to bolster the part of the population that is neither Aboriginal, European, nor North American, they have since been overshadowed by the return of Chinese immigration.

In the 1980s and 1990s, the third wave of Chinese newcomers arrived. These several waves are, in retrospect, distinguished by source demography and by motivations. Although the first wave was made up mostly of poor Guangdonese peasants following the Pacific Rim gold and rail booms of the nineteenth and early twentieth centuries, the mid-twentieth-century wave was chiefly about family reunification and sponsored immigration that occurred against a backdrop of sequential tightening and slight liberalizing of legislative regulation. The third wave for the first time drew heavily (though not exclusively) upon a population with a very different socio-economic status and was actively recruited – not by twentieth-century Onderdonks but by a federal and provincial state eager to take advantage of changing circumstances in South Asia. Between 1981 and 1991, nearly two-thirds of BC's immigrants came from Asia.

The period between 1985 and 1997 witnessed the sharpest increase in immigration for decades. At the start, there were hardly more than 12,000 new arrivals; a dozen years later, this had more than quadrupled to 53,235 in a year. This was not necessarily foreseen in 1981, when there were only 96,910 British Columbians of Chinese ancestry in the province, nearly 84,000 of whom lived in Vancouver.[55] By 2001, the greatest number of these new British Columbians (39 percent of the provincial immigrant stream) were from the People's Republic of China, Taiwan, and Hong Kong, in that order. Add on recent immigration from India, the Philippines, and South Korea, and the total from Asia jumps to 63 percent.[56] In real numbers, this is very nearly three times the births in the province in the same year. The current Chinese population in British Columbia – most of which is situated in the Greater Vancouver area – numbers more than 350,000, or one in six of the metro population. At the current rate, the number of Asian immigrants in the population will double to 860,000 by 2018.

This growth will result in a more "Asian" population. It is not merely a numbers game. Although it is true to say that the late twentieth-century waves of immigrants from Asia did not cluster in enclaves like "Chinatown" or "Little Tokyo," as was the case for the first wave of Asian newcomers, nor has the second wave demonstrated an even dispersal across the province. Fewer than 10 percent of new Chinese immigrants find themselves living outside of metro Vancouver, and the greatest number there are clustered in Richmond.[57] This is hardly a Chinatown in the pre-millennial sense, but it is definitely a critical mass, one that sustains an array of commercial and cultural services that cannot be found elsewhere in BC. Likewise, the Indo-Canadian community, though more evenly distributed around the province, is not ubiquitous. But dispersal is no longer the principal element in cultural transformation arising from demographic change. Market capitalism, which generates and tailors its services to suit demand, reflects (and, yes, moulds) the tastes of an evolving community. To that end, chain-retailers across the province stock products that announce the tastes of the changing metropolis. As well, Vancouver's unchallenged position as the centre of media concentration in the province ensures the Asianizing of journalism and entertainment. In this regard, the province – once conceived as a bulwark against Asian populations – has been and will continue to be re-imagined.

Conclusion

What has the last century or so of immigration taught us on this subject?

First, that "identity politics" are historically less about personal choice than about bureaucratic impulses. Racial and national categories simplified the census takers' task of counting newcomers, just as the Indian Act had the effect of counting in and counting out various British Columbians of mixed ancestry. Nativity – place of birth – was used as a blunt tool with which to assign racial identities and assumptions about the kinds of people who were coming to this part of Canada.

We also learn that, in terms of sources of immigration, the surest paths are soon abandoned. Latin America, the Caribbean, and Africa have not yet begun in earnest to provide this province with settlers. The very large country to our south might at any time open the vents, producing a gale of American immigrants. Influences closer to home, too, are bound to have an impact on this process: Aboriginal numbers have demonstrated a remarkable recovery curve, and Aboriginal economic and political muscle has not yet been fully flexed. The point is that any discussion about the future of our population hinges perilously on conjecture and assumptions. To date, what we can say for certain is that our population is more Canadian, not nearly as British, nor quite as Asian as it was a little over a century ago.

In this context, it is critical to appreciate that the demographic fates of recently populated communities (and of households in those communities) are to some degree tied to the very nature of settler selection. Migrants within North America and those crossing either the Atlantic or the Pacific have historically tended to trace the footsteps of their predecessors. Sometimes referred to as "wave migrations" (by which it is meant that one small wave is followed by others), the process has also been described as one of "migration fields." Populations in newcomer settlements in BC were likely to be derived from specific sources in Britain, the US, China, or elsewhere in Canada where economic activities or ambitions shared some connection with the frontier. In short, colliery towns begat the bulk of emigrants for coal-mining frontiers such as eastern Vancouver Island and Fernie, whereas tin-miners from Cornwall were a notable presence in the goldfields of the Cariboo. One author has observed that vital rates in the originating community might be far worse than those prevailing in the newcomer communities (the example of eighteenth- and nineteenth-century London is the one repeatedly offered), or the connection between the source and the colonial populations might define a common set of vital rates. Under these latter circumstances, immigrants are said to have brought their demography with them, including "diseases, a standard of living, and notions of appropriate age at marriage and family size."[58] Although one might argue that the process of globalization has led to a flattening out of demographic behavioural differences across cultures, it is also true that regional, occupational, and cultural distinctions continue to survive around the planet. As a place to which newcomers are invited, British Columbia will continue to combine its own demographic rhythms with those of immigrant peoples.

And this will be the case because one demographic pattern, in particular, shows no signs of going away soon. The low birthrate continues to demand augmentation by immigrants (whether they come from other countries or other provinces). This was as true in the Edwardian period as it is today. Less than 20 percent of population growth from 1891 to 1901 can be attributed to natural increase; from 1901 to 1911, more than 200,000 people were added to the total (that is, a 149 percent increase), of which only 28,213 – roughly 13 percent – came from natural increase. The situation in the twenty-first century is remarkably similar. Now, if there were a low mortality rate to match flagging fertility, the immigration imperative would be less powerful. But, as the next chapter reveals, death rates are very healthy indeed.

7
The Mourning After: Mortality

According to government medical records, a suspected case of "pig typhoid or cholera" in Nanaimo was brought to the attention of the local doctor, E.A. Praeger, in 1890. He urged the provincial secretary to introduce a Public Health Act immediately so that steps might be taken to quarantine infected livestock. Praeger's appeal to officials for action, though prudent for the long term, was no answer to the immediate problem. According to Praeger, the Chinese swine owners pursued a folk cure. Putting a monkey among their hogs evidently had the desired effect: the typhoid scare vanished as quickly as it had appeared.[1] The government agent, Marshall Bray, was soon joking with the deputy attorney general that what really lay behind Praeger's continued protests was the fact that "the monkey [was] not ... a registered practitioner."

In Nanaimo, however, Bray showed less good humour. He admonished Praeger, saying that he was "not fit for this country and had better go back to England." Praeger then complained to Victoria that he was the butt of jokes on the streets of Nanaimo. He sank into an unprofessional sulk: "For the future ... I shall keep as close as an oyster on any matter affecting the public welfare – even if smallpox or cholera should break out among an unappreciative public – outside my health district."[2]

Dr. Praeger's frustration might have been better vented on the provincial government than on the public. As early as 1864, petitions were circulating in Victoria and London describing the Nanaimoites' concern about the "sanitary regulations" or lack thereof in their town. Waste, for example, was being dumped directly into the streets.[3] Chinese graves were another source of worry, and in 1890 Nanaimo's constable was anxious that the Asian community's burial practices (mainly, the use of shallow graves) might lead to the outbreak of disease.[4] A little over a decade later, there were typhoid scares all along the east coast of Vancouver Island, a concern that had plagued the mining, whaling, and fishing towns for years. Praeger might have felt vindicated by an 1898 report written by Edward Mohun, a specialist appointed by the provincial government. Mohun's study revealed that, in the absence of a coherent sewerage system, Nanaimo's fecal waste was being disposed of in a variety of unsatisfactory ways. Most of the businesses and homes in the town centre dumped their sewage into Commercial Inlet or the nearby ravine (a practice that was disclosed with every low tide). A "rudimentary sewer" linked the courthouse with a few residences, but that was all that passed for infrastructure. It was found as well that some of the homes on Front Street "discharge their sewage into the abandoned coal workings beneath them." Elsewhere in Nanaimo, a night soil "scavenger" served more than a quarter of the town's homes, carting the waste two miles to the Vancouver Coal Company's farm, where it was used for manure. A great many local residents, possibly the majority, used human waste to manure their own gardens, and this practice very probably extended to the majority of British Columbian households at the time. Nonetheless, the special social and economic circumstances of turn-of-the-century Nanaimo – a fifty-year-old mining community with a relatively high population density – set the town apart from junior cities such as Rossland and Vancouver and from the less industrialized centres of Victoria and Kamloops. Under these circumstances, the availability of reasonably fresh water was perhaps all that spared Nanaimoites from higher mortality rates.[5]

The state began its long and meandering reply to hygiene questions as early as 1869, when Victoria introduced "An Ordinance for Promoting the Public Health." In 1872, municipalities were made responsible for the regulation of abattoirs, local streams, sewers, and the "preservation of the public health" generally.[6] Legislation creating a Provincial Board of Health was passed in 1893, but it was not proclaimed until 1895, and a board structure was not in place before 1899.[7] It was only at the dawn of the twentieth century, therefore, that the bureaucratic instruments were at last in place for improving the physical well-being of British Columbians. And none too soon. Mohun, a civic engineer reporting to the attorney general in the late 1890s, described a parlous situation in the province's largest centres. At New Westminster, for example, he found

> nothing in the city which by any stretch of courtesy can be called a system of sewerage. A certain number of the buildings (and it is thought most of those having water closets), discharge their crude sewage through box drains direct into the river, others have cesspools, or earth closets, in which it is feared that the use of earth is dispensed with ... The town has been in existence about forty years, and though an ample supply of water of good quality has for the last few years been furnished to the public, no systematic means has been adopted for the disposal of liquid and excrementitious wastes.[8]

Even in smaller communities located close to freshwater sources, as was the case in Kamloops in 1898, Mohun's expert opinion was that the need for sewer systems was urgent.[9] A successful public health program was, however, difficult to realize in the context of a boom-bust economy.[10] There was plenty of boosterist support when the towns were on the rise, but once they began to stabilize or decline, interest in pouring tax dollars into public health slid. In addition, local control over sewage and water meant persistent sharp differentials in the quality of infrastructure and thus in mortality rates. Regional hospitals might be liberally distributed by the provincial government, but, of course, some newcomer nodes were located far from any medical facilities worthy of the name, a situation that remained common until the second half of the twentieth century.[11] Health care, hygiene levels, and mortality rates were bound to differ from town to town, from city to city.

In the nineteenth and twentieth centuries, the urge to modernize involved a battle between, on the one hand, superstition and folk responses to ailments and death, and scientific, empirically verifiable understandings of germs, viruses, and the human body on the other. In British Columbia, this pitted modernists like Edward Mohun against not only traditionalists and "quacks" among the white population but also against the various less privileged populations within the colonial enterprise that was British Columbia.[12] Chinese medicine and understandings of death came under attack, as did Aboriginal codes of behaviour. Cole Harris and Mary-Ellen Kelm have made this point: the reserve system and the residential schools demonstrated intolerance toward alternative interpretations of illness and health, and these new imperial institutions subjected their occupants to a foreign regime that sought to colonize not just land and people, but bodies as well.[13] Isolation – geographic, political, social, medical, and economic – and the imposition of culturally embedded European ideas about health and appropriate bio-cultural practices muddied the demographic current of Aboriginal life.

As is the case with depopulation, sex ratios, and fertility, British Columbia's record of mortality is distinct in several respects. First, the rates of mortality have historically run at relatively high levels. Second, it is unusual in its experience: mortality occurred under circumstances and in ways that were and are unique in Canada. Third, the experience of infant and maternal mortality exhibits behaviours that demand further research. These characteristics are explored in this chapter.

The British Columbian Way of Death

Even more so than birth, mortality in a community is episodic. Outbreaks of disease and war, in particular, produce peaks as sharp as any in the Monashees, although workplace disasters of the greatest magnitude were also considerations in British Columbia. These various mortality spikes – to a considerable extent, even those of the two world wars – were typically local-ized events, epidemics hardly less so than mining accidents. It is not surpris-ing, as well, to find that the spatial compartmentalizing of populations in British Columbia produced specific mortality patterns along socially con-structed "racial" lines. Chinatowns and Native reserves had the effect of isolating and confirming distinct morbidities and mortalities on specific peoples.

At one extreme, there was Darcy Island. Located near Sydney, this was a turn-of-the-century leper colony; its inmates, though few in number, were all Chinese immigrants. They lived in dire conditions, according to South Vancouver medical health board chairman Dr. F.W. Brydone-Jack, who complained of the policy of "marooning Lepers for life on an island in the Gulf under no Medical treatment and with very little, if any, supervision, beyond the sending over of food supplies at stated periods and the raising of a flag (if the patient is capable of doing so) which may or may not be seen from a passing boat or from the adjacent island, if help is required."[14] Around the same time, the secretary of the Provincial Board of Health, C.J. Fagan, wrote of the lazaretto, "There is no pretension made to give medical treat-ment, or nursing, and no effort made to relieve pain."[15] In the case of Darcy Island, racial antipathy combined with revulsion at an ancient disease to produce a visceral neglect; for all intents and purposes, the Chinese lepers had been sentenced to death.

First Nations mortality rates produced their own peculiarities, quite apart from massive die-outs from diseases such as smallpox. For example, on the Northwest Coast, at Kincolith, 185 burials were recorded at the local mission from 1869 to the end of 1899, of which 19 were younger than six months, another 16 were between six and twelve months of age, and a further 27 between one and five years; thus, infant burials account for fully one-third of the total.[16] This example points to higher than average infant mortality rates among a people whose territories were becoming progressively trun-cated, their access to resources leaner and leaner. As Aboriginal people turned to opportunities in waged-labour, mortality rates took a new direction. From the 1880s on, segregation in the workplace guaranteed that Asians and Ab-originals alike would be spared some of the many kinds of injuries and deaths that were the lot of the white working-class population, but the fisheries in particular took a heavy toll on coastal Native communities. The Kincolith registers record five deaths at sea and one from "internal injury sustained ... whilst logging," a reminder that the human costs of resource extraction were felt across the province.[17]

In fact, appalling working conditions are often disguised in statistics by euphemisms such as "environmental factors." The resource-extraction in-dustries that are the heart and lungs of the provincial economy take a terrible toll on the hearts, lungs, sinews, and bones of its working people. This was an industrializing hinterland in which work was as dangerous as imaginable. Hard-rock mines, with their heavy reliance on dynamite to speed along the process, were killers. Mine explosions on the Vancouver Island coalfield in 1884, 1887, and 1888 caused nearly 300 fatalities, and these were followed by mine disasters at Wellington in 1901 (68 dead), at Fernie in 1902, 1908, and 1917 (128, 10, and 34 dead, respectively), and at Princeton's Blakeburn Colliery in 1930 (45 dead).[18] Above ground, other calamities took a toll: a fire at Twenty Mile Creek in the Cariboo claimed the lives of 11 Chinese goldminers in 1869. Two-thirds of the 90 Canadians who died by asphyxiation in 1901 due to the inhalation of noxious gas did so in BC, most of them in mines.[19] Perhaps worse, mineworkers might face a lingering death from injuries or from respiratory problems acquired by inhaling dust. Conditions in the forest industry were also very dangerous. Gordon Hak reports that the first recorded logging death occurred in the summer of 1867 and that the decade from 1909 to 1919 averaged more than 12 deaths annually.[20] As lumber production became industrialized, the possibilities for untimely deaths in that sector also increased. One has to keep in mind that these were horrific ways to go. Tom Hall, newly arrived from England in the spring of 1889, took a job at a steam-powered sawmill in the Thompson Valley; a momentary lapse in concentration cost him his life on his first day at work. "Tom Hall was," according to one account, "essentially chopped to pieces."[21] The fisheries was another sector in which untimely deaths occurred with alarming frequency, as was the construction of the Canadian Pacific Railway through the Fraser Canyon, a stretch that infamously devoured Chinese labourers wholesale.[22] Accidental deaths on the railway regularly occurred once the line was up and running but were registered in small numbers – that is, usually in ones. With few exceptions, only a handful and not hundreds of lives would be lost at work in places such as Revelstoke, Fort George, and Lytton.[23] In all of these cases, the exposed population was comprised of young men. As Hak writes of an early fatality in a Burrard Inlet sawmill, he "had recently moved to Vancouver in hopes that the coastal climate would benefit his wife's health. He was thirty years old and left two small children."[24] Other catastrophes deserve a place on this grim list: the Point Ellice Bridge in Victoria collapsed in 1896 killing 57; the wreck of the *Valencia* in 1906 claimed 115; twelve years later, the *Princess Sophia* went down in Lynn Canal, claiming 342 lives.[25] A youthful, vigorous newcomer population thus did not necessarily preclude a high rate of deaths in the first fifty years after Confederation.

In the more bucolic corners of the province, workplace dangers were of a much lower magnitude. One account of death in the Okanagan, written in 1892, captures the rural ideal of mortality: "Everybody dies a natural death, and people are buried in either backyards or under their favorite fruit trees. It is perfectly delightful."[26] But only a fraction of the Interior was given over to farming and orcharding enclaves; the greater agricultural activity was ranching, with different attendant dangers. But if one were to look to the "wild west" elements of the Interior frontier for additional cheerless accounts of abbreviated lives, one would do so in vain. John Mara, a Kamloops politician and entrepreneur, wrote to the attorney general in 1872, describing the hazards of frontier life and complaining of the need "for a Constable and Jail or Lock up of some kind." What with "Drovers coming and going, Packers and others from the Wagon Road, and men connected with the [railway] survey," the respectable permanent elements in the population sought to guarantee the reputation of their town. Mara added that "Kamloops had a very unenviable notoriety last winter, Pistols and Knives were frequently drawn, in one case it was little short of a miracle than a man was not shot."[27] In fact, shootings were very rare indeed, and they became more so as the new century got under way.[28] Whether in cattle country or in the "sunny Okanagan," the "death from external causes" column made for brief reading in the pre-war years. Nevertheless, it is worth noting that the rosy image of death hardly pertained. Table 7.1 describes the funerals and/or burials conducted by the Kamloops Methodist Church at the turn of the century. Of sixteen burials, five were for infants; three others were for non-whites/non-Aboriginals; three were for elderly men; four might be described

Table 7.1

Kamloops Fourth Avenue Methodist Church, burials, 1902-04

Date	Name	Description
25/08/1902	Ernest Pottroff	Infant under 15 days old
04/10/1902	Infant (9 months)	Male
22/10/1902	James Lektock	Elderly man
07/11/1902	"A Japanese"	"Fell off train"
10/11/1902	"A Japanese"	"Killed by train"
16/01/1903	Edward Nield	17 years old; consumption
16/01/1903	Unnamed man from provincial jail	Brain tumour
27/02/1903	W.R. Pollock	Crushed by a load of saw logs
18/07/1903	Mr. McRae	From Provincial Home
18/10/1903	Mrs. Ann Crawford of Revelstoke	Stroke/heart failure
30/12/1903	Freddie Goddend	10 yrs, 1 mo.
27/01/1904	Jack Ladner	Railway death
30/01/1904	Infant	Son of Mr. & Mrs. Shafer
07/03/1904	Infant	Son of Mrs. & Mr. Richardson
25/03/1904	Alexander Williams	"Old Colored Gentleman"
31/03/1904	James, infant (6 weeks old)	Son of Mr. & Mrs. Humphreys

Source: Burials, 1902-04, Kamloops Fourth Avenue Methodist Church Records, United Church Archives, Vancouver School of Theology, Vancouver, BC.

as workplace-related deaths; the death of a prisoner in the provincial jail may have been the result of violent treatment (was "brain tumour" a euphemism for a severe head injury?); and only three of the adult deaths were ascribed to physiological failures. In sum, burials registered by the Methodist Church in Kamloops were not typically for those aged citizens who went (gentle or not) into that good night.

Climate was another environmental factor that probably played a role in differentiating between mortality rates in the Interior and on the coast. Southern Vancouver Island and the Lower Mainland enjoy year-round moderate temperatures; the Okanagan and Thompson Valleys, by contrast, are semi-arid regions with climates marked by extremes. Table 7.2 compares morbidity in the "Vancouver" and "Yale and Cariboo" Census Districts, the former covering the central-east coast of Vancouver Island. With the exception of the dramatic effect of a February 1901 mine disaster, the island record shows fewer deaths in most months and muted seasonal fluctuations. On the plateau, however, peaks appear exactly where one would expect to find them: at the end of winter and in late summer. In the Thompson Valley (the population epicentre of Yale and Cariboo), there was a greater than usual snowfall in the first two months of 1901, an average temperature of -5.1°C with a low point of -26.7°C in January. These factors would have produced conditions that were particularly unfavourable for the elderly and the less well off. Day-to-day winter chores were far more demanding in the Interior

Table 7.2

Seasonality of death, Nanaimo and Kamloops, 1901

Month	Vancouver Census District		Yale and Cariboo Census District	
	Number	Rank (worst of 12)	Number	Rank (worst of 12)
January	35	2	30	3
February	84	1	25	5
March	29	3	40	1
April	20	5	24	7
May	14	11	14	12
June	16	9	25	5
July	13	12	19	10
August	15	10	26	4
September	17	8	33	2
October	18	7	21	9
November	19	6	22	8
December	26	4	16	11
Totals	306		295	

Source: Census of Canada, 1901, vol. 1: *Population* (Ottawa: Queen's Printer, 1903), 247-79.

than along the mild southwest coast of BC. "On account of the poor houses the climate seemed very severe," wrote one contemporary, "at 28° below zero [F.] those little board houses with no walls laid on[,] just sheet iron heaters[, it] was no luxury. For water we had to go down to the River and dip it into a bucket and carry back to the house, if any dripped over it would freeze on the kitchen floor as you carried it and we had to take an axe down to chip through the ice hole to reach the water."[29] The late winter/early spring mortality peak in Kamloops may be explained by neonatal deaths. May and June were the most popular months of the year for marriages and – one may presume – for conception. Thus, February and March saw the largest number of births and, necessarily, the highest incidence of neonatal deaths and maternal mortalities. (In 1891 the March mortality spike for females was 2.56 per 1,000, whereas nationally it was only 1.48.)[30] As for the summertime increase in deaths on the plateau, these may be partly explained by swelteringly high temperatures – as hot as 37.2°C in August with an average of 22.3°C night and day. With nil precipitation in a near-desert environment, conditions would have been dangerous for infants, due to the combined risks of dehydration, street filth that was not dissipated by rainfall, and deteriorating water quality as the level of the Thompson Rivers fell to its annual low.[31] Given its climate, the Thompson Valley was not likely to be British Columbia's "vale of health."

The incidence of fatal infectious diseases was conditioned by environmental factors as well. Illnesses on the Vancouver Island coalfield, for example, point to miners' occupationally induced weaknesses. The most feared ailments were associated with lung diseases, particularly tuberculosis and bronchial pneumonia, both of which were linked with the inhalation of coal dust.[32] Between the two, they claimed more than half the lives lost in and around Nanaimo at the turn of the century.[33] Treatment was not overwhelmingly effective: of sixty-two tuberculosis patients admitted to the Tranquille Sanatorium near Kamloops in 1907 and 1908, thirty-seven succumbed to the illness, most within a year of their arrival.[34] Tuberculosis was in retreat throughout Britain in the same period due, it is claimed, to improved living standards and public health provisions.[35] But throughout British Columbia, the presence of a vulnerable Native population was a factor in driving up the frequency of TB, as were conditions in the province's mines.

Tuberculosis, in fact, was a unifying element in pre-war British Columbia. Sanatoria were constructed in the dry-belt of the Interior, and many a played-out coastal coalminer found his way to Kamloops, a number of whom made it their final resting place.[36] Myth making about the salubrious High Country air began some time during the construction of the Canadian Pacific Railway, and it was to grow in circulation and in the extravagance of its claims. As early as 1887, local boosters were selling Kamloops as "a great resort for invalids."[37] This was echoed in the 1894 *British Columbia Directory,* which described the valley as "a favorite health resort, especially for consumptives and those suffering from bronchial and lung infections."[38] Likewise, an 1897 flyer on Kamloops Mining Camp claimed that "On account of the dryness and equability of its climate, and its possession of all the conditions necessary for the cure of lung troubles Kamloops is destined to be one of the great health resorts of the West."[39] From the outset, a dearth of acute "rheumatism, pneumonia and acute Bright's Disease" and phthisis was observed.[40] According to Robert Service, who spent about four months in Kamloops in 1904, the Bank of Commerce regularly transferred its consumptive employees to the Thompson Valley, and by 1907 the "bracing air" had already attracted many of the bank's "suspected lungers."[41] One result of this often disingenuous campaign was that mortality was relocated from the four corners of the province to the hub town.[42] For example, in 1913, 44 of 295 deaths in BC from tuberculosis (that is, 15 percent) occurred in Kamloops, presumably a reflection of the magnetic role played by the Tranquille Sanatorium. (In the same year, only 16 died from tuberculosis in Nanaimo.)

Generally speaking, the quantitative and qualitative evidence points to more disease-related death in the Interior than on the coast. Accounts from the first thirteen years of the century highlight some local peculiarities. In Fort George, by way of an example, typhoid claimed 16 lives in 1913 (17.6 percent of the provincial total), and another 15 fell prey to the disease in Kamloops; this was a fairly typical year in that typhoid was consistently more dangerous in the Interior than it was on the coast. Heart disease claimed 66 percent more people in Kamloops than it did in Nanaimo, and pneumonia caused 24 deaths in Kamloops against only 5 in the much larger coaltown. In fact, Kamloops in 1913 had a total of 299 deaths, whereas only 149 occurred in Nanaimo.[43]

Local undertakers' records, though problematic, reveal this much: the annual average age of Kamloopsian men and women at burial in the 1890s could be as low as 22.4 years and as high as 63 years.[44] The same records, shown in Table 7.3, reveal that the average age – for men, at least – was climbing steadily, settling at around 50 years at death at the turn of the century. This trend was partly due to Kamloops' emerging role as a "retirement centre." By 1894 Kamloops was officially a city, and it boasted both the Royal Inland Hospital and the Provincial (or Old Men's) Home, which was both a hospital and hostel for the aged. In 1891 the *Kamloops Inland Sentinel* newspaper observed that the annual number of deaths in the community "would leave the impression that ours is a very unhealthy district, whereas the reverse is the case."[45] Whatever the merits of the boosterist newspaper's argument, the local mortality pattern was in fact slightly skewed by the presence of a substantial population of aging and played-out Mexican, Chilean, Prussian, Jamaican, Dutch, Swedish, and Anglo-North American

Table 7.3

Average age at death for burials, age fifteen or older, Kamloops, 1889-99, 1905-08

Year	Males	Females
1889	45.6	38.0
1890	35.0	30.0
1891	38.7	44.6
1892	22.4	34.0
1893	44.5	23.0
1894	46.1	19.3
1895	47.2	0
1896	53.7	29.0
1897	45.2	43.5
1898	62.9	29.8
1899	57.2	65.7
1905	56.8	34.5
1906	49.9	37.8
1907	52.6	35.6
1908	53.6	52.6

Sources: Client Records, 1888-March 1898, 1898-1905, and Funeral Register, June 1905-September 1913, Schoening Funeral Service (1961) Ltd., Kamloops, BC.

prospectors, some of whom had hung on since the days of the Fraser River and Cariboo gold rushes.[46] When Alex Lord visited the northern Interior in 1915, he encountered an elderly but sardonic miner "who announced, 'I am on my way to Hazelton to get my commitment papers to the Old Men's Home in Kamloops to die.'" The Home was, indeed, the last stop for many immigrants who were drawn to British Columbia by the promise of easy wealth.[47] Turn-of-the-century Kamloops was importing *natural* mortality from elsewhere in the province.

Whereas working-class men were exposed to many kinds of life-threatening occupational hazards, British Columbian women were at special risk from maternal mortality.[48] One of the consequences of a rising curve of fertility before the Great War (see Chapter 5) was frequent exposure to the risks entailed in pregnancy. In 1890-91 nearly 3 percent of all female deaths on the Vancouver Island coalfield were attributed to childbirth; the figure for contemporary Ontario was 1.79 percent. Of the thirty-four women buried by the Anglican Church in Nanaimo from 1881 to 1894, four (11.7 percent) died in childbirth.[49] When Kamloopsian Maria Marche died in childbirth in 1911, she was buried alongside her stillborn infant – an experience and arrangement that was not exceptional.[50] For women residing in more remote centres of human occupation, the absence of a physician and/or a midwife could be telling.[51]

More numerically significant and temporally compressed was the mortality of international conflicts into which Canada was drawn in the twentieth century. Of these, the Great War claimed the greatest number of lives. It is reckoned that 6,225 British Columbians died between August 1914 and the armistice, although perhaps many more provincial residents enlisted in and died as part of other Canadian or British regiments and so would not be recorded as British Columbians.[52] This catastrophe carried off at least one in sixty-six British Columbians; to put it another way, British Columbia contributed nearly 10 percent of Canada's war dead, even though the province's share of national population was less than half that amount. The province was, in fact, the national leader in wartime deaths. Whole communities were gutted, most notably newly established towns and villages, especially those containing large numbers of recent British immigrants.[53] Across the province, widowhood followed in the wake of war. The Second World War culled significantly fewer from a population that had grown since 1914: British Columbia contributed 3,789 to Canada's war dead between 1939 and 1945.[54]

And yet, none of these mortality events had the singular impact of the 1862 smallpox epidemic. It claimed some lives among the non-Aboriginal population, but the First Nations communities of the southwest, the north coast, and the plateau suffered worst of all (as described in Chapters 2 and 3). Every subsequent mortality event – including two world wars – pales in contrast to the 1862-63 smallpox epidemic. One must ask why there is no monument memorializing this most lamentable event in the region's history. Its lack is all the more remarkable for the extent to which the mortality events that followed are more widely remembered.

What, then, was the general experience of death in British Columbia down to the interwar period? It must be allowed that the rate of deaths in BC was – indeed, is – apt to be under-reported. Of the three principal vital events in Anglo-Canadian culture – birth, marriage, and death – mortality is the least likely to be recorded because fewer consequences attach to the failure to do so. Of course, a landscape of remote farmsteads, mining claims, and isolated communities worked against the comprehensive maintenance of any official registry. Because births, too, were inconsistently registered, infant deaths were inevitably under-reported as well. As historian Tony Wrigley notes in an examination of European mortality rates, if children died prior to being baptized, the likelihood is greater that the death would not be recorded on local parish registers.[55] The same was true, after a fashion, in British Columbia. What is more, adult deaths and burials in the Far West were probably under-reported as well: in the nineteenth and early twentieth centuries (and in some quarters to the present), it was simply practical to bury farmers and ranchers on their own property, very often with little in the line of a headstone or marker to indicate the details.[56] Even the Hudson's Bay Company's dignified physician, John Helmcken, buried his two children in his James Bay garden, although he later had them re-interred in a nearby churchyard when his young wife passed away.[57] A comprehensive accounting of colonial and early provincial mortality is thus inconceivable.[58] What is available is, however, enlightening.

Mortality Rates

Rates of mortality can be assembled and represented in a variety of ways. The crude death rate (CDR) is the simplest, showing the number of deaths per 1,000 population. A standardized death rate (SDR) endeavours to adjust the rate to distinctive age structures, for example. Incomplete vital statistics records make accurate SDRs impossible for this period; therefore, CDRs are primarily relied upon here, along with statistics on the infant mortality rate (IMR).

CDR

The crude death rate (CDR) is a simple means of tracking changes in the rate of mortality. Be aware: it can be impacted by the age of the population (infants and the elderly are more at risk than other populations, and British Columbia has plenty of both). Social histories of death (called *thanatological histories*) draw attention to the fact that the ways in which communities experience changes in death rates can vary so sharply that the CDR might be rising at a time when awareness of death is actually declining. That aside, the formula looks like so:

$$CDR = \frac{\text{Deaths in year}}{\text{Population at mid-year}} \times 1,000$$

SDR

The crude death rate does not take account of age differences in populations; the standardized death rate (SDR) does. There are direct and indirect measures, plus age standardized death rates (ASDRs). These all require a comparison of expected and observed mortalities, but the former are not always available. Sometimes SDRs are referred to as standardized mortality rates, or SMRs.

IMR

Because the first five years of life are so filled with risks and because mortality in those years has become a benchmark of social progress, many demographies make use of the infant mortality rate (IMR):

$$IMR = \frac{\text{Deaths under age 1 in year}}{\text{Live births in year}} \times 1{,}000$$

To this information, we can add one detail. The CDR for Victoria in the 1880s was in the area of 17 per 1,000. Of British Columbia's cities and towns, Victoria probably had the greatest bureaucratic machinery in place, and we might expect that city's vital statistics to have been gathered rather more effectively than in, say, Gastown. The fact that the city's CDR falls slightly below that of the province as a whole, which was 20 per 1,000, suggests that the provincial figure was not heavily inflated and that, at least in some communities west of the Rockies, mortality rates were comparable to those in the seven leading mortality cities in the country.[59]

The pre-war provincial CDR shows a dramatic fall from 1881 to 1891 followed by remarkable resilience from 1891 to c. 1911. The high figure for 1881 reflects the costs of both underground mining and railway construction in that year. The stability of the CDR from 1891 to 1911 is a phenomenon for which several explanations are possible. First, improvements in public health and professional medicine made little difference before the Great War, although they probably played roughly equivalent roles in lowering the mortality rate and raising life expectancies. Changes in sewerage systems – recall Mohun – had more definitive impacts. Victoria built its first public sewage system in 1894, which brought about an immediate effect: the CDR fell from more than 21 per 1,000 to 16.76 per 1,000 in the space of two years. Even so, only about half the buildings in Victoria were on the system, and though local authorities felt that the CDR should be brought down to about 12 per 1,000, this proved an elusive goal.[60] Second, the infant mortality rate remained a significant factor until it began a long-term retreat in the 1920s. Overall, then, BC's mortality and infant mortality rates were slow to change, but, notably, they were somewhat higher than those of Canada as a whole.

This empirical evidence thus contradicts the frontier caricature of pioneer virility and environmental purity.[61] As one version has it, "settlers usually

Table 7.4

Mortality, Kamloops and Nanaimo regions, 1881-1901

	\multicolumn{6}{c}{Deaths (by age cohorts)}					
	0-1	1-5	0-5	All ages	Pop'n	CDR
Yale and Cariboo Census District (includes Kamloops)						
1881	13	25	38	266	16,750	15.8
1891	58	61	119	298	19,180	15.5
1901	65	35	100	315	61,889	5.1
Vancouver Census District (includes Nanaimo)						
1881	38	26	64	171	9,991	17.1
1891	74	76	150	432	18,229	23.7
1901	27	33	60	309	27,198	11.4

Sources: Census of Canada, 1881, vol. 1 (Ottawa, 1882), 94-95; *Census of Canada, 1891,* vol. 4 (Ottawa, 1891), 424-25; *Census of Canada, 1901,* vol. 4: *Vital Statistics,* 348.

were healthy, they ate good, uncontaminated food; they breathed unpolluted air; and they had plenty of good exercise."[62] By rights, a generally young and healthy adult pioneer population (like the one described by Peter Ward and Jean Barman) should have influenced the overall mortality figures in a positive way. Measured against the British record – in the period 1896-1900, the British CDR was 18.8 – the British Columbian figures look somewhat better, but against the Canadian average they do not.[63]

The mortality figures for both the Kamloops and Nanaimo areas help to flesh out the provincial patterns before the Great War (Table 7.4).[64] Crude death rates in the two towns were typically higher than those for Canada and British Columbia. A combination of factors, including living environment, a significantly higher than average incidence of infectious diseases, and resilient infant mortality rates (considered below) contributed to these high CDRs.

Although the death rate per 1,000 population among the non-Aboriginal community was fairly stable from 1926 to 1960, remaining between 8.4 and 10.1, the rate among Aboriginal British Columbians was consistently higher.[65] Tuberculosis took the place of smallpox in the late nineteenth century and throughout the twentieth was the principal killer; moreover, TB sufficiently weakened Aboriginal populations and thus raised morbidity due to measles, whooping cough, and influenza, all of which became lethal.[66] The conditionally good news is that the gap between Aboriginal and non-Aboriginal mortality rates closed, for the most part, by 1960. So, in 1926-30, "Indian Mortality" was 22.7 per 1,000 – nearly three times the rate among non-Aboriginals – rising to a high of 27.4 in 1936-40, falling to 15.6 in 1951-55, and then to 11.3 in 1960 – at which time the non-Aboriginal mortality rate was 9.1 per 1,000. By c. 1990, the mortality rate among "Status Indians" in

British Columbia was actually slightly lower than the general provincial rate.[67]

Causes of death otherwise fluctuated throughout the twentieth century, not all tending to move in a downward curve. Definitions of diseases are fluid, and reporting is naturally uneven. But the broad categories of morbidity and mortality provide some instructive trends. For example, infectious diseases claimed nearly 3 per 1,000 in the decade of the First World War, falling thereafter but especially in the 1950s. (To be sure, it was falling from an artificially high plateau: the end of the Great War brought to Canada both Spanish influenza and a spike in cases of venereal disease, the latter infecting as many as one in four members of the Canadian Expeditionary Force.)[68] By the 1960s, the rate of death from infectious disease was a mere 0.5 per 1,000, and it continued to fall in the 1970s to 0.29 per 1,000, rebounding slightly in the 1980s, presumably due to AIDS. Diseases of the heart and respiratory system (which include tuberculosis, pneumonia, and influenza) increased their harvest of lives from 1910 in every decade to 1960, when they peaked at 3.79 per 1,000, falling off slightly thereafter. Cancers (referred to in medical parlance as "neoplasms") were a rising cause of death in every decade of the century, although they never claimed more than 1.89 per 1,000 in a decade.[69] If we set aside environmental factors (including exposure to a growing list of carcinogens), part of the increase in cancer deaths can be attributed to medical science's ability to diagnose neoplasms before the host died of other, related killers such as pneumonia.[70] In addition, the rise in cancer deaths (and heart disease morbidity as well) can be ascribed to improved life expectancy – people now live long enough to die of these diseases, whereas in the Victorian and Edwardian eras, in particular, men and women in their forties were considered old. This can be observed in a negative correlation between the rate of heart-disease-related deaths and neoplasm deaths: that is to say, as the former fell, the latter rose. In short, British Columbians were increasingly likely to get cancer precisely because they were less likely to die of heart disease. Swings, as they say, and roundabouts.

From 1921 to the mid-1940s, the crude death rate (CDR) climbed in British Columbia, whereas it was falling across Canada as a whole (see Figure 7.1).[71] At the end of the Second World War, the British Columbian CDR began a steady but uneven descent, briefly meeting the national rate in the early 1980s, after which it again ran higher than the national average (though somewhat lower than the Maritime provinces, Manitoba, and Saskatchewan). When compared to the CDR of its nearest Canadian neighbours, the British Columbian rate was typically and often significantly higher, improving in this respect only in the 1970s when it slipped below the Manitoba and Saskatchewan CDRs. Perhaps remarkably, the CDR for Alberta has pushed well below the British Columbian rate since the 1960s. The two westernmost provinces ended the twentieth century with distinctive patterns of mortality – Alberta's rate in the 1980s and '90s was around 5.6 deaths per 1,000 population, whereas British Columbia's remained in the 7.1 to 7.4 range.[72]

The consequences of a higher CDR paired to fewer births in the Pacific province were observed by Peter Ward in 1983. He wrote, "On the prairies, relatively high fertility has combined with low mortality to sustain rates of natural increase that historically have either exceeded or closely resembled national norms. British Columbia, however, has had a long history of low fertility and above average mortality, which together yielded the lowest rates of natural increase in Canada during the first seven decades of the twentieth century."[73] Without immigration, this is a recipe for population shrinkage, but immigration is, in part, the problem. Statistics from 2001 illustrate this point. Alberta, with a smaller population overall, had 35,938 births and 17,508 deaths for a net gain of 18,430; British Columbia recorded 40,165 births against 27,582 deaths for a net gain of only 12,583. What stands out in this respect is the contrast between the ratios of births to deaths (2.05:1 in Alberta and 1.45:1 in BC), as well as the evidently higher fecundity of Albertans. These differences can be explained in part by intensified labour recruitment to Alberta's oil patch from the 1980s on, which would have significantly reduced and kept low the average age in that province. But they are also an indication that Alberta exports its elderly (and thus its mortality) to the milder west coast, the Okanagan, and elsewhere in BC. This has four

Figure 7.1

Crude death rates, Canada and BC, 1921-91

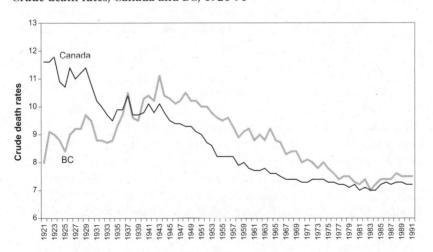

Source: Surinder Wadhera and Jill Strachan, *Selected Mortality Statistics, Canada, 1921-1990*, catalogue no. 82-548 (Ottawa: Statistics Canada, 1994), 35-36.

effects: first, it necessarily reduces the death rate east of the Rockies; second, it raises the rate of apparent natural increase in Alberta; third, the mortality rate *west* of the Rockies is inflated by retirees whose life expectancy as British Columbians is necessarily short; and fourth, this reduces BC's net natural increase.[74] Other measures further highlight regional differences.

In terms of life expectancy and average age at death, British Columbia is unusual once again, certainly in the Canadian West. Whereas the average age at death for men in the Prairie provinces in 1921 ranged from 26.6 in Saskatchewan to 31.3 in Manitoba, in British Columbia it was 42.9. Higher infant mortality rates on the Prairies no doubt played a role in distorting these figures in the early twentieth century, and it is true that the average age at death in the Prairie provinces rose steadily thereafter. Nonetheless, the British Columbian figure stayed reliably ahead of the western pack until the late 1960s when an aging population in Manitoba and Saskatchewan caught up.[75] Throughout the century, the average age at death for Albertan men is consistently lower than for their British Columbian counterparts. The same is true for women. As is the case nationally, the life expectancy gap between men and women in BC was widest in the mid-1970s.[76] Again, this may be explained in part by the arrival of older migrants.

What is more, government estimates suggest that life expectancy at birth improved significantly and varied sharply around BC. Table 7.5 shows an improvement from 60.3 years for males and 64.2 for females in 1921 to, re-spectively, 78.0 and 82.9 in 1991. As to variety of regional experiences toward the end of the century, in 1987-91 the range ran from a low of 66.92 years in the Snow Country Local Health Area (LHA) of the northwest to highs of 84.2 and 84.3 in Windermere and Telegraph Creek LHAs respectively. In 1996-2000 the troughs and peaks were marked, respectively, by Vancouver's "Downtown Eastside" LHA at 70.41 (although, curiously, Telegraph Creek was nearly as bad) and Stikine at 84.96 years. On the whole, life expectancy at birth improved for British Columbians, rising from 77.98 to 79.9 over the 1987-2001 period.[77] Similarly, life expectancy at age 65 improved through the twentieth century and continues to inch upward. In the early 1950s, the average time left on this earth for men and women at their sixty-fifth birthday was fourteen and a half years; by the millennium, another five years had been added on.[78] Life expectancy climbed for both men and women, although, at the start of this century, female life expectancy remains significantly higher (82.23) than male life expectancy (76.82). The ramifica-tions of this fact for geriatric policy planning and public spending are, of course, significant, though hardly apocalyptic.[79] Pension funds must stretch 33 percent further over the average lifespan while eldercare (and deathcare) facilities expand in numbers, size, and variety.

Published data may reveal something of the First Nations experience, but they are far less helpful in teasing out significant socio-economic differentials

Table 7.5

Life expectancy, males and females, 1921-2001		
Year	Male	Female
1921	60.3	64.2
1931	62.0	65.4
1941	63.5	68.9
1951	66.7	72.3
1961	68.9	75.4
1971	69.9	76.9
1981	72.6	79.6
1991	74.9	81.2
2001	78.0	82.9

Sources: British Columbia, The Nineteen Eighties: A Statistical Resource for a Decade of Vital Events in British Columbia (Victoria: Ministry of Health and Ministry Responsible for Seniors, 1994), 19; Statistics Canada, "Life Expectancy, Abridged Life Table, at Birth and at Age 65, by Sex, Canada, Provinces and Territories," CANSIM table 102-0125 (2002).

of death. Nevertheless, national studies on the subject – and studies performed in Britain and the United States – point undeniably in one direction: class, even more than gender, has a profound effect on life expectancy. Although the mortality gap between the middle and higher classes had closed by the third quarter of the twentieth century, "the relative risk of death for the least privileged class [remains] much higher than that for the other classes."[80] From the nineteenth century onward, rising living standards provided the nutrition necessary to stave off a great many illnesses, but those standards were not rising at the same rate across the board; nor were they rising for everyone.[81] Nor have socio-economic differentials that impact mortality gone away since. Cancers, pneumonia, bronchitis, cirrhosis of the liver, suicide, and, of course, workplace accidents kill off working-class Canadians with greater frequency than they do middle- and upper-class men and women.[82] Infant mortality rates barely differ across socio-economic boundaries now, but that was not the case as recently as 1986. As for life expectancies at birth, one Statistics Canada study shows that the poorest Canadian males reach seventy-three years on average, whereas the richest Canadians get an additional five years.[83] British Columbia's economy is changing, but the legacy of long dependence on resource-extraction industries will class-differentiate life expectancies for many years to come.

Infant Mortality Rates
Historically, infant mortality rates varied sharply across the province, but they were especially bad in the early twentieth century (see Appendix D). It is reckoned that, in 1891, the rate for both Vancouver and the whole of the

province stood at about 122 deaths per 1,000 births (which, incidentally, places British Columbia well below the median for Canadian cities and provinces).[84] Compared to infant death rates in Montreal (285 per 1,000; outside of Quebec, the rate falls below 200), those in Vancouver look like acceptable losses.[85] Victoria's infant mortality rate, however, was reckoned to be about 300 per 1,000. The smaller communities in BC also recorded high infant mortality rates. Nanaimo's, which stood at 250 in the 1880s and 229 in the 1890s, was shockingly high.[86] Remarkably, infant mortality was higher in the south-central part of the Interior. At Kamloops in 1891, the infant mortality rate reached 380 deaths per 1,000 live births. By 1901, infant death rates across British Columbia had reached 179; in some communities, especially in the coastal mining towns, the rates were much higher to at least 1914, a sign of both the continuing hardships faced by the Aboriginal communities and the shortcomings of the small and isolated newcomer settlements. Stillbirths were common enough, too. Norah Lewis observes that, of the 8,008 babies born in British Columbia in 1912, 598 were still-births or were dead within the year.[87] As elsewhere in the history of humanity, it was true in BC that, "under the age of one, and to a lesser degree under the age of five, life is desperately hazardous."[88] We need to note, then, that emigrating to the westernmost frontier was not an effective strategy for prolonging infant life; in many parts of the province, infant mortality was high, and it was a nagging feature of the generation before 1914. Also, we need to ask why this was the case.

The premier consideration is that we are comparing aggregate province-wide statistics with local figures. Provincial estimates are less severe than local reports, but (and probably *because*) they are incomplete. I suspect this has to do with the greater likelihood of mortality events being recorded at the local level. Certainly, in Britain this appears to have been the case in the nineteenth century, and in some British locales one in four children died before their fifth birthday.[89] Wherever the infant mortality figures in BC were high, however, the likely explanations come from two directions.

As the settler population increased, it did so most dramatically in urbanizing areas, and in doing so, it often outstripped the housing supply. Despite the availability of relatively cheap land (admittedly less available than on the prairies), overcrowded urban living spaces were common in the resettlement era. By 1881, Barkerville and Richfield had room to spare, for housing densities ran to 2.87 persons per dwelling (half of which were, to be sure, "shanties"). But that was not the case along the Thompson from Kamloops to Lytton, where densities ran to 6.24 per unit. On the Vancouver Island coalfield and in Rossland at the turn of the century, housing densities ran to 4.79 and 4.19 persons per dwelling respectively – an observation that loses its force unless we recall how very small and painfully basic "housing" was in these mining towns.[90] These conditions, especially in communities such as Nanaimo, which contained a considerable number of children, were conducive to the spread of measles, meningitis, whooping cough, influenza, and pneumonia, afflictions that claimed a great many infant lives.

A second factor contributing to the high infant mortality rates was the water supply. Diarrhea and enteritis were chronic problems across the province and were extremely telling on the under-one cohort, as was the related problem of "unsanitary" bottle-feeding.[91]

Whatever the underlying causes, infant death was a fact of life in settler communities. If one rhyme can be described as ubiquitous from cemetery to cemetery in the province, it is this maudlin piece of turn-of-the-century mortuary doggerel: "Short was your stay, but long will be your rest, / God took you hence, because he thought it was best." Naturally, the likelihood of infant mortality striking in any given household increased with the number of children born (and earlier first marriages, enabled by a badly skewed sex ratio, probably drove up the infant mortality rate as well).[92] Although, statistically, about one child may have died for every ten or eleven live births in BC in 1891, in household terms, the rate could be much higher. For example, the Malpass family of Nanaimo, headed by a couple from the town's initial South Staffordshire cohort, had a fearsome fecundity: but they lost three infants out of seventeen live births.[93] Sarah Crease, an upper-middle-class immigrant from England, carried seven pregnancies to full term between 1854 and 1872 but may have lost as many as six others.[94] In the First Nations population, the situation was worse. It has been estimated that, generally, fewer than half of the children born to First Nations families would reach adulthood; the culling was most dreadful for infants.[95] At Nanaimo's Indian Mission, eighty-nine burials were recorded between 1886 and 1906, of which thirty-three (37 percent) were of children under the age of five.[96] Among the settler communities, the situation was not much better. Although Kamloops' civic boosters claimed a "nil" incidence of infant mortality in 1894, other sources do not bear out their assertion. In 1892, 1893, and 1894, the Kamloops Anglican burial registers alone indicate six deaths among the under-fives.[97] An examination of an undertaker's registers discloses that as many as one in every four Kamloops funerals for female residents in the years before the First World War involved infant girls. This one firm conducted a dozen or more infant and childhood funerals at the start and end of the 1890s, a rate that rose fairly steadily to two dozen in 1911. And of all the children's funerals performed in Kamloops, as Table 7.6 reveals, the vast majority were for under-ones.[98]

One can conclude from this evidence that the social and psychological crucible of pre-war British Columbia was bound to be shaped in part by the knowledge that a large proportion of children were fated to die before they were old enough to enter school, and that, insofar as infant mortality rates can be used as a barometer of nutrition, environmental conditions, and the

Table 7.6

Infant and child burials, Kamloops, 1891-99, 1905-13

	Childhood deaths by age group					
	Under 1 year		1 to 5 years		5 to 13 years	
Year	(#)	(%)	(#)	(%)	(#)	(%)
1891	6	52	3	22	3	26
1892	8	70	3	30	0	–
1893	1	100	0	–	0	–
1894	6	61	1	16	2	23
1895	2	50	2	50	0	–
1896	1	24	2	52	1	24
1897	3	42	3	45	1	13
1898	5	62	2	26	1	12
1899	12	73	3	19	1	8
1905	9	68	2	15	2	17
1906	5	44	2	15	5	41
1907	7	59	3	22	2	19
1908	4	37	5	43	2	20
1909	15	76	3	12	2	12
1910	8	55	4	25	3	20
1911	10	40	9	36	6	24
1912	8	52	2	14	5	34
1913	9	59	6	41	0	–

Sources: Client Records, 1888-March 1898, 1898-1905, and Funeral Register, June 1905-September 1913, Schoening Funeral Service (1961) Ltd., Kamloops, BC.

general standard of living, the experience of Aboriginals and early settlers in BC was not uniformly good.

The improvement in infant mortality rates through the twentieth century has already been noted in the context of fertility changes (Chapter 5). Not everyone, however, experienced the same degree of relief from infant deaths. In both neonatal and infant mortality categories, Aboriginal British Columbians were subjected to a much more severe trend. James Teit recorded harrowing numbers at Spences Bridge among the Nlaka'pamux: of forty-three lives that began in or after 1884, twenty-five concluded before 1894.[99] Although the rates moved downward throughout the century, Aboriginal neonatal death rates were above 50 per 1,000 live births through most of the 1930s, dropping erratically and slowly to 34.3 in 1951 and 25.3 in 1960; non-Aboriginal rates fell from about 20 in the 1930s and '40s to 17.4 in 1951 and 14.8 in 1960. In the last decade of the twentieth century, these distinctions survived in the rate of post-neonatal deaths (that is, among infants of more than twenty-eight days old but younger than one year), which stood at 9.6 per 1,000 live births among Status Indians and 2.9 among the rest of the provincial population. Similarly, Aboriginal infant deaths (in the one-to four-year-old category) were a staggering 128 per 1,000 live births in 1951, falling by half to 66 per 1,000 live births in 1960; the comparable figures for the non-Aboriginal population were a mere 24.6 and 21.1 per 1,000 live births.[100] Aboriginal infant deaths continued to hover above non-Aboriginal rates, however slightly, until 2000, at which point the differences became fractional.[101]

As to causes of infant deaths, in the half decade of 1955-60, Aboriginal infants were vastly more likely to die of pneumonia, diarrhea, and enteritis than were non-Aboriginal infants. On the other hand, Aboriginal infants were less prone to fatal encounters with bronchitis; nor were they as suscept-ible to death due to prematurity, injury at birth, and congenital malforma-tions. Care during delivery did not seem to make much difference to the figures for either group. Location, however, was a considerable factor. In the mid-1950s, children born in rural areas were at significantly greater risk than those born in the metropolitan centres of Vancouver and Victoria. On the southern tip of Vancouver Island, for example, the neonatal morality rate stood at 12.9; rates topped 20 deaths per 1,000 live births in the East Koote-nays, the Selkirk health district, and the Skeena but were worse still in the south-central Interior at 21.5 deaths.[102]

Infant mortality rates began their long-term retreat in the twenties, if not earlier, falling from 71.4 per 1,000 live births in 1921 to 49.4 in 1931. The statistics to confirm an earlier fall in infant mortality are unavailable, but one suspects that the institutionalization of birthing in British Columbia – well under way by the mid-1920s – contributed most profoundly to these improved rates. Even in the first half of the interwar period, over half of the reported births took place in hospitals or comparable institutions. By 1941-45, the share was over 90 percent, reaching 96 percent at the end of the war.[103]

Maternal Mortality Rates
Hospital births improved maternal survival chances as well. In the 1920s, the rate of maternal mortality in British Columbia was close to 7 per 1,000.[104] As one study shows, in that decade, British Columbia had the lowest birth rate of any province, but it topped the tables for maternal mortalities, which translates to fewer but more dangerous births.[105] The maternal mortality rate fell thereafter but not very smoothly, as can be seen in Table 7.7. Its decline was halted and reversed briefly in the 1930s. Angus McLaren and Arlene Tigar McLaren are no doubt correct in their argument that a significant contribution was made to the rising rate by declining living standards and dangerous practices associated with abortions, especially during the Depres-sion years.[106] Nevertheless, the fact that between 1936 and 1956, the likeli-hood of a woman dying in childbirth fell from about 0.4 percent to 0.03

Table 7.7

Maternal mortality rates (per 1,000 live births), BC and Canada, 1922-66

Year	BC	Canada	Year	BC	Canada	Year	BC	Canada
1922	6.2	5.1	1937	4.5	4.9	1952	0.6	0.9
1923	6.3	5.0	1938	3.9	4.3	1953	0.6	0.8
1924	6.8	5.3	1939	3.1	4.3	1954	0.4	0.7
1925	5.8	4.9	1940	3.1	4.0	1955	0.5	0.8
1926	6.5	5.6	1941	2.7	3.6	1956	0.4	0.6
1927	6.7	5.5	1942	2.7	3.1	1957	0.4	0.5
1928	5.9	5.6	1943	2.5	2.9	1958	0.4	0.6
1929	5.6	5.7	1944	2.6	2.8	1959	0.4	0.5
1930	5.8	5.8	1945	2.7	2.3	1960	0.5	0.4
1931	6.3	5.1	1946	1.7	1.8	1961	0.3	0.5
1932	5.3	5.0	1947	1.2	1.6	1962	0.5	0.4
1933	4.7	5.0	1948	1.1	1.5	1963	0.3	0.3
1934	5.1	5.3	1949	1.0	1.5	1964	0.5	0.3
1935	5.2	4.9	1950	1.0	1.1	1965	0.3	0.3
1936	4.7	5.6	1951	0.7	1.1	1966	0.4	0.4

Sources: British Columbia, *The Nineteen Eighties: A Statistical Resource for a Decade of Vital Events in British Columbia* (Victoria: Ministry of Health and Ministry Responsible for Seniors, 1994), 23; F.H. Leacy, ed., *Historical Statistics of Canada*, 2nd ed. (Ottawa: Statistics Canada, 1983), B51-B58.

percent is surely one of the great medical success stories of the twentieth century. This remarkable reduction in maternal mortality, on which only marginal improvements have since been made, has been ascribed principally to improvements in medicine, including better and more readily available supplies of blood for transfusions. As well, developments in prenatal care are thought to have played a pivotal role, as did the aggressive move to almost universal hospital births.[107] This last factor, perhaps provocative to those who favour home birthing, needs to be considered seriously because of the sharp drop in maternal deaths that came precisely as the fertility rate took off in the mid-1940s.[108] What we know of the baby boom indicates that it depended on more women giving birth once or twice rather than somewhat fewer women having a greater number of babies each. This means that a greater number of women were exposed to the risks of maternal mortality at the very moment when the rate of maternal mortality was sinking. The fact that these changes took place within the context of an expanding public health regime was no coincidence.

By Canada's centennial year, British Columbia had the lowest maternal mortality rate of all provinces. Manitoba and Alberta were not far behind, but the rates of the next nearest – Saskatchewan and Nova Scotia – were about 33 percent higher. What is most remarkable in the data presented in Figure 7.2 is the contrast between British Columbia and Quebec. In the latter,

Figure 7.2

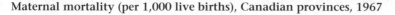

Maternal mortality (per 1,000 live births), Canadian provinces, 1967

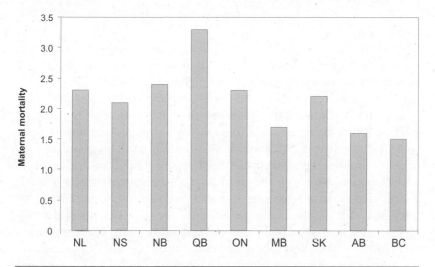

Source: Dr. A.J.J.G. Nuyens, "Maternal Mortality in Ontario," n.d., 191, Health Consultants – Adult Health – General Maternal Mortality, Health Services and Promotion Branch, RG 29, vol. 51, file 6756-1-3, Library and Archives Canada.

a long-delayed fertility transition arrived in the 1960s, so the fact that we find twice as many maternal deaths in a province where active fertility was sharply in decline is remarkable. This statistic, perhaps more than any other, distinguishes the two low-birth-rate provinces demographically. Quebec had a low fertility rate, but, simply stated, a pregnancy in that province was a more dangerous proposition than anywhere else in Canada; in British Columbia, fertility fell, and the safeguards for those women who continued to produce children were evidently first-rate.

At least, that was the case for non-Aboriginal women. For First Nations women in British Columbia, the picture was not so bright. While non-Aboriginal maternal mortality began a steady decline in the mid-1930s, the Aboriginal rate simultaneously moved upward to a high of roughly 13 deaths per 1,000 live births. The late 1930s were arguably exceptional years in this respect, but the rate began to stabilize only in the 1940s at more than double its non-Aboriginal equivalent. In the 1950s, too, the rates refused to meet completely. There were 1.1 Aboriginal maternal deaths per 1,000 live births in 1951, actually rising through the decade to a high of 2.8 in 1954, and falling to 1.3 in 1960; in the same three years, the non-Aboriginal numbers were 0.7, 0.3, and 0.4 per 1,000 live births. From 1955 to 1966, First Nations cases of maternal mortality constituted more than 16 percent of the provincial total, despite the fact that Native peoples were only 2.4 percent of the population. In terms of maternal mortality, as in every other category, the demographic complexion of Aboriginal life (and death) stands apart from that of the rest of British Columbia.[109]

Conclusion

Much more could be said about mortality and death in British Columbia, but this study can deal only with the *statistical* features of death: that is, with mortality rates. The *cultural* phenomenon of death, however, plays out differently from place to place as social and demographic circumstances change. How and when and where people die is one thing: what an emerging and fluid settler society makes of those events is quite another. If we remember that cemeteries were (and in some places in BC, still are) segregated by race, it is immediately evident that death means more than a cessation of bodily functions. Moreover, the early evidence suggests that rituals surrounding death in BC have often been elaborate and very public, presumably to compensate for the absence of mourning family members. Benevolent societies sprang up to meet both the social and mortal needs of a largely male, unmarried, or spouseless society of newcomers. One could argue that the rise of early trade unions and fraternal lodges was, in part, sustained and promoted by the province's peculiar mortality regime.

But let's place some of this chapter's findings into perspective. What we know is that the province registered comparatively high crude mortality and infant mortality rates since the nineteenth century. The net effect of which practically cancelled out the addition of population through natural means. We can see, then, how a community with a relatively (and historically) low fertility rate would, of necessity, come to depend on immigration to build up its numbers. This link has not been recognized as fully in the literature on immigration and social change in British Columbia as perhaps it should be. Ultimately, what drives immigration isn't the market for labour: it's the market for coffins.

8

The British Columbia Clearances: Some Conclusions

Taken as a whole, the story of British Columbia's population since the eighteenth century has been one of dramatic and repeated transformation. At almost every turn, we find British Columbia at the extremes of Western world demographic trends. The consequences of imperialism for Aboriginal populations were catastrophic elsewhere, but the numbers involved in this region – even the lowball numbers – appear to dwarf all others in what is now Canada and the United States. The speed of newcomer arrival in the gold rush years had but one Canadian echo, in the Klondike. The diversity on the ground makes the history of Victorian agonizing over Irish Catholic minorities in Ontario and New Brunswick look ridiculous by contrast. Sex ratios, fertility trends, divorce rates, and urbanization distinguish British Columbia from even its nearest Canadian neighbours. The collapse of fertility in mid-twentieth-century Quebec absorbs much national interest, and for important reasons, but it is startling to find British Columbian demography breathing down Quebec's neck in various categories or, indeed, surging ahead. At the start of a new century, we see the westernmost province stabilizing within Canadian and North American demographic norms, but huge distinctions remain. The population is aging in ways unlike that of the rest of Canada; it is Asianizing as well, and feminizing. Several writers have already pointed to Vancouver's rise as a regional super/metro/cosmo-polis, one with a diminishing link to its own provincial hinterland but also one that models an emergent variation on urbanism that syncretizes – to an extent unlike any other North American city – European and Asian forms.[1] To employ a metaphor with local resonance, the demographic history and the probable demographic future of British Columbia resemble the great, aging wooden roller coaster at the Pacific National Exhibition: seemingly beyond control and continually flirting with disaster – imagined or real.

What has happened, demographically, is only part of the question historians must address. If the population history of British Columbia has been consistently unusual, is there One Big Theory that can be used to explain patterns of exceptionality? Perhaps we may go that far.

Because I am a Marxist informed by feminist and post-colonial theory, my interpretation predictably turns on questions of historical economic structures and consequent power relations. The intrusion of eighteenth-century Europeans occurred at a time when one kind of imperialism (emblematized by the Spanish and, to a lesser extent, the Russians) collided with an emerging capitalistic variant (played out by the British and Americans). The changes taking place in European economic structures were forces that lay behind the unprecedented four-way race to dominate the west coast, albeit at a huge distance from home ports. The gendering of "exploration," Enlightenment science, and commerce placed men in this particular frame and left women outside. In other words, a "Man's Province" doesn't just happen: it exposes prevailing values in the dominant society at the time, especially when pressed by contingent factors such as the cost of long-distance travel. The history of capital accumulation based on colonial exploitation positioned these players to engage in their globe-trotting commerce and territorial occupation. Enlightenment-era wealth and productive capacity equipped them for travel to the Pacific slope and for material domination over Aboriginal peoples. It also facilitated what the French historian Emmanuel Le Roy Ladurie long ago correctly called the "unification of the globe by disease."[2] The demographic history of British Columbia in the century that followed can be understood only within the context of industrial capitalism. The gold rush, the establishment of coal- and silver-mining communities, and investment in canneries and sawmills were trademarks of British and British North American capitalist expansion in the age of steam and telegraph. They each required and effected the proletarianization of labour, nowhere more so than in British Columbia. Aboriginal peoples were drawn into this process, as were European, Euro-North American, and Asian peasants and wage-labourers. On the prairies, this would clearly not be the case, notwithstanding the eruption of colliery towns such as Drumheller: these excrescences would prove the exception to the rule of the family-run farm as the principal unit of production. In British Columbia, the typical colonist was a male wage-labourer, the colonized "Other" was a subsistence-oriented Native, and the colonial demography was built on those two facts. Proletarianization under industrial capitalism permitted and endorsed immigration of adult males without reference to natural increase or the needs of settlers themselves (let alone the needs of Aboriginal peoples). Indeed, this is the context, too, of Aboriginal economic marginalization: why proletarianize anew a population that has its own economic reality when there is plenty of surplus, already proletarianized labour milling about on the docks in Guangdong, San Francisco, Halifax, or Liverpool? And if the Natives aren't prepared to be useful under these terms, spatial isolation from the *real business* of nineteenth-century industrial colonialism is one obvious solution.

Industrialization dominated the backstory in Victorian and Edwardian British Columbia, and it was hardly less so across the "short twentieth century" from 1914 to 1989. Canada emerged as a semi-autonomous participant in an increasingly integrated global economic order. There is no clearer demonstration of that development than the economic depression of the 1930s. British Columbia's special degree of adversity in that decade stems precisely from both the rise of the international commodities market and the inherent rootlessness of free industrial labour – even agricultural wage-labour on the prairies – that culminated in profound economic dislocation on the west coast. Natural-resource-extraction industries continued to exploit mobile (or economically "free") adult males and even families in a market-place that was increasingly fragile; the army of unemployed that poured into Vancouver in the 1930s was proof of that, and it was the foundation of the demographic changes that followed on the heels of *Anschluss* and Pearl Harbor. Had labour in the port city not been readily available, it is unlikely that the reindustrialization of the shipbuilding industry along Burrard Inlet and False Creek in 1939-40 would have taken place with such speed. Coupled to wartime employment, the postponement of marriage among the unemployed and underemployed contributed to a marriage boom and thus a baby boom that led Canadian rates of rising fertility. Arguably, nothing has so informed the post-war culture and economy as that singular constellation of demographic events.

Global capitalism entered into its consumerist phase before the Cold War began, but the ideological friction between Eastern Bloc and Western Alliance served to drive demographic values in particular directions.[3] This was a phenomenon experienced widely in the West and certainly not exclusively in British Columbia. What strikes me as exceptional in this context, however, is how quickly a Man's Province made up of what Adele Perry calls "hardy backwoodsmen" became reconceptualized as a suburban, material-istic, and nuclear-family-dominated society. (Ontario and Alberta, by way of contrast, did not have to travel nearly so far in this respect.) As prosperity became an essential weapon against communism at home and abroad, there followed a rise in the rate of natural increase. This was part of a package of changes in socio-economic behaviour, as material expectations and standards changed, especially among working-class families who now sought the prosperity, security, and comforts that were previously the exclusive lot of their social betters. Thus, prosperity required the creation of a new under-class prepared to perform the entry-level wage-labour that was now beneath the standards of so many British Columbians. Immigration does not occur in a vacuum but within a matrix of economic needs, and the midcentury rise of an Indo-British Columbian community, for example, can be understood only within this setting. Racist barriers had outlived their usefulness by the 1970s and had to be challenged, generating a post-modern British Columbia in which prescribed identities dating back to the gold rush were reconsidered. That this took place on the eve of the Hong Kong crisis was probably coincidental, but it certainly facilitated the arrival and integration of the largest immigration since the nineteenth century. From the Atlantic perspective of New York and London, the Cold War may have ended in 1989, but Tiananmen Square underlined its persistence on the Pacific Rim. Through the 1990s, Asian immigration accelerated, driven and facilitated by capitalism and by ideological and material fears of the People's Republic.

The newest of newcomers might be forgiven for thinking that the current boom in housing prices on the coast derives from the impact of Asian immigration or from the 2010 Winter Olympics. In point of fact, no economic activity so defined life in twentieth-century Vancouver as real estate. The bard of imperialism, Rudyard Kipling, tried to flip property in the Terminal City prior to 1914, and residents, visitors, and international investors have been doing the same before and since.[4] The housing marketplace, especially in Vancouver and Victoria but increasingly throughout all the southern cities on the island and the mainland, has made fortunes for some, but it has also determined the shape of the family. For example, prices rocketed upward in the 1980s when second-wave feminism generated the possibility of many two-income households. Since that time, per capita floorspace in new Vancouver homes has fallen. This is both a signal of, and a factor in, decreasing family size.

Not to belabour the point, but the specific economic infrastructure of British Columbia has framed mortality rates as well. Whether we look to industrial death, infant and maternal mortality, or the experience of widowhood, it is inescapable that these phenomena occur within the context of a resource-extraction economic order. A counter-argument would no doubt claim that commercial- and administrative-urban centres, such as Vancouver and Victoria, offer a different pattern, and indeed they do. But it is a bourgeois pattern in the truest sense. Being of the *bourg,* or town, a great many middle- and upper-class British Columbians have escaped the mortality regime that is the lot of the majority in this province. To look to other urbanites – those whose livelihood is found in the canneries, the mills, the dockyards, and the naval bases – is to remind one how much of demography is determined by socio-economic class, even within the bourg. In a deindustrializing global economy, the contours of a blue-collar demography become the subject of nostalgia for some, but they persist in life expectancies and can be tracked down without difficulty in East Vancouver, in mining, smelter, and greenchain towns, and on reserves across the province.

It is important to situate, too, the unique-in-Canada phenomenon of a demographic boom among seniors, the significance of which should not be underestimated. Although every province watches with concern the greying of the population, British Columbia (and its frayed social safety net) faces double jeopardy – a cohort of newly arrived retirees and another that is homegrown. Given that, under the Canadian federal system, socially funded eldercare (like health care) is a burden carried principally by the provinces, this singular demographic feature, combined with an especially low rate of natural increase, is guaranteed to become a political football. Fear of a beggared provincial treasury (and fearmongering of the same) seems to drive upward the stock of neo-conservative politicians committed to reducing state obligations to the old. Much of the debate over public- versus private-sector engagement in these fields arises from demographics, although, to be sure, the burden of carrying the costs of eldercare (traditionally shouldered by welfare-statists on the left) and the opportunities of making money from services rendered to the elderly (readily seized by the right) are starkly and instinctively ideological.[5]

A Marxian approach to demography is neither reductionist nor nostalgic: it comprehends the chain that links economics, class, and life. It is important to register this ideological perspective because Whiggish liberal understandings of demography are so dominant. As indicated at the outset, so long as studies of population in Canada remain invested with notions of bigger and better, we cannot hope for a critical appreciation of change over time and its various manifestations. The overall story of British Columbia's population is one of growth, but against that one must note the several milestones of disaster, stagnation, and repeated periods of decline. These contrary currents in the grand narrative of expansion are the moments that test the larger project and its assumptions. The process of becoming British Columbia is not linear nor is it progressive nor, for that matter, is it a case of ebbs and flows; whole generations spent themselves struggling against the ebb tides, and their hardships contribute to whatever understanding of the place unfolds. In point of fact, demographic downturn – indeed, demographic suffering – has been consciously, wilfully inflicted upon British Columbians by other British Columbians. This is an ugly demographic theme that runs throughout the history of British Columbia, and it, too, is unusual though not unique.

From the imperial period on, there are incidents in which people – in this sense, human communities with functioning biological engines of growth – are removed in whole or in part. The British Columbian Clearances start with Aboriginal communities. In some instances, one First Nations group displaced another to be closer to European trade resources, but the European colonizers quickly developed the habit of pushing Aboriginal villages to one side. This occurred on Vancouver Island at Victoria and Nanaimo as elsewhere, but more severely in the Fraser Canyon during the gold rush. The 1860s witnessed a wholesale reallocation of land resources under the auspices of the imperial regime, an event that has been thoroughly documented by Cole Harris. One community of First Nations after the next found itself contained on reserves, which is to say *cleared* from the non-reserved land on which it had previously lived. Newcomer railway and road construction, necessarily pinched into what valleys and alleys occur in a mountainous terrain, saw Native communities evacuated, sometimes repeatedly, and well into the twentieth century.[6]

Asian communities also found their spatial tenure in British Columbia negotiable. Kay Anderson has demonstrated how "Chinatown" was a constructed space similar in some respects to reserves, and she usefully reminds us of "the underlying European racial frame of reference" to population and community that is still in effect.[7] Closed, forbidding, and exotic in the eyes of many non-Chinese, Chinatown – whether in Victoria, Nanaimo, or Vancouver – was lived by its residents as under-serviced, neglected, and vulnerable. Although it is true that Chinese medical practitioners did not face the kind of suppression visited upon traditional Aboriginal health care practitioners, suspicion of Chinese drug trafficking and barriers to treatment in "white" hospitals had undeniable impacts, as did immigration laws. Women were not "cleared" from Chinatown, to be sure; they were merely barred from entering its demographic equation. Other groups suffered similarly. Racism oppressed people in their day-to-day existence but also in their very biological fabric and certainly in their life-course. In this instance, as Mary-Ellen Kelm's study of the "colonization of bodies" demonstrates, the numbers do not lie: *History,* that juggernaut of imperial mission, had powerful implications for births, marriages, fertility, movement, and mortality for subject peoples.[8]

Euro-British Columbians did not escape these processes. Through the nineteenth and twentieth centuries, company towns rose and fell, and almost every cycle entailed the forced relocation of large numbers of white households. This happened repeatedly on the Vancouver Island coalfield as the people of Wellington relocated to Extension and from Extension to Ladysmith. Likewise, hard-rock mining towns in the southeast were built by (largely foreign) capital and closed at its whim.

The experience of children in this tale of community cleansing draws together the sagas of First Nations and newcomers. Children have long been targets of human relocation schemes in the province, beginning with Aboriginal children who were forcibly packed off to residential schools and continuing through the "Sixties Scoop" of still more Aboriginal children.[9] This sorry tale and the apprehension and relocation of more than a hundred Doukhobor children in 1953 remain acts of stark inhumanity, against which voices were raised at the time and for which no individual has yet been held to account.[10]

Growing state power and a modernizing, impersonal bureaucracy led to further displacements. In the 1930s nearly six hundred Sons of Freedom were incarcerated on Piers Island for the especially devised criminal offence of public nudity. This was, in effect, a forced relocation at the hands of the state that gutted communities from Grand Forks through the Slocan for three years. In the 1950s and '60s, the W.A.C. Bennett administration cleared other remote "hinterland" villages wholesale. Perhaps the most single-minded example in the relatively recent past was the destruction of entire healthy communities to enable the flooding of the Arrow Lakes with an eye to generating cheap electricity for urban consumers.[11] Even city-dwellers were not immune to these twentieth-century clearances. The urban working class and poor have been pushed aside to make way for gentrification (typically a gradual process) or urban renewal (sometimes marked by blitzkrieg subtlety). The Central School District in downtown Vancouver – a densely packed working-class neighbourhood and left-wing civic ward – was effectively rezoned out of existence beginning in 1927, though it has lately become a bijou postal code carpeted by converted warehouse apartments and expensive high-rises. The "hobo jungles" of the (mostly white) homeless unemployed in the Depression were razed in 1931, many of the residents finding themselves exiled to men-only relief camps in the Interior. Residents of Vancouver's Gastown, Chinatown, and Strathcona mostly stayed the hand of "redevelopment" in the 1950s and '60s, but whole city blocks were nonetheless bulldozed and the residents removed to grim housing projects. Many well-established False Creek residents succumbed to similar urban renewal pressures in the 1970s and 1980s. Urban Aboriginal communities have fared especially badly: Kitsilano Point and Whoi-Whoi (a.k.a. Lumberman's Arch) are two familiar sites from which Native occupants were banished. The bureaucratic herding of the poor and socially "deviant" into "Skid Row" (itself a spatial and demographic problem) has been brilliantly charted and critiqued elsewhere.[12]

The Japanese evacuation in 1942 is widely perceived as anomalous, but it is not. Relocations affected thousands of British Columbians. Native. Asian. White. Families. Children. And this list does not begin to consider those potential British Columbians who were forbidden entry and thus were never really *cleared away*. Nor, because they did not constitute a functioning biological community, does it include the hundreds of inmates of the province's mental hospitals who were either deported or sterilized.[13] In this context, however, the passengers on the *Komagata Maru* and the unfortunates of Essondale can be seen as part of something larger, something more than racist or eugenicist, something downright demographic.[14]

It is hardly surprising to find that these are the very categories to which the dominant patriarchal Anglo-British Columbian elite only reluctantly extended full citizenship.[15] These clearances took place within ideological frameworks that provided an invariably "forward-looking" justification. They were, in the fewest words, all about making way for the future. Some writers have celebrated British Columbia's lack of a historical consciousness. Douglas Coupland, for example, writes "If you're a Vancouverite, you find the city's lack of historical luggage liberating – it dazzles with a sense of limitless possibility."[16] I was born a second-generation Vancouverite and I cannot agree. The banishing of the past from our consciousness is liberating only insofar as it lifts the burden of responsibility. If we are dazzled with the possibility of crushing the populations of remote valleys and nearby neighbourhoods, well, fine. The future then becomes the thing, and much may be justifiably sacrificed to its will.

The continual forced movement or containment or restriction of population is ideological, but it is also demographic in its origins. And, as a demographic history, this is where the present study must conclude. Population is political. The right kind of population in the right place at the right time is the authentic goal of the modern state since before the 1850s. British Columbia bears that stamp. Successive regimes have understood "population" differently, but all have engaged with demographic concerns, for good or ill. If the central project of human societies is encouraging stable or growing numbers, managing movement in and out, and handling the multifaceted question of mortality, then it is incumbent on academics, policy makers, and the citizenry to take population seriously. Demography is not *all*, one need not be a reductionist.[17] But one must be alert to efforts to "landscape the human garden."[18] Such urges on the part of the state, the elite, outsiders, and insiders lie at the heart of our communities' and our personal histories.

Appendices

Appendix A
Leading Settlements/Towns/Cities, BC, 1871-1951

1871

Community (100+)	Population	Community (100+)	Population
Victoria	3,720	Lytton	250
Nanaimo	2,500	Cowichan Bay	224
New Westminster	2,000	Langley	200
Barkerville	1,000	Lillooet	200
Yale	500	Comox	102

1881

Community (100+)	Population	Community (100+)	Population
Victoria	5,925	Cowichan Bay	221
New Westminster	2,500	Kamloops	200
Nanaimo	1,645	Sooke	200
Burrard Inlet	1,200	Cloverdale	180
Wellington	1,000	Alexandria	165
Yale	1,000	Comox	102
Barkerville	500	Hope	100
Lillooet	300	Langley	100
Lytton	300	Quesnel	100

1891

Community (500+)	Population	Community (500+)	Population
Victoria	16,841	Rossland/Trail	2,000
Vancouver	13,709	Kamloops	1,500
New Westminster	6,678	Union Bay	1,500
Nanaimo	4,595	Comox	1,000
Wellington/Northfield	2,400	Greenwood	1,000
New Denver to Kaslo	2,300	Revelstoke/Farwell	900
Nelson	2,000	Cedar	800

1891

Community (500+)	Population	Community (500+)	Population
Esquimalt	700	Cumberland	500
Grand Forks	700	Duncan	500
Port Essington	700	Fort Steele	500
Ainsworth	600	Golden	500
Vernon	600	Hastings	500
Burrard Inlet (North Vancouver)	500	Ladner	500
Chilliwack	500	Nakusp	500
Cranbrook	500	Ymir	500

1901

Community (500+)	Population	Community (500+)	Population
Vancouver	26,133	Phoenix	866
Victoria	20,816	Vernon	802
Rossland/Trail	7,519	Cedar	800
(Rossland = 6,159; Trail = 1,360)		Ladner	800
New Westminster	6,499	Port Essington	750
Nanaimo	6,130	Ladysmith	746
Nelson	5,273	Cumberland	732
Kaslo	1,680	Golden	705
Fernie	1,640	Trout Lake	700
Revelstoke (Farwell)	1,600	Ainsworth	600
Kamloops	1,594	Coquitlam	600
Atlin	1,500	Moyie	582
Comox	1,500	Sandon	551
Greenwood	1,359	Port Moody	539
Esquimalt	1,200	Barkerville	520
Cranbrook	1,196	Alberni	502
Union Bay	1,149	Sechelt	500
Grand Forks	1,012	Slocan	500

1911

Community (500+)	Population	Community (500+)	Population
Vancouver	120,847	Revelstoke (Farwell)	3,017
Victoria	31,660	Rossland	2,826
South Vancouver	16,126	Vernon	2,371
New Westminster	13,199	Hosmer	2,019
North Vancouver	8,196	Kelowna	1,661
Nanaimo	6,254	Chilliwack	1,657
Nelson	4,476	Grand Forks	1,577
Point Grey	4,320	Michel	1,515
Prince Rupert	4,184	Trail	1,460
Esquimalt	4,001	Cumberland	1,237
Kamloops	3,772	Golden	932
Ladysmith	3,295	Alberni	891
Fernie	3,060	Enderby	835

1911

Community (500+)	Population	Community (500+)	Population
Summerland	835	Mission City	600
Armstrong	810	Morrissey	600
Ladner	800	Arrowhead	560
Penticton	800	Hazelmere	550
Stewart	800	Hazelton	550
Greenwood	778	Port Moody	550
Kaslo	722	Ashcroft	535
Merritt	703	Atlin	500
Port Alberni	700	Chemainus	500
Port Essington	700	Duncan	500
New Michel	662	Keremeos	500
Phoenix	662	Midway	500
Clearbrook	650	Moyie	500
Ymir	650	Silverton	500
Marysville	600	Wardner	500

1921

Community (500+)	Population	Community (500+)	Population
Vancouver	163,220	Duncan	1,178
Victoria and Esquimalt	38,727	Port Coquitlam	1,178
New Westminster	14,495	Steveston	1,100
North Vancouver	7,652	Port Simpson	1,030
Nanaimo	6,559	Princeton	1,000
Prince Rupert	6,393	Kaslo	950
Nelson	5,230	Golden	900
Kamloops	4,501	Port Hammond	900
Penticton	4,000	Williams Lake	900
Vernon	3,685	Courtenay	800
Summerland/W. Summerland	3,300	Michel	800
Trail	3,020	Enderby	783
Fernie	2,802	Creston	700
Revelstoke (Farwell)	2,782	Keremeos	700
Cranbrook	2,725	Smithers	650
Kelowna	2,520	Salmon Arm	627
Rossland	2,097	Inverness	600
Prince George	2,056	Nakusp	600
Ladysmith	1,967	Sandon	600
Chilliwack	1,767	Ashcroft	500
Port Alberni/Alberni	1,596	Cassidy	500
Pouce Coupe	1,500	Corbin	500
Grand Forks	1,469	Hedley	500
Merritt	1,389	Ioco	500
Mission City	1,200	Natal	500
Sidney	1,200	Peachland	500
Cumberland	1,179	Port Essington	500

1921

Community (500+)	Population	Community (500+)	Population
Quesnel	500	Squamish	500
South Wellington	500	Vananda	500

1931

Community (500+)	Population	Community (500+)	Population
Vancouver	246,593	Port Haney	1,000
Victoria and Esquimalt	39,082	Princeton	1,000
New Westminster	17,524	Steveston	1,000
North Vancouver	8,510	Summerland	1,000
Trail	7,573	Smithers	999
Nanaimo	6,745	Armstrong	989
Prince Rupert	6,350	Port Hammond	950
Kamloops	6,167	Cumberland	907
Nelson	5,992	Fraser Mills	900
Kelowna	4,655	Salmon Arm	830
Penticton	4,000	Sidney	800
Vernon	3,937	Port Simpson	725
Kimberley	3,500	Creston	695
Cranbrook	3,067	Port Alice	650
Port Alberni/Alberni	3,058	Somenos	610
Rossland	2,848	Golden	600
Revelstoke	2,736	Squamish	600
Fernie	2,732	White Rock	600
Prince George	2,479	Enderby	555
Chilliwack	2,461	Kaslo	523
Ocean Falls	2,000	Abbotsford	510
Duncan	1,843	Ashcroft	500
Britannia Beach	1,700	Atlin	500
Anyox	1,500	Canoe	500
Coquitlam	1,500	Cassidy	500
Ladysmith	1,443	Cloverdale	500
Mission City	1,314	Corbin	500
Port Coquitlam	1,312	Dewdney	500
Grand Forks	1,298	Fort Langley	500
Merritt	1,296	Hedley	500
Port Moody	1,260	Ioco	500
Courtenay	1,219	Milner	500
Campbell River	1,200	Pouce Coupe	500
Yarrow	1,067	Sointula	500
Buckley Bay	1,000	Somenos	500
Michel	1,000		

1941

Community (700+)	Population	Community (700+)	Population
Vancouver	275,353	Ladysmith	1,706
Victoria and Esquimalt	44,068	Chemainus	1,679
New Westminster	21,967	Ocean Falls	1,556
Surrey	14,840	Port Coquitlam	1,539
Richmond	10,370	Port Moody	1,512
Trail	9,392	Princeton	1,380
North Vancouver	8,914	Grand Forks	1,259
Coquitlam	7,949	Creston	1,153
West Vancouver	7,669	Natal	1,117
Prince Rupert	6,714	Copper Mountain	1,106
Nanaimo	6,635	Yarrow	1,067
Port Alberni/Alberni	6,391	Michel	1,066
Kamloops	5,959	Rutland	1,004
Nelson	5,912	Fruitvale	994
Vernon	5,209	Armstrong	977
Kelowna	5,118	Lumby	959
Chilliwack	3,675	Merritt	940
Rossland	3,657	Agassiz	911
Cranbrook	2,568	Bralorne	894
Fernie	2,545	Cumberland	885
Duncan	2,189	Woodfibre	860
Revelstoke	2,106	Salmon Arm	836
Prince George	2,057	Port Alice	807
Summerland	2,054	Powell River	782
Mission City	1,957	Smithers	759
White Rock	1,814	Golden	756
Ladner	1,800	Haney	733
Courtenay	1,737		

1951

Community (1,500+)	Population	Community (1,500+)	Population
Vancouver	344,833	Kelowna	8,517
Victoria and Esquimalt	51,331	Vernon	7,822
Surrey	33,670	Nanaimo	7,196
Burnaby	30,328	Nelson	6,772
New Westminster	28,639	Kimberley	5,933
Richmond	19,186	Chilliwack	5,663
Coquitlam	15,697	Summerland/ W. Summerland	5,056
North Vancouver	15,687	Prince George	4,703
West Vancouver	13,990	Rossland	4,604
Trail	11,430	Cranbrook	3,621
Port Alberni/Alberni	11,168	White Rock	3,441
Penticton	10,548	Port Coquitlam	3,232
Kamloops/North Kamloops	9,998	Ocean Falls	2,825
Prince Rupert	8,546	Duncan	2,784

	1951		
Community (1,500+)	*Population*	*Community (1,500+)*	*Population*
Mission City	2,668	Rutland	1,976
Courtenay	2,553	Hope	1,668
Fernie	2,551	Chemainus	1,661
Port Moody	2,246	Sidney	1,648
Princeton	2,147	Grand Forks	1,646
Ladysmith	2,094	Lake Cowichan	1,628
Prince George	2,074	Creston	1,626
Central Saanich	2,069	Quesnel	1,587
Campbell River	1,986	Haney	1,512

Sources: Riley Moffat, *Population History of Cities and Towns in Canada, Australia, and New Zealand: 1861-1996* (London: Scarecrow Press, 2001), 12-20; *Census of Canada, 1981,* catalogue no. 93-934 (Ottawa: Statistics Canada), table 2.

Appendix B
Total Population, BC, 1867-2006 (Rounded to 000s)

Year	Total	Year	Total	Year	Total	Year	Total
1867	32,000	1902	199,000	1937	759,000	1972	2,302,000
1868	33,000	1903	220,000	1938	775,000	1973	2,367,000
1869	34,000	1904	242,000	1939	792,000	1974	2,443,000
1870	36,000	1905	264,000	1940	805,000	1975	2,500,000
1871	36,000	1906	279,000	1941	818,000	1976	2,534,000
1872	37,000	1907	309,000	1942	870,000	1977	2,570,000
1873	39,000	1908	330,000	1943	900,000	1978	2,614,000
1874	37,000	1909	350,000	1944	932,000	1979	2,663,000
1875	42,000	1910	370,000	1945	949,000	1980	2,743,000
1876	43,000	1911	393,000	1946	1,003,000	1981	2,824,000
1877	44,000	1912	407,000	1947	1,044,000	1982	2,873,000
1878	45,000	1913	424,000	1948	1,082,000	1983	2,906,000
1879	46,000	1914	442,000	1949	1,113,000	1984	2,946,000
1880	48,000	1915	450,000	1950	1,137,000	1985	2,974,000
1881	49,000	1916	456,000	1951	1,165,000	1986	3,004,000
1882	54,000	1917	464,000	1952	1,205,000	1987	3,050,000
1883	59,000	1918	474,000	1953	1,248,000	1988	3,115,000
1884	64,000	1919	488,000	1954	1,295,000	1989	3,198,000
1885	69,000	1920	507,000	1955	1,342,000	1990	3,291,000
1886	74,000	1921	525,000	1956	1,399,000	1991	3,374,000
1887	78,000	1922	541,000	1957	1,482,000	1992	3,469,000
1888	83,000	1923	555,000	1958	1,538,000	1993	3,568,000
1889	88,000	1924	571,000	1959	1,567,000	1994	3,676,000
1890	93,000	1925	588,000	1960	1,602,000	1995	3,777,000
1891	98,000	1926	606,000	1961	1,629,000	1996	3,874,000
1892	106,000	1927	623,000	1962	1,660,000	1997	3,949,000
1893	114,000	1928	641,000	1963	1,699,000	1998	3,983,000
1894	122,000	1929	659,000	1964	1,745,000	1999	4,011,000
1895	130,000	1930	676,000	1965	1,797,000	2000	4,039,000
1896	138,000	1931	694,300	1966	1,874,000	2001	4,079,000
1897	146,000	1932	707,000	1967	1,945,000	2002	4,115,000
1898	154,000	1933	717,000	1968	2,003,000	2003	4,155,000
1899	162,000	1934	727,000	1969	2,060,000	2004	4,203,000
1900	170,000	1935	736,000	1970	2,128,000	2005	4,258,000
1901	179,000	1936	745,200	1971	2,240,000	2006	4,311,000

Source: Statistics Canada, Ottawa, prepared by BC Stats, Ministry of Labour and Citizen's Services, Victoria, http://www.bcstats.gov.bc.ca/data/pop/pop/BC1867on.csv.

Appendix C
Age and Sex Distributions, BC, 1891-2001

Thanks to the baby boom and the subsequent aging of the Canadian popula-tion, the general public now has some passing acquaintance with population pyramids. What appears below in Figures C.1 to C.13, however, looks very un-pyramidish, so some explanation is necessary.

Proper pyramidal shapes reflect certain demographic conditions. If the birth rate is high but child mortality chews away at young cohorts, if adulthood is perilous due to childbirth risks or chronic health issues or recurrent violent conflict but not in such a way as to favour a heavily male or heavily female population, and if few individuals graduate into old age, the resultant shape will be very much like a pyramid: wide at the bottom, narrowing to a peak at the top. Developing countries and Aboriginal populations alike tend to produce distributions of this order. Economies and societies that enjoy sufficient wealth distribution and a general application of public health practices, however, tend to produce a pattern that is far more columnar: roughly even on either side, tapering suddenly at the top like a soft ice-cream cone. By further contrast, com-munities that experience adult immigration tend to bloat in the middle ranges. Finally, an aging population that is not supported by large younger cohorts is likely to present a lightbulb shape. This is, of course, the worrying scenario set forth for the years after 2015 when the boomer bulge floats further upward like a helium balloon.

In some respects, age and sex pyramids are brutish tools: a whole population reduced to a pile of stacking Lego blocks without distinctions between ethnic/racial groups and rural/urban communities. Their appeal, however, is in their deceptive simplicity: a glance, most people think, tells us all we need to know. (And, indeed, a glance at Figure C.13 tells us that female retirement migration is the fastest-growing demographic of 2001.) But population pyramids invite more rigorous analysis and use. Look not only at the oversupply of males (some-times females) in any given year, but also at how each gender cohort compares with that above or below it. The cohort of twenty-five- to twenty-nine-year-old males, for example, was clearly in economic demand from 1891 through 1911 (Figures C.2 to C.4); the impact on the under-thirties of war and a maturing economy can be seen affecting this age group in 1921 and 1931 (Figures C.5 and C.6). Also, look at the share of the under-fives in 1931 relative to the five- to fourteen-year-olds in that year and then look at the same cohort relationships in 1921 (Figures C.5 and C.6); as a share of population, babies were becoming less evident. Follow a single cohort across the decades, from zero to four years of age to ten to fourteen, twenty to twenty-four, thirty to thirty-four, and so on. How does its demographic reality change? Specifically, follow the twenty-fives to twenty-nines of 1911 through the decades. They literally stick out of the pack through their seventies. Notice, too, how a rising life expectancy creates a grow-ing capstone shelf of individuals over the age of seventy-five. And see how Gen-X reveals itself in 1971 and 1981 as a shrinking foundation, overburdened by boomers. A more discerning approach to population (a.k.a. age and sex) pyramids can thus produce insights into the life-course of a whole community.

A note about structure. Pyramids are often presented in percentages. This is fine when both the male and the female slopes are roughly the same, but it tends to diminish intergender differences. Take a look at the two pyramids for 1911 in Figure C.1.

Percents represent the female population as smaller than its male counterpart, but not dwarfed; the use of real numbers produces a very different effect while

Figure C.1a and C.1b

Sex ratios, BC, 1911

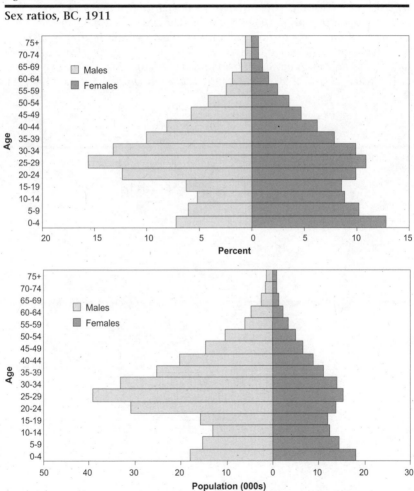

Sources: BC Stats, http://www.bcstats.gov.bc.ca/data/pop/pop/project/bctab7.asp, http://www. bcstats.gov.bc.ca/data/pop/pop/project/bctab8.asp, 1 May 2007; Statistics Canada, "Age Groups and Sex for Population, for Canada, Provinces and Territories, 1921 to 2001 Censuses – 100 percent Data," Online catalogue no. 97F0003XCB2001002; Julie M. Macdonald, "Vital Statistics in British Columbia: An Historical Overview of 100 Years, 1891 to 1990," *Vital Statistics Quarterly Digest* 4, 1 (June 1994): 20.

not losing the internal, gender-specific sense of proportions across age cohorts. For that reason, I have departed from customary practice and have used real numbers as the basis of the pyramids below. The distortions disappear around 1941; thereafter, the percentage and real number versions are almost identical. Be aware, too, that the numbers jump up so sharply after 1951 that the scale on the Y-axis increases abruptly, giving the impression that the total population size has collapsed.

The Figures C.2 to C.13 are drawn from the following sources: BC Stats, http://www.bcstats.gov.bc.ca/data/pop/pop/project/bctab7.asp, http://www.bcstats.gov.bc.ca/data/pop/pop/project/bctab8.asp, 1 May 2007; Statistics Canada, "Age Groups and Sex for Population, for Canada, Provinces and Territories, 1921 to 2001 Censuses – 100 percent Data," Online catalogue no. 97F0003XCB2001002; Julie M. Macdonald, "Vital Statistics in British Columbia: An Historical Overview of 100 Years, 1891 to 1990," *Vital Statistics Quarterly Digest* 4, 1 (June 1994): 20.

Figure C.2

Sex ratios, BC, 1891

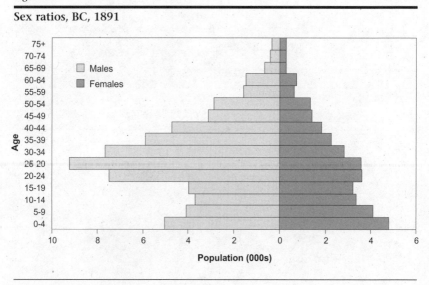

Figure C.3

Sex ratios, BC, 1901

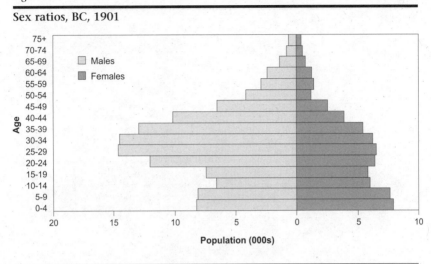

Figure C.4

Sex ratios, BC, 1911

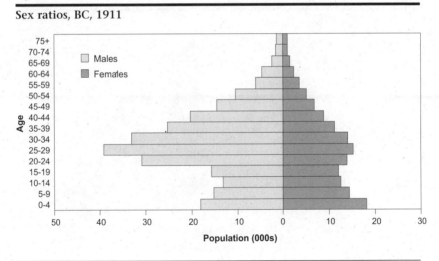

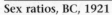

Figure C.5

Sex ratios, BC, 1921

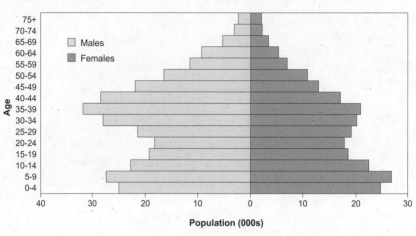

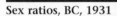

Figure C.6

Sex ratios, BC, 1931

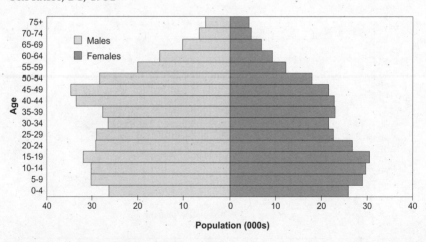

Figure C.7

Sex ratios, BC, 1941

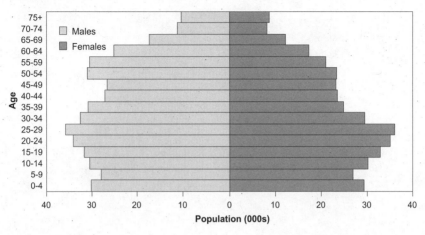

Figure C.8

Sex ratios, BC, 1951

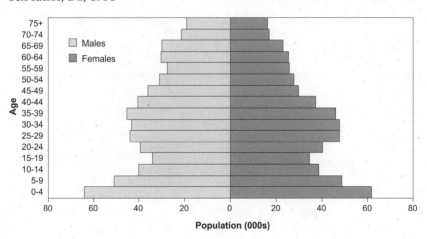

Figure C.9

Sex ratios, BC, 1961

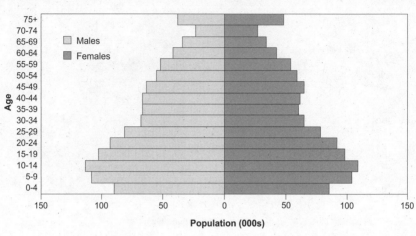

Figure C.10

Sex ratios, BC, 1971

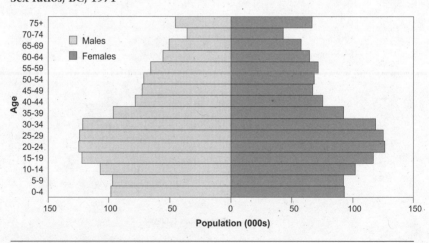

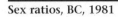

Figure C.11

Sex ratios, BC, 1981

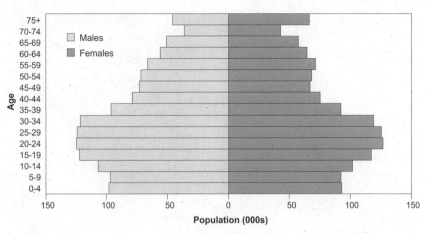

Figure C.12

Sex ratios, BC, 1991

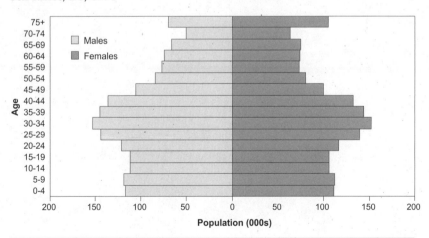

Figure C.13

Sex ratios, BC, 2001

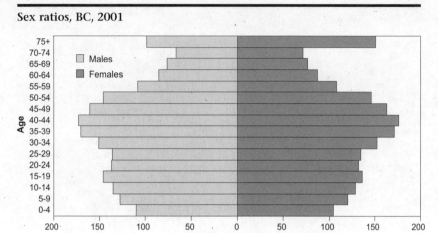

Appendix D
Infant Mortality Rates (IMR), BC, 1922-2002

Year	IMR	Year	IMR	Year	IMR
1922	68.35	1949	31.43	1976	13.33
1923	66.79	1950	29.69	1977	12.97
1924	56.72	1951	29.88	1978	12.46
1925	55.02	1952	29.17	1979	10.56
1926	58.43	1953	27.06	1980	10.50
1927	60.10	1954	25.80	1981	9.92
1928	50.46	1955	25.25	1982	9.61
1929	55.41	1956	26.05	1983	8.53
1930	51.72	1957	28.29	1984	8.28
1931	49.40	1958	27.21	1985	7.70
1932	46.70	1959	24.87	1986	8.20
1933	45.81	1960	23.58	1987	8.48
1934	43.41	1961	24.49	1988	8.28
1935	45.94	1962	23.03	1989	8.10
1936	43.99	1963	23.45	1990	7.32
1937	55.86	1964	21.03	1991	6.33
1938	44.57	1965	20.29	1992	5.96
1939	39.04	1966	23.41	1993	5.33
1940	38.08	1967	20.94	1994	5.89
1941	36.71	1968	19.47	1995	5.87
1942	35.46	1969	16.19	1996	4.92
1943	37.80	1970	16.58	1997	4.55
1944	40.37	1971	18.22	1998	4.06
1945	41.96	1972	16.46	1999	3.78
1946	37.68	1973	16.04	2000	3.70
1947	36.48	1974	15.40	2001	4.01
1948	33.41	1975	13.53	2002	4.44

Sources: British Columbia, *The Nineteen Eighties: A Statistical Resource for a Decade of Vital Events in British Columbia* (Victoria: Ministry of Health and Ministry Responsible for Seniors, 1994), 23; P.R.W. Kendall, *A Review of Infant Mortality in British Columbia: Opportunities for Prevention* (Victoria: Ministry of Health, 2003), 9.

Notes

Chapter 1: Cradle to Grave: An Introduction

1   Ged Martin, *Past Futures: The Impossible Necessity of History* (Toronto: University of Toronto Press, 2004), 199.

2   There are, inevitably, many editions of Malthus to choose from. An excellent choice is Thomas Robert Malthus, *An Essay on the Principle of Population,* ed. Philip Appleman (New York: Norton, 1976). The classic historical demographies include Peter Laslett, *The World We Have Lost,* 2nd ed. (1965; repr., London: Methuen, 1975); E.A. Wrigley, *Population and History* (New York: McGraw-Hill, 1969); John Demos, *A Little Commonwealth: Family Life in Plymouth Colony* (London: Oxford University Press, 1970); Tamara K. Hareven, *Family Time and Industrial Time: The Relationship between the Family and Work in a New England Industrial Community* (Cambridge: Cambridge University Press, 1982); Louise Dechêne, *Habitants and Merchants in Seventeenth-Century Montréal,* trans. Liana Vardi (Montreal and Kingston: McGill-Queen's University Press, 1992); Gérard Bouchard, *Quelques arpents d'Amérique: population, économie, famille au Saguenay, 1838-1971* (Montreal: Boréal, 1996); and Bouchard, "Mobile Populations, Stable Communities: Social and Demographic Processes in the Rural Parishes of the Saguenay, 1840-1911," *Continuity and Change* 6, 1 (1991): 59-86. See also Peter R. Knights, *The Plain People of Boston, 1830-1860: A Study in City Growth* (New York: Oxford University Press, 1971).

3   See Warren E. Kalbach and Wayne W. McVey, *The Demographic Bases of Canadian Society* (Toronto: McGraw-Hill, 1971); Roderic Beaujot and Kevin McQuillan, *Growth and Dualism: The Demographic Development of Canadian Society* (Toronto: Gage, 1982); and their essay "The Social Effects of Demographic Change, Canada 1851-1981," in *Perspectives on Canada's Population: An Introduction to Concepts and Issues,* Frank Trovato and Carl F. Grindstaff, eds. (Don Mills: Oxford University Press, 1994), 35-47. Beaujot and Donald Kerr have produced what is the standard text: *Population Change in Canada,* 2nd ed. (Don Mills: Oxford University Press, 2003). Other important titles include Michael Barrett, *Population and Canada,* 3rd ed. (Toronto: Faculty of Education, University of Toronto, 1982); Donald Kerr and Bali Ram, *Population Dynamics in Canada* (Ottawa: Statistics Canada, 1994); Wayne W. McVey Jr. and Warren E. Kalbach, *Canadian Population* (Toronto: Nelson Canada, 1995); and Sylvia T. Wargon, *Demography in Canada in the Twentieth Century* (Vancouver: UBC Press, 2002).

4   E.A. Wrigley, "Population History in the 1980s," *Journal of Interdisciplinary History* 12, 2 (Autumn 1981): 218.

5   See, for example, two studies in *Child and Family Welfare in British Columbia: A History,* Diane Purvey and Chris Walmsley, eds. (Calgary: Detselig, 2005): Diane Purvey, "The Alexandra Orphanage, 1892-1938," 53-76, and Veronica Strong-Boag, "Interrupted Relations: The Adoption of Children in Twentieth Century British Columbia," 139-64.

6   Not every jurisdiction begins the business of writing its demographic history from the same starting line. In older communities with a long tradition of church record keeping, the

possibilities for assembling large quantities of data and also for applying family reconstitu-
tion techniques are vastly superior than they are in Canada's West. The efflorescence of
demographic history in Quebec reveals how, in this respect, the rest of North America has
suffered for its Protestantism.

7 This process of dissemination is ably described and critiqued in Bruce Curtis, *The Politics
of Population: State Formation, Statistics, and the Census of Canada, 1840-1875* (Toronto:
University of Toronto Press, 2001), 19-22.

8 An isolated survey in 1851, for example, showed Nanaimo to have a population of 151
whites, but it indicated little else. James Douglas to Lord John Russell, 21 August 1855,
Colonial Office Papers 305(6), Public Records Office (PRO), Kew, UK.

9 This is referred to in the literature as the "historic period," meaning the period of written
records. It has to be said that Aboriginal peoples in the years before contact with Russians,
Spaniards, and English very likely did not see themselves as living in a world without history.
This is obvious, but the division between a "historic" past since the eighteenth century and
an "ethnographic" or "archaeological" past before that time is intellectually frustrating and
sometimes even dishonest. One relatively recent study, for example, surveys the competition between European interests for territorial dominance in the region without setting it
in the context of the pre-existing Aboriginal dominance. See Paul F. Thomas, "Geopolitical
Development: An Overview," in *British Columbia, the Pacific Province: Geographical Essays,*
Canadian Western Geographical Series 36, Colin J.B. Wood, ed. (Victoria: Western Geographical Press, 2001), 97-131.

10 Henry Pellew Crease, Attorney General, to the Officer Administering the Government, copy,
28 April 1866, Colonial Office Papers 60(24), PRO.

11 Frederick Seymour to the Duke of Buckingham and Chandos, 11 August 1868, Colonial
Office Papers 60(33), PRO.

12 Governor Anthony Musgrave to the Earl of Kimberley, 14 December 1870, Colonial Office
Papers 60(41), PRO.

13 Jean Barman, "The West beyond the West: The Demography of Settlement in British Columbia," *Journal of Canadian Studies* 25, 3 (Autumn 1990): 7.

14 Eric Sager, "The Canadian Families Project and the 1901 Census," *Historical Methods* 33, 4
(Fall 2000): 180; Bettina Bradbury, "Single Parenthood in the Past," *Historical Methods* 33,
4 (Fall 2000): 213. See also Linda S. Williams, *Families and the Canadian Census: A Brief Cri-
tique of Current Methodology and Some Suggested Improvements,* Occasional Papers in Social
Policy Analysis 4 (Toronto: Department of Sociology in Education, Ontario Institute for
Studies in Education, 1984); John R. Miron, *Housing in Postwar Canada: Demographic Change,
Household Formation, and Housing Demand* (Kingston and Montreal: McGill-Queen's Uni-
versity Press, 1988), 25-26; Alan A. Brookes, "'Doing the Best I Can': The Taking of the 1861
New Brunswick Census," *Histoire sociale/Social History* 9, 17 (May 1976): 90.

15 It is not known whether the British Columbian enumerators were as "underpaid, badly in-
formed, and often poorly educated" as those in Ontario, described in David Gagan, *Hopeful
Travellers: Families, Land, and Social Change in Mid-Victorian Peel County, Canada West* (Toronto:
University of Toronto Press, 1981), 63. See also comments on the use of the Canadian census
in Eric W. Sager and Peter Baskerville, "Locating the Unemployed in Urban British Columbia:
Evidence from the 1891 Census," *Journal of Canadian Studies* 25, 3 (Fall 1990): 39.

16 In this instance the writer was responsible for a thousand individuals. Eric Duncan, *Fifty-
Seven Years in the Comox Valley* (Courtenay, BC: Comox Argus, 1934), 42-43.

17 Patrick Dunae, "Making the 1891 Census in British Columbia," *Histoire sociale/Social History*
31, 62 (November 1998): 225.

18 See Jean-Pierre Beaud and Jean-Guy Prevost, "Statistics and Eugenics: Measuring Racial
Origins in Canada," *Canadian Ethnic Studies/Etudes ethniques au Canada* 27, 2 (1996):
1-24.

19 Patricia E. Roy, *A White Man's Province: British Columbia Politicians and Chinese and Japanese
Immigrants, 1858-1914* (Vancouver: UBC Press, 1989); Rob Watts, "Making Numbers Count
on the Racial Frontier: An Historical Sociology of the Birth of the Census, Victoria (Australia),
1835-1840," *Histoire sociale/Social History* 35 (November 2002): 423-46; Kay J. Anderson,

Vancouver's Chinatown: Racial Discourse in Canada, 1875-1980 (Montreal and Kingston: McGill-Queen's University Press, 1991), 44-47. See also Bruce Curtis, "On the Local Construction of Statistical Knowledge: Making Up the 1861 Census of the Canadas," *Journal of Historical Sociology* 7, 4 (1994): 416-34.

20 Robert Galois and Cole Harris, "Recalibrating Society: The Population Geography of British Columbia, 1881," *Canadian Geographer* 38, 1 (1994): 37.

21 The path grows more tangled still as, with assimilation into settler society, Leung evidently accepted and grew accustomed to the new name – which he shared with his store in Kamloops' Chinatown – although he subsequently refined a new public identity as "Chong Lee." Leung's children were to participate in these multiple identities from birth: his first son was known to the family as Leung Kwong Fat but to the community at large (and to the census taker) as Charles Lee. Charles Lee Jr., "Two Chinese Families of the British Columbia Interior: A Short History of the Family of Charles Lee of Kamloops and of His Wife Jessie Hing" (unpublished paper in the author's collection, courtesy of Ms. Rose Delap), 2.

22 Dunae, "Making the 1891 Census in British Columbia," 232.

23 Mary-Ellen Kelm, *Colonizing Bodies: Aboriginal Health and Healing in British Columbia, 1900-50* (Vancouver: UBC Press, 1998), 182-83.

24 Sager and Baskerville, "Locating the Unemployed," 39. See also Peter Baskerville and Eric Sager, "Finding the Work Force in the 1901 Census of Canada," *Histoire sociale/Social History* 28, 56 (November 1995): 521-39.

25 Dunae, "Making the 1891 Census in British Columbia," 232.

26 Michael Anderson, "Historical Demography after *The Population of England*," *Journal of Interdisciplinary History* 15, 4 (Spring 1985): 599.

27 Wrigley, "Population History in the 1980s," 217, 219.

28 A good example of demographic research that exploits unusual source material is Jacalyn Duffin, "Census versus Medical Daybooks: A Comparison of Two Sources on Mortality in Nineteenth Century Ontario," *Continuity and Change* 12, 2 (August 1997): 199-219.

29 For example, the extent of the franchise is seldom considered in accounts of British Columbia's political history. The importance of doing so can be illustrated by the following figures: The population in 1891 was reckoned by the Dominion census to be 92,797, of which 25,661 were First Nations. Of those 67,000 or so whites, only 15,560 had the vote. Keeping in mind that the settler population was overwhelmingly male, what does this imply for the dominant discourse of liberal democratic political history? See British Columbia, "Census of British Columbia," *Sessional Papers*, 1892, 411-15.

30 I make this case more fully in "The West We Have Lost: British Columbia's Demographic Past and an Agenda for Population History," *Western Historical Quarterly* 29, 1 (Spring 1998): 25-47.

31 Howay's 1930 essay was reprinted as "The Settlement and Progress of British Columbia, 1871-1914," in *Historical Essays on British Columbia,* J. Friesen and H.K. Ralston, eds. (Toronto: McClelland and Stewart, 1976), 23-43.

32 Ward's survey does go some distance toward suggesting links between demographic history and the cultural life of BC. Although his objective is to describe both important differences and similarities across Western Canada, he emphasizes evidence in the demographic record that sets BC apart from its neighbours. Ward sees as the foremost of British Columbia's peculiar qualities its long-term reliance on immigration (rather than natural increase) to drive forward its growth, and the high proportion of Canadian migrants within the newcomer category. Also outstanding is a regionally (though not nationally) high mortality rate, a skewed sex ratio that reflects the sustained impact of male immigration, and a relatively low level of dependence (some of which the current study challenges). W. Peter Ward, "Population Growth in Western Canada: 1901-1971," in *The Developing West: Essays in Honour of Lewis H. Thomas,* John E. Foster, ed. (Edmonton: University of Alberta Press, 1983), 155-77. Ward also suggests a correlation between demographic trends and "populist politics" in Western Canada as a whole. This is a subject that merits a subtle and applied assessment, one that goes beyond what is done in Martin Robin, "The Social Basis of Party Politics in British Columbia," *Queen's Quarterly* 77 (1966): 675-90. For the Prairies, see David Laycock,

Populism and Democratic Thought in the Canadian Prairies, 1910-1945 (Toronto: University of Toronto Press, 1990).

33 Central to Barman's assessment is the belief that almost every generation of British Columbians from 1858 on transformed their society and its values in a manner that was distinctive in Canada. Barman is more sensitive than Ward to ethnic demographies, finding links between the shifting discourses of racism and new infusions of population. One might complain that she takes this emphasis too far, perceiving in racial and ethnic definitions the key to the demographic map of BC: class, age, occupation, and religion are neglected. Barman, "West beyond the West," 5-18, and *The West beyond the West: A History of British Columbia* (Toronto: University of Toronto Press, 1991), especially 129-50 and 363-75. (The University of Toronto Press published revised editions of *The West beyond the West* in 2001 and 2007.)

34 Jean Barman, "Neighbourhood and Community in Interwar Vancouver: Residential Differentiation and Civic Voting Behaviour," *BC Studies* 69-70 (Spring-Summer 1986): 97-141; Galois and Harris, "Recalibrating Society," 37-53; Allen Seager and Adele Perry, "Mining the Connections: Class, Ethnicity, and Gender in Nanaimo, British Columbia, 1891," *Histoire sociale/Social History* 30, 59 (May 1997): 67-73; Perry, "'Oh I'm Just Sick of the Faces of Men': Gender Imbalance, Race, Sexuality, and Sociability in Nineteenth-Century British Columbia," *BC Studies* 105-6 (Spring-Summer 1995): 27-44; Perry, *On the Edge of Empire: Gender, Race, and the Making of British Columbia, 1849-1871* (Toronto: University of Toronto Press, 2001); Jeremy Mouat, *Roaring Days: Rossland's Mines and the History of British Columbia* (Vancouver: UBC Press, 1995), especially Chapter 6; John Douglas Belshaw, *Colonization and Community: The Vancouver Island Coalfield and the Making of the British Columbian Working Class* (Montreal and Kingston: McGill-Queen's University Press, 2002); Belshaw, "Rurality Check: Demographic Boundaries on the British Columbian Frontier," in *Beyond the City Limits: Rural History in British Columbia,* Ruth Sandwell, ed. (Vancouver: UBC Press, 1999), 195-211; Ruth Sandwell, "Peasants on the Coast? A Problematique of Rural British Columbia," in *Canadian Papers in Rural History,* vol. 10, Donald Akenson, ed. (Gananoque: Langdale, 1996); and Sandwell, *Contesting Rural Space: Land Policy and Practices of Resettlement on Saltspring Island, 1859-1891* (Montreal and Kingston: McGill-Queen's University Press, 2006). James R. Gibson, "Smallpox on the Northwest Coast, 1835-1838," *BC Studies* 56 (Winter 1982-83): 61-81; Robert Galois, *Kwakwa̲ka'wakw Settlements, 1775-1920: A Geographical Analysis and Gazetteer* (Vancouver: UBC Press, 1994); Galois, "Measles, 1847-1850: The First Modern Epidemic in British Columbia," *BC Studies* 109 (Spring 1996): 31-46; and Robert Boyd, "Smallpox in the Pacific Northwest: The First Epidemics," *BC Studies* 101 (Spring 1994): 5-40. (For a more complete review of the literature on smallpox, see Chapter 3, below.) W. Peter Ward, *White Canada Forever: Popular Attitudes and Public Policy towards Orientals in British Columbia* (Montreal and Kingston: McGill-Queen's University Press, 1990); Roy, *A White Man's Province;* Roy, *The Oriental Question: Consolidating a White Man's Province, 1914-41* (Vancouver: UBC Press, 2003); and Roy, *The Triumph of Citizenship: The Japanese and Chinese in Canada, 1941-67* (Vancouver: UBC Press, 2007). See also Donald H. Avery, *Reluctant Hosts: Canada's Response to Immigrant Workers, 1896-1994* (Toronto: McClelland and Stewart, 1995), Chapter 2. Robert Malatest, *British Columbia Population: Growth Profiles and Perspectives* (Vancouver: BC Telephone Company, 1984); Leslie Foster and Michael Edgell, eds., *The Geography of Death: Mortality Atlas of British Columbia, 1985-1989,* Western Geographical Series 26 (Victoria: Western Geographical Press, 1992); Julie M. Macdonald, "Vital Statistics in British Columbia: An Historical Overview of 100 Years, 1891-1990," *Vital Statistics Quarterly Digest* 4, 1 (June 1994): 19-45; and Herbert C. Northcott and P. Jane Milliken, *Aging in British Columbia: Burden or Benefit?* (Calgary: Detselig, 1998). See also the essays collected and edited by Ellen M. Gee and Gloria M. Gutman, *The Overselling of Population Aging: Apocalyptic Demography, Intergenerational Challenges, and Social Policy* (Toronto: Oxford University Press, 2000). Also see Robert Rutherdale, "Approaches to Community Formation and the Family in the Provincial North: Prince George and British Columbia's Central Interior," *BC Studies* 104 (Winter 1994-95): 103-26; and Robert A.J. McDonald, "Lumber Society on the Industrial Frontier: Burrard Inlet, 1863-1886," *Labour/Le Travail* 33 (Spring 1994): 69-96.

35 Dorothy E. Chunn, "Sex and Citizenship: (Hetero)Sexual Offences, Law and 'White' Settler Society in British Columbia, 1885-1940," in *Contesting Canadian Citizenship: Historical Readings*, Robert Adamoski, Dorothy E. Chunn, and Robert Menzies, eds. (Peterborough, ON: Broadview Press, 2002), 363; Adele Perry, "Hardy Backwoodsmen, Wholesome Women, and Steady Families: Immigration and the Construction of a White Society in Colonial British Columbia, 1849-1871," *Histoire sociale/Social History* 33, 66 (November 2000): 347; Tina Loo, *Making Law, Order, and Authority in British Columbia, 1821-1871* (Toronto: University of Toronto Press, 1994) and Jean Barman, *Growing Up British in British Columbia: Boys in Private School* (Vancouver: UBC Press, 1984), 6, 11, 12. See also Jean Barman, "Ethnicity in the Pursuit of Status: British Middle and Upper-Class Emigration to British Columbia in the Late Nineteenth and Early Twentieth Centuries," *Canadian Ethnic Studies* 18, 1 (1986): 32-51. The extent to which the colonial regime sought to put a specifically British stamp on British Columbia and Vancouver Island is suggested in the account of T. Griffiths, a Welsh captain in the Salvation Army. In 1889 he wrote that, "at Nanaimo, for the first time in Canada, did I think it prudent to speak, sing and pray in my own native language." Griffiths, *Cambrian* 9, 8 (August 1889): 255. The rarity of this cultural environment is made clear in William D. Jones, *Wales in America: Scranton and the Welsh, 1860-1920* (Cardiff: University of Wales Press, 1993).
36 Galois and Harris, "Recalibrating Society," 39. See also Susan Greenhalgh, "The Social Construction of Population Science: An Intellectual, Institutional, and Political History of Twentieth-Century Demography," *Comparative Studies in Society and History* 38 (1996): 26-66. Some historical demographers find the idea of the linguistic turn intruding on their field as difficult to imagine. See Russell R. Menard, "Whatever Happened to Early American Population History?" *William and Mary Quarterly*, 3rd ser., 50, 2 (1993): 357.
37 Perry makes a similar observation in "Hardy Backwoodsmen," 345.
38 *Saturday Sunset*, 10 August 1907, reproduced in Anderson, *Vancouver's Chinatown*, 87. Similarly, Margaret Ormsby wrote in 1958, with respect to the multitude of sources for populating Vancouver after 1886, that "All these newcomers – with the exception of the Chinese, as the riots of January, 1887, indicated – could be absorbed into the society of the newest and fastest growing city in Canada." Not only are Asians regarded as inherently external to "the society" that does the absorbing, but First Nations are not mentioned as participants in the populating process. Ormsby, *British Columbia: A History* (Toronto: MacMillan of Canada, 1958), 299-300.
39 Allan Smith, "The Writing of British Columbia History," *BC Studies* 45 (Spring 1980): 80-81.
40 Ormsby, *British Columbia*, between pages 310 and 311.
41 Norbert MacDonald, "Population Growth and Change in Seattle and Vancouver, 1880-1960," *Pacific Historical Review* 39 (August 1970): 315.
42 Anderson, *Vancouver's Chinatown*, 46.
43 Roy, *A White Man's Province*, vi, 23.
44 For a lively intervention into the debate over the place of "race" in the writing of BC history, see two articles by Rennie Warburton, "Race and Class in British Columbia: A Comment," *BC Studies* 49 (Spring 1981): 79-85, and "The Workingmen's Protective Association, Victoria, BC, 1878: Racism, Intersectionality and Status Politics," *Labour/Le Travail* 43 (Spring 1999): 105-20. To be fair to Roy and Ward, their work appeared long before the debates on the new social/cultural history had taken off, although there were at the time voices questioning the dialectics of development.
45 Arthur R.M. Lower, "The Growth of Population in Canada," in *Canadian Population and Northern Colonization*, V.W. Bladen, ed. (Toronto: University of Toronto Press, 1962), 58. In large measure, the scholarly discussion of the "Other" has shifted to questions of citizenship, which is to say the very demographic question of "who counts." See Robert Menzies, Robert Adamoski, and Dorothy E. Chunn, "Rethinking the Citizen in Canadian Social History," in Adamoski, Chunn, and Menzies, *Contesting Canadian Citizenship*, 11-42, and Veronica Strong-Boag, "Who Counts? Late Nineteenth- and Early Twentieth-Century Struggles about Gender, Race, and Class in Canada," in *Citizenship in Transformation in Canada*, Yvonne M. Hébert, ed. (Toronto: University of Toronto Press, 2002), 37-56.

46 McDonald, "Lumber Society," 71 See also Robert A.J. McDonald, "Vancouver's 'Four Hundred': The Quest for Wealth and Status in Canada's Urban West, 1886-1914," *Journal of Canadian Studies* 25 (1990): 55-73; MacDonald, "Population Growth," 300. See also Daniel Scott Smith, "A Malthusian-Frontier Interpretation of United States Demographic History before c. 1815," *Urbanization in the Americas: The Background in Comparative Perspective*, Woodrow Borah, Jorge Hardoy, and Gilbert A. Stelter, eds. (Ottawa: National Museum of Man, 1980), 15-24.

47 Roderic Beaujot, *Population Change in Canada: The Challenges of Policy Adaptation* (Toronto: McClelland and Stewart, 1991), 45; Michel Foucault, "On Governmentality," *Ideology and Consciousness*, vol. 6 (1979), 5-22, cited in Watts, "Making Numbers Count," 427; Anderson, *Vancouver's Chinatown*, 25-26; *New Westminster Columbian*, 21 April 1900, quoted in Ward, *White Canada Forever*, 92. I am mindful here of the objections raised by Robert Wright in his article "Historical Underdosing: Pop Demography and the Crisis in Canadian History," *Canadian Historical Review* 81, 4 (December 2000): 646-67.

48 To facilitate this kind of study, I undertook in 1989 to convert to computer-readable form data from the Canada census manuscripts of the last century that cover much of the south-central Interior. With the assistance of students employed under summer and work study programs, I was able to compile a very large database, most of which is now accessible through the Living Landscapes website, http://www.livinglandscapes.bc.ca/thomp-ok/census/index.html. Combining this material with information gleaned from church registers of baptisms/births, funerals/deaths, and marriages made it possible to determine much more about the private life-course of a larger number of British Columbians than ever before. These resources allow insights into how, for example, the preponderance of males in British Columbia from 1858 until the last half of the twentieth century affected marriage rates, age at first marriage for females, and the fertility of the population.

49 Paul Ehrlich, *The Population Bomb* (New York: Ballantine, 1971); David Cork with Susan Lightstone, *The Pig and the Python: How to Prosper from the Aging Baby Boom* (Toronto: Stoddart Books, 1996); David K. Foot with Daniel Stoffman, *Boom, Bust and Echo: How to Profit from the Coming Demographic Shift* (Toronto: Macfarlane Walter and Ross, 1996); Mary S. Hartman, *The Household and the Making of History: A Subversive View of the Western Past* (Cambridge: Cambridge University Press, 2004).

Chapter 2: Weddings, Funerals, Anything: The British Columbian Demographic Narrative

1 Richard Somerset Mackie, *The Wilderness Profound: Victorian Life on the Gulf of Georgia* (Victoria: Sono Nis Press, 1995), 48-49. Another study places greater emphasis on conflict than on disease, stating that the Pentlatch were "already nearly exterminated by Nootkan raids" before the 1860s. Dorothy I.D. Kennedy and Randall T. Bouchard, "Northern Coast Salish," *Handbook of North American Indians*, vol. 7: *Northwest Coast* (Washington: Smithsonian Institution, 1990), 449. This is echoed in Harry Assu, *Assu of Cape Mudge: Recollections of a Coastal Indian Chief*, Harry Assu with Joy Inglis (Vancouver: UBC Press, 1989), 10-11nn8-9. Inglis observes in the footnotes that the Comox were, themselves, being forced south and that ultimately their principal village became "socially and politically Kwagiulth."

2 William M. Denevan, ed., *The Native Population of the Americas in 1492* (Madison: University of Wisconsin Press, 1976), 7.

3 The earliest known site of human occupation is currently Charlie Lake Cave near Fort St. John. See Knut R. Fladmark, "The Prehistory of Charlie Lake Cave," in *Early Human Occupation in British Columbia*, Roy L. Carlson and Luke Dalla Bona, eds. (Vancouver: UBC Press, 1996), 11-20. Although it is possible that the Interior has been occupied for longer than the coast, it is more likely the case that archaeological evidence on the Pacific has been lost to the sea, into which the coastline has been continually sinking. Roy L. Carlson and Philip M. Hobler, "The Pender Canal Excavations and the Development of Coast Salish Culture," *BC Studies* 99 (Autumn 1993): 29, 36.

4 James Teit, *The Salishan Tribes of the Western Plateaus*, Bureau of American Ethnology, Annual Report 45 (Washington: Government Printing Office, 1930), 213.

5 David Wyatt, "Nicola," *Handbook of North American Indians,* vol. 12: *Plateau* (Washington: Smithsonian Institution, 1998), 224-25.
6 Nothing could make the task of estimating contact-era numbers more fraught with problems. Defining territories, nations, and communities is very difficult outside of insular groups on the coast such as the Haida. Ethnologists once used language families as the defining principle, but it has become clear that these overlapped in valleys and along inlets, causing uncertainty over identity. Moreover, anthropologists, historians, and First Nations groups themselves have further complicated things by continually redefining Aboriginal self-identities. This leads to problems of double-counting. For example, the Sekani are comprised, ethnically, of Dunne-za, Dene-thah, and Sekani ancestries; likewise, the Dunne-za (known to generations of newcomers as the Beaver) contain elements of Dene-thah and Sekani ethnicity. It is typically impossible to determine whether censuses in the region are territory- or ethnic-specific.
7 Wendy C. Wickwire, "To See Ourselves as the Other's Other: Nlaka'pamux Contact Narratives," *Canadian Historical Review* 75, 1 (1994): 4; Cole Harris, "The Fraser Canyon Encountered," *BC Studies* 94 (Summer 1992): 11.
8 Brian Hayden and Jim Spafford, "The Keatley Creek Site and Corporate Group Archaeology," *BC Studies* 99 (Autumn 1993): 106-14.
9 Arnoud Stryd, "The Later Prehistory of the Lillooet Area, British Columbia" (PhD diss., University of Calgary, 1973), 76.
10 Charles Hill-Tout, "Notes on the Ntlakapamuq," in *The Salish People: The Local Contribution of Charles Hill-Tout,* vol. 1: *The Thompson and the Okanagan,* Ralph Maud, ed. (Vancouver: Talonbooks, 1978), 58.
11 Robert Muckle, *The First Nations of British Columbia: An Anthropological Survey* (Vancouver: UBC Press, 1998), 30. Heavy reliance on the salmon migration along the Fraser River system has been pointed to as a factor that set upward limits on population. See Richard Somerset Mackie, *Trading beyond the Mountains: The British Fur Trade on the Pacific, 1793-1843* (Vancouver: UBC Press, 1997), 85, 184.
12 In Collaboration, "Ktunaxa," in *Aboriginal Peoples of Canada: A Short Introduction,* Paul Robert Magocsi, ed. (Toronto: University of Toronto Press, 2002), 181.
13 John A. Cherrington, *The Fraser Valley: A History* (Madeira Park, BC: Harbour, 1992), 36; Margaret A. Ormsby, *British Columbia: A History* (Toronto: Macmillan, 1958), 37; David M. Schaepe et al., "Changing Households, Changing Houses," in *A Stó:lō Coast Salish Historical Atlas,* Keith Thor Carlson, ed., with Albert (Sonny) McHalsie, cultural advisor (Vancouver: Douglas and McIntyre, 2001), 42-43.
14 John Boit, 1792, quoted in George Woodcock, *British Columbia: A History of the Province* (Vancouver: Douglas and McIntyre, 1990), 57; Daniel W. Clayton, *Islands of Truth: The Imperial Fashioning of Vancouver Island* (Vancouver: UBC Press, 2000), 132.
15 Muckle, *The First Nations of British Columbia,* 37.
16 Jean Barman, *The West beyond the West: A History of British Columbia* (Toronto: University of Toronto Press, 1991), 363.
17 Jody F. Decker, "Tracing Historical Diffusion Patterns: The Case of the 1780-82 Smallpox Epidemic among the Indians of Western Canada," *Native Studies Review* 4, 1 and 2 (1988): 20-21; Robin Fisher, *Contact and Conflict: Indian-European Relations in British Columbia, 1774-1890,* 2nd ed. (Vancouver: UBC Press, 1977), 131. Although it is widely believed that First Nations peoples in the Americas were rendered more vulnerable to European-introduced diseases by their relative genetic homogeneity, there are dissenting views. See Francis Black, "Why Did They Die? Genetic Homogeneity in New World Populations," *Science,* 11 December 1992, 1739-40; Peter J. Bianchine and Thomas A. Russo, "The Role of Epidemic Infectious Diseases in the Discovery of America," in *Columbus and the New World: Medical Implications,* Guy A. Settipane, ed. (Providence, RI: Oceanside, 1995), 13; Robert McCaa, "Spanish and Nahuatl Views on Smallpox and Demographic Catastrophe in Mexico," *Journal of Interdisciplinary History* 25 (1994-95): 419-20. I am grateful to Robert McCaa for these references.
18 Sarah K. Campbell, *PostColumbian Culture History in the Northern Columbia Plateau, A.D. 1500-1900* (New York: Garland, 1990).

19 Wilson Duff, *The Indian History of British Columbia*, vol. 1: *The Impact of the White Man*, new ed. (Victoria: Royal British Columbia Museum, 1997), 54, 58; Robert T. Boyd, "Demographic History, 1774-1874," *Handbook of North American Indians*, vol. 7: *Northwest Coast*, 138.

20 Elizabeth A. Fenn, *Pox Americana: The Great Smallpox Epidemic of 1775-82* (New York: Hill and Wang, 2001), 226-58.

21 Boyd, "Demographic History," *Handbook*, vol. 7, 136-38. James R. Gibson, "Smallpox on the Northwest Coast, 1835-1838," *BC Studies* 56 (Winter 1982-83): 61-81.

22 Boyd, "Demographic History, 1774-1874," 141; Fisher, *Contact and Conflict*, 45.

23 Gibson, "Smallpox on the Northwest Coast," 79.

24 Less extensive reports are available for the 1830s epidemic. See Jonathan R. Dean, "'Those Rascally Spackaloids': The Rise of Gispaxlots Hegemony at Fort Simpson, 1832-40," *BC Studies* 101 (Spring 1994): 55-60. On the 1875 smallpox outbreak, see Robert Boyd, *The Coming of the Spirit of Pestilence: Introduced Infectious Diseases and Population Decline among Northwest Coast Indians, 1774-1874* (Vancouver: UBC Press, 1999), 302-4. Boyd, "Demographic History, 1774-1874," 142. See also Daisy Sewid-Smith, "In Time Immemorial," *BC Studies* 89 (Spring 1991): 26-27.

25 Elsewhere a scorched-earth policy was implemented in the hopes of burning out the bacilli. See the account of Francis Poole, *Queen Charlotte Islands: A Narrative of Discovery and Adventure in the North Pacific*, John W. Lyndon, ed. (Vancouver: J.J. Douglas, 1972), 158-59. For the Bella Coola source of the outbreak in the Cariboo, see Marie Elliott, *Gold and Grand Dreams: Cariboo East in the Early Years* (Victoria: Horsdal and Schubert, 2000), 60.

26 Boyd, *Coming of the Spirit of Pestilence*, 183-86; Cole Harris, "The Lower Mainland, 1820-81," in *Vancouver and Its Region*, Graeme Wynn and Timothy Oke, eds. (Vancouver: UBC Press, 1992), 57-58.

27 James Alexander Teit, *The Thompson Indians of British Columbia*, vol. 1, part 4 of *The Jesup North Pacific Expedition*, Franz Boas, ed. (1900; repr., Merritt, BC: Nicola Valley Museum Archives Association, 1997), 176; Robert Boyd, "Population Decline from Two Epidemics on the Northwest Coast," in *Disease and Demography in the Americas*, John W. Verano and Douglas H. Ubelaker, eds. (Washington: Smithsonian Institution, 1992), 249-55; Reminiscences of John (Jack "Long Gun") Irvine (1861-1948), 17, Irvine Family fonds, Originals, 1851-1942, Add Mss 322, BC Archives, Victoria, BC; Lieutenant H. Spencer Palmer, *Report of a Journey from Victoria to Fort Alexander via North Bentick Arm* (New Westminster: Royal Engineer Press, 1863), 7-8; Duff, *Indian History*, 59; Andrew Yarmie, "Smallpox and the British Columbia Indians: Epidemic of 1862," *British Columbia Library Quarterly* 31, 3 (1969): 13-21.

28 Cole Harris, "Social Power and Cultural Change in Pre-Colonial British Columbia," *BC Studies* 115-16 (Autumn-Winter 1997-98): 51.

29 See John Sutton Lutz, *Makúk: A New History of Aboriginal-White Relations* (Vancouver: UBC Press, 2008); Elliot Fox-Povey, "How Agreeable Their Company Would Be: The Meaning of the Sexual Labour of Slaves in the Nuu-chah-nulth – European Sex Trade at Nootka Sound in the Eighteenth Century," *British Columbia Historical News* 36, 3 (Summer 2003): 1-10.

30 James R. Gibson, *Otter Skins, Boston Ships, and China Goods: The Maritime Fur Trade of the Northwest Coast, 1785-1841* (Montreal and Kingston: McGill-Queen's University Press, 1992), 273. See also Christon I. Archer, "The Transient Presence: A Re-Appraisal of Spanish Attitudes toward the Northwest Coast in the Eighteenth Century," in *British Columbia: Historical Readings*, W. Peter Ward and Robert A.J. McDonald, eds. (Vancouver: Douglas and McIntyre, 1981), 56-57.

31 It is impossible to determine whether "prostitution" or the "sale of sexual favours" was widespread before the arrival of Europeans, though some authors maintain that it was "alien to native society," arising only to meet a newfound market among sailors. See Douglas Cole and David Darling, "History of the Early Period," *Handbook of North American Indians*, vol. 7: *Northwest Coast*, 130; Jennifer Windecker, "The Prostitution of Native Women of the North Coast of British Columbia," *British Columbia Historical News* 30, 3 (Summer 1997): 29-33; Carol Cooper, "Native Women of the Northern Pacific Coast: An Historical Perspective, 1830-1900," *Journal of Canadian Studies* 27 (Winter 1992-93): 58; and Jo-Anne Fiske,

"Colonization and the Decline of Women's Status: The Tsimshian Case," *Feminist Studies* 17, 3 (Fall 1991): 523.

32 Robert T. Boyd, "Demographic History until 1990," *Handbook of North American Indians,* vol. 12: *Plateau,* 473.

33 For a description of indigenous ailments, see Steven Acheson, "Culture Contact, Demography and Health among the Aboriginal Peoples of British Columbia," in *A Persistent Spirit: Towards Understanding Aboriginal Health in British Columbia,* Canadian Western Geographical Series 31, Peter H. Stephenson, Susan J. Elliott, Leslie T. Foster, and Jill Harris, eds. (Victoria: Western Geographical Press, 1995), 9-10.

34 Cholera was a particular concern in mid-nineteenth-century urbanizing North America. For the closest outbreak, see Mitchell Roth, "Cholera, Community, and Public Health in Gold Rush Sacramento and San Francisco," *Pacific Historical Review* 66, 4 (November 1997): 527-51.

35 Robert Galois, "Measles, 1847-1850: The First Modern Epidemic in British Columbia," *BC Studies* 109 (Spring 1996): 31-43.

36 Madge Wolfenden, ed., "John Tod: Career of a Scotch Boy," *British Columbia Historical Quarterly* 18, 3-4 (1954): 224-27; Boyd, "Demographic History until 1990," 474.

37 Galois, "Measles," 35; Cole Harris, *Making Native Space: Colonialism, Resistance, and Reserves in British Columbia* (Vancouver: UBC Press, 2002), 24.

38 Teit, *The Thompson Indians,* 175.

39 Roderic Beaujot and Donald Kerr, *Population Change in Canada,* 2nd ed. (Don Mills: Oxford University Press, 2003), 21.

40 Fisher, *Contact and Conflict,* 118.

41 Clayton, *Islands of Truth,* 142.

42 Duff, *Indian History,* 61; Alan D. McMillan, *Since the Time of the Transformers: The Ancient Heritage of the Nuu-chuh-nulth, Ditidaht, and Makah* (Vancouver: UBC Press, 1999), 185-87; Patricia E. Roy and John Herd Thompson, *British Columbia: Land of Promises* (Don Mills: Oxford University Press, 2005), 25. The Okanagan murders are described in Fisher, *Contact and Conflict,* 98-99, and in Daniel P. Marshall, "No Border: American Miner-Soldiers at War with the Nlaka'pamux of the Canadian West," in *Parallel Destinies: Canadian-American Relations West of the Rockies,* Kenneth Coates and John M. Findlay, eds. (Seattle: University of Washington Press, 2002), 36-39, 41-46; Woodcock, *British Columbia,* 126-27.

43 Chris Arnett, *The Terror of the Coast: Land Alienation and Colonial War on Vancouver Island and the Gulf Islands, 1849-1863* (Burnaby: Talonbooks, 1999); Woodcock, *British Columbia,* 134-35; Fisher, *Contact and Conflict,* 168; Barman, *West beyond the West,* 77. For a critical account of the Chilcotin incident, see Tina Loo, *Making Law, Order, and Authority in British Columbia, 1821-1871* (Toronto: University of Toronto Press, 1994), 134-56. Fisher, *Contact and Conflict,* 169.

44 On the subject of colonizers' "surveillance" of Aboriginal populations, see John Lutz, "'Relating to the Country': The Lekwammen and the Extension of European Settlement, 1843-1911," in *Beyond the City Limits: Rural History in British Columbia,* Ruth Sandwell, ed. (Vancouver: UBC Press, 1999), 22-26.

45 See Michael Kew, "Making Indians," in *Workers, Capital and the State in British Columbia: Selected Papers,* Rennie Warburton and David Coburn, eds. (Vancouver: UBC Press, 1988), 24-34.

46 Boyd, *Coming of the Spirit of Pestilence,* 55.

47 Susan Scott and Christopher J. Duncan, *Biology of Plagues: Evidence from Historical Populations* (Cambridge: Cambridge University Press, 2001), 389-93.

48 Fiske, "Colonization and the Decline of Women's Status," 523; Fisher, *Contact and Conflict,* 115.

49 Boyd, *Coming of the Spirit of Pestilence,* 272-73.

50 Counting Aboriginal people in the twentieth and twenty-first centuries is further complicated by the phenomenon of self-definition. Census forms typically ask for one racial or ethnic identity, and it has not always been the case that individuals of mixed ancestry would choose to self-identify as Aboriginal if there was another plausible option available

to them. See Nancy Shoemaker, *American Indian Population Recovery in the Twentieth Century* (Albuquerque: University of New Mexico Press, 1999), 6.

51 David Chuen-yan Lai, "Chinese Communities," in *British Columbia: Its Resources and People,* Canadian Western Geographical Series 32, Charles N. Forward, ed. (Victoria: Western Geographical Press, 1987), 336.

52 See Fox-Povey, "How Agreeable Their Company Would Be," 10. For a less sanitized version of events, see Peter S. Webster, *As Far as I Know: Reminiscences of an Ahousat Elder* (Campbell River, BC: Campbell River Museum and Archives, 1983), 59.

53 Duane Thomson and Marianne Ignace, "'They Made Themselves Our Guests': Power Relationships in the Interior Plateau Region of the Cordillera in the Fur Trade Era," *BC Studies* 146 (Summer 2005): 11. Fort Langley, established on the Fraser River in 1827, contained eighteen HBC employees in 1830, seventeen of whom were married to Aboriginal women. Along with the handful of children they had produced by that time, the total population was only forty-seven. Mary Cullen, *The History of Fort Langley, 1827-1896,* Canadian Historic Sites 20 (Ottawa: National Historic Parks and Sites Branch, Parks Canada: Indian and Northern Affairs, 1979), 85. See also Cole Harris, *The Resettlement of British Columbia: Essays on Colonialism and Geographical Change* (Vancouver: UBC Press, 1997), 39, 78. Fiske, "Colonization and the Decline of Women's Status," 522. See also Jean Barman, "Family Life at Fort Langley," *British Columbia Historical News* 32, 4 (Fall 1999): 16-23, and Bruce M. Watson, "Family Life at Fort Langley," *British Columbia Historical News* 32, 4 (Fall 1999): 24-30.

54 Robin Fisher, "Contact and Trade, 1774-1849," in *The Pacific Province: A History of British Columbia,* Hugh J.M. Johnston, ed. (Vancouver: Douglas and McIntyre, 1996), 63.

55 Ormsby, *British Columbia,* 100-1.

56 See John Douglas Belshaw, *Colonization and Community: The Vancouver Island Coalfield and the Making of the British Columbian Working Class* (Montreal and Kingston: McGill-Queen's University Press, 2002), 23-24.

57 Jay Nelson, "'A Strange Revolution in the Manners of the Country': Aboriginal-Settler Intermarriage in Nineteenth Century British Columbia," in *Regulating Lives: Historical Essays on the State, Society, the Individual, and the Law,* John McLaren, Robert Menzies, and Dorothy E. Chunn, eds. (Vancouver: UBC Press, 2002), 26. Orkneyman quoted in Adele Perry, *On the Edge of Empire: Gender, Race, and the Making of British Columbia, 1849-1871* (Toronto: University of Toronto Press, 2001), 58. Judith Hudson Beattie and Helen M. Buss, eds., *Undelivered Letters to Hudson's Bay Company Men on the Northwest Coast of America, 1830-57* (Vancouver: UBC Press, 2003), 348; Mackie, *Trading beyond the Mountains,* 308; Massimo Livi-Bacci, *A Concise History of World Population,* 4th ed. (London: Blackwell, 2007), 48.

58 Tom Koppel, *Kanaka: The Untold Story of Hawaiian Pioneers in British Columbia and the Pacific Northwest* (Vancouver: Whitecap Books, 1995), 12-16; Mackie, *Trading beyond the Mountains,* 162-63; Morag Maclachlan, ed., *The Fort Langley Journals, 1827-30* (Vancouver: UBC Press, 1998), 100.

59 See Jeremy Mouat, "Situating Vancouver Island in the British World, 1846-49," *BC Studies* 145 (Spring 2005): 5-30.

60 Sharon Meen, "Colonial Society and Economy," in Johnston, *The Pacific Province,* 103, 115. The Canada census of 1901 muddies the water on this subject considerably. In that year, 1,058 people claimed to have arrived in the territory before 1855, half of them before 1851. *Census of Canada, 1901,* vol. 1: *Population* (Ottawa: Queen's Printer, 1903), 452.

61 It is a point often made by Richard Mackie, and rightly so, that the small HBC-era colonial population proved prolific, especially on Vancouver Island.

62 Barman, *West beyond the West,* 65.

63 Cheryl Coull, *A Traveller's Guide to Aboriginal BC* (Vancouver: Whitecap Books, 1996), 68, 76, 115.

64 See Adele Perry, "Hardy Backwoodsmen, Wholesome Women, and Steady Families: Immigration and the Construction of a White Society in Colonial British Columbia, 1849-1871," *Histoire sociale/Social History* 33, 66 (November 2000): 346.

65 Edgar Wickberg et al., *From China to Canada: A History of the Chinese Communities in Canada* (Toronto: McClelland and Stewart, 1982), 13-14, 16.

66 Patricia K. Wood, "Borders and Identities among Italian Immigrants in the Pacific Northwest, 1880-1938," in Coates and Findlay, *Parallel Destinies,* 109. The cemetery of each of the colliery communities provides a vivid reminder of the nineteenth-century Italian presence in the form of elaborate mortuary.

67 Quoted in Elliott, *Gold and Grand Dreams,* xxii.

68 Meen, "Colonial Society," 130n64; Cyril Edel Leonoff, *Pioneers, Pedlars, and Prayer Shawls: The Jewish Communities in British Columbia and the Yukon* (Victoria: Sono Nis Press, 1978), 83-142.

69 British Columbia, "British Columbia," Report of the Hon. H.L. Langevin, C.B., Minister of Public Works, *Sessional Papers,* 1872, no. 10, 22.

70 Adele Perry, "Bachelors in the Backwoods," *Beyond the City Limits: Rural History in British Columbia,* Ruth Sandwell, ed. (Vancouver: UBC Press, 1999), 182; Perry, *On the Edge of Empire,* 147-49. Examples of marriages between goldminers and Aboriginal women abound, but see Andrea Laforet and Annie York, *Spuzzum: Fraser Canyon Histories, 1808-1939* (Vancouver: UBC Press, 1998), 138-40.

71 T.W. Murdoch to F.F. Elliot, 26 April 1867 (marginal notes), Colonial Office Papers 60(30), Public Records Office, Kew, UK. Perry considers the impact of immigrant recruitment in *On the Edge of Empire,* 125-38.

72 See, for example, Roy and Thompson, *British Columbia,* 33.

73 Mackie, *The Wilderness Profound,* 50.

74 Meen, "Colonial Society," 116-17; Harris, "Lower Mainland," 49; Barman, *West beyond the West,* 84 (Yale), 73 (Barkerville).

75 See James R. Gibson, *The Lifeline of the Oregon Country: The Fraser-Columbia Brigade System, 1811-47* (Vancouver: UBC Press, 1997). Ken Favrholdt, "Domesticating the Drybelt: Agricultural Settlement in the Hills around Kamloops, 1860-1960," in Sandwell, *Beyond the City Limits,* 103-4.

76 Meen, "Colonial Society," 117; Lai, "Chinese Communities," 339.

77 Jean Barman, "Invisible Women: Aboriginal Mothers and Mixed-Race Daughters in Rural Pioneer British Columbia," in Sandwell, *Beyond the City Limits,* 165.

78 By way of an example, the Nuxalk collapsed what were as many as twenty villages into one at Bella Coola. See John Barker and Douglas Cole, eds., *At Home with the Bella Coola Indians: T.F. McIlwraith's Field Letters, 1922-4* (Vancouver: UBC Press, 2003), 11. See also Duane Thomson, "The Response of Okanagan Indians to European Settlement," *BC Studies* 101 (Spring 1994): 100.

79 Harris, "Lower Mainland," 52, 58.

80 *British Columbian,* 4 July 1866, quoted in Barman, *West beyond the West,* 91.

81 Mackie, *The Wilderness Profound,* 68.

82 Stella Higgins, "Colonial Vancouver Island and British Columbia as Seen through British Eyes, 1849-1871" (M.A. thesis, University of Victoria, 1972), 183.

83 Barman, *West beyond the West,* 99-100; Barman, "Invisible Women," 171.

84 Ormsby, *British Columbia,* 261.

85 For the argument that British Columbia entered Confederation so as to tap into Canadian population resources, see Perry, "Hardy Backwoodsmen," 359. On the railway-era Chinese immigrants and conditions, see Wickberg et al., *From China to Canada,* 22; Meen, "Colonial Society," 129n47; F.W. Howay, "The Settlement and Progress of British Columbia, 1871-1914," in *Historical Essays on British Columbia,* J. Friesen and H.K. Ralston, eds. (Toronto: McClelland and Stewart, 1976), 39; Tamara Adilman, "A Preliminary Sketch of Chinese Women and Work in British Columbia 1858-1950," in *Not Just Pin Money: Selected Essays on the History of Women's Work in British Columbia,* Barbara K. Latham and Roberta J. Pazdro, eds. (Victoria: Camosun College, 1984), 55. The theme of Canadian imperialism was taken up long ago by Walter N. Sage in "British Columbia Becomes Canadian, 1871-1901," *Queen's Quarterly* 52, 2 (1945): 168-83, reprinted in Friesen and Ralston, *Historical Essays on British Columbia,* 57-69. Sage concluded that the "Canadianization of British Columbia was fairly well complete" by 1901, something that he regards as singularly good despite the fact that he does not reflect on what constitutes "Canadian."

86 Wood, "Borders and Identities among Italian Immigrants," 112. The literature on the Doukhobor experience continues to grow. Insights to official attitudes in the 1950s may be gleaned from Harry B. Hawthorn, ed., *The Doukhobors of British Columbia* (Vancouver: University of British Columbia and J.M. Dent, 1955). Allen Seager, "The Resource Economy," in Johnston, *The Pacific Province*, 229; David Dendy, "The Worm in the Apple: Contesting the Codling Moth in British Columbia," in Sandwell, *Beyond the City Limits*, 144-45.

87 The trade-off between the possibility of relative prosperity and the negative aspects of a long voyage, an uncertain environment, loss of families, etc., was arguably more difficult to strike in recruiting for remote BC than in almost all of the rest of North America. And if one subscribes to the view suggested in the 1960s that there is a direct correlation between the psychic costs of migration and the distance to be covered, then for all but a few newcomers British Columbia would represent the relative psychic cost equivalent of the Wall Street Crash. T.W. Schultz, "Reflections on Investment in Man," and L.A. Sjaasted, "The Costs and Returns of Human Migration," both in *Journal of Political Economy* 70, supplement (October 1962): 1-8, 80-93, cited in Johannes Overbeek, *Population and Canadian Society* (Toronto: Butterworths, 1980), 97-98.

88 Paul M. Koroscil, "Boosterism and the Settlement Process in the Okanagan Valley, British Columbia, 1890-1914," in *Canadian Papers in Rural History*, vol. 5, Donald Akenson, ed. (Gananoque: Langdale, 1986), 77-78.

89 Working with the nominal census returns and making allowances for unenumerated Aboriginal peoples, Cole Harris estimates the 1881 population as "just over 53,000." In the present study, however, the published census numbers are used exclusively. Harris, *Resettlement*, 138.

90 Hugh J.M. Johnston, "Native Peoples, Settlers and Sojourners, 1871-1916," in Johnston, *The Pacific Province*, 170.

91 For information on the Asian newcomer population in the 1880s, see Canada, "Report of the Royal Commission on Chinese Immigration," *Sessional Papers*, 1885, no. 54a (Ottawa: Printed by order of the Commission, 1885).

92 Barman, *West beyond the West*, 99-100. See also Crawford Killian, *Go Do Some Great Thing: The Black Pioneers of British Columbia* (Vancouver: Douglas and McIntyre, 1978).

93 Lieutenant Governor of British Columbia, Report of his Executive Council with reference to the population of British Columbia, September 1893, RG 6, series A-1, vol. 83, docket 4905, Library and Archives Canada, Ottawa.

94 Howay, "Settlement and Progress of British Columbia," 27.

95 Harris, *Resettlement*, 138; Barman, *West beyond the West*, 369.

96 *Census of Canada, 1881*, vol. 4 (Ottawa, 1882), 86.

97 Favrholdt, "Domesticating the Drybelt," 102-14; F.H. Leacy, ed., *Historical Statistics of Canada*, 2nd ed. (Ottawa: Statistics Canada, 1983), A337.

98 *Census of Canada, 1890-91* (Ottawa, 1893), vol. 2, 2-5, table 1; *Census of Canada, 1901*, vol. 1: *Population*, 2, table 4; *Census of Canada, 1911*, vol. 1: *Areas and Population by Provincial Districts and Subdistricts* (Ottawa: Census and Statistics Office, 1912), 38-39; *Census of Canada, 1911*, vol. 2, 156. For the "bush gentry" and their place in Edwardian British Columbia, see Richard Mackie, "Cougars, Colonists, and the Rural Settlement of Vancouver Island," in Sandwell, *Beyond the City Limits*, 126.

99 Wickberg et al., *From China to Canada*, 21, 23.

100 Arn Keeling, "Sink or Swim: Water Pollution and Environmental Politics in Vancouver, 1889-1975," *BC Studies* 142 (Summer-Autumn 2004): 75.

101 *Census of Canada, 1901*, vol. 1: *Population*.

102 Ruth Sandwell, "Negotiating Rural: Policy and Practice in the Settlement of Saltspring Island, 1859-91," in Sandwell, *Beyond the City Limits*, 89.

103 Perry, "Hardy Backwoodsmen," 352.

104 Robert A.J. McDonald, *Making Vancouver: Class, Status, and Social Boundaries, 1863-1913* (Vancouver: UBC Press, 1996), 54.

105 Quoted in Perry, "Bachelors in the Backwoods," 182.

106 Cole Harris and Elizabeth Phillips, eds., *Letters from Windermere, 1912-1914* (Vancouver: UBC Press, 1984), 9, 13, 67.

107   For a superb visual/cartographic overview from the 1850s to the 1980s, see Bruce Macdonald, *Vancouver: A Visual History* (Vancouver: Talonbooks, 1992). Robert A.J. McDonald has assembled a thorough and thoughtful analysis of Vancouver's early population changes in *Making Vancouver*, especially 13, 21, 23-25. On Native communities, see Harris, "Lower Mainland," 58. The growing sanctions against intermarriage are considered by several British Columbian historians. See, for example, Perry, *On the Edge of Empire*, 48-78; Barman, "Invisible Women," 159-79; and Brett Christophers, *Positioning the Missionary: John Booth Good and the Confluence of Cultures in Nineteenth-Century British Columbia* (Vancouver: UBC Press, 1998), 59-62.

108   Harris, "Lower Mainland," 52; *Census of Canada, 1921*, vol. 1 (Ottawa: King's Printer, 1924), 3 and 234, tables 1 and 12: 3 and 234, Allen Seager, "Workers, Class, and Industrial Conflict in New Westminster, 1900-1930," in Warburton and Coburn, *Workers, Capital and the State*, 118-19. Competition between Vancouver and Victoria was not graciously ceded by the latter. After the 1891 census found slightly fewer than seventeen thousand in the provincial capital, the city council produced a separate and ostensibly more thorough survey. As was reported in the pages of the *Victoria Colonist* newspaper, the city claimed to have found an additional six thousand people. Victoria's Census, Add Mss 1908, microfilm A-1356, BC Archives. Norbert MacDonald, *Distant Neighbors: A Comparative History of Seattle and Vancouver* (Lincoln: University of Nebraska Press, 1987), 155; Walter G. Hardwick, *Vancouver* (Don Mills: Collier-Macmillan Canada, 1974), 4.

109   Norbert MacDonald, "A Critical Growth Cycle for Vancouver, 1900-1914," in *The Canadian City: Essays in Urban History*, Gilbert Stelter and Alan F.J. Artibise, eds. (Toronto: Macmillan, 1979), 144.

110   McDonald, *Making Vancouver*, 54, 58.

111   Marvin McInnis notes that British Columbia in 1901 was "dominated" by Vancouver, but he wrongly projects this precedence backward to 1891 in some of his tables. McInnis, "The Population of Canada in the Nineteenth Century," in *A Population History of North America*, Michael R. Haines and Richard H. Steckel, eds. (Cambridge: Cambridge University Press, 2000), 424.

112   Harris, *Resettlement*, 200.

113   Though could one be sure? One traveller, writing about Kamloops in 1907, commented that the population "was 2500, 3000 and 5000, according respectively to the census officers, the local inhabitants and the real estate agents." Stanton Hope, *Rolling Round the World – for Fun* (London, n.d.), 17, quoted in Wayne Norton, "When the Travellers Come to Town," in *Kamloops: One Hundred Years of Community, 1893-1993*, Wayne Norton and Wilf Schmidt, eds. (Merritt: Sonotek, 1992), 20.

114   It is only fair to add that the Victoria Cougars won the Stanley Cup in 1925.

115   Julie M. Macdonald, "Vital Statistics in British Columbia: An Historical Overview of 100 Years, 1891-1990," *Vital Statistics Quarterly Digest* 4, 1 (June 1994): 44.

116   Richard Frederick Corless Sr. fonds, Add Mss 348, BC Archives.

117   Mary-Ellen Kelm, *Colonizing Bodies: Aboriginal Health and Healing in British Columbia, 1900-50* (Vancouver: UBC Press, 1998), 12-13.

118   Margaret W. Andrews, "Epidemic and Public Health: Influenza in Vancouver, 1918-1919," *BC Studies* 34 (Summer 1977): 21, 24, 41.

119   J. Lewis Robinson, "Vancouver: Changing Geographical Aspects of a Multicultural City," *BC Studies* 79 (Autumn 1988): 64.

120   The Japanese community mounted a remarkable birth rate during the decade of the Great War: forty per one thousand population. See Patricia E. Roy, *The Oriental Question: Consolidating a White Man's Province, 1914-41* (Vancouver: UBC Press, 2003), 56-57. Aspects of soldier settlement schemes and, indeed, the remaking of rural British Columbia are considered in James Murton, *Creating a Modern Countryside: Liberalism and Land Resettlement in British Columbia* (Vancouver: UBC Press, 2007). W. Peter Ward, "Population Growth in Western Canada: 1901-1971," in *The Developing West: Essays in Honour of Lewis H. Thomas*, John E. Foster, ed. (Edmonton: University of Alberta Press, 1983), 159.

121   A fine account of the effects of the immigration legislation on the Chinese Canadian population is Denise Chong, *The Concubine's Children: Portrait of a Family Divided* (Toronto:

Penguin, 1995). Contrast the restrictions on Chinese immigration with the fact that 8,037 Japanese women immigrated in the same period. See Karen Van Dieren, "The Response of the Women's Missionary Society to the Immigration of Asian Women, 1888-1942," in Latham and Pazdro, *Not Just Pin Money*, 89. Sky Lee, *Disappearing Moon Café* (Vancouver: Douglas and McIntyre, 1990), 68; W. Peter Ward, *White Canada Forever: Popular Attitudes and Public Policy towards Orientals in British Columbia* (Montreal and Kingston: McGill-Queen's University Press, 1990), 164-65; Roy and Thompson, *British Columbia*, 137. See also Yuen-Fong Woon, *The Excluded Wife* (Montreal and Kingston: McGill-Queen's University Press, 1998), and Wing Chung Ng, *The Chinese in Vancouver, 1945-80: The Pursuit of Identity and Power* (Vancouver: UBC Press, 1999), 16.

122 Richmond P. Hobson Jr., *Grass beyond the Mountains: Discovering the Last Great Cattle Frontier on the North American Continent* (Toronto: Lippincott, 1951), 18; Patricia E. Roy, "Vancouver: 'The Mecca of the Unemployed,' 1907-1929," in *Town and City: Aspects of Western Canadian Urban Development*, Alan Artibise, ed. (Regina: Canadian Plains Research Center, 1981), 393-413; Canada, Bureau of Statistics, *Vital Statistics of Canada, 1929-1939* (Ottawa: King's Printer, 1940), 57; *Vancouver Daily Province*, 25 September 1937.

123 Statistics Canada, *Canada E-Stats*, Series A33.

124 Angus McLaren, *A History of Contraception from Antiquity to the Present Day* (Oxford: Blackwell, 1990), 238; David K. Foot with Daniel Stoffman, *Boom, Bust and Echo: How to Profit from the Coming Demographic Shift* (Toronto: Macfarlane Walter and Ross, 1996), 18-19.

125 For the immediate impact this flurry of family formation had in Vancouver, see Jill Wade, *Houses for All: The Struggle for Social Housing in Vancouver, 1919-50* (Vancouver: UBC Press, 1994), 95-96.

126 In 1959, 1961, and 1962, for example, the unemployment rates in BC and Ontario were, respectively, around 8.5 percent and 5.5 percent. These were British Columbia's worst years in the post-war boom period but the gap was consistently about the same, at least proportionately. See Leacy, *Historical Statistics of Canada*.

127 Frank Zelko, "Making Greenpeace: The Development of Direct Action Environmentalism in British Columbia," *BC Studies* 142-43 (Summer-Autumn 2004): 197.

128 Trip of the Minister [of Citizenship and Immigration] to Immigration offices overseas and proposed visit in the Province of BC, RG 26, series A-1-a, vol. 75, file 1-1-8, Library and Archives Canada.

129 Paul M. Koroscil, *British Columbia: Settlement History* (Burnaby: Department of Geography, Simon Fraser University, 2000), 148-68.

130 For a somewhat dated but encyclopedic survey of various immigrant groups, see John Norris, *Strangers Entertained: A History of the Ethnic Groups of British Columbia* (Vancouver: Evergreen Press, 1971).

131 Too much should not be made of the legislative changes in 1947: they remained highly restrictive. See Ng, *Chinese in Vancouver*, 19-20. Jean R. Burnet with Howard Palmer, *"Coming Canadians": An Introduction to the History of Canada's People* (Toronto: McClelland and Stewart, 1988), 171; Wickberg et al., *From China to Canada*, 245.

132 Roderic Beaujot and Kevin McQuillan, *Growth and Dualism: The Demographic Development of Canadian Society* (Toronto: Gage, 1982), 98. See also Lai, "Chinese Communities," 348-50.

133 On Indian immigration to British Columbia, see Tara Singh Bains and Hugh Johnston, *The Four Quarters of the Night: The Life Journey of an Emigrant Sikh* (Montreal and Kingston: McGill-Queen's University Press, 1995), 71, 240, and Kamala Elizabeth Nayar, *The Sikh Diaspora in Vancouver: Three Generations amid Tradition, Modernity, and Multiculturalism* (Toronto: University of Toronto Press, 2004).

134 As a recent survey puts it, the 1976 legislation "reinforced existing policy. It explicitly affirmed the fundamental objectives of Canadian immigration laws, including family reunification, non-discrimination, concern for refugees, and the promotion of Canada's demographic, economic and cultural goals." Beaujot and Kerr, *Population Change in Canada*, 101-2. Statistics Canada, *Canada's Changing Immigrant Population*, catalogue no. 96-311E (Ottawa: Statistics Canada, 1994), table 1.2. Government of British Columbia, BC Stats: Population, http://www.bcstats.gov.bc.ca/data/pop/mig/immLandC.pdf.

135   Robin Brunet, "Goodbye 'British' Columbia: Media Cheers Cannot Hide the Problems of Vancouver's Ethnic Transformation," *BC Report*, 1 December 1997, 18-21.
136   In 1991 the median years of schooling for Canadian-born males and females in BC was 12.6 years; for male and female immigrants to the province, it was 13.2 and 12.7 years respectively. See Statistics Canada, *Canada's Changing Immigrant Population*, 43. There were, inevitably, outbreaks of racist backlash, for some of which the Ku Klux Klan acted as a lightning rod. For the history of the Klan in Canada, see Martin Robin, *Shades of Right: Nativist and Fascist Politics in Canada, 1920-1940* (Toronto: University of Toronto Press, 1992). For the situation on the west coast, see British Columbia, Ministry of Labour, *Report Arising out of Activities of the Ku Klux Klan in British Columbia* (Victoria: Ministry of Labour, 1981). On mainstream suspicion of and hostility toward Asian newcomers, see Brunet, "Goodbye 'British' Columbia." Tim Gallagher, "The Hongcouver Backlash: Racism Rears Its Head as Vancouver Property Values Soar," *Western Report*, 24 October 1988, 15. See also Ng, *Chinese in Vancouver*, 140. James Stafford, "Welcome but Why? Recent Changes in Canadian Immigration Policy," in *Perspectives on Canada's Population: An Introduction to Concepts and Issues*, Frank Trovato and Carl F. Grindstaff, eds. (Don Mills: Oxford University Press, 1994), 337.
137   Quoted in Norman Knowles, "Religious Affiliation, Demographic Change and Family Formation among British Columbia's Chinese and Japanese Communities: A Case Study of Church of England Missions, 1861-1942," *Canadian Ethnic Studies* 27, 2 (1995): 5.
138   Herbert C. Northcott and P. Jane Milliken, *Aging in British Columbia: Burden or Benefit?* (Calgary: Detselig, 1998), 28; Donald Kerr and Bali Ram, *Population Dynamics in Canada* (Ottawa: Statistics Canada, 1994), 6-7, 21-22. See Statistics Canada, "Estimates of Population, by Age Group and Sex for July 1, Canada, Provinces and Territories, Annual (Persons Unless Otherwise Noted)," CANSIM table 051-0001 (2007).
139   See N. Fast, "AIDS/HIV Related Mortality in British Columbia: 1985 to 1994," *Vital Statistics Quarterly Digest* 5, 1 (May 1995): 21, 22, 26, 28; Z. Kashaninia, "The Impact of Infectious Diseases on Mortality in BC, 1990-1997," *Vital Statistics Quarterly Digest* 8, 3 (March 1999): 21-35.
140   Department of Health Services and Hospital Insurance, British Columbia, *Vital Statistics of the Province of British Columbia, Eighty-Ninth Report, 1960* (Victoria: Queen's Printer, 1961), J27, J28; Macdonald, "Vital Statistics in British Columbia," 40-41; E. Demaere, "Accident Fatality in British Columbia, 1987-1995," *Vital Statistics Quarterly Digest* 6, 3 (January 1997): 25; British Columbia Vital Statistics Agency, *Selected Vital Statistics and Health Status Indicators, Annual Report 2005*, 83, http://www.vs.gov.bc.ca/stats/annual/2005/pdf/deaths.pdf; Health Canada, Medical Services Branch, and BC Division of Vital Statistics, "Status Indians in British Columbia: A Vital Statistical Overview," *Vital Statistics Quarterly Digest* 4, 2 (August 1994): 25. The dominance of males over females in drowning deaths continues to the present. In the 1990s male British Columbians were more likely than women to drown in all manner of activities on or beneath the waves, though women were more than twice as likely as men to drown in bathtubs. See Z. Kashaninia, J. Macdonald, and R. Armour, "Drowning and Other Water-Related Accidental Fatalities, British Columbia, 1990-1998," *Vital Statistics Quarterly Digest* 9, 1 and 2 (October 1998): 37.
141   A. Romaniuc, *Current Demographic Analysis: Fertility in Canada: From Baby-Boom to Baby-Bust* (Ottawa: Statistics Canada, 1984), 55-56.
142   Vijaya Krishnan, "Contraceptive Sterilization among Canadians, 1984-1995," *Canadian Studies in Population* 31, 1 (2004): 16-17.
143   Kerr and Ram, *Population Dynamics in Canada*, 36.
144   On divorce law generally, see Roderick Phillips, *Untying the Knot: A Short History of Divorce* (Cambridge: Cambridge University Press, 1991), 213, 219. On the Canadian experience in the nineteenth century, see Peter Ward, *Courtship, Love, and Marriage in Nineteenth-Century English Canada* (Montreal and Kingston: McGill-Queen's University Press, 1990), 37. For incidence of divorce, see Department of Health Services and Hospital Insurance, British Columbia, *Vital Statistics of the Province of British Columbia, Ninety-Second Report for the Year 1963* (Victoria: Queen's Printer, 1965), 45, and John Porter, *Canadian Social Structure* (Toronto: McClelland and Stewart, 1967), 60.

145 O.B. Adams and D.N. Nagnur, *Marriage, Divorce and Mortality: A Life-Table Analysis for Canada and Regions* (Ottawa: Statistics Canada, 1988), 15. See also Lynn Barr, *Basic Facts on Families in Canada, Past and Present,* catalogue no. 89-516 (Ottawa: Statistics Canada, 1993), 16.

146 See Tina Block, "'This Crowd of Spiritual Outcasts': Class, Gender, Region, and Irreligion in Postwar British Columbia" (paper presented at the Canadian Historical Association Conference, Halifax, 31 May 2003). See also the following sources, provided by Block in "'Families That Pray Together, Stay Together': Religion, Gender, and Family in Postwar Victoria, British Columbia," *BC Studies* 145 (Spring 2005): Lynne Marks, "Exploring Regional Diversity in Patterns of Religious Participation: Canada in 1901," *Historical Methods* 33, 4 (2000): 247-54, and Bob Stewart, "That's the BC Spirit! Religion and Secularity in Lotus Land," *Canadian Society of Church History Papers* (1983): 22-35.

147 See Carl Grindstaff, "A Vanishing Breed: Women with Large Families, Canada in the 1980s," *Canadian Studies in Population* 19, 2 (1993): 145-62.

148 The "New Home Economics" school of the 1980s championed this position, but its model has since been critiqued as superficial. See, for example, Michael Anderson, "British Population History, 1911-1991," in *British Population History from the Black Death to the Present Day,* Michael Anderson, ed. (Cambridge: Cambridge University Press, 1996), 390.

149 Douglas Coupland, *Generation X: Tales for an Accelerated Culture* (New York: St. Martin's Press, 1991).

150 Northcott and Milliken, *Aging in British Columbia,* 27-47. Although the stereotype is, in the case of Victoria, at least viable, both the capital and Kelowna are eclipsed by Penticton, where the senior population constitutes 23 percent of the total. Ibid., 23, 27-47. See also Charles N. Forward, "Relationships between Elderly Population and Income Sources in the Urban Economic Bases of Victoria and Vancouver," *BC Studies* 36 (Winter 1977-78): 34.

151 A cautionary note as regards city populations is in order: although these are based on census counts, urban boundaries are inherently fluid, and it is clear from the large number of towns with populations of, say, five hundred or twenty-five hundred, that rounding of figures was almost certainly practised. Nevertheless, one gets a good sense of how distribution and growth were experienced in this period, however inaccurate the specific figures may be.

152 J. Lewis Robinson and Walter G. Hardwick, *British Columbia: One Hundred Years of Geographical Change* (Vancouver: Talonbooks, 1973), 38.

153 See David Mitchell, *WAC Bennett and the Rise of British Columbia* (Vancouver: Douglas and McIntyre, 1995).

154 *Census of Canada, 1951,* vol. 1: *Population* (Ottawa: Queen's Printer, 1951), xv.

155 Veronica Strong-Boag, "Society in the Twentieth Century," in Johnston, *The Pacific Province,* 309n9.

156 The connections between suburbanization and the Canadian baby boom are explored in Veronica Strong-Boag, "Home Dreams: Women and the Suburban Experiment in Canada, 1945-60," *Canadian Historical Review* 72, 4 (1991): 471-504.

157 Geoffrey J. Matthews and Robert Morrow Jr., *Canada and the World: An Atlas Resource,* 2nd ed. (Scarborough: Prentice Hall, 1994), 182; Françoise Singh, *Growth of the Canadian Metropolitan Population, 1971-1976* (Ottawa: Statistics Canada, 1979), 10-11.

158 Norbert MacDonald, "Population Growth and Change in Seattle and Vancouver, 1880-1960," *Pacific Historical Review* 39 (August 1970): 321.

159 Statistics Canada, *The 1999 Canada Year Book* (Ottawa: Ministry of Industry, 1998), 94.

160 Government of British Columbia, BC Stats: Population, http://www.bcstats.gov.bc.ca/data/pop/mig/comp_RD2002.pdf.

161 Statistics Canada, *Profile of the Canadian Population: Where We Live,* catalogue no. 96F0030 (Ottawa: Statistics Canada, 2002), cited in Beaujot and Kerr, *Population Change in Canada,* 138.

162 Robert Burkinshaw, *Pilgrims in Lotus Land: Conservative Protestantism in British Columbia, 1917-1981* (Montreal and Kingston: McGill-Queen's University Press, 1995), 242-43.

163 At 11,430, Trail was less than half the size of New Westminster (28,639), a shade more than one-fifth the population of Victoria (51,331), and a fraction of Vancouver (344,833). See *Census of Canada, 1951,* vol. 1: *Population,* table 3. On Kelowna, see Robinson and Hardwick, *British Columbia,* 46-47. City of Kamloops, *Kamloops: A Demographic Profile* (Kamloops: City

of Kamloops, 1989), 2-3; Claude Marchand and Janine Charland, *The Depopulation of Canadian Communities, 1981-86* (Toronto: ICURR Press, 1991), 20, figure 5; Statistics Canada, *Profile of the Canadian Population,* cited in Beaujot and Kerr, *Population Change in Canada,* 137-38.
164 Woodcock, *British Columbia,* 267.
165 Tony F. Arruda, "'You Would Have Had Your Pick': Youth, Gender, and Jobs in Williams Lake, British Columbia, 1945-75," in Sandwell, *Beyond the City Limits,* 225-26.
166 Victoria and Vancouver had densities of 7.1 and 7.89 respectively in 1950. *Census of Canada, 1951,* vol. 1: *Population,* table 3.
167 British Columbia Vital Statistics Agency, "Municipalities Greater than 5,000 Population 1996-2001 Percent Growth, 10 Highest and 10 Lowest Rates," http://www.bcstats.gov.bc. ca/data/cen01/munlohi2.gif.
168 In some districts, but particularly in the southeast, the demands of metropolitan capitalism hurried along the decline and disappearance of whole communities. This was most dramatically the case along the central Arrow Lakes during the 1960s when the construction of the Columbia River hydroelectricity dams forced the relocation of more than a thousand people. See J.W. Wilson, *People in the Way: The Human Aspects of the Columbia River Project* (Toronto: University of Toronto Press, 1973).
169 Comparisons with California might be invoked. I would argue that the history of European-Aboriginal contact there was a much more drawn out and very differently organized proposition, that San Francisco's ascendancy during the gold rush produced a different pattern of capital and population accumulation in the northern half of the state, that the Spanish presence alone differentiates the two regions, and that the territory was aggressively Americanized before the gold rush and thus far less "international" and certainly less British than was the case in BC.
170 Perry, "Hardy Backwoodsmen," 344.
171 See Neil Sutherland, *Children in English Canadian Society: Framing the Twentieth-Century Consensus* (Toronto: University of Toronto Press, 1976), 155-226.
172 British Columbia, *The Nineteen Eighties: A Statistical Resource for a Decade of Vital Events in British Columbia* (Victoria: Ministry of Health and Ministry Responsible for Seniors, 1994), 12.

Chapter 3: The West We Have Lost: First Nations Depopulation

1 One monograph on the subject of Aboriginal depopulation compellingly describes the history of military assaults on Natives in both North and South America since the fifteenth century and shows how what can only be described as genocidal policies and tactics have been underplayed, if not ignored utterly, in historical texts. However, it tars with the same brush those scholars who have favoured lower pre-Columbian numbers. The disparaging tone used to describe historians and anthropologists who present evidence contrary to that of the high counters is a mark of how academic freedom of discussion is under threat. By way of an example – "While upward revision of estimates to conform with the evidence has elicited all manner of howls from paleoconservatives and allegedly 'responsible' academics about the need for exercising 'proper scientific caution' in such matters, the fact is that it is orthodoxy itself which threw both science and caution to the winds in deliberately low-counting the pre-invasion population of the continent. Estimates approximating those of Dobyns and Thornton have, after all, been available to anyone who cared to use them since at least as early as 1860. As Jennings observes, they 'simply ignored' such inconveniences." Proof that there was a deliberate conspiracy to undercount or that the estimates from the 1860s carried with them any kind of legitimacy is not provided by the author; nor, for that matter, does he help his case much in minimizing the methodological efforts exerted by Henry Dobyns and Russell Thornton. The fact that the author is openly and confessedly polemical in his style and political in his goals is cold comfort: low counters are aligned with neo-Nazis and Holocaust-deniers such as Ernst Zundel. One can only hope that this knee-jerk censorship of debate on the demography of First Nations has subsided. Ward Churchill, *A Little Matter of Genocide: Holocaust and Denial in the Americas, 1492 to the Present* (Winnipeg: Arbeiter Ring, 1998), 11, 135.

2 See Marlita A. Reddy, ed., *Statistical Record of Native North Americans* (Detroit: Gale, 1993), 1. It has been widely accepted, perhaps erroneously, that the Spanish imperial regime was more careful and assiduous than other imperial powers in assembling population accounts. Aspects of the Spanish bureaucratic system, which contrasts sharply with the North American regimes, can be found in Daniel T. Reff, *Disease, Depopulation, and Culture Change in Northwestern New Spain, 1518-1764* (Salt Lake City: University of Utah Press, 1991), 7-9. Alfred W. Crosby Jr., *The Columbian Exchange: Biological and Cultural Consequences of 1492* (Westport, CN: Greenwood Press, 1972), provides one version of the widely accepted view of catastrophic impact. A more critical and more circumspect approach can be found in D. Ann Herring, "Toward a Reconsideration of Disease and Contact in the Americas," *Prairie Forum* 17, 2 (Fall 1992): 153-66. See also Keith Basso, "History of Ethnological Research," *Handbook of North American Indians*, vol. 9: *Southwest* (Washington: Smithsonian Institution, 1979), 14-21; Robert McCaa, "Spanish and Nahuatl Views on Smallpox and Demographic Catastrophe in Mexico," *Journal of Interdisciplinary History* 25 (1994-95): 397-431; and A. Zambardino, "Mexico's Population in the Sixteenth Century: Demographic Anomaly or Mathematical Illusion?" *Journal of Interdisciplinary History* 11 (1980): 1-27.

3 For a very good example of the public face of this discussion, see Charles C. Mann, "1491," *Atlantic* 289 (March 2002): 41-53.

4 Henry F. Dobyns, "Estimating Aboriginal American Populations, I: An Appraisal of Techniques with a New Hemispheric Estimate (and Comments)," *Current Anthropology* 7, 4 (1966): 395-416, 425-49; Harold E. Driver, *Indians of North America*, 2nd ed. (Chicago: University of Chicago Press, 1969), 63. For Mooney, see Douglas H. Ubelaker, "The Sources and Methodology for Mooney's Estimates of North American Indian Populations," in *The Native Population of the Americas in 1492*, William M. Denevan, ed. (Madison: University of Wisconsin Press, 1976), 243-88. For Kroeber, see Douglas H. Ubelaker, "North American Indian Population Size: Changing Perspectives," in *Disease and Demography in the Americas*, John W. Verano and Douglas H. Ubelaker, ed. (Washington: Smithsonian Institution, 1992), 172-73.

5 Henry F. Dobyns, *Their Number Become Thinned: Native American Population Dynamics in Eastern North America* (Knoxville: University of Tennessee Press, 1983). These figures are all taken from Russell Thornton, *American Indian Holocaust and Survival: A Population History since 1492* (Norman: University of Oklahoma Press, 1987), 26.

6 Olive Dickason, *Canada's First Nations: A History of Founding Peoples from Earliest Times*, 3rd ed. (Don Mills: Oxford University Press, 2002), 45.

7 Ronald Wright, *Stolen Continents: The "New World" through Indian Eyes since 1492* (Toronto: Penguin Books Canada, 1992), 123. Erring too much on the side of caution, a standard text, *Canadian Population*, states that what is now "Canada was thought to have been inhabited by about 200,000 aboriginals when the Europeans first began their exploration and colonization of the New World," without indicating that there is the slightest debate on this subject. Wayne W. McVey Jr. and Warren E. Kalbach, *Canadian Population* (Toronto: Nelson Canada, 1995), 342.

8 Wilson Duff, *The Indian History of British Columbia*, vol. 1: *The Impact of the White Man*, new ed. (Victoria: Royal British Columbia Museum, 1997), 55.

9 Jean Barman, *The West beyond the West: A History of British Columbia* (Toronto: University of Toronto Press, 1991), 14; Robin Fisher, *Contact and Conflict: Indian-European Relations in British Columbia, 1774-1890*, 2nd ed. (Vancouver: UBC Press, 1977), xv-xvi. Barman recently signed off on this statement, which suggests a change of heart on the subject: "In 1900 only some 175,000 people lived in British Columbia, probably fewer than had inhabited the same space one hundred and fifty years earlier." Cole Harris and Jean Barman, "Editorial at the End of a Century," *BC Studies* 124 (Winter 1999-2000): 3.

10 Roy Carlson, "The First British Columbians," in *The Pacific Province: A History of British Columbia*, Hugh J.M. Johnston, ed. (Vancouver: Douglas and McIntyre, 1996), 31.

11 Robert T. Boyd, "Demographic History, 1774-1874," *Handbook of North American Indians*, vol. 7: *Northwest Coast* (Washington: Smithsonian Institution, 1990), 147. Some of these peoples lived south of Juan de Fuca Strait, whereas others could be found on the Alaska Panhandle.

12 Robert T. Boyd, "Demographic History until 1990," *Handbook of North American Indians,* vol. 12: *Plateau* (Washington: Smithsonian Institution, 1998), 472. Duane Thomson and Marianne Ignace describe Boyd's figures for the Northern Plateau as "conservative" but do not provide reasons for doing so. Thomson and Ignace, "'They Made Themselves Our Guests': Power Relationships in the Interior Plateau Region of the Cordillera in the Fur Trade Era," *BC Studies* 146 (Summer 2005): 7n14.

13 Arthur C. Aufderheide, "Summary on Disease before and after Contact," in *Disease and Demography in the Americas,* John W. Verano and Douglas H. Ubelaker, eds. (Washington: Smithsonian Institution, 1992), 166.

14 Cole Harris, *Making Native Space: Colonialism, Resistance, and Reserves in British Columbia* (Vancouver: UBC Press, 2002), 47.

15 Paul Tennant, *Aboriginal Peoples and Politics: The Indian Land Question in British Columbia, 1849-1989* (Vancouver: UBC Press, 1990).

16 Robert Muckle, *The First Nations of British Columbia: An Anthropological Survey* (Vancouver: UBC Press, 1998), 37; Dobyns, *Their Number Become Thinned,* 38-39.

17 David E. Stannard, *American Holocaust: The Conquest of the New World* (New York: Oxford University Press, 1992), 21.

18 One study that straddles the divide between scholarly and popular history claims that there were 300,000 indigenous peoples in BC before the arrival of Europeans, citing Cole Harris' work as its source. Remarkably, there is nothing on the page cited that refers to the figure of 300,000. Kathryn Bridge, *By Snowshoe, Buckboard and Steamer: Women of the Frontier* (Victoria: Sono Nis Press, 1998), 17. A similarly positioned examination of life in the Gulf Islands refers to "a smallpox epidemic spread by infected Europeans in 1769," for which there is no scholarly support. Charles Kahn, *Salt Spring: The Story of an Island* (Madeira Park, BC: Harbour, 1998), 22. Finally, a popular history of the province claims that an epidemic in 1780 killed "an estimated 60,000" among the Haida and Tlingit alone. The assertion of a certain year and a certain number (both of which are doubtful) is reckless enough, but the sin is worsened by the lack of references. Geoffrey Molyneux, *British Columbia: An Illustrated History* (Vancouver: Raincoast, 2002), 33.

19 Sarah K. Campbell, *PostColumbian Culture History in the Northern Columbia Plateau, A.D. 1500-1900* (New York: Garland, 1990), 186-87. Even Daniel Reff, who has to be included in those who favour higher numbers for Mexico's First Nations, argues that "The evidence for hemispheric pandemics ... is still meager or contradictory." Reff, *Disease,* 5.

20 On recovery, see Ann F. Ramenofsky, *Vectors of Death: The Archaeology of European Contact* (Albuquerque: University of New Mexico Press, 1987), 12-13.

21 Jody F. Decker, "Tracing Historical Diffusion Patterns: The Case of the 1780-82 Smallpox Epidemic among the Indians of Western Canada," *Native Studies Review* 4, 1 and 2 (1988): 15-18.

22 What is striking from this account is the role *not* played by Europeans in the spread of smallpox. Horses had reached the plains and were being widely used by American Indians as early as the 1730s, and this would have facilitated the movement of contagions, but the riverine economy and culture of the Woods Cree was, evidently, equally effective. Cole Harris, *The Resettlement of British Columbia: Essays on Colonialism and Geographical Change* (Vancouver: UBC Press, 1997), 17; Robert Boyd, "Smallpox in the Pacific Northwest: The First Epidemics," *BC Studies* 101 (Spring 1994): 5-40. Elizabeth A. Fenn, *Pox Americana: The Great Smallpox Epidemic of 1775-82* (New York: Hill and Wang, 2001), 252-57.

23 Duff, *Indian History,* 54.

24 Boyd's exhaustive search for accounts of eighteenth-century epidemics in BC comes up almost entirely dry. He provides much better evidence out of Russian Alaska and Washington's Columbia Valley. The sharpness of those peripheral accounts stands in stark contrast to the elliptical allusions and uncritical assertions of smallpox on the British Columbian land mass. The report of signs of smallpox among the Ditidaht of southern Vancouver Island in 1791 is certainly direct but not as critical and reflective – and therefore, not as easily accepted – as the accounts from the southern and northern borderlands. Robert Boyd, *The Coming of the Spirit of Pestilence: Introduced Infectious Diseases and Population Decline among Northwest Coast Indians, 1774-1874* (Vancouver: UBC Press, 1999), 31.

25 Robert Galois, *Kwakwaka'wakw Settlements, 1775-1920: A Geographical Analysis and Gazetteer* (Vancouver: UBC Press, 1994); Alan D. McMillan, *Since the Time of the Transformers: The Ancient Heritage of the Nuu-chuh-nulth, Ditidaht, and Makah* (Vancouver: UBC Press, 1999), 191-92; Daniel W. Clayton, *Islands of Truth: The Imperial Fashioning of Vancouver Island* (Vancouver: UBC Press, 2000), 148. Boyd includes an account of a late eighteenth-century population collapse at Quatsino Sound in his evidence for a 1770s smallpox epidemic in the Kwakwaka'wakw territory but acknowledges that "the passage is not definitive proof" because of counterclaims for depopulation by warfare. Boyd, *Coming of the Spirit of Pestilence*, 27.

26 Harris, *Resettlement*, 4.

27 See also Diamond Jenness, *Faith of a Coast Salish Indian* (Victoria: British Columbia Provincial Museum, Department of Education, 1955); Harris, *Resettlement*, 10.

28 Cole Harris, "Social Power and Cultural Change in Pre-Colonial British Columbia," *BC Studies* 115-16 (Autumn-Winter 1997-98): 54.

29 Robert Boyd, "Commentary on Early Contact-Era Smallpox in the Pacific Northwest," *Ethnohistory* 43 (1996): 318.

30 Harris, *Resettlement*, 8.

31 Harris, *Making Native Space*, 47.

32 Boyd, "Smallpox," 10, 16; Steven Acheson, "Culture Contact, Demography and Health among the Aboriginal Peoples of British Columbia," in *A Persistent Spirit: Towards Understanding Aboriginal Health in British Columbia*, Canadian Western Geographical Series 31, Peter H. Stephenson, Susan J. Elliott, Leslie T. Foster, and Jill Harris, eds. (Victoria: Western Geographical Press, 1995), 10.

33 Robin Fisher, "The Northwest from the Beginning of Trade with Europeans to the 1880s," *The Cambridge History of the Native Peoples of the Americas*, vol. 1: *North America Part 2* (Cambridge: Cambridge University Press, 1996), 145. See also McMillan, *Since the Time of the Transformers*, 192-93.

34 Boyd, "Smallpox," 17.

35 Robert Galois, "Measles, 1847-1850: The First Modern Epidemic in British Columbia," *BC Studies* 109 (Spring 1996): 31-46.

36 Boyd, *Coming of the Spirit of Pestilence*, 21.

37 Fenn, *Pox Americana*, 227, 257-58.

38 This opinion is shared by one of Boyd's reviewers. See Theodore Binnema, "Disease History on the Northwest Coast: A Microcosm, or a Unique Region?" review of *The Coming of the Spirit of Pestilence*, by Robert Boyd, H-Environment, H-Net Reviews, April 2000, http://www. h-net.org/reviews/.

39 Douglas Cole and Bradley Lockner, eds., *To the Charlottes: George Dawson's 1878 Survey of the Queen Charlotte Islands* (Vancouver: UBC Press, 1993), 53, 68, 163-65.

40 T. Manby Journal, December 1790-June 1793, 43, William Robertson Coe Collection, Yale University, quoted in Harris, *Resettlement*, 12.

41 Harris, *Resettlement*, 16.

42 Galois, "Measles," 42.

43 Clayton, *Islands of Truth*, 132-34.

44 Boyd, "Demographic History, 1774-1874," 138; Harris, *Resettlement*, 19.

45 Keith Thor Carlson, "The Numbers Game: Interpreting Historical Stó:lō Demographics," in *A Stó:lō Coast Salish Historical Atlas*, Keith Thor Carlson, ed., with Albert (Sonny) McHalsie, cultural advisor (Vancouver: Douglas and McIntyre, 2001), 77.

46 Russell Thornton, Jonathan Warren, and Tim Miller, "Depopulation in the Southeast after 1492," in Verano and Ubelaker, *Disease and Demography in the Americas*, 193.

47 Acheson, "Culture Contact, Demography and Health," 12.

48 See, for example, Jonathan R. Dean, "'Those Rascally Spackaloids': The Rise of Gispaxlots Hegemony at Fort Simpson, 1832-40," *BC Studies* 101 (Spring 1994): 55-60.

49 James R. Gibson, "Smallpox on the Northwest Coast, 1835-1838," *BC Studies* 56 (Winter 1982-83): 69, 71.

50 This refers to the impact an epidemic disaster would have on the sex ratio within the context of culturally imposed marriage customs. Simply stated, customs could curtail marriage and mating where "appropriate" partners were no longer available.

51 Robert Boyd, "Population Decline from Two Epidemics on the Northwest Coast," in Verano and Ubelaker, *Disease and Demography in the Americas,* 249-55. Boyd's numbers invite some further examination. It took sixty years for the Haida to reach their nadir. That is precisely the interval between the 1780s epidemic and the HBC census of 1841. Let us assume for a moment that the 1841 population was itself a nadir, a low point following on the 1782-83 smallpox mortality (as well as following on the c. 1800 and 1830s epidemics). The point of this exercise is not to provide a new figure for the Haida in the 1780s, but to show how inconsistently the methodology of "retrojection" has been applied.
52 Thornton, Warren, and Miller, "Depopulation in the Southeast after 1492," 192-93.
53 Decker, "Tracing Historical Diffusion Patterns," 12, 20.
54 Harris, *Resettlement,* 15; Ralph Maud, "Introduction," in *The Salish People: The Local Contribution of Charles Hill-Tout,* vol. 1: *The Thompson and the Okanagan,* Ralph Maud, ed. (Vancouver: Talonbooks, 1978), 44; George MacDonald, *Kitwanga Fort Report* (Ottawa: Canadian Museum of Civilization, 1989), 4. Elliot Fox-Povey argues that European mariners' demand for sexual relations with Native women spurred on the practice of raiding for slaves in the late eighteenth century. Fox-Povey, "How Agreeable Their Company Would Be: The Meaning of the Sexual Labour of Slaves in the Nuu-chah-nulth – European Sex Trade at Nootka Sound in the Eighteenth Century," *British Columbia Historical News* 36, 3 (Summer 2003): 7-9.
55 Jerome S. Cybulski, "Human Biology," *Handbook of North American Indians,* vol. 7: *Northwest Coast,* 58-59; Jay Miller, "Tsimshian Ethno-Ethnohistory: A 'Real' Indigenous Chronology," *Ethnohistory* 45, 4 (Fall 1998): 657-74; Jo-Anne Fiske, "Colonization and the Decline of Women's Status: The Tsimshian Case," *Feminist Studies* 17, 3 (Fall 1991): 521.
56 Clayton, *Islands of Truth,* 145; McMillan, *Since the Time of the Transformers,* 193.
57 Quoted in Galois, "Measles," 36.
58 Lieutenant H. Spencer Palmer, *Report of a Journey from Victoria to Fort Alexander via North Bentick Arm* (New Westminster: Royal Engineer Press, 1863), 7.
59 See Harry Assu, *Assu of Cape Mudge: Recollections of a Coastal Indian Chief, Harry Assu with Joy Inglis* (Vancouver: UBC Press, 1989), 14-15.
60 Thomson and Ignace, "'They Made Themselves Our Guests,'" 9.
61 See James Teit, *The Salishan Tribes of the Western Plateaus,* Bureau of American Ethnology, Annual Report 45 (Washington: Government Printing Office, 1930), 257.
62 Horses arrived in the southern Interior some time in the first half of the eighteenth century; at approximately the same time iron shows up in the region. Duane Thomson, "The Response of Okanagan Indians to European Settlement," *BC Studies* 101 (Spring 1994): 98; Robert L. Wilson and Catherine Carlson, *The Archaeology of Kamloops,* Simon Fraser University Department of Archaeology Publications 7 (Burnaby: SFU Dept. of Archaeology, 1980), 9.
63 David Wyatt, "Nicola," *Handbook of North American Indians,* vol. 12: *Plateau,* 221.
64 Duane Thomson, "Hwistensmexe'qen, Nicola, (1785-1859) Indian Chief, Warrior, Hunter, Trader, Guide, Farmer," 2007, http://www.livinglandscapes.bc.ca/thomp-ok/river-post/nicola.html.
65 Teit, *Salishan Tribes of the Western Plateaus,* 268.
66 *Victoria Colonist,* 23 April 1864, quoted in John Lutz, "Work, Sex, and Death on the Great Thoroughfare: Annual Migrations of 'Canadian Indians' to the American Pacific Northwest," in *Parallel Destinies: Canadian-American Relations West of the Rockies,* Kenneth Coates and John M. Findlay, eds. (Seattle: University of Washington Press, 2002), 90.
67 McMillan, *Since the Time of the Transformers,* 192.
68 Duff, *Indian History,* 61. The utility of firearms in close-quarters fighting and raiding is questioned by many academics. See Clayton, *Islands of Truth,* 121-22.
69 See Lutz, "Work, Sex, and Death," 89, 91.
70 See Leland Donald, *Aboriginal Slavery on the Northwest Coast of North America* (Berkeley: University of California Press, 1997), 103-20.
71 Ralph Maud, "Introduction," 11. Charles Hill-Tout adds to this his conviction that slaves were *not* executed at the death of their owners, a mortality factor that may have occurred elsewhere but not in the Thompson-Fraser River area. Hill-Tout, "Notes on the Ntlakapamuq," in Maud, *The Salish People,* 49.

72 The status of slaves in Tsimshian communities envisioned some reproductive contribution: "Slaves were permitted to marry (but only high-ranking captive women married freemen, almost always chiefs)." It is unclear if and to what extent these practices changed over the course of the eighteenth and nineteenth centuries. See Fiske, "Colonization and the Decline of Women's Status," 513; Donald, *Aboriginal Slavery,* 116-17.

73 Fenn, *Pox Americana,* 231.

74 James R. Gibson, "The Maritime Trade of the North Pacific Coast," *Handbook of North American Indians,* vol. 4: *History of Indian-White Relations* (Washington: Smithsonian Institution, 1998), 390.

75 Keith Thor Carlson, "Intercommunity Conflicts," in Carlson and McHalsie, *A Stó:lō Coast Salish Historical Atlas,* 48-49. See also Dean, "'Those Rascally Spackaloids,'" 66-68.

76 Harris, *Making Native Space,* 25.

77 Fenn, *Pox Americana,* 226.

78 Russell Thornton, *The Cherokees: A Population History* (Lincoln: University of Nebraska Press, 1990), 14; Thornton, *American Indian Holocaust,* 22.

79 A discussion of Mooney's "conservative" methodology can be found in Douglas H. Ubelaker, "The Sources and Methodology for Mooney's Estimates of North American Indian Populations," in *The Native Population of the Americas in 1492,* William M. Denevan, ed. (Madison: University of Wisconsin Press, 1976), 243-88.

80 See, for example, McMillan, *Since the Time of the Transformers,* 193. McMillan endorses the estimates of Nuu-chah-nulth population compiled by John Meares in 1788 without giving a reason for doing so. Meares was making estimates based, it would seem, on what he was told by his First Nations informants, all of whom may have had reasons to inflate their numbers. Meares himself offers the view that, in the context of trade, the Europeans were "dupes of [Aboriginal] cunning." And it was Meares, we should remind ourselves, who "usurped" Aboriginal land at Yuquot (a fact verified by McMillan) and who characterized Maquinna as a cannibal. Without wanting to sound an ad hominem attack, one must ask how far – if at all – is Meares to be trusted as a source? See Fisher, *Contact and Conflict,* 9, 75.

81 Henry F. Dobyns, "Estimating Aboriginal American Populations, I: An Appraisal of Techniques with a New Hemispheric Estimate (and Comments)," *Current Anthropology* 7, 4 (1966): 395-416, 425-49.

82 Patrick Dunae, "Making the 1891 Census in British Columbia," *Histoire sociale/Social History* 31, 62 (November 1998): 232.

83 For the most comprehensive critique, see David Henige, *Numbers from Nowhere: The American Indian Contact Population Debate* (Norman: University of Oklahoma Press, 1998), but see also Ramenofsky, *Vectors of Death,* 1-14.

84 Boyd, *Coming of the Spirit of Pestilence,* 263-66.

85 This list includes Tennant, *Aboriginal Peoples and Politics;* Muckle, *The First Nations of British Columbia;* and Gibson, "Smallpox on the Northwest Coast."

86 Harris, *Making Native Space,* 346n10; Boyd, "Commentary," 323.

87 New research is now challenging the fact of smallpox epidemics in sixteenth-century Mexico. Whether it will become part of a new orthodoxy on the subject, it is too early to say. But one study suggests that indigenous viruses similar to the Ebola or hantavirus were to blame for the Aztec decline in the mid-1500s. Bruce Stutz, "Megadeath in Mexico," *Discover* 27, 2 (February 2006): 44-51.

88 Anatole Romaniuc, "Aboriginal Population of Canada: Growth Dynamics under Conditions of Encounter of Civilizations," *Canadian Journal of Native Studies* 20, 1 (2000): 98. Romaniuc's general observations are worth noting, but his study is otherwise entirely devoted to the eastern woodlands areas in the past.

89 A good example of this more nuanced approach is Clarence Bolt's *Thomas Crosby and the Tsimshian: Small Shoes for Feet Too Large* (Vancouver: UBC Press, 1992). See also Brett Christophers, *Positioning the Missionary: John Booth Good and the Confluence of Cultures in Nineteenth-Century British Columbia* (Vancouver: UBC Press, 1998).

90 Elizabeth Furniss, "Pioneers, Progress, and the Myth of the Frontier: The Landscape of Public History in Rural British Columbia," *BC Studies* 115-16 (Autumn-Winter 1997-98): 10.

91 Harris, *Resettlement,* 29. These points are also made in Reff, *Disease,* 10-12.
92 Richard Somerset Mackie, *The Wilderness Profound: Victorian Life on the Gulf of Georgia* (Victoria: Sono Nis Press, 1995), 46.
93 Harris develops these themes in his book *Making Native Space,* especially xv-xxxi.
94 Carlson, "The Numbers Game," 76-77. See also the fairly recent recapitulation of the debate in Charles C. Mann, *1491: New Revelations of the Americas before Columbus* (New York: Alfred A. Knopf, 2005), 92-96, 132-33.
95 Harris, *Resettlement,* 28.
96 Galois, "Measles," 43.
97 Gibson, "Maritime Trade," 390.
98 Carlson provides a description of the methodology in "The Numbers Game," 76-77.

Chapter 4: Girl Meets Boys: Sex Ratios and Nuptiality

1 Richard Somerset Mackie, *The Wilderness Profound: Victorian Life on the Gulf of Georgia* (Victoria: Sono Nis Press, 1995), 66.
2 Robin Fisher, "Matter for Reflection: *BC Studies* and British Columbia History," *BC Studies* 100 (Winter 1993-94): 75.
3 W. Kaye Lamb, ed., "The Census of Vancouver Island, 1855," *British Columbia Historical Quarterly* 4, 1 (1940): 51-58; Colonial Office, Blue Books of Statistics, British Columbia, 1861-70, *British Parliamentary Papers* (London, 1871). Typically, sex ratios are presented as a single number with the ratio implied (e.g., 19.3). For the sake of clarity, I have opted to include the ratio indicator, thus 19.3:1.
4 Adele Perry, "Hardy Backwoodsmen, Wholesome Women, and Steady Families: Immigration and the Construction of a White Society in Colonial British Columbia, 1849-1871," *Histoire sociale/Social History* 33, 66 (November 2000): 352.
5 Peter Ward, *Courtship, Love, and Marriage in Nineteenth-Century English Canada* (Montreal and Kingston: McGill-Queen's University Press, 1990), 59.
6 Mackie, *The Wilderness Profound,* 66, 271.
7 Colonial Office, *Reports on the Present State of Her Majesty's Colonial Possessions, 1868,* Part 2 (London, 1870), 7-9.
8 R.T. Williams, ed., *The British Columbia Directory, 1882/83* (Victoria, 1883), 293; Hugh J.M. Johnston, "Native Peoples, Settlers and Sojourners, 1871-1916," in *The Pacific Province: A History of British Columbia,* Hugh J.M. Johnston, ed. (Vancouver: Douglas and McIntyre, 1996), 181.
9 Eva MacLean, *The Far Land* (Prince George: Caitlin Press, 1993), 24-25; Lucill K. Adems, "1913-14: The Homestead at Finlay Forks," in *Peace River Chronicles,* Gordon E. Bowes, ed. (Vancouver: Prescott, 1963), 317.
10 *Census of Canada, 1911,* vol. 1: *Areas and Population by Provincial Districts and Subdistricts* (Ottawa: Census and Statistics Office, 1912), 38-39.
11 Thornhill also believed "that unless a man 'packed a woman in with him' he had little chance of succeeding as a farmer" in the Interior. J.B. Thornhill, *British Columbia in the Making* (London: Constable, 1913), 85. Kathryn Bridge, *Henry and Self: The Private Life of Sarah Crease, 1826-1922* (Victoria: Sono Nis Press, 1996), 94.
12 Lynne Marks, "Exploring Regional Diversity in Patterns of Religious Participation: Canada in 1901," *Historical Methods* 33, 4 (2000): 248.
13 See Peter Johnson, *Voyages of Hope: The Saga of the Bride Ships* (Victoria: TouchWood Editions, 2002), and Brett Christophers, *Positioning the Missionary: John Booth Good and the Confluence of Cultures in Nineteenth-Century British Columbia* (Vancouver: UBC Press, 1998), 53-59.
14 Jeremy Mouat, *Roaring Days: Rossland's Mines and the History of British Columbia* (Vancouver: UBC Press, 1995), 110-11. This was as evident in new British industrial towns (where male labour prevailed completely after reforms in the 1840s) as it was in British Columbia. In English mining towns where other occupational niches could be found – as in Wigan, for example – rates of female employment were much higher than in mono-industrial colliery towns elsewhere. One consequence was that women left the older coalfields and avoided the newer ones. See Ellen Jordan, "Female Unemployment in England and Wales 1851-1911:

An Examination of the Census Figures for 15-19 Year Olds," *Social History* 13, 2 (May 1988): 188; Angela John, *By the Sweat of Their Brow: Women Workers at Victorian Coal Mines* (London: Croom Helm, 1984); Edward Higgs, "Women, Occupations and Work in the Nineteenth Century Censuses," *History Workshop* 23 (Spring 1987): 59-80; and Marjorie Griffen Cohen, *Women's Work, Markets, and Economic Development in Nineteenth-Century Ontario* (Toronto: University of Toronto Press, 1988), 128-34.

15 Duncan George Forbes Macdonald, *British Columbia and Vancouver's Island: Comprising a Description of These Dependencies* (Victoria, 1863), 70, 378.

16 W. Peter Ward, "Population Growth in Western Canada: 1901-1971," in *The Developing West: Essays in Honour of Lewis H. Thomas,* John E. Foster, ed. (Edmonton: University of Alberta Press, 1983), 170. I am grateful to Jeremy Mouat for sharing statistics on Rossland for 1901.

17 Marie Elliott, *Gold and Grand Dreams: Cariboo East in the Early Years* (Victoria: Horsdal and Schubert, 2000), 114; *Kamloops Inland Sentinel,* 24 January 1891, 1.

18 Charles Lee Jr., "Two Chinese Families of the British Columbia Interior: A Short History of the Family of Charles Lee of Kamloops and of His Wife Jessie Hing" (unpublished paper in the author's collection, courtesy of Ms. Rose Delap), 2.

19 Wing Chung Ng, *The Chinese in Vancouver, 1945-80: The Pursuit of Identity and Power* (Vancouver: UBC Press, 1999), 11.

20 Johnston, "Native Peoples, Settlers and Sojourners," 191.

21 Tamara Adilman, "A Preliminary Sketch of Chinese Women and Work in British Columbia 1858-1950," in *Not Just Pin Money: Selected Essays on the History of Women's Work in British Columbia,* Barbara K. Latham and Roberta J. Pazdro, eds. (Victoria: Camosun College, 1984), 56-59.

22 Adele Perry, *On the Edge of Empire: Gender, Race, and the Making of British Columbia, 1849-1871* (Toronto: University of Toronto Press, 2001), 17.

23 Cole Harris, *The Resettlement of British Columbia: Essays on Colonialism and Geographical Change* (Vancouver: UBC Press, 1997), 142.

24 Robert A.J. McDonald, *Making Vancouver: Class, Status, and Social Boundaries, 1863-1913* (Vancouver: UBC Press, 1996), 21.

25 This was a far sight better than in California's goldfields, where miners were faced with a 9:1 ratio, or in the hard-rock towns of Montana, where there were four men for every woman. See Rodman Paul, *Mining Frontiers of the Far West, 1841-1880* (New York: Holt, Rinehart and Winston, 1963), 17, 40. In a sample of mining camps in Idaho, the average female proportion was 26.3 percent in 1880. Elliot West, "Five Idaho Mining Towns: A Computer Profile," *Pacific Northwest Quarterly* 73, 3 (July 1982): 110.

26 Veronica Strong-Boag, "Society in the Twentieth Century," in Johnston, *The Pacific Province,* 273.

27 Dorothy D'Arcy (Clippingdale) Goldrick, Reminiscences, 21, Add Mss 1072, BC Archives, Victoria, BC.

28 See, for example, Sarjeet Singh Jagpal, *Becoming Canadians: Pioneer Sikhs in Their Own Words* (Madeira Park, BC: Harbour, 1994), 52-54.

29 Nelson Riis, "The Walhachin Myth: A Study of Settlement Abandonment," *BC Studies* 17 (Spring 1973): 22-24.

30 Ng, *Chinese in Vancouver,* 16.

31 Department of Health Services and Hospital Insurance, British Columbia, *Vital Statistics of the Province of British Columbia, Eighty-Ninth Report, 1960* (Victoria: Queen's Printer, 1961), J13; Julie M. Macdonald, "Vital Statistics in British Columbia: An Historical Overview of 100 Years, 1891-1990," *Vital Statistics Quarterly Digest* 4, 1 (June 1994): 20.

32 Ng indicates that the ratio among Chinese across Canada, not only in British Columbia, had improved to about 2:1 in 1961. Ng, *Chinese in Vancouver,* 25.

33 Herbert C. Northcott and P. Jane Milliken, *Aging in British Columbia: Burden or Benefit?* (Calgary: Detselig, 1998), 19, 21.

34 Statistics Canada, "Age Groups and Sex for Population, for Canada, Provinces and Territories, 1921 to 2001 Censuses – 100 percent Data," Online catalogue no. 97F0003XCB 2001002.

35 Annie McQueen to her mother, 10 March 1888, McQueen Family Papers, Add Mss 860, BC Archives.
36 An important study in the early 1980s indicated no evidence for sex ratio differences in nineteenth-century English community newborns. This is in stark contrast with what is found in British Columbia. See Dov Friedlander and Eliahu Ben-Moshe, "Occupations, Migration, Sex Ratios, and Nuptiality in Nineteenth Century English Communities: A Model of Relationships," *Demography* 23, 1 (February 1986): 1.
37 This was not the case among the Aboriginal population. There, we find female surpluses in the zero- to four-year-old cohorts for 1929, 1939, and 1949. Among adult cohorts, however, the male surplus – or at least near parity – reasserted itself in most years. See Mary-Ellen Kelm, *Colonizing Bodies: Aboriginal Health and Healing in British Columbia, 1900-50* (Vancouver: UBC Press, 1998), 5.
38 Infant Mortality and Stillbirths, Vancouver, 1948, PD2084, City of Vancouver Archives, Vancouver, BC.
39 Department of Health Services and Hospital Insurance, *Vital Statistics, 1960,* J19.
40 See, for example, E.A. Hammell, Sheila R. Johansson, and Caren A. Ginsberg, "The Value of Children during Industrialization: Sex Ratios in Childhood in Nineteenth Century America," *Journal of Family History* 8, 1 (Winter 1983): 346-47. See also Robert P. Swierenga, "Demography of Dutch Emigration," *Journal of Family History* 5 (Winter 1980): 395.
41 Department of Health Services and Hospital Insurance, *Vital Statistics, 1960,* J13.
42 With respect to the treatment of the elderly, see Megan J. Davies, *Into the House of Old: A History of Residential Care in British Columbia* (Montreal and Kingston: McGill-Queen's University Press, 2003).
43 Ng, *Chinese in Vancouver,* 21.
44 Edgar Wickberg et al., *From China to Canada: A History of the Chinese Communities in Canada* (Toronto: McClelland and Stewart, 1982), 152.
45 Paul Yee, *Saltwater City: An Illustrated History of the Chinese in Vancouver* (Vancouver: Douglas and McIntyre, 1988), 108.
46 W.L. Morton, ed., *God's Galloping Girl: The Peace River Diaries of Monica Storrs, 1929-1931* (Vancouver: UBC Press, 1979), 139.
47 The Northwest Coast practice of cross-cousin marriage is described in Harold E. Driver, *Indians of North America,* 2nd ed. (Chicago: University of Chicago Press, 1969), 227-29; Wayne Suttles, *Coast Salish Essays* (Vancouver: Talonbooks, 1987), 220; Bruce Miller, "The 'Really Real' Border and the Divided Salish Community," *BC Studies* 112 (Winter 1996-97): 65-66. Jerome S. Cybulski, "Human Biology," *Handbook of North American Indians,* vol. 7: *Northwest Coast* (Washington: Smithsonian Institution, 1990), 56.
48 Dorothy I.D. Kennedy and Randall T. Bouchard, "Lillooet," *Handbook of North American Indians,* vol. 12: *Plateau* (Washington: Smithsonian Institution, 1998), 448; Eugene Arima and John Dewhurst, "Nootkans of Vancouver Island," *Handbook of North American Indians,* vol. 7: *Northwest Coast,* 405.
49 Father A.J. Brabant, *Mission to Nootka, 1874-1900,* ed. Charles Lillard (Sydney: Gray's, 1977), 76.
50 Charles Hill-Tout, "Notes on the Ntlakapamuq," in *The Salish People: The Local Contribution of Charles Hill-Tout,* vol. 1: *The Thompson and the Okanagan,* Ralph Maud, ed. (Vancouver: Talonbooks, 1978), 48.
51 Kennedy and Bouchard, "Lillooet," 448.
52 Douglas Cole and David Darling, "History of the Early Period," *Handbook of North American Indians,* vol. 7: *Northwest Coast,* 148.
53 This was, it is thought, a break from tradition: his grandfather and his father (Pelkamulox II and Pelkamulox III) had four and two wives respectively. Shirley Lewis, *Q'Sapi: A History of the Okanagan People as Told by Okanagan Families* (Penticton: Theytus Books, 2003), 55-57. See also Duane Thomson, "Hwistensmexe'qen, Nicola (1785-1859), Indian Chief, Warrior, Hunter, Trader, Guide, Farmer," 2007, http://www.livinglandscapes.bc.ca/thomp-ok/river-post/nicola.html.
54 Arima and Dewhurst, "Nootkans," 406.
55 Ibid., 405; Kennedy and Bouchard, "Lillooet," 448.

56 Mrs. H.M. Dallain, "What I Remember: Memories of a Pioneer Daughter," 24, British Columbia Centennial '58 Committee, Anthology Material, GR2080, microfilm B9771, BC Archives.
57 M.E. Armstrong, "Country Dances," *Okanagan History* 49 (1985): 160.
58 Annie McQueen to her mother, 7 January 1888, McQueen Family Papers, Add Mss 860, BC Archives. For a full account of McQueen's experience of demographic scarcity, see Jean Barman, *Sojourning Sisters: The Lives and Letters of Jessie and Annie McQueen* (Toronto: University of Toronto Press, 2003), 67-75. I take a rather different view of the connections between marriage and household formation on the one hand, and agency in the case of Annie McQueen on the other. See John Douglas Belshaw, "Rurality Check: Demographic Boundaries on the British Columbian Frontier," in *Beyond the City Limits: Rural History in British Columbia*, Ruth Sandwell, ed. (Vancouver: UBC Press, 1999), 207-10.
59 Perry, *On the Edge of Empire*, 171.
60 Arthur R.M. Lower, "The Growth of Population in Canada," in *Canadian Population and Northern Colonization*, V.W. Bladen, ed. (Toronto: University of Toronto Press, 1962), 47.
61 Marvin McInnis, "The Population of Canada in the Nineteenth Century," in *A Population History of North America*, Michael R. Haines and Richard H. Steckel, eds. (Cambridge: Cambridge University Press, 2000), 407.
62 First United [Presbyterian] Church, Ladysmith, BC, Marriage Register, 1904-19, United Church Archives, Vancouver School of Theology, Vancouver, BC.
63 John R. Hinde, *When Coal Was King: Ladysmith and the Coal-Mining Industry on Vancouver Island* (Vancouver: UBC Press, 2003), 53.
64 See, for example, Paul Phillips, *No Power Greater: A Century of Labour in British Columbia* (Vancouver: British Columbia Federation of Labour and Boag Foundation, 1967), 163. See also Adele Perry, "'Oh I'm Just Sick of the Faces of Men': Gender Imbalance, Race, Sexuality, and Sociability in Nineteenth-Century British Columbia," *BC Studies* 105-6 (Spring-Summer 1995): 29.
65 The Nanaimo figure refers to the proportion of Nanaimo women, aged twenty-five to thirty-four, who were listed as married in the 1891 census.
66 John Douglas Belshaw, "The Standard of Living of British Miners on Vancouver Island, 1848-1900," *BC Studies* 84 (Winter 1989-90): 37-64.
67 Patrick Dunae, "Making the 1891 Census in British Columbia," *Histoire sociale/Social History* 31, 62 (November 1998): 233. See also Peter A. Baskerville, "'She Has Already Hinted at "Board"': Enterprising Women in British Columbia, 1863-1896," *Histoire sociale/Social History* 26, 52 (November 1993): 219.
68 Charles H. Scott Gallery, *The Photographs of Hannah Maynard: 19th Century Portraits* (Vancouver: Emily Carr College of Art and Design, 1992); Wilf Schmidt, "Mary Spencer: Kamloops Photographer 1899-1909," in *Kamloops: One Hundred Years of Community, 1893-1993*, Wayne Norton and Wilf Schmidt, eds. (Merritt: Sonotek, 1992), 41.
69 The connection between a "marriage career" and a "business career" is considered in Baskerville, "'She Has Already Hinted at "Board,"'" 220.
70 Perry, *On the Edge of Empire*, 172.
71 Henry Pellew Crease, Attorney General, Crease to the Officer Administering the Government, copy, 28 April 1866, Colonial Office Papers 60, Public Records Office, Kew, UK.
72 First United [Presbyterian] Church, Ladysmith, BC, Marriage Register, 1904-19, United Church Archives, Vancouver School of Theology, Vancouver, BC.
73 Register of Marriages, 1884-1912, Cariboo Diocese, Anglican Provincial Synod of BC and Yukon Archives, Vancouver, BC (Anglican Synod).
74 Kathryn Bridge, *By Snowshoe, Buckboard and Steamer: Women of the Frontier* (Victoria: Sono Nis Press, 1998), 16.
75 *Census of Canada, 1881*, vol. 1 (Ottawa, 1882), 182-83, table 10; *Census of Canada, 1891*, vol. 4 (Ottawa, 1891), 414-15; *Census of Canada, 1911*, vol. 1: *Areas and Population*, 245-49; First United [Presbyterian] Church, Ladysmith, BC, Marriage Register, 1904-19, United Church Archives, Vancouver School of Theology. British demographers have argued that "an intimate connection between the employment and industrial complexion of a community and its fertility, courtship and nuptiality characteristics can be expected." Eilidh

Garrett et al., *Changing Family Size in England and Wales: Place, Class and Demography, 1891-1911* (Cambridge: Cambridge University Press, 2001), 13.

76 Charles Lee Jr., "Two Chinese Families of the British Columbia Interior: A Short History of the Family of Charles Lee of Kamloops and of His Wife Jessie Hing" (unpublished paper in the author's collection, courtesy of Ms. Rose Delap), 5.

77 Ward, *Courtship*, 56; *Census of Canada, 1881,* vol. 1, 135-37, 164, 182, tables 8, 9, and 10. On elite marriage networks, see Patrick Dunae, *Gentlemen Emigrants: From the British Public Schools to the Canadian Frontier* (Vancouver: Douglas and McIntyre, 1981), 46-47; *Kamloops Inland Sentinel,* 9 May 1891, 1.

78 Jean Barman, "Neighbourhood and Community in Interwar Vancouver: Residential Differentiation and Civic Voting Behaviour," *BC Studies* 69-70 (Spring-Summer 1986): 106, 108.

79 Ward surveyed the English Canadian "marriage age and marriage market," but his figures derive entirely from what became Ontario. Ward, *Courtship*, 51-56. An excellent work in this area is Dov Friedlander, "The British Depression and Nuptiality: 1873-1896," *Journal of Interdisciplinary History* 23, 1 (Summer 1992): 19-37.

80 Ward, *Courtship*, 53.

81 Ellen Gee, "Fertility and Marriage Patterns in Canada: 1851-1971" (PhD diss., University of British Columbia, 1978), 221; Jean Barman, *The West beyond the West: A History of British Columbia* (Toronto: University of Toronto Press, 1991), 370. For the colonial period, see Perry, *On the Edge of Empire,* 172.

82 Ward, *Courtship*, 27.

83 Census takers were not concerned about age at marriage, but they recorded enough data to allow some assessment of nuptiality. Deducting the age of the eldest co-resident child from that of his or her married white mother under thirty-five, as recorded in the census manuscripts, produces an estimate of the mother's probable age at marriage or, more correctly, her age at the time of her first surviving live birth. Miscarriages, of course, cannot be factored in; nor can the loss of a child before the census enumerator arrived on the doorstep. However, the effect is only to overestimate the age of local women at the time of marriage, a fact that merely reinforces the conclusions reached here. For a discussion of this type of method, see John Demos, "Families in Colonial Bristol, Rhode Island: An Exercise in Historical Demography," *William and Mary Quarterly,* 3rd ser., 25 (1963): 102-3.

84 Missionary activity at Kincolith was aggressive. And it was not above flattery when it came to government relations. One account describes how, in 1888, the mission received the stipendiary magistrate for Vancouver Island, the Welsh immigrant J.P. Planta, with a brass band playing "March of the Men of Harlech," a Welsh air. *Cambrian* 9, 4 (April 1889): 125. Marriage Register, 1871-1907, Kincolith Indian Mission fonds, microfilm 25A(1), BC Archives.

85 Sacred Heart Cathedral, Kamloops, Marriage Registers, 1880-1920.

86 Ibid.

87 Instances can be discerned from these records of weddings that took place after a pregnancy had begun, but there is every indication that these were exceptional in the extreme. Register of Marriages, 1884-1912, Cariboo Diocese, Anglican Provincial Synod of BC and Yukon Archives, Vancouver, BC (Anglican Synod). The Cariboo Diocese was created in 1912; before that time Kamloops was included in the Columbia (aka: New Westminster) Diocese.

88 Sacred Heart Cathedral, Kamloops, Marriage Registers, 1880-1920. Instances can be discerned from these records of weddings that took place after a pregnancy had begun, but there is every indication that these were exceptional in the extreme. The sample includes ninety records for men and eighty-nine for women over the period 1885-88 and 1904-12. See the caveat on sample size provided in Ward, *Courtship,* 52.

89 See R.B. Outhwaite, "Age at First Marriage in England from the Late Seventeenth Century to the Nineteenth Century," *Transactions of the Royal Historical Society,* 5th ser., 23 (1973): 55-70.

90 Ruth M. Crofts, "Madeley: A Mining Community in the Third Quarter of the Nineteenth Century" (master's thesis, Wolverhampton Polytechnic, 1983), 33.

91 One historical case study maintains that late marriages can be attributed almost entirely to poor farming conditions and local economic difficulties, but in that instance both men and women married late. The exceptional thing about the Vancouver Island mining community is that only the men married late. See Robert E. Bieder, "Kinship as a Factor in Migration," *Journal of Marriage and the Family* 35, 3 (1973): 426-39. St. Paul's Nanaimo, 1861-81, text 330, box 8, Archives of the Anglican Diocese of British Columbia, Victoria, BC.

92 First United [Presbyterian] Church, Ladysmith, BC, Marriage Register, 1904-19, United Church Archives, Vancouver School of Theology.

93 See, for example, Russell R. Menard and Lorena S. Walsh, *The Demography of Somerset County, Maryland: A Progress Report,* Newberry Papers in Family and Community History 81-2 (Chicago: Newberry Library, 1981), 18-21. This trend is, however, reversed in the Mennonite communities studied in Royden K. Loewen, *Family, Church and Market: A Mennonite Community in the Old and the New Worlds, 1850-1930* (Toronto: University of Toronto Press, 1993), 229-30.

94 Birth, Marriage and Baptismal Records, St. Andrew's Presbyterian Church (Victoria) fonds, Add Mss 1507, BC Archives. First United [Presbyterian] Church, Ladysmith, BC, Marriage Register, 1904-19, United Church Archives, Vancouver School of Theology.

95 D.E.C. Eversley, "Population, Economy and Society," in *Population in History: Essays in Historical Demography,* D.V. Glass and D.E.C. Eversley, eds. (London: Edward Arnold, 1965), 63. Susan A. McDaniel, "Reconceptualizing the Nuptiality/Fertility Relationship in Canada in a New Age," *Canadian Studies in Population* 16, 2 (1989): 165.

Chapter 5: Ahead by a Century: Fertility

1 Reminiscences of John (Jack "Long Gun") Irvine (1861-1948), 17, Originals, 1851-1942, Irvine Family fonds, Add Mss 322, BC Archives, Victoria, BC.

2 Farming households around Kamloops at the turn of the century had large families, many including more than six children, but few in double digits. See Ken Favrholdt, "Domesticating the Drybelt: Agricultural Settlement in the Hills around Kamloops, 1860-1960," in *Beyond the City Limits: Rural History in British Columbia,* Ruth Sandwell, ed. (Vancouver: UBC Press, 1999), 109-15. For Vancouver Island, see Richard Somerset Mackie, *The Wilderness Profound: Victorian Life on the Gulf of Georgia* (Victoria: Sono Nis Press, 1995), 224-25.

3 The definitive work on this subject is Ansley J. Coale and Susan Cotts Watkins, eds., *The Decline of Fertility in Europe* (Princeton: Princeton University Press, 1986).

4 Roderic Beaujot, *Population Change in Canada: The Challenges of Policy Adaptation* (Toronto: McClelland and Stewart, 1991), 73.

5 See Eilidh Garrett et al., *Changing Family Size in England and Wales: Place, Class and Demography, 1891-1911* (Cambridge: Cambridge University Press, 2001), 8-10. New research by David Hacker suggests that the fertility decline among white Americans was delayed until about 1840. This argument places the American transition into closer harmony with marital fertility changes across the English-speaking world. See J. David Hacker, "Rethinking the 'Early' Decline of Marital Fertility in the United States," *Demography* 40, 4 (November 2003): 605-20.

6 See John Hajnal, "European Marriage Patterns in Perspective," in *Population in History: Essays in Historical Demography,* D.V. Glass and D.E.C. Eversley, eds. (London: Edward Arnold, 1965), 101-43. See also Mary S. Hartman, *The Household and the Making of History: A Subversive View of the Western Past* (Cambridge: Cambridge University Press, 2004).

7 The literature on Mennonite settlement in the Far West is scant, but see Leonard N. Neufeldt, ed., *Village of Unsettled Yearnings: Yarrow, British Columbia: Mennonite Promise* (Victoria: TouchWood Editions, 2002). On the Doukhobor settlements, see Paul M. Koroscil, *British Columbia: Settlement History* (Burnaby: Department of Geography, Simon Fraser University, 2000), 121-47.

8 Jacques Henripin, *Trends and Factors of Fertility in Canada* (Ottawa: Statistics Canada, 1972), 18, 21, 357-66, 373-76.

9 Barman's reference is confusing in this respect: in the first edition she cites *Vital Statistics: Births,* 1: 1972, 64-74, and 1984, 8-9, but neither of these sources offer data on the 1891 to

1911 period. Jean Barman, *The West beyond the West: A History of British Columbia* (Toronto: University of Toronto Press, 1991), 370. The data and reference are unchanged in the second edition. Also, see W. Peter Ward, "Population Growth in Western Canada: 1901-1971," in *The Developing West: Essays in Honour of Lewis H. Thomas,* John E. Foster, ed. (Edmonton: University of Alberta Press, 1983), 162, where Henripin's account is reproduced.

10 Marvin McInnis, "The Population of Canada in the Nineteenth Century," in *A Population History of North America*, Michael R. Haines and Richard H. Steckel, eds. (Cambridge: Cambridge University Press, 2000), 371-432, and McInnis, "Canada's Population in the Twentieth Century," in ibid., 432-599.

11 Some qualifications are in order. McInnis disaggregates his figures between "Cities" and "Ex-Cities," or hinterlands; the I_f of 0.344 is for "ex-urban" BC. The I_f for Vancouver in 1891, however, is 0.343, which is higher than that for any other major city apart from Quebec City and Trois-Rivières. As for the marital fertility index (I_g), Vancouver sits at 0.464 (lower than any other major centre), and ex-urban British Columbia is at 0.464 (also the lowest provincial rate). This apparent anomaly is explained by the record-setting rate of nuptiality (I_m) across urban and ex-urban British Columbia – there were 50 percent more women married as a proportion of the population in the westernmost province than in PEI and Nova Scotia. (More married women as a share of total population means that marital fertility would be statistically deflated.)

12 Julie M. Macdonald, "Vital Statistics in British Columbia: An Historical Overview of 100 Years, 1891-1990," *Vital Statistics Quarterly Digest* 4, 1 (June 1994): 19-45.

13 As Figure 5.1 shows, Macdonald's 1891 GFR is 53.3. Of course, had she added the forty-five to forty-nine cohort to the equation, the GFR would have dropped even further (and indeed it does: the fifteen to forty-nine figure is 49.3).

14 If Henripin had applied the number of children under the age of one year (as per the 1891 *Census of Canada*) in lieu of the number born in that year, his GFR for BC would still have been significantly higher than that produced by the provincial Vital Statistics data. However, such a revised figure would be less than half of what Henripin and Barman published.

15 Newell, *Methods and Models*, 48.

16 McInnis, "Canada's Population in the Twentieth Century," 549.

17 Specifically, McInnis started from age cohorts reported in the Canada census and adjusted for infant mortality in order to generate an approximate GFR. I am grateful to Professor McInnis for making his material on British Columbian fertility available to me. For an example of national trends, see Roderic Beaujot and Kevin McQuillan, "The Social Effects of Demographic Change, Canada 1851-1981," in *Perspectives on Canada's Population: An Introduction to Concepts and Issues,* Frank Trovato and Carl F. Grindstaff, eds. (Don Mills: Oxford University Press, 1994), 37.

18 *Statistical Yearbook, 1893* (Ottawa, 1894), 34. Because the figures in the *Yearbook* measure like with like, they are valid for comparative purposes, but they do not square with those provided in Macdonald, "Vital Statistics in British Columbia," 25.

19 These data are now accessible on-line. For Kamloops, see Living Landscapes: Thompson/ Okanagan: Past, Present and Future, "Nominal Census Data for the Southern Interior of BC," http://www.livinglandscapes.bc.ca/thomp-ok/census/index.html. For Nanaimo, see viHistory.ca, "Vancouver Island 1881 Census," http://vihistory.ca/content/census/census. php, and viHistory.ca, "Vancouver Island 1891 Census," http://vihistory.ca/content/ census/census.php.

20 Newell, *Methods and Models*, 37.

21 A tract that appeared toward the end of the Second World War argued that increased life expectancy would lead to a rise in public taxation, which, inevitably, would discourage Canadian couples from producing more dependants themselves. This case was made, of course, on the eve of the baby boom. See C.E. Silcox, *The Revenge of the Cradles* (Toronto: Ryerson Press, 1945), 14.

22 Beaujot, *Population Change,* 76. See also Angus McLaren, *A History of Contraception from Antiquity to the Present Day* (Oxford: Blackwell, 1990), 199-202.

23 Peter Gossage, *Families in Transition: Industry and Population in Nineteenth-Century Saint-Hyacinthe* (Montreal and Kingston: McGill-Queen's University Press, 1999), 141. Gossage

provides a useful survey of the debate in Quebec over regional changes in fertility rates. See also Dov Friedlander, Barbara S. Okun, and Sharon Segal, "The Demographic Transition Then and Now: Processes, Perspectives, and Analyses," *Journal of Family History* 24, 3 (October 1999): 497-505, and Robert Woods, *The Population History of Britain in the Nineteenth Century* (Cambridge: Cambridge University Press, 1995), 35-40.

24 Simon Szreter, *Fertility, Class and Gender in Britain, 1860-1940* (Cambridge: Cambridge University Press, 1996), 444.

25 McLaren points out that the economics-driven approach to fertility limitation (i.e., as material life improves, fertility declines) can be put to the test by observing fertility behaviour in twentieth-century recessions and depressions. Fertility in Western Europe and much of North America came down in the nineteenth century, carried on falling until the Second World War, and in no way turned around during economic reversals. This was not the case in British Columbia. McLaren, *A History of Contraception*, 202. See also John C. Caldwell, "Towards a Restatement of Demographic Transition Theory," in *Population and Society: Selected Readings*, Frank Trovato, ed. (Don Mills: Oxford University Press, 2002), 158-77. One study of the transition in Belgium and France argues that even in rural areas, where the classic modernization explanation cannot be said to apply and where living standards were actually falling, there was a decline in fertility. In that instance, it appears that the poor economic situation led to postponement of marriages and thus of marital fertility. That option, delaying marriage, was nullified in British Columbia by the sex ratio and the comparative availability of land. See R. Lesthaeghe, "Beyond Economic Reductionism: The Transformation of the Reproductive Regimes in France and Belgium in the Eighteenth and Nineteenth Centuries," in *Fertility Transitions, Family Structures, and Population Policy*, Calvin Goldscheider, ed. (Boulder: Westview Press, 1992), 1-44.

26 McLaren, *A History of Contraception*, 202.

27 Gossage, *Families in Transition*, 143.

28 Szreter, *Fertility, Class and Gender*, 445.

29 Garrett et al., *Changing Family Size*, 16-17.

30 P.E.H. Hair, "Children in Society," in *Population and Society in Britain, 1850-1980*, Theo Barker and Michael Drake, eds. (London: Batsford, 1982), 40-41. See also T.H.C. Stevenson, "The Fertility of Various Social Classes in England and Wales from the Middle of the Nineteenth Century to 1911," *Journal of the Royal Statistical Society* 83 (1920): 420-32; Dov Friedlander, "Demographic Patterns and Socioeconomic Characteristics of the Coal-Mining Population in England and Wales in the Nineteenth Century," *Economic Development and Cultural Change* 22, 1 (October 1973): 43; and Michael Haines, "Fertility, Nuptiality, and Occupation: A Study of Coal Mining Population and Regions in England and Wales in the Mid-Nineteenth Century," *Journal of Interdisciplinary History* 8, 2 (Autumn 1977): 253, 256.

31 Quoted in Lynne Bowen, *Three Dollar Dreams* (Lantzville, BC: Oolichan Books, 1987), 133.

32 For a range of quantitative approaches to fertility measurement, see J. Dennis Willigan and Katherine A. Lynch, *Sources and Methods of Historical Demography* (London: Academic Press, 1982), 102-3, and Jim Potter, "The Growth of Population in America, 1700-1860," in Glass and Eversley, *Population in History*, 674-75.

33 *Census of Canada, 1881*, vol. 1 and vol. 2, 132-39, table 8 (Ottawa, 1882). Macdonald, "Vital Statistics in British Columbia," 20.

34 John Douglas Belshaw, *Colonization and Community: The Vancouver Island Coalfield and the Making of the British Columbian Working Class* (Montreal and Kingston: McGill-Queen's University Press, 2002), 72-73.

35 Ibid., 105-9.

36 McInnis, "Canada's Population in the Twentieth Century," 552.

37 Barman, *West beyond the West*, 370. Barman cites *Vital Statistics: Births*, 1: 1972, 64-74, and 1984, 8-9. The figures are the same in the 1991, 2001, and 2007 editions.

38 Wayne W. McVey Jr. and Warren E. Kalbach, *Canadian Population* (Toronto: Nelson Canada, 1995), 273-75.

39 This pattern is supported by McInnis' twentieth-century figures. His data also point to a falling GFR for BC, something that is *not* sustained by other evidence. McInnis, "Canada's Population in the Twentieth Century," 548-49.

40 Mary F. Bishop, "Vivian Dowding: Birth Control Activist 1892-," in *Not Just Pin Money: Selected Essays on the History of Women's Work in British Columbia,* Barbara K. Latham and Roberta J. Pazdro, eds. (Victoria: Camosun College, 1984), 327; Kate Fisher and Simon Szreter, "'They Prefer Withdrawal': The Choice of Birth Control in Britain, 1918-1950," *Journal of Interdisciplinary History* 34, 2 (Autumn 2003): 263-91; Eric G. Moore and Brian S. Osborne, "Marital Fertility in Kingston, 1861-1881: A Study of Socio-Economic Differentials," *Histoire sociale/Social History* 20, 39 (May 1987): 10.
41 It has been argued that urban life "generated ... alternative pleasures and distractions and provided a clear incentive to save on children in order to spend on other indulgences and leisure" and that it was this missing materialist option that led to high fertility rates in British mining communities. If so, can the falling fertility rate among British miners on Vancouver Island be taken as evidence of improved recreational options? See F.M.L. Thompson, *The Rise of Respectable Society: A Social History of Victorian Britain* (Cambridge, MA: Cambridge University Press, 1988), 80.
42 See Angus McLaren and Arlene Tigar McLaren, *The Bedroom and the State: The Changing Practices of Contraception and Abortion in Canada, 1880-1997,* 2nd ed. (Toronto: Oxford University Press, 1997), 47-50. The complexity of cultural factors is surveyed in Barbara A. Anderson, "Regional and Cultural Factors in the Decline of Marital Fertility in Europe," in Coale and Watkins, *The Decline of Fertility in Europe,* 293-313.
43 A. Romaniuc, *Current Demographic Analysis: Fertility in Canada: From Baby-Boom to Baby-Bust* (Ottawa: Statistics Canada, 1984), 14-15.
44 Hugh J.M. Johnston, "Native Peoples, Settlers and Sojourners, 1871-1916," in *The Pacific Province: A History of British Columbia,* Hugh J.M. Johnston, ed. (Vancouver: Douglas and McIntyre, 1996), 170, 183.
45 Robert S. Hogg, "Evaluating Historic Fertility Change in Small Reserve Populations," *BC Studies* 101 (Spring 1994): 79-95.
46 Department of Health Services and Hospital Insurance, British Columbia, *Vital Statistics of the Province of British Columbia, Eighty-Ninth Report, 1960* (Victoria: Queen's Printer, 1961), J16.
47 Wilson Duff, *The Indian History of British Columbia,* vol. 1: *The Impact of the White Man,* new ed. (Victoria: Royal British Columbia Museum, 1997), 63.
48 Indian and Northern Affairs Canada, "2.1 Fertility and Mortality," 1997, http://www.ainc-inac.gc.ca/pr/ra/execs/rece-1_e.html.
49 Anatole Romaniuc, "Aboriginal Population of Canada: Growth Dynamics under Conditions of Encounter of Civilizations," *Canadian Journal of Native Studies* 20, 1 (2000): 97; Health Canada, Medical Services Branch, and BC Division of Vital Statistics, "Status Indians in British Columbia: A Vital Statistical Overview," *Vital Statistics Quarterly Digest* 4, 2 (August 1994): 20.
50 Romaniuc, "Aboriginal Population," 111-13, speculates that the rising Aboriginal birth rate reflected increased numbers of hospital births and the decline of nursing in favour of bottle-feeding. He argues that Aboriginal society generally lags behind Euro-Canada "by a considerable margin on major scores of socio-economic development" and therefore "has not reached the developmental 'critical threshold' necessary to sustain the declining path of fertility."
51 Romaniuc, *Current Demographic Analysis,* 13.
52 McInnis, "Canada's Population in the Twentieth Century," 532; Jennifer Dayne, "The Impact of a Reduced Fertility Rate on Women's Health," *Women's Health Surveillance Report: A Multidimensional Look at the Health of Canadian Women* (30 September 2005), http://secure.cihi.ca/cihiweb/products/WHSR_Chap_10_e.pdf.
53 McLaren, *A History of Contraception,* 239-42.
54 McInnis, "Canada's Population in the Twentieth Century," 551.
55 Canada, Bureau of Statistics, *Vital Statistics, 1882-1939* (Ottawa: King's Printer, 1941), tabulated in John Douglas Belshaw, "The Administration of Relief to the Unemployed in Vancouver during the Great Depression" (M.A. thesis, Simon Fraser University, 1982), 81-82.
56 See, for example, Ward, "Population Growth," 161.

57 The Depression and the war held back the fertility of women born between 1920 and 1924 in particular. In 1945, for the only time in the period from 1941 to 1961, the twenty-five- to twenty-nine-year-old cohort had more births per 1,000 women than the twenty to twenty-four cohort.

58 British Columbia, *The Nineteen Eighties: A Statistical Resource for a Decade of Vital Events in British Columbia* (Victoria: Ministry of Health and Ministry Responsible for Seniors, 1994), 16.

59 Department of Health Services and Hospital Insurance, *Vital Statistics, 1960*, J14-J15.

60 City of Vancouver Planning Department, "The Vancouver Monitoring Program Information Update: Births and Deaths, 1941-1990" (December 1991), 4-6, City of Vancouver Archives, Vancouver, BC.

61 British Columbia, *Fertility Rates in British Columbia* (Victoria: Bureau of Economics and Statistics, Government of British Columbia, 1971), 8.

62 Anatole Romaniuc, "Fertility in Canada: Retrospective and Prospective," in Trovato and Grindstaff, *Perspectives on Canada's Population*, 218.

63 Department of Health Services and Hospital Insurance, *Vital Statistics, 1960*, J13. In the first half of the century, dependency in Aboriginal communities was typically much higher than in their non-Aboriginal counterparts. Mary-Ellen Kelm, *Colonizing Bodies: Aboriginal Health and Healing in British Columbia, 1900-50* (Vancouver: UBC Press, 1998), 6.

64 Michael Barrett, *Population and Canada*, 3rd ed. (Toronto: Faculty of Education, University of Toronto, 1982), 25.

65 Woods, *The Population History of Britain in the Nineteenth Century*, 35. See also Francine van de Walle, "Infant Mortality and the European Demographic Transition," in Coale and Watkins, *The Decline of Fertility in Europe*, 201-60.

66 The connection between falling fertility and falling infant mortality (the former ought, by rights, to follow the latter) has lately been challenged. In Britain, for example, evidence points to a reversal of the pattern. See Garrett et al., *Changing Family Size*, 8.

67 Surinder Wadhera and Jill Strachan, *Selected Mortality Statistics, Canada, 1921-1990*, catalogue no. 82-548 (Ottawa: Statistics Canada, 1994), 94-95; M.C. Urquhart and K.A.H. Buckley, *Historical Statistics of Canada*, 2nd ed. (Ottawa: Statistics Canada, 1983), B51-B58. See also Veronica Strong-Boag, *The New Day Recalled: Lives of Girls and Women in English Canada, 1919-1939* (Markham: Penguin, 1988), 170-71.

68 Infant Mortality Rates, Vancouver 1918-1948, c. 1964, PD2084, City of Vancouver Archives. The decline in infant mortality across Canada was nonetheless steady, although a spike occurred in every province in 1937 in the depths of the Great Depression. In Quebec, the rate was more than twice the British Columbian level and, in Ontario, nearly a third higher. Statistics Canada, "Infant Mortality Rates, by Province and Territory (Both Sexes)," http://www40.statcan.ca/l01/cst01/health21a.htm.

69 Indeed, years ago John Porter noted that, in Canada in 1961, British Columbian women led the provinces in the highest age at first marriage. John Porter, *Canadian Social Structure* (Toronto: McClelland and Stewart, 1967), 59.

70 Strong-Boag, *New Day Recalled*, 82.

71 On the subject of age at marriage and sex ratios, see Peter Ward, *Courtship, Love, and Marriage in Nineteenth-Century English Canada* (Montreal and Kingston: McGill-Queen's University Press, 1990), 56-58.

72 Ellen Gee, "Fertility and Marriage Patterns in Canada: 1851-1971" (PhD diss., University of British Columbia, 1978), 221.

73 Department of Health Services and Hospital Insurance, *Vital Statistics, 1960*, J17.

74 In 1964 the rate rose from 22.1 to 22.3, but in the very next year the CBR stood at 18.7, hardly better than in the year Pearl Harbor was struck. Z. Kashaninia, "Marriage and Family in British Columbia: 1931-1994," *Vital Statistics Quarterly Digest* 6, 2 (October 1996): 18.

75 F.H. Leacy, ed., *Historical Statistics of Canada*, 2nd ed. (Ottawa: Statistics Canada, 1983); Kashaninia, "Marriage and Family in British Columbia," 21.

76 The elusive information here is whether a rising cost of living index or the falling incidence of fertility among younger women was driving female workforce participation. For rates of female workforce participation earlier in the twentieth century, see Eric W. Sager, "Women

in the Industrial Labour Force: Evidence for British Columbia, 1921-53," *BC Studies* 149 (Spring 2006): 39-62.

77 The female share of the population with a bachelor's degree rose from about 30 percent in 1961 to nearly half in 1991. Kashaninia, "Marriage and Family in British Columbia," 23.

78 Y.C. MacNab, J. Macdonald, and T.A. Tuk, "Increased Maternal Age and the Outcome of Pregnancy: An Eight Year Population Based Study, British Columbia, 1987-1994," *Vital Statistics Quarterly Digest* 6, 1 (July 1996): 18.

79 O.B. Adams and D.N. Nagnur, *Marriage, Divorce and Mortality: A Life-Table Analysis for Canada and Regions* (Ottawa: Statistics Canada, 1988), 15.

80 Ellen M. Gee, "Early Canadian Fertility Transition: A Components Analysis of Census Data," *Canadian Studies in Population* 6 (1979): 28, 30.

81 Ibid.

82 These changes cannot be fully explained by the rather modest efforts on the part of Victoria to regulate marriage in the interwar period. See James G. Snell and Cynthia Comacchio Abeele, "Regulating Nuptiality: Restricting Access to Marriage in Early Twentieth-Century English-Speaking Canada," *Canadian Historical Review* 69, 4 (1988): 484-85, 489.

83 Jill Wade, *Houses for All: The Struggle for Social Housing in Vancouver, 1919-50* (Vancouver: UBC Press, 1994), 24.

84 J. Lewis Robinson and Walter G. Hardwick, *British Columbia: One Hundred Years of Geographical Change* (Vancouver: Talonbooks, 1973), 28.

85 Canada, Bureau of Statistics, *Vital Statistics, 1882-1939,* tabulated in Belshaw, "Administration of Relief," 81-82.

86 For the broader Canadian pattern, see Susan A. McDaniel, "Reconceptualizing the Nuptiality/ Fertility Relationship in Canada in a New Age," in Trovato and Grindstaff, *Perspectives on Canada's Population,* 276-79.

87 See Veronica Strong-Boag, "Home Dreams: Women and the Suburban Experiment in Canada, 1945-60," *Canadian Historical Review* 72, 4 (1991): 484-88.

88 Kashaninia, "Marriage and Family in British Columbia," 18.

89 In 1945-49 the provincial rate was 59 per 1,000, climbing to 126 per 1,000 in 1965-69. By comparison, the rates in Quebec and Ontario were often half the BC figures. George Emery, "Age-Parity and Marital Status Compositional Influences on the Maternal Mortality Rate in Canada, 1930-1969: A Regional Comparison," *Histoire sociale/Social History* 25, 50 (November 1992): 242, table 2; J.L. Gayton (Senior Medical Officer, Vancouver) to Dr. J.L.M. Whitbread (Senior Medical Officer, Victoria), 2 February 1964, Medical Health Officer Reports, 1886-1988, Health Department fonds, Vancouver (BC), series 101, loc. 146-B-6, file 6, City of Vancouver Archives.

90 Wartime rates of illegitimacy gave rise to concerns over juvenile pregnancies after 1945. For many religious leaders, the sacrament of marriage and the institution of the family were at stake. See Tina Block, "'Boy Meets Girl': Constructing Heterosexuality in Two Victoria Churches, 1945-1960," *Journal of the Canadian Historical Association,* n.s., 10 (1999): 282-83.

91 Department of Health Services and Hospital Insurance, *Vital Statistics, 1960,* J17-J18. See also Emery, "Age-Parity and Marital Status," 242.

92 A comprehensive bibliography published in the 1990s of historical and social scientific studies on women in BC contained no reference to studies that were specifically demographic, nor (with the exception of McLaren and McLaren, *The Bedroom and the State*) were there any devoted to fertility, nuptiality, or mortality experiences among the female population. Theresa Healey, "Finding Women in British Columbia: A Select Bibliography," in *British Columbia Reconsidered: Essays on Women,* Gillian Creese and Veronica Strong-Boag, eds. (Vancouver: Press Gang, 1992), 431-49. On the process of redefining ideals of Canadian and British Columbian womanhood after 1945, see, for example, respectively, Mona Gleason, *Normalizing the Ideal: Psychology, Schooling, and the Family in Postwar Canada* (Toronto: University of Toronto Press, 1999), and Diane B. Purvey, "Perceptions of Wife-Beating in Post-World War II English Speaking Canada: Blaming Women for Violence against Wives" (PhD diss., University of British Columbia, 2001).

93 Division of Vital Statistics, *Selected Vital Statistics and Health Status Indicators, One Hundred Thirtieth Annual Report, 2001* (Victoria: Ministry of Health Planning, 2001), http://www.vs.gov/bc.ca/stats/annual/2001/tab08.html.

94 From 1891 to 1911, the share of the population living in urban areas was higher in British Columbia than in any other province and for Canada as a whole. Leroy O. Stone, *Urban Development in Canada* (Ottawa: Dominion Bureau of Statistics, 1967), 38-39; Leroy O. Stone and Claude Marceau, *Canadian Population Trends and Public Policy through the 1980s* (Montreal and Kingston: McGill-Queen's University Press, 1977), 13.

Chapter 6: Strangers in Paradise: Immigration and the Experience of Diversity

1 Canada, Department of the Interior, Topographical Surveys Branch, *Description of Surveyed Land in the Railway Belt of British Columbia, Part No. 2 – Central Division* (Ottawa: Department of the Interior, 1915), 23, BC Archives, Victoria, BC.

2 John R. Hinde, *When Coal Was King: Ladysmith and the Coal-Mining Industry on Vancouver Island* (Vancouver: UBC Press, 2003), 51.

3 Quoted in Jim Potter, "The Growth of Population in America, 1700-1860," in *Population in History: Essays in Historical Demography,* D.V. Glass and D.E.C. Eversley, eds. (London: Edward Arnold, 1965), 643.

4 As a rule in late twentieth-century Canada, recent immigrants differ from their late nineteenth-century counterparts in that they bring with them a level of fertility that is lower than or at least not significantly greater than that of the host community. Roderic P. Beaujot, "Immigration and Demographic Structures," in *Immigrant Canada: Demographic, Economic, and Social Challenges,* Shiva S. Halli and Leo Driedger, eds. (Toronto: University of Toronto Press, 1999), 95-96.

5 A chronology of immigration laws and events is provided in Colin J.B. Wood, "Population and Ethnic Groups," in *British Columbia: Its Resources and People,* Canadian Western Geographical Series 32, Charles N. Forward, ed. (Victoria: Western Geographical Press, 1987), 322.

6 Patricia E. Roy, *The Oriental Question: Consolidating a White Man's Province, 1914-41* (Vancouver: UBC Press, 2003), 55.

7 Statistics Canada, "Destination of Immigrants," *1991 Census,* catalogue no. 93-332 (Ottawa: Statistics Canada, 1993); Beaujot, "Immigration and Demographic Structures," 100-1.

8 T.R. Balakrishnan and Feng Hou, "Residential Patterns in Cities," in Halli and Driedger, *Immigrant Canada,* 122, 124-25.

9 By 2001 the share of British Columbians whose mother tongue was other than French (still 1.4 percent) or English (now 73 percent) had risen to 24.3 percent. BC Stats, *2001 Census Profile: British Columbia, a Province of Canada,* Fall 2003 and September 2005, http://www.bcstats.gov.bc.ca/data/cen01/profiles/59000000.pdf.

10 Statistics Canada, *The 1999 Canada Year Book* (Ottawa: Ministry of Industry, 1998), 99.

11 Emigration from British Columbia in the early twentieth century is difficult to track. By the start of the Depression, hardly more than 250 British Columbians had moved to Washington State out of a total of 552 US-bound emigrants. These are not significant numbers. See Bruno Ramirez, *Crossing the 49th Parallel: Migration from Canada to the United States, 1900-1930* (Ithaca: Cornell University Press, 2001), 106-9, 113.

12 BC Stats, "British Columbia Regional District Migration Components," http://www.bcstats.gov.bc.ca/data/pop/mig/comp_RD2002.pdf.

13 Statistics Canada, "Components of Population Growth, Provinces and Territories, Annual, (Persons), 6 November 2005," CANSIM table 051-0004 (2004/2005).

14 Statistics Canada, "In-, Out- and Net-Migration Estimates, by Provincial Regions and Age Group, Annual (Number)," CANSIM table 111-0028 (2007).

15 Jean Dumas and Alain Belanger, *Report on the Demographic Situation in Canada 1994,* catalogue no. 91-209 (Ottawa: Statistics Canada, 1994), 81.

16 Annie McQueen of the Nicola Valley (mentioned earlier) was a Presbyterian Nova Scotian who evinced suspicion of, and even hostility toward, Methodists on her arrival in British Columbia. Nevertheless, she married a Methodist. John Douglas Belshaw, "Rurality Check:

Demographic Boundaries on the British Columbian Frontier," in *Beyond the City Limits: Rural History in British Columbia,* Ruth Sandwell, ed. (Vancouver: UBC Press, 1999), 208.

17 British Columbia, "Report of the Registrar-General," *Sessional Papers,* 1879, 814; British Columbia, "Report of the Registrar-General," *Sessional Papers,* 1882, 223.

18 Jean Barman, "Invisible Women: Aboriginal Mothers and Mixed-Race Daughters in Rural Pioneer British Columbia," in Sandwell, *Beyond the City Limits,* 160.

19 Madeline A. Kalbach, *Ethnic Groups and Marital Choices: Ethnic History and Marital Assimilation in Canada, 1871 and 1971* (Vancouver: UBC Press, 1991), 116.

20 Ibid.

21 That is, three or four years after Semlin arrived in British Columbia in 1862 or 1863.

22 Barman, "Invisible Women," 165.

23 The Aboriginal female surplus was not evenly distributed. Among the Nisga'a and the Kwakwaka'wakw in 1881, for example, there were more men than women in the young adult cohorts, but among the Secwepemc, there were more teenaged males than females. Also, Native women were found in considerable numbers in trading centres such as Victoria where they outnumbered the Native male population by large margins, depending on the season. See Cole Harris, *The Resettlement of British Columbia: Essays on Colonialism and Geographical Change* (Vancouver: UBC Press, 1997), 147-49, and Adele Perry, *On the Edge of Empire: Gender, Race, and the Making of British Columbia, 1849-1871* (Toronto: University of Toronto Press, 2001), 97-123.

24 Methodist Petitioners to Hon. Theo Davie, A-G and Premier, and Members of the Cabinet, c. 21 January 1895, Attorney General, Correspondence Inward, Originals, GR429, box 3, file 2, BC Archives.

25 See Jay Nelson, "'A Strange Revolution in the Manners of the Country': Aboriginal-Settler Intermarriage in Nineteenth Century British Columbia," in *Regulating Lives: Historical Essays on the State, Society, the Individual, and the Law,* John McLaren, Robert Menzies, and Dorothy E. Chunn, eds. (Vancouver: UBC Press, 2002), 32-34, 39, 41-49.

26 Estate of John Smith of Mayne Island, Attorney General, Correspondence Inward, Originals, GR429, box 4, file 2, 1932/98, BC Archives.

27 McPhillips Wooton and Barnard to Attorney General, 5 May 1903, ibid., box 10, file 2.

28 See Sylvia Van Kirk, "The Role of Native Women in the Creation of Fur Trade Society in Western Canada, 1670-1830," in *The Women's West,* Susan Armitage and Elizabeth Jameson, eds. (Norman: University of Oklahoma Press, 1987), 53-62.

29 Charles Lee Jr., "Two Chinese Families of the British Columbia Interior: A Short History of the Family of Charles Lee of Kamloops and of His Wife Jessie Hing" (unpublished paper in the author's collection, courtesy of Ms. Rose Delap).

30 I am grateful to Jean Barman for this information, which she gleaned from the Canada census enumerators' manuscripts for 1881 and 1891. Pockets of Chinese settlement were established throughout the mainland during the various 1860s gold rushes. Osoyoos was one of the largest, containing nearly 200 in 1868, compared to the Fraser Canyon with 465 and the Cariboo District with 736. United Kingdom, Colonial Office, Blue Books of Statistics, Colony of British Columbia, 1868, 210, quoted in David Chuen-yan Lai, "Chinese Communities," in Forward, *British Columbia,* 339.

31 Peter Ward, *Courtship, Love, and Marriage in Nineteenth-Century English Canada* (Montreal and Kingston: McGill-Queen's University Press, 1990), 61.

32 Hugh J.M. Johnston, "Native Peoples, Settlers and Sojourners, 1871-1916," in *The Pacific Province: A History of British Columbia,* Hugh J.M. Johnston, ed. (Vancouver: Douglas and McIntyre, 1996), 187.

33 It is not my intention to be oblique here. "Some" Native ancestry reflects the fact that there were, in addition to the large Secwepemc population in and around Kamloops, individuals and whole families whose race or origin the enumerators described as "Iroquois," as well as many more who were descendants of the Plains Cree, or who described themselves alternately as Metis or Half-breeds (not necessarily the same thing). See Theodore J. Kamaranski, "The Iroquois and the Fur Trade of the Far West," *Beaver* 312 (Spring 1982): 4-13.

34 W. Peter Ward, "Population Growth in Western Canada: 1901-1971," in *The Developing West: Essays in Honour of Lewis H. Thomas,* John E. Foster, ed. (Edmonton: University of Alberta Press, 1983), 174-75.

35 Jean Barman, *The West beyond the West: A History of British Columbia* (Toronto: University of Toronto Press, 1991), 364.

36 Statistics Canada, *1999 Canada Year Book,* 90.

37 In 1971, for example, British Columbia contributed only 114,000 migrants to the Canadian total of 2.47 million. That is the third-lowest count in the country, following only Prince Edward Island and Newfoundland. In 1996 nearly eighty thousand British Columbians originated in Atlantic Canada; across the four easternmost provinces, there were fewer than ten thousand British Columbians. Statistics Canada, *Canada E-Stats,* Series A32; Statistics Canada, *1999 Canada Year Book,* 90.

38 See Paul M. Koroscil, *British Columbia: Settlement History* (Burnaby: Department of Geography, Simon Fraser University, 2000), 169-231; Eric Faa, *Norwegians in the Northwest: Settlement in British Columbia, 1858-1918* (Victoria: Runestad, 1994), 113-260; Duncan Stacey and Susan Stacey, *Salmonopolis: The Steveston Story* (Madeira Park, BC: Harbour, 1994), 65-98; Daphne Marlatt, *Steveston Recollected* (Victoria: Provincial Archives of British Columbia, 1975); Ken Favrholdt, "Domesticating the Drybelt: Agricultural Settlement in the Hills around Kamloops, 1860-1960," in Sandwell, *Beyond the City Limits,* 111-12; Paula Wild, *Sointula: Island Utopia* (Madeira Park, BC: Harbour, 1995), 25; Roy, *The Oriental Question,* 55-56; *Census of Canada, 1951,* vol. 1: *Population* (Ottawa: Queen's Printer, 1951), table 33.

39 Wing Chung Ng identifies a "second stage" of Chinese arrivals to Vancouver's Chinatown, running from 1911 to 1921, during which time the community's population nearly doubled. Ng, *The Chinese in Vancouver, 1945-80: The Pursuit of Identity and Power* (Vancouver: UBC Press, 1999), 14.

40 The literature on anti-Asian racism is now extensive. See, for example, the two volumes by Patricia E. Roy, *A White Man's Province: British Columbia Politicians and Chinese and Japanese Immigrants, 1858-1914* (Vancouver: UBC Press, 1989), and *The Oriental Question;* David Chuen-yan Lai's several studies but especially, "Chinese: The Changing Geography of the Largest Visible Minority," in *British Columbia, the Pacific Province: Geographical Essays,* Canadian Western Geographical Series 36, Colin J.B. Wood, ed. (Victoria: Western Geographical Press, 2001), 147-71; Ng, *Chinese in Vancouver,* especially 10-18; and Kay J. Anderson, *Vancouver's Chinatown: Racial Discourse in Canada, 1875-1980* (Montreal and Kingston: McGill-Queen's University Press, 1991).

41 Lai, "Chinese: The Changing Geography," 152.

42 Marie Elliott, *Gold and Grand Dreams: Cariboo East in the Early Years* (Victoria: Horsdal and Schubert, 2000), 15, 84-85, 120. See also the representations of Cariboo-Chilcotin residents compiled by C.D. Hoy and Faith Moosang, *C.D. Hoy: Portraits from the Cariboo* (North Vancouver: Presentation House Gallery, 2005).

43 *Census of Canada, 1881,* http://www.livinglandscapes.bc.ca/thomp-ok/census/index. html.

44 David Chuen-yan Lai, *The Forbidden City within Victoria: Myth, Symbol and Streetscape of Canada's Earliest Chinatown* (Victoria: Orca Books, 1991), 7.

45 British Columbia, "Statement Showing the Chinese, Japanese and Indian Populations of British Columbia, According to the Government Census of 1901," *Sessional Papers,* 1902, 841-42.

46 Lai, "Chinese: The Changing Geography," 160.

47 See Edgar Wickberg et al., *From China to Canada: A History of the Chinese Communities in Canada* (Toronto: McClelland and Stewart, 1982), 63-64, and Karen Van Dieren, "The Response of the Women's Missionary Society to the Immigration of Asian Women, 1888-1942," in *Not Just Pin Money: Selected Essays on the History of Women's Work in British Columbia,* Barbara K. Latham and Roberta J. Pazdro, eds. (Victoria: Camosun College, 1984), 79.

48 A scholarly yet fictionalized account of this period of families divided by an ocean and shadowy immigration is Yuen-Fong Woon, *The Excluded Wife* (Montreal and Kingston: McGill-Queen's University Press, 1998).

49 Lai, *Forbidden City*, 10.
50 Kamala Elizabeth Nayar, *The Sikh Diaspora in Vancouver: Three Generations amid Tradition, Modernity, and Multiculturalism* (Toronto: University of Toronto Press, 2004), 16-17.
51 Ng, *Chinese in Vancouver*, 24.
52 Patricia E. Roy and John Herd Thompson, *British Columbia: Land of Promises* (Don Mills: Oxford University Press, 2005), 182.
53 Ng, *Chinese in Vancouver*, 7.
54 Sarjeet Singh Jagpal, *Becoming Canadians: Pioneer Sikhs in Their Own Words* (Madeira Park, BC: Harbour, 1994), 33; Nayar, *The Sikh Diaspora*, 18. A biographical approach to Sikh community affairs in Canada is Tara Singh Bains and Hugh Johnston, *The Four Quarters of the Night: The Life Journey of an Emigrant Sikh* (Montreal and Kingston: McGill-Queen's University Press, 1995).
55 Statistics Canada, *Canada's Changing Immigrant Population*, catalogue no. 96-311E (Ottawa: Statistics Canada, 1994), table 1.2. *Census of Canada, 1981*, catalogue no. 93-934 (Ottawa: Statistics Canada, 1981), table 2.
56 In terms of real numbers and proportionally, British Columbians from these sources do not add much weight in the aggregate, but at the local level their communities are substantial. For a discussion of the Filipina experience of immigration since the 1970s and the rise of a female-dominated immigrant workforce, see Geraldine Pratt in collaboration with the Ugnayan Ng Kabataang Pilipino Sa Canada/Filipino-Canadian Youth Alliance, "Between Homes: Displacement and Belonging for Second-Generation Filipino-Canadian Youths," *BC Studies* 140 (Winter 2003-04): 44-45.
57 Lai, "Chinese: The Changing Geography," 165.
58 Russell R. Menard, "Whatever Happened to Early American Population History?" *William and Mary Quarterly*, 3rd ser., 50, 2 (1993): 359-60.

Chapter 7: The Mourning After: Mortality

1 Yes, one has to wonder: where *did* they get a monkey? I can provide no answer.
2 Dr. E.A. Praeger to John Robson, Provincial Secretary, 14 July 1890, Attorney General's Paper's, Correspondence Inward, Originals, GR429, box 2, file 3, BC Archives, Victoria, BC.
3 Arthur Edward Kennedy to the Rt. Hon. Edward Cardwell, 22 November 1864, Colonial Office Papers 305(23), Public Records Office, Kew, UK.
4 Attorney General, Correspondence Inward, Originals, GR429, box 2, file 3, BC Archives.
5 Report on Nanaimo, 5 July 1898, ibid., box 4, file 2, 1047/98.
6 S.B.C. 1871, s. 108.
7 Mona Gleason, "Race, Class and Health: School Medical Inspection and 'Healthy' Children in British Columbia, 1890 to 1930," in *Children, Teachers and Schools in the History of British Columbia*, 2nd ed., Jean Barman and Mona Gleason, eds. (Calgary: Detselig, 2003), 133.
8 Report on New Westminster sewerage, 31 May 1898, Attorney General, Correspondence Inward, Originals, GR429, box 4, file 2, 1047/98, BC Archives.
9 Report on Kamloops sewerage, 17 May 1898, ibid., 1046/98.
10 Vancouver City's encounter with Mohun and sewerage is explored in Arn Keeling, "Sink or Swim: Water Pollution and Environmental Politics in Vancouver, 1889-1975," *BC Studies* 142 (Summer-Autumn 2004): 69-101.
11 Settlers at Blue River, for example, found themselves squarely between hospitals at Kamloops and Jasper, both of which were in excess of two hundred kilometres away. An "Outpost Hospital" (consisting of three beds) was established only in 1948, prior to which time the Canadian National Railway and canoes down the North Thompson River served as the local ambulance service. Clearwater and District History Book Committee, *North Thompson Reflections* (Altona, MB: Friesens, 1996), 45-48.
12 Gleason, "Race, Class and Health," 134. See also Norah Lewis, "Physical Perfection for Spiritual Welfare: Health Care of the Urban Child, 1900-1939," in *Studies in Childhood History: A Canadian Perspective*, R.L. Schnell and Patricia T. Rooke, ed. (Calgary: Detselig, 1982), 135-66.

13 Cole Harris, *Making Native Space: Colonialism, Resistance, and Reserves in British Columbia* (Vancouver: UBC Press, 2002), 290; Mary-Ellen Kelm, *Colonizing Bodies: Aboriginal Health and Healing in British Columbia, 1900-50* (Vancouver: UBC Press, 1998).
14 Provincial Board of Health to Hon. C. Wilson, Attorney General, 21 October 1904, Attorney General, Correspondence Inward, Originals, GR429, box 11, file 5, BC Archives.
15 C.J. Fagan, Secretary, Provincial Board of Health, to Attorney General, 1 August 1905, ibid., box 1, file 12.
16 Burial Register, 1869-1914, Kincolith Indian Mission fonds, microfilm 25A(1), BC Archives.
17 Ibid. On the subject of Aboriginal British Columbians and the newcomer economy, see Rolf Knight, *Indians at Work: An Informal History of Native Indian Labour in British Columbia, 1858-1930* (1978; rev. ed., Vancouver: New Star, 1996); Richard Mackie, "The Colonization of Vancouver Island, 1849-58," *BC Studies* 96 (Winter 1992-93): 3-40; and John Lutz, "Work, Sex, and Death on the Great Thoroughfare: Annual Migrations of 'Canadian Indians' to the American Pacific Northwest," in *Parallel Destinies: Canadian-American Relations West of the Rockies,* Kenneth Coates and John M. Findlay, eds. (Seattle: University of Washington Press, 2002), 80-103. For the later period, see Dianne Newell, *Tangled Webs of History: Indians and the Law in Canada's Pacific Coast Fishery* (Toronto: University of Toronto Press, 1993), especially Chapter 4.
18 Paul Phillips, *No Power Greater: A Century of Labour in British Columbia* (Vancouver: British Columbia Federation of Labour and Boag Foundation, 1967), 8-9; Ben Moffat, "A Community of Working Men: The Residential Environment of Early Nanaimo, British Columbia, 1875-1891" (M.A. thesis, University of British Columbia, 1981), 77, table 4; D. Morton and T. Copp, *Working People: An Illustrated History of the Canadian Labour Movement* (Ottawa: Deneau and Greenberg, 1980), 50.
19 *Census of Canada, 1901,* vol. 4: *Vital Statistics* (Ottawa, 1902), 72-88, table 5.
20 Gordon Hak, *Turning Trees into Dollars: The British Columbia Coastal Lumber Industry, 1858-1913* (Toronto: University of Toronto Press, 2000), 140.
21 Jean Barman, *Sojourning Sisters: The Lives and Letters of Jessie and Annie McQueen* (Toronto: University of Toronto Press, 2003), 68.
22 Edgar Wickberg et al., *From China to Canada: A History of the Chinese Communities in Canada* (Toronto: McClelland and Stewart, 1982), 23-24; Anthony B. Chan, *Gold Mountain: The Chinese in the New World* (Vancouver: New Star, 1983), 65-66.
23 The place name "Fort George" changed to "Prince George" in 1915.
24 Hak, *Turning Trees into Dollars,* 160.
25 Julie M. Macdonald, "Vital Statistics in British Columbia: An Historical Overview of 100 Years, 1891-1990," *Vital Statistics Quarterly Digest* 4, 1 (June 1994): 44; Marie Elliott, *Gold and Grand Dreams: Cariboo East in the Early Years* (Victoria: Horsdal and Schubert, 2000), 81-82.
26 Quoted in Colin Coates, "Death in British Columbia, 1850-1950" (M.A. thesis, University of British Columbia, 1984), 93-94.
27 John Mara to Attorney-General, "Conditions in Kamloops," 21 July 1872, Attorney General, Correspondence Inward, Originals, GR429, box 1, file 1, BC Archives.
28 This is not to say that shooting deaths never occurred. Drunken brawls rather than set-piece shootouts were, however, more likely events. See, for example, Richard Somerset Mackie, *The Wilderness Profound: Victorian Life on the Gulf of Georgia* (Victoria: Sono Nis Press, 1995), 68.
29 Mrs. H.M. Dallain, "What I Remember: Memories of a Pioneer Daughter," British Columbia Centennial '58 Committee, Anthology Material, 23, GR2080, microfilm B9771, BC Archives.
30 *Census of Canada, 1891,* vol. 4 (Ottawa, 1891), 424-25.
31 I am grateful to my former colleague Mr. Jim Miller for this historical climate data. British and European historical demographers John Knodel, Tony Wrigley, and R.S. Schofield have observed that as little as a one degree Fahrenheit drop in average winter temperatures, for example, will have an almost immediate effect on population mortality. John E. Knodel,

Demographic Behaviour in the Past: A Study of Fourteen German Village Populations in the Eighteenth and Nineteenth Centuries (Cambridge: Cambridge University Press, 1988), 60-61; E.A. Wrigley and R.S. Schofield, *The Population History of England, 1541-1871: A Reconstruction* (Cambridge: Cambridge University Press, 1981), 284-98. On the seasonality of infant death, see also Patricia A. Thornton and Sherry Olson, "Family Context of Fertility and Infant Survival in Nineteenth-Century Montréal," *Journal of Family History* 16, 4 (1991): 406.

32 For the links between mining, silicosis, tuberculosis, and pneumonia, see Alan Derickson, *Workers' Health, Workers' Democracy: The Western Miners' Struggle, 1891-1925* (Ithaca: Cornell University Press, 1988), 39-51.

33 *Census of Canada, 1901,* vol. 4: 232-35, table 6. Comparable material on the situation in Central Canada can be found in David Gagan and Rosemary Gagan, "Working-Class Standards of Living in Late-Victorian Urban Ontario: A Review of the Miscellaneous Evidence on the Quality of Material Life," *Journal of the Canadian Historical Association*, 1, 1 (1990): 189.

34 Tranquille Sanatorium Admissions Book, British Columbia Anti-Tuberculosis Society Papers, vol. 7, Add Mss 1916, BC Archives.

35 E.H. Hunt, *British Labour History, 1815-1914* (London: Weidenfeld and Nicolson, 1981), 50.

36 Wayne Norton, *A Whole Little City by Itself: Tranquille and Tuberculosis* (Kamloops: Plateau Press, 1999), 22-30.

37 *Victoria Colonist,* Holiday number 1887, 14, BC Archives.

38 *The Williams' Official British Columbia Directory, 1894* (Victoria, 1895), 95.

39 *Kamloops Mining Camp* (Kamloops, 1897), 17, BC Archives.

40 Richmond P. Hobson Jr., *Grass beyond the Mountains: Discovering the Last Great Cattle Frontier on the North American Continent* (Toronto: Lippincott Dodd, 1951), 18.

41 Robert Service, *Ploughman of the Moon* (New York: Mead and Co., 1945), 301; Canada, Department of the Interior, Topographical Surveys Branch, *Description of Surveyed Land in the Railway Belt of British Columbia, Part No. 2 – Central Division* (Ottawa: Department of the Interior, 1915), 22, BC Archives.

42 See, for example, Marie Elliott, ed., *Winifred Grey: A Gentlewoman's Remembrances of Life in England and the Gulf Islands of British Columbia, 1871-1910* (Victoria: Gulf Islands Press, 1994), 166.

43 British Columbia, "Register of Births, Deaths and Marriages for the Province of British Columbia, Abstract 1913," *Sessional Papers,* 1914, J15-J20.

44 Client Records, 1888-March 1898, 1898-1905, and Funeral Register, June 1905-September 1913, Schoening Funeral Service (1961) Ltd., Kamloops, BC. Figures do not include burials of convicts executed at Kamloops Gaol, although suicides and accidental deaths are incorporated. During the years covered, there was only one undertaker in Kamloops, so in this respect the record is a complete one. This Table 7.3 includes only those individuals buried in Kamloops for whom an age at death is supplied. The words "Baby" or "Infant" are frequently used in the case of neonatal deaths; in those instances, an age of less than one year is assumed.

45 *Kamloops Inland Sentinel,* 7 March 1891.

46 *Census of Canada, 1881,* http://www.livinglandscapes.bc.ca/thomp-ok/census/index.html.

47 John Calam, ed., *Alex Lord's British Columbia: Recollections of a Rural School Inspector, 1915-1936* (Vancouver: UBC Press, 1991), 43; Megan J. Davies, *Into the House of Old: A History of Residential Care in British Columbia* (Montreal and Kingston: McGill-Queen's University Press, 2003), 59-60.

48 The occupational hazards associated with the sex trade were, of course, faced almost exclusively by women. See Susan J. Johnston, "Twice Slain: Female Sex-Trade Workers and Suicide in British Columbia, 1870-1920," *Journal of the Canadian Historical Association* 5, 1 (1994): 147-66.

49 *Census of Canada, 1891,* vol. 2, 106-9, table 11. St. Paul's (Nanaimo), text 330, box 8, Archives of the Anglican Diocese of British Columbia, Victoria, BC.

50 Funeral Register, June 1905-September 1913, Schoening Funeral Service.
51 See, for example, Lucill K. Adems, "1913-14: The Homestead at Finlay Forks," in *Peace River Chronicles,* Gordon E. Bowes, ed. (Vancouver: Prescott, 1963), 317.
52 Macdonald, "Vital Statistics in British Columbia," 94-95.
53 One Thompson River community comprised almost entirely of recent British immigrants could claim "the highest enlistment rate per capita of any city in Canada." Joan Weir, *Walhachin: Catastrophe or Camelot?* (Surrey: Hancock House, 1984), 86-88. See also, Nelson Riis, "The Walhachin Myth: A Study of Settlement Abandonment," *BC Studies* 17 (Spring 1973): 3-24.
54 Macdonald, "Vital Statistics in British Columbia," 44.
55 E.A. Wrigley, "Mortality and the European Marriage System," in *Food, Diet and Economic Change Past and Present,* Catherine Geissler and Derek J. Oddy, eds. (Leicester: Leicester University Press, 1993), 38.
56 Helen C. Pullem, *The Not so Gentle Art of Burying the Dead* (New Westminster: Bridges to Yesterday, 1992), 50.
57 Dorothy B. Smith, *The Reminiscences of Doctor John Sebastien Helmcken* (Vancouver: UBC Press, 1975), 215n2.
58 It is likely that the mortality figures for BC as a whole are slightly affected as well by the out-migration of the terminally ill. Take the fairly dramatic example of Mary Lawless, the daughter of a Nanaimo-area carpenter, who was a relatively recent arrival on Vancouver Island. In the early 1890s, Miss Lawless was sent to San Francisco to seek medical attention for an affliction that quickly took her life. Although it may be tempting to regard areas of recent settlement in British Columbia as ones to which the newcomers evinced only a partial attachment, Mary's tragic last letters to her father tell us otherwise. In what proved to be her final correspondence to Nanaimo, she requested that her remains be returned to the island, where she could be buried alongside her sister. Mary Lawless to her father, 1893, Lawless Family fonds, code 22, box 12, Nanaimo Community Archives, Nanaimo, BC.
59 Montreal steadily led the pack with about 30 per 1,000; Fredericton recorded a much better rate of 12 per 1,000. For the situation in what was then Canada's largest city, see Patricia A. Thornton and Sherry Olson, "Infant Vulnerability in Three Cultural Settings in Montréal, 1880," in *Infant and Child Mortality in the Past,* Alain Bideau, Bertrand Desjardins, and Héctor Pérez Brignoli, eds. (Oxford: Oxford University Press, 1997), 216-44; Marvin McInnis, "Infant Mortality in Late Nineteenth-Century Canada," in ibid., 262-75; and Thornton and Olson, "Family Context of Fertility and Infant Survival," 406.
60 Report on Health Conditions in Victoria, 20 June 1898, Attorney General, Correspondence Inward, Originals, GR429, box 4, file 2, 1186/98, BC Archives.
61 A recent study of Edwardian British demography argues that "'environment' is consistently able to explain more variance in infant and child mortality" than are social class and/or occupational categories. One might reply that the former is very often informed by the latter. Eilidh Garrett et al., *Changing Family Size in England and Wales: Place, Class and Demography, 1891-1911* (Cambridge: Cambridge University Press, 2001), 10.
62 Jan Gould, *Women of British Columbia* (Saanichton, BC: Hancock House, 1975), 117.
63 P.D. Logan, "Mortality in England and Wales from 1848 to 1947," *Population Studies* 4, 2 (September 1950-51): 134-35.
64 Census districts changed size and shape throughout this period. Kamloops, however, was included in either the "Yale" or the "Yale and Cariboo District," and Nanaimo fell within the "Vancouver District." In both cases the cities under study were only tiny fragments of their respective census district, but they were consistently the dominant centres.
65 Department of Health Services and Hospital Insurance, British Columbia, *Vital Statistics of the Province of British Columbia, Eighty-Ninth Report, 1960* (Victoria: Queen's Printer, 1961), J16.
66 Kelm, *Colonizing Bodies,* 10-14; Hugh J.M. Johnston, "Native Peoples, Settlers and Sojourners, 1871-1916," in *The Pacific Province: A History of British Columbia,* Hugh J.M. Johnston, ed. (Vancouver: Douglas and McIntyre, 1996), 171.
67 Health Canada, Medical Services Branch, and BC Division of Vital Statistics, "Status Indians in British Columbia: A Vital Statistical Overview," *Vital Statistics Quarterly Digest* 4, 2 (August

1994): 21. Despite improvements in some mortality levels, deaths from suicide continued to claim Status Natives at a rate "3.6 times greater than the rate for the rest of the BC population." The incidence of homicide as the cause of death was higher still: nearly six times that of the non-Aboriginal community. See T.A. Tuk and J. Macdonald, "Suicide, Homicide, and Gun Deaths, British Columbia, 1985 to 1993," *Vital Statistics Quarterly Digest* 5, 2 (August 1995): 30, 38.

68 Jacques Bernier, *Disease, Medicine and Society in Canada: A Historical Overview*, Historical Booklet 63 (Ottawa: Canadian Historical Association, 2003), 14.

69 Macdonald, "Vital Statistics in British Columbia," 36. For additional information on the impact of tuberculosis, influenza, and other respiratory diseases in the late twentieth century, see Y.C. MacNab, J. Macdonald, and T.A. Tuk, "Respiratory Disease Mortality in British Columbia, 1985 to 1994," *Vital Statistics Quarterly Digest* 5, 3 (November 1995): 19-50.

70 For a discussion of the ways in which the cause of death is determined and the extent to which suspicion of this information ought to prevail, see Simon P. Thomas and Steve E. Hrudey, *Risk of Death in Canada: What We Know and How We Know It* (Edmonton: University of Alberta Press, 1997), especially 101-2.

71 For the national record, see Robert Bourbeau, "Canadian Mortality in Perspective: A Comparison with the United States and Other Developed Countries," *Canadian Studies in Population* 29, 2 (2002): 313-69.

72 Surinder Wadhera and Jill Strachan, *Selected Mortality Statistics, Canada, 1921-1990*, catalogue no. 82-548 (Ottawa: Statistics Canada, 1994), 35-36; Statistics Canada, *The 1999 Canada Year Book* (Ottawa: Ministry of Industry, 1998), 89.

73 W. Peter Ward, "Population Growth in Western Canada: 1901-1971," in *The Developing West: Essays in Honour of Lewis H. Thomas*, John E. Foster, ed. (Edmonton: University of Alberta Press, 1983), 163.

74 It has a fifth consequence: a growing geriatric migration in the late twentieth century means that Vancouver, Victoria, Kelowna, and Penticton especially are home to a thriving trade in funerals. Undertaker extraordinaire Ray Loewen based his multinational deathcare operation in a manorial South Burnaby funeral home, from which he expanded across North America in the 1980s and '90s. See Herbert C. Northcott and P. Jane Milliken, *Aging in British Columbia: Burden or Benefit?* (Calgary: Detselig, 1998), 30-47.

75 Wadhera and Strachan, *Selected Mortality Statistics*, 76-77.

76 François Nault, "Narrowing Mortality Gaps, 1978 to 1995," *Health Reports* (Statistics Canada) 9, 1 (Summer 1997): 37.

77 BC Stats, "Life Expectancy," 2006, http://www.bcstats.gov.bc.ca/data/pop/pop/dynamic/LifeExpectancy.asp.

78 BC Stats, "British Columbia Life Expectancy at Age 65: 1951-2001," 2005, http://www.bc-stats.gov.bc.ca/data/pop/vital/exp65_bc.csv.

79 See Ellen M. Gee, "Population and Politics: Voodoo Demography, Population Aging, and Canadian Social Policy," in *The Overselling of Population Aging: Apocalyptic Demography, Intergenerational Challenges, and Social Policy*, Ellen M. Gee and Gloria M. Gutman, eds. (Toronto: Oxford University Press, 2000), 5-25.

80 Andre Billette and Gerry B. Hill, "Social Inequalities of Mortality in Canada," ii, 2, (1964) Social Inequalities of Mortality in Canada, Health Programs and Services Branch, 3, RG 29, vol. 49, file 6755-1-22, Library and Archives Canada, Ottawa.

81 Roderic Beaujot and Donald Kerr, *Population Change in Canada*, 2nd ed. (Don Mills: Oxford University Press, 2003), 44-46. See also Eleanor Bartlett, "Real Wages and the Standard of Living in Vancouver, 1901-1920," *BC Studies* 51 (Autumn 1981): 3-62.

82 On suicides and social class in BC, see Tuk and Macdonald, "Suicide, Homicide, and Gun Deaths," 24.

83 Russell Wilkins, Jean-Marie Berthelot, and Edward Ng, "Trends in Mortality by Neighbourhood Income in Urban Canada from 1971 to 1996," *Supplement to Health Reports* (Statistics Canada) 13 (2002): 6-7, http://www.statcan.ca/english/freepub/82-003-SIE/2002001/pdf/82-003-SIE2002007.pdf.

84 The differentiation between Vancouver and the rest of the province in 1891 is not particularly helpful, given that the ex-Vancouver figures include the still sizable communities of

Victoria and New Westminster – both of which probably exhibited similar urban trends, thus lowering the rates evident elsewhere in the hinterland. Marvin McInnis, "The Population of Canada in the Nineteenth Century," in *A Population History of North America,* Michael R. Haines and Richard H. Steckel, eds. (Cambridge: Cambridge University Press, 2000), 403. See also B.R. Mitchell, *International Historical Statistics: The Americas 1750-1988,* 2nd ed. (Basingstoke, UK: Macmillan, 1993), 83-84.

85 The death rate of the provincial capital's five- to twenty-year-old cohort was, at 121 per 1,000, the worst of all major Canadian cities in 1889. Canada, Department of Agriculture, *The Statistical Yearbook of Canada for 1889* (Ottawa, 1890), 94.

86 See the 1871-1911 Minister of Mines Reports in British Columbia, *Sessional Papers.* For infant mortality rates in Britain and the American Pacific states, see Logan, "Mortality in England and Wales from 1848 to 1947," 134-35.

87 Norah Lewis, "'Reducing Maternal Mortality," in *Not Just Pin Money: Selected Essays on the History of Women's Work in British Columbia,* Barbara K. Latham and Roberta J. Pazdro, ed. (Victoria: Camosun College, 1984), 337.

88 Wrigley, "Mortality," 35.

89 Michael Haines, "Fertility, Nuptiality, and Occupation: A Study of Coal Mining Population and Regions in England and Wales in the Mid-Nineteenth Century," *Journal of Interdisciplinary History* 8, 2 (Autumn 1977): 248-49. See also C.H. Lee, "Regional Inequalities in Infant Mortality in Britain, 1861-1971: Patterns and Hypotheses," *Population Studies* 45 (1991): 55-65.

90 *Census of Canada, 1881,* vol. 1 (Ottawa, 1882), 94-95, table 1; *Census of Canada, 1901,* vol. 1: *Population,* 6, table 2; *Census of Canada, 1901,* vol. 4: *Vital Statistics,* 348, table 16.

91 *Census of Canada, 1901,* vol. 4: *Vital Statistics,* 72-88, table 5. See also W. Peter Ward and Patricia C. Ward, "Infant Birth Weight and Nutrition in Industrializing Montréal," *American Historical Review* 89, 2 (April 1984): 324-45, and Louise Tilly and Joan Scott, *Women, Work, and Family* (New York: Holt, Rinehart and Winston, 1978), 173.

92 See Haines, "Fertility, Nuptiality, and Occupation," 274.

93 Beck Family fonds, 1892, A-06-01, box 1, Nanaimo Community Archives.

94 Kathryn Bridge, *Henry and Self: The Private Life of Sarah Crease, 1826-1922* (Victoria: Sono Nis Press, 1996), 13, 90, 114n10.

95 Johnston, "Native Peoples, Settlers and Sojourners," 170.

96 Baptisms 1886-1906 – Burials, Nanaimo Indian Mission, United Church Archives, Vancouver School of Theology, Vancouver, BC.

97 Register of Burials, Columbia (aka: New Westminster) Diocese Kamloops, BC (Anglican Archives).

98 Client Records, 1888-April 1905, and Funeral Register, June 1905-3 February 1923, Schoening Funeral Service.

99 James Alexander Teit, *The Thompson Indians of British Columbia,* vol. 1, part 4 of *The Jesup North Pacific Expedition,* ed. Franz Boas (1900; repr., Merritt, BC: Nicola Valley Museum Archives Association, 1997), 176-77.

100 Kelm, *Colonizing Bodies,* 7-9; Harris, *Making Native Space,* 290; Health Canada, Medical Services Branch, and BC Division of Vital Statistics, "Status Indians," 22.

101 Department of Vital Statistics, British Columbia, *Regional Analysis of Health Statistics for Status Indians in British Columbia, 1992-2002* (Victoria: Ministry of Health, 2004), 21.

102 Department of Health Services and Hospital Insurance, *Vital Statistics, 1960,* J29; British Columbia, Division of Vital Statistics, *Special Report Number 43: Infant Mortality in British Columbia, 1952-1957,* part 2 (Victoria: Department of Health Services and Hospital Insurance, February 1960), 16-17.

103 By contrast, the institutionalization of death was much slower and far less complete. The percentage share of all deaths that occurred in institutions in 1926-30 is 41.2, and although this rose through the midcentury, it did not reach 70 percent before 1960. Department of Health Services and Hospital Insurance, *Vital Statistics, 1960,* J19.

104 British Columbia, *The Nineteen Eighties: A Statistical Resource for a Decade of Vital Events in British Columbia* (Victoria: Ministry of Health and Ministry Responsible for Seniors, 1994), 23.

105 Veronica Strong-Boag and Kathryn McPherson, "The Confinement of Women: Childbirth and Hospitalization in Vancouver, 1919-1939," *BC Studies* 69-70 (Spring-Summer 1986): 144-46.

106 Angus McLaren and Arlene Tigar McLaren, *The Bedroom and the State: The Changing Practices of Contraception and Abortion in Canada, 1880-1997*, 2nd ed. (Toronto: Oxford University Press, 1997), 47-50.

107 Dr. A.J.J.G. Nuyens, "Maternal Mortality in Ontario," n.d., 191, Health Consultants – Adult Health – General Maternal Mortality, Health Services and Promotion Branch, RG 29, vol. 51, file 6756-1-3, Library and Archives Canada; Strong-Boag and McPherson, "Confinement of Women," 145-46.

108 For a balanced yet critical account of the hospitalization of birth, see Veronica Strong-Boag, *The New Day Recalled: Lives of Girls and Women in English Canada, 1919-1939* (Markham: Penguin, 1988), 153-62.

109 Kelm, *Colonizing Bodies*, 7. W.S. Thomas, "Maternal Mortality in Native British Columbia Indians, a High-Risk Group," in *Population Issues in Canada*, Carl Grindstaff, Craig L. Boydell, and Paul C. Whitehead, eds. (Toronto: Holt, Rinehart and Winston, 1971), 54-60; Department of Health Services and Hospital Insurance, *Vital Statistics, 1960*, J29.

Chapter 8: The British Columbia Clearances: Some Conclusions

1 See, for example, the collection of essays in *Vancouver: Representing the Postmodern City*, Paul Delany, ed. (Vancouver: Arsenal Pulp Press, 1994), especially the editor's introduction, 1-24. Another (more cohesive and coherent) discourse on the subject is Lance Berelowitz, *Dream City: Vancouver and the Global Imagination* (Vancouver: Douglas and McIntyre, 2005).

2 Emmanuel Le Roy Ladurie, "A Concept: The Unification of the Globe by Disease (14th to 17th Centuries)," *The Mind and Method of the Historian*, trans. Sian Reynolds and Ben Reynolds (Chicago: University of Chicago Press, 1981), 28-83.

3 See Michael Dawson, *Selling British Columbia: Tourism and Consumer Culture, 1890-1970* (Vancouver: UBC Press, 2004).

4 For a recent reflection on the pre-war real estate bubble, see Derek Hayes, *Historical Atlas of Vancouver and the Lower Fraser Valley* (Vancouver: Douglas and McIntyre, 2005), 76-83. For working-class participation in speculation, see Robert A.J. McDonald, *Making Vancouver: Class, Status, and Social Boundaries, 1863-1913* (Vancouver: UBC Press, 1996), 138-40. On Kipling's flutter, see Eric Nicol, *Vancouver* (Toronto: Doubleday Canada, 1978), 110.

5 Herbert C. Northcott and P. Jane Milliken argue that attitudes toward seniors should not be based on a "mercenary calculus of their relative costs and benefits." They conclude that "There is a need to do what must be done to provide a decent quality of life for all of society's members, young and old alike" but do so without recognizing that this is both a moral and an ideological charge. Northcott and Milliken, *Aging in British Columbia: Burden or Benefit?* (Calgary: Detselig, 1998), 14-15, 30-31, 123-24. See also Michael J. Prince, "Apocalyptic, Opportunistic, and Realistic Demographic Discourse: Retirement Income and Social Policy or Chicken Littles, Nest-Eggies, and Humpty Dumpties," in *The Overselling of Population Aging: Apocalyptic Demography, Intergenerational Challenges, and Social Policy*, Ellen M. Gee and Gloria M. Gutman, eds. (Toronto: Oxford University Press, 2000), 100-2.

6 Cole Harris, *Making Native Space: Colonialism, Resistance, and Reserves in British Columbia* (Vancouver: UBC Press, 2002).

7 Kay J. Anderson, *Vancouver's Chinatown: Racial Discourse in Canada, 1875-1980* (Montreal and Kingston: McGill-Queen's University Press, 1991), 19.

8 Mary-Ellen Kelm, *Colonizing Bodies: Aboriginal Health and Healing in British Columbia, 1900-50* (Vancouver: UBC Press, 1998).

9 It is difficult to place numbers on the "Sixties Scoop." What can be said for certain is that the number of Aboriginal children in provincial government care rose from 1,100 in 1962 to 2,825 in 1973. See Christopher Walmsley, *Protecting Aboriginal Children* (Vancouver: UBC Press, 2005), 13-14, 21-22.

10 John McLaren, "The State, Child Snatching, and the Law: The Seizure and Indoctrination of Sons of Freedom Children in British Columbia, 1950-60," in *Regulating Lives: Historical Essays on the State, Society, the Individual, and the Law*, John McLaren, Robert Menzies, and

Dorothy E. Chunn, eds. (Vancouver: UBC Press, 2002), 59-93. Although the provincial government has recognized and "regrets" the way in which the Doukhobor people were treated, it has – significantly – stopped short of an apology.

11 A wrenching personal account of the dislocation of the Arrow Lakes populations is Linda Kendall, "Death of a Community," *BC Studies* 142-43 (Summer-Autumn 2004): 153-55. A scholarly examination of the same events is Tina Loo, "People in the Way: Modernity, Environment, and Society on the Arrow Lakes," *BC Studies* 142-43 (Summer-Autumn 2004): 161-96.

12 See Anderson, *Vancouver's Chinatown*, 188-209; Wing Chung Ng, *The Chinese in Vancouver, 1945-80: The Pursuit of Identity and Power* (Vancouver: UBC Press, 1999), 97-102; Jean Barman, *Stanley Park's Secret: The Forgotten Families of Whoi Whoi, Kanaka Ranch, and Brockton Point* (Madeira Park, BC: Harbour, 2005); and Jeff Sommers and Nick Blomley, "'The Worst Block in Vancouver,'" in *Stan Douglas: Every Building on 100 West Hastings*, Reid Shier, ed. (Vancouver: Contemporary Art Gallery, 2002), 18-61.

13 Robert Menzies has charted the rise of eugenicist and social Darwinist liberalism in the region and the "removal" of the mentally unfit (variously defined) from the 1850s through the 1930s. He describes the interwar years as "Deportation's Golden Age" and details the expulsion of 553 individuals between 1921 and 1938, including the mass deportation in 1935 of sixty-five Chinese inmates of British Columbia's asylums. See Robert Menzies, "Governing Mentalities: The Deportation of 'Insane' and 'Feebleminded' Immigrants out of British Columbia from Confederation to WWII," in *Crime and Deviance in Canada: Historical Perspectives*, Chris McCormick, ed. (Toronto: Canadian Scholars Press, 2005), 161-86, and Menzies, "Race, Reason, and Regulation: British Columbia's Mass Exile of Chinese 'Lunatics' Aboard the *Empress of Russia*, 9 February 1935," in McLaren, Menzies, and Chunn, *Regulating Lives*, 196-230.

14 See *Hugh Johnston, The Voyage of the Komagata Maru: The Sikh Challenge to Canada's Colour Bar*, 2nd ed. (Vancouver: UBC Press, 1995). But by all means see Angus McLaren, *Our Own Master Race: Eugenics in Canada, 1885-1945* (Toronto: McClelland and Stewart, 1990).

15 See, for one correlation, Veronica Strong-Boag, "'The Citizenship Debates': The 1885 Franchise Act," in *Contesting Canadian Citizenship: Historical Readings*, Robert Adamoski, Dorothy E. Chunn, and Robert Menzies, eds. (Peterborough: Broadview Press, 2002), 69-94. The fact that, as a group, children remain without full citizenship rights should not be overlooked.

16 Douglas Coupland, *City of Glass: Douglas Coupland's Vancouver* (Vancouver: Douglas and McIntyre, 2000), 58.

17 An accusation that is often (and often fairly) levelled at works such as David K. Foot with Daniel Stoffman, *Boom, Bust and Echo: How to Profit from the Coming Demographic Shift* (Toronto: Macfarlane Walter and Ross, 1996), and David Cork with Susan Lightstone, *The Pig and the Python: How to Prosper from the Aging Baby Boom* (Toronto: Stoddart Books, 1996).

18 Amir Weiner, ed., *Landscaping the Human Garden: Twentieth-Century Population Management in a Comparative Framework* (Stanford: Stanford University Press, 2003), 1-18.

Suggested Reading

Primary sources such as censuses and the products of the Vital Statistics Division, Statistics Canada, or BC Stats have been cited fully in the endnotes, as have any secondary sources of information, data, or opinion. This section highlights studies of particular merit to the field of historical demography, especially as it pertains to British Columbia.

However much historical demography grows across the English-speaking world, its heart continues to beat in Cambridge. The titles below (arranged chronologically) exemplify best practices and include a classic and a good global survey:

Peter Laslett, *The World We Have Lost*, 2nd ed. (1965; repr., London: Methuen, 1975).
Michael Anderson, "Historical Demography after *The Population of England*," *Journal of Interdisciplinary History* 15, 4 (Spring 1985): 595-608.
Robert Woods, *The Population History of Britain in the Nineteenth Century* (Cambridge: Cambridge University Press, 1995).
Massimo Livi-Bacci, *A Concise History of World Population*, 4th ed. (London: Blackwell, 2007).

The method of the historical demographer is complicated by the kinds of information sources at our disposal. The best studies of the field comprehend and articulate the negotiable qualities of the data:

J. Dennis Willigan and Katherine A. Lynch, *Sources and Methods of Historical Demography* (London: Academic Press, 1982).
Chad Gaffield, "Theory and Method in Canadian Historical Demography," *Archivaria* 14 (Summer 1982): 123-36.
Linda S. Williams, *Families and the Canadian Census: A Brief Critique of Current Methodology and Some Suggested Improvements*, Occasional Papers in Social Policy Analysis 4 (Toronto: Ontario Institute for Studies in Education, University of Toronto, 1984).
George Emery, *Facts of Life: The Social Construction of Vital Statistics, Ontario 1869-1952* (Montreal and Kingston: McGill-Queen's University Press, 1993).
Susan Greenhalgh, "The Social Construction of Population Science: An Intellectual, Institutional, and Political History of Twentieth-Century Demography," *Comparative Studies in Society and History* 38 (1996): 26-66.
Bruce Curtis, *The Politics of Population: State Formation, Statistics, and the Census of Canada, 1840-1875* (Toronto: University of Toronto Press, 2001).

Two studies that examine the experience of the census taker – and thus open a window on the ways in which Canadian population was understood in the past – are

Alan A. Brookes, "'Doing the Best I Can': The Taking of the 1861 New Brunswick Census," *Histoire sociale/Social History* 9, 17 (May 1976): 70-91.

Patrick Dunae, "Making the 1891 Census in British Columbia," *Histoire sociale/Social History* 31, 62 (November 1998): 223-39.

The literature on Canadian demography is dominated by the work of sociologists. Regional work is, however, more likely to reveal the hand of the historian. As models of what might be done, I particularly recommend the works of Patricia Thornton and Gérard Bouchard. The Canadian Families Project, which carefully examines a national 1901 census sample, may be monitored at http://web.uvic.ca/hrd/cfp. A subsequent nationwide project – the Canadian Century Research Infrastructure Project, led by Chad Gaffield – reveals that a more sophisticated approach to demographic questions is well under way (at http://www. canada.uottawa.ca/ccri/). Up-to-date lists of new scholarship in this field can be found in the bibliography on the history of Canadian population and historical demography in Canada, which appears annually in the journal *Histoire sociale/Social History*. Otherwise, general surveys and important regional works include

Sheva Medjuk, "Family and Household Composition in the Nineteenth Century: The Case of Moncton, New Brunswick 1851-1871," *Canadian Journal of Sociology* 4, 3 (1979): 275-86.

David Gagan, *Hopeful Travellers: Families, Land, and Social Change in Mid-Victorian Peel County, Canada West* (Toronto: University of Toronto Press, 1981).

Gordon Darroch and Michael Ornstein, "Family Coresidence in Canada in 1871: Family Life-Cycles, Occupations and Networks of Mutual Aid," *Canadian Historical Association, Historical Papers* (1983): 30-55.

Patricia Thornton, "Newfoundland's Frontier Demographic Experience: The World We Have Lost," *Newfoundland Studies* 1, 2 (Fall 1985): 141-62.

Patricia A. Thornton and Sherry Olson, "Family Context of Fertility and Infant Survival in Nineteenth-Century Montréal," *Journal of Family History* 16, 4 (1991): 401-18.

Louise Dechêne, *Habitants and Merchants in Seventeenth-Century Montréal*, trans. Liana Vardi (Montreal and Kingston: McGill-Queen's University Press, 1992).

Gérard Bouchard, *Quelques arpents d'Amérique: Population, économie, famille au Saguenay, 1838-1971* (Montreal: Boréal, 1996).

Peter Gossage, *Families in Transition: Industry and Population in Nineteenth-Century Saint-Hyacinthe* (Montreal and Kingston: McGill-Queen's University Press, 1999).

Sylvia Wargon, *Demography in Canada in the Twentieth Century* (Vancouver: UBC Press, 2002).

Roderic Beaujot and Donald Kerr, *Population Change in Canada*, 2nd ed. (Don Mills: Oxford University Press, 2003).

Popular demographic studies in Canada enjoyed their salad days in the 1990s. The two most widely read studies are

David Cork with Susan Lightstone, *The Pig and the Python: How to Prosper from the Aging Baby Boom* (Toronto: Stoddart Books, 1996).

David K. Foot with Daniel Stoffman, *Boom, Bust and Echo: How to Profit from the Coming Demographic Shift* (Toronto: Macfarlane Walter and Ross, 1996).

Studies on British Columbia are surveyed in Chapter 1, which allows me to highlight a handful here. The works of Barman, Harris, and Strong-Boag are of special significance, and one should turn first to

Jean Barman, "The West beyond the West: The Demography of Settlement in British Columbia," *Journal of Canadian Studies* 25, 3 (Autumn 1990): 5-18.

–, *The West beyond the West: A History of British Columbia* (Toronto: University of Toronto Press, 1991). (The University of Toronto Press published revised versions of this book in 2001 and 2007.)

Cole Harris, *The Resettlement of British Columbia: Essays on Colonialism and Geographical Change* (Vancouver: UBC Press, 1997).

–, "Social Power and Cultural Change in Pre-Colonial British Columbia," *BC Studies* 115-16 (Autumn-Winter 1997-98): 45-82.

Veronica Strong-Boag, "Who Counts? Late Nineteenth- and Early Twentieth-Century Struggles about Gender, Race, and Class in Canada," in *Citizenship in Transformation in Canada*, Yvonne Hébert, ed. (Toronto: University of Toronto Press, 2002), 37-56.

–, "Interrupted Relations: The Adoption of Children in Twentieth Century British Columbia," in *Child and Family Welfare in British Columbia: A History,* Diane Purvey and Chris Walmsley, eds. (Calgary: Detselig, 2005), 139-64.

British Columbian histories that engage directly with demographic issues and/or with the laws that frame demographic behaviour include

Peter Baskerville and Eric Sager, "Finding the Work Force in the 1901 Census of Canada," *Histoire sociale/Social History* 28, 56 (November 1995): 521-39.

Adele Perry, *On the Edge of Empire: Gender, Race, and the Making of British Columbia, 1849-1871* (Toronto: University of Toronto Press, 2001).

Jay Nelson, "'A Strange Revolution in the Manners of the Country': Aboriginal-Settler Intermarriage in Nineteenth Century British Columbia," in *Regulating Lives: Historical Essays on the State, Society, the Individual, and the Law,* John McLaren, Robert Menzies, and Dorothy E. Chunn, eds. (Vancouver: UBC Press, 2002), 23-62.

Christopher A. Clarkson, *Domestic Reforms: Political Visions and Family Regulation in British Columbia, 1862-1940* (Vancouver: UBC Press, 2007).

James Murton, *Creating a Modern Countryside: Liberalism and Land Resettlement in British Columbia* (Vancouver: UBC Press, 2007).

There are many histories of Aboriginal experience in the farthest West, although few resolve population issues. See, for example,

Robert Muckle, *The First Nations of British Columbia: An Anthropological Survey* (Vancouver: UBC Press, 1998).

Keith Thor Carlson, ed., with Albert (Sonny) McHalsie, cultural advisor, *A Stó:lō Coast Salish Historical Atlas* (Vancouver: Douglas and McIntyre, 2001).

It is ironic that the most urbanized province lacks a strong tradition of scholarly urban histories. Much of the twentieth century remains uncharted in terms of city studies, but major centres such as Victoria, the Thompson-Okanagan conurbation, and Prince George have almost nothing to show for as much as 150 years of experience. The best of the urban studies and two community-focused studies (including my own) are

Graeme Wynn and Timothy Oke, eds., *Vancouver and Its Region* (Vancouver: UBC Press, 1992).

Jeremy Mouat, *Roaring Days: Rossland's Mines and the History of British Columbia* (Vancouver: UBC Press, 1995).

Robert A.J. McDonald, *Making Vancouver: Class, Status, and Social Boundaries 1863-1913* (Vancouver: UBC Press, 1996).

Ruth Sandwell, *Contesting Rural Space: Land Policy and Practices of Resettlement on Saltspring Island, 1859-1891* (Montreal and Kingston: McGill-Queen's University Press, 2006).

John Douglas Belshaw, *Colonization and Community: The Vancouver Island Coalfield and the Making of the British Columbian Working Class* (Montreal and Kingston: McGill-Queen's University Press, 2002).

Of late, stories of the collision between Europe and the Americas emphasize the widespread and disastrous diffusion of exotic disease. The study of this process has circled out from Hispaniola and Meso-America to include every quarter of the hemisphere. The following list, ordered chronologically, includes seminal works, an early synthesis, and the increasingly biologically focused literature:

Henry F. Dobyns, "Estimating Aboriginal American Populations, I: An Appraisal of Techniques with a New Hemispheric Estimate (and Comments)," *Current Anthropology* 7, 4 (1966): 395-416, 425-49.

Alfred W. Crosby Jr., *The Columbian Exchange: Biological and Cultural Consequences of 1492* (Westport, CN: Greenwood Press, 1972).

William M. Denevan, ed., *The Native Population of the Americas in 1492* (Madison: University of Wisconsin Press, 1976).

Emmanuel Le Roy Ladurie, "A Concept: The Unification of the Globe by Disease (14th to 17th Centuries)," in *The Mind and Method of the Historian,* trans. Sian Reynolds and Ben Reynolds (Chicago: University of Chicago Press, 1981), 28-83.

Henry F. Dobyns, *Their Number Become Thinned: Native American Population Dynamics in Eastern North America* (Knoxville: University of Tennessee Press, 1983).

Ann F. Ramenofsky, *Vectors of Death: The Archaeology of European Contact* (Albuquerque: University of New Mexico Press, 1987).

Russell Thornton, *American Indian Holocaust and Survival: A Population History since 1492* (Norman: University of Oklahoma Press, 1987).

Francis Black, "Why Did They Die? Genetic Homogeneity in New World Populations," *Science,* 11 December 1992, 1739-40.

John W. Verano and Douglas H. Ubelaker, eds., *Disease and Demography in the Americas* (Washington: Smithsonian Institution, 1992).

Elizabeth A. Fenn, *Pox Americana: The Great Smallpox Epidemic of 1775-82* (New York: Hill and Wang, 2001).

Susan Scott and Christopher J. Duncan, *Biology of Plagues: Evidence from Historical Populations* (Cambridge: Cambridge University Press, 2001).

Studies focusing on the depopulation on the Northwest Coast and in the Columbia basin exploded onto the scene in the 1990s. These are remarkably detailed works, a sampling of which is arranged here by author:

Robert T. Boyd, *The Coming of the Spirit of Pestilence: Introduced Infectious Diseases and Population Decline among Northwest Coast Indians, 1774-1874* (Vancouver: UBC Press, 1999).

–, "Demographic History, 1774-1874," *Handbook of North American Indians,* vol. 7: *Northwest Coast* (Washington: Smithsonian Institution, 1990), 135-48.

–, "Demographic History until 1990," *Handbook of North American Indians,* vol. 12: *Plateau* (Washington: Smithsonian Institution, 1998), 467-83.

–, "Smallpox in the Pacific Northwest: The First Epidemics," *BC Studies* 101 (Spring 1994): 5-40.

Sarah K. Campbell, *PostColumbian Culture History in the Northern Columbia Plateau, A.D. 1500-1900* (New York: Garland, 1990).

Jerome Cybulski, "Culture Change, Demographic History, and Health and Disease on the Northwest Coast," in *In the Wake of Contact: Biological Responses to Contact,* Clark Spencer Larsen and George R. Milner, eds. (New York: Wiley-Liss, 1994), 75-86.

Jody F. Decker, "Tracing Historical Diffusion Patterns: The Case of the 1780-82 Smallpox Epidemic among the Indians of Western Canada," *Native Studies Review* 4, 1 and 2 (1988): 1-24.

Robert Galois, "Measles, 1847-1850: The First Modern Epidemic in British Columbia," *BC Studies* 109 (Spring 1996): 31-46.

James R. Gibson, "Smallpox on the Northwest Coast, 1835-1838," *BC Studies* 56 (Winter 1982-83): 61-81.

There is, as well, a smaller body of work on post-collapse demographics:

Steven Acheson, "Culture Contact, Demography and Health among the Aboriginal Peoples of British Columbia," in *A Persistent Spirit: Towards Understanding Aboriginal Health in British Columbia,* Canadian Western Geographical Series 31, Peter H. Stephenson, Susan J. Elliott, Leslie T. Foster, and Jill Harris, eds. (Victoria: Western Geographical Press, 1995), 1-42.
Mary-Ellen Kelm, *Colonizing Bodies: Aboriginal Health and Healing in British Columbia, 1900-50* (Vancouver: UBC Press, 1998).
Anatole Romaniuc, "Aboriginal Population of Canada: Growth Dynamics under Conditions of Encounter of Civilizations," *Canadian Journal of Native Studies* 20, 1 (2000): 95-137.

"Hajnal's Line" first appeared on demographers' maps in 1965. Since that time, the distinctive qualities of Western nuptial trends have been used to explain the fertility transition, industrialization, urbanization, and the rise of liberal democracy.

John Hajnal, "European Marriage Patterns in Perspective," in *Population in History: Essays in Historical Demography,* D.V. Glass and D.E.C. Eversley, eds. (London: Edward Arnold, 1965), 101-43.
Dov Friedlander, Barbara S. Okun, and Sharon Segal, "The Demographic Transition Then and Now: Processes, Perspectives, and Analyses," *Journal of Family History* 24, 3 (October 1999): 497-505.
Eilidh Garrett, Alice Reid, Kevin Schurer, and Simon Szreter, *Changing Family Size in England and Wales: Place, Class and Demography, 1891-1911* (Cambridge: Cambridge University Press, 2001).
David Hacker, "Rethinking the 'Early' Decline of Marital Fertility in the United States," *Demography* 40, 4 (November 2003): 605-20.
Mary S. Hartman, *The Household and the Making of History: A Subversive View of the Western Past* (Cambridge: Cambridge University Press, 2004).

The literature on changes to Canadian nuptiality and fertility trends was dominated by the late Ellen Gee. This list focuses on the debates, not the case studies·

Ellen M. Gee, "Early Canadian Fertility Transition: A Components Analysis of Census Data," *Canadian Studies in Population* 6 (1979): 23-32.
–, "Marriage in Nineteenth-Century Canada," *Canadian Review of Sociology and Anthropology* 19 (1982): 311-25.
Jamie G. Snell and Cynthia Comacchio Abeele, "Regulating Nuptiality: Restricting Access to Marriage in Early Twentieth-Century English-Speaking Canada," *Canadian Historical Review* 69, 4 (1988): 466-89.
Carl Grindstaff, "A Vanishing Breed: Women with Large Families, Canada in the 1980s," *Canadian Studies in Population* 19, 2 (1993): 145-62.
Anatole Romaniuc, "Fertility in Canada: Retrospective and Prospective," in *Perspectives on Canada's Population: An Introduction to Concepts and Issues,* Frank Trovato and Carl F. Grindstaff, eds. (Don Mills: Oxford University Press, 1994), 214-30.
John C. Caldwell, "Towards a Restatement of Demographic Transition Theory," in *Population and Society: Selected Readings,* Frank Trovato, ed. (Don Mills: Oxford University Press, 2002), 158-77.

The literature on counter-fertility and counter-nuptiality (that is, contraception and divorce) includes

Angus McLaren, *A History of Contraception from Antiquity to the Present Day* (Oxford: Blackwell, 1990).

Angus McLaren and Arlene Tigar McLaren, *The Bedroom and the State: The Changing Practices of Contraception and Abortion in Canada, 1880-1997,* 2nd ed. (Toronto: Oxford University Press, 1997).

Kate Fisher and Simon Szreter, "'They Prefer Withdrawal': The Choice of Birth Control in Britain, 1918-1950," *Journal of Interdisciplinary History* 34, 2 (Autumn 2003): 263-91.

Roderick Phillips, *Untying the Knot: A Short History of Divorce* (Cambridge: Cambridge University Press, 1991).

British Columbia's overtly racist foundations have attracted generations of scholars, many of whom have studied the field with an eye upon immigration demographics. In this field, Patricia Roy has made the greatest concerted and sustained effort:

Patricia E. Roy, *A White Man's Province: British Columbia Politicians and Chinese and Japanese Immigrants, 1858-1914* (Vancouver: UBC Press, 1989).

–, *The Oriental Question: Consolidating a White Man's Province, 1914-41* (Vancouver: UBC Press, 2003).

–, *The Triumph of Citizenship: The Japanese and Chinese in Canada, 1941-67* (Vancouver: UBC Press, 2007).

Contrasting views and supplementary data on the Asian experience of immigration regulation include

W. Peter Ward, *White Canada Forever: Popular Attitudes and Public Policy towards Orientals in British Columbia* (Montreal and Kingston: McGill-Queen's University Press, 1990).

Kay J. Anderson, *Vancouver's Chinatown: Racial Discourse in Canada, 1875-1980* (Montreal and Kingston: McGill-Queen's University Press, 1991).

Wing Chung Ng, *The Chinese in Vancouver, 1945-80: The Pursuit of Identity and Power* (Vancouver: UBC Press, 1999).

Kamala Elizabeth Nayar, *The Sikh Diaspora in Vancouver: Three Generations amid Tradition, Modernity, and Multiculturalism* (Toronto: University of Toronto Press, 2004).

Roderic P. Beaujot, "Immigration and Demographic Structures," in *Immigrant Canada: Demographic, Economic, and Social Challenges,* Shiva S. Halli and Leo Driedger, eds. (Toronto: University of Toronto Press, 1999), 93-115.

Studies of mortality tend to fall into three camps: causes, numbers, and meaning. What there is, is tantalizing; what is needed to round out the field is quite a bit more.

Colin Coates, "Death in British Columbia, 1850-1950" (M.A. thesis, University of British Columbia, 1984).

Leslie Foster and Michael Edgell, eds., *The Geography of Death: Mortality Atlas of British Columbia, 1985-1989,* Western Geographical Series 26 (Victoria: Western Geographical Press, 1992).

Surinder Wadhera and Jill Strachan, *Selected Mortality Statistics, Canada, 1921-1990,* catalogue no. 82-548 (Ottawa: Statistics Canada, 1994).

Robert Bourbeau, "Canadian Mortality in Perspective: A Comparison with the United States and Other Developed Countries," *Canadian Studies in Population* 29, 2 (2002): 313-69.

On the greying of British Columbia, see these three studies:

Herbert C. Northcott and P. Jane Milliken, *Aging in British Columbia: Burden or Benefit?* (Calgary: Detselig, 1998).

Ellen M. Gee and Gloria M. Gutman, eds., *The Overselling of Population Aging: Apocalyptic Demography, Intergenerational Challenges, and Social Policy* (Toronto: Oxford University Press, 2000).

Megan J. Davies, *Into the House of Old: A History of Residential Care in British Columbia* (Montreal and Kingston: McGill-Queen's University Press, 2003).

Easily the most useful thing available to anyone working in the field of BC population studies is the wealth of publications produced by the Department of Vital Statistics. I am happy to close with

Julie M. Macdonald, "Vital Statistics in British Columbia: An Historical Overview of 100 Years, 1891-1990," *Vital Statistics Quarterly Digest* 4, 1 (June 1994): 19-45.

Index

ENVIRONMENTAL BENEFITS STATEMENT

UBC Press saved the following resources by printing the pages of this book on chlorine free paper made with 100% post-consumer waste.

TREES	WATER	ENERGY	SOLID WASTE	GREENHOUSE GASES
9	3,150	6	405	759
FULLY GROWN	GALLONS	MILLION BTUs	POUNDS	POUNDS

Calculations based on research by Environmental Defense and the Paper Task Force.
Manufactured at Friesens Corporation